To the memory of
George Ewart Hobbs
A Swindon wordsmith

A SWINDON WORDSMITH

The Life, Times and Works of
George Ewart Hobbs

Noel Ponting & Graham Carter

Published on behalf of Swindon Heritage by
The Hobnob Press
8 Lock Warehouse, Severn Road, Gloucester GL1 2GA

The Authors hereby assert their moral rights to be identified as the authors of the work.

All rights reserved. No part of this publication may be reproduced, stored in a retrieval system, or transmitted in any form or by any means, electronic, mechanical, photocopying, recording or otherwise, without the prior permission of the publisher and copyright holder.

British Library cataloguing in publication data:
a catalogue record for this book is available from the British Library.

Design and typesetting by Graham Carter

The text is set in Adobe Garamond Pro in 11pt/14pt

© Noel Ponting and Graham Carter,
and the Estate of George Ewart Hobbs 2019

ISBN 978-1-906978-76-1 (paperback edition)
ISBN 978-1-906978-77-8 (hardback edition)

Contents

Preface • 7
A Note to Readers • 11
A Short Biography of George Ewart Hobbs • 13
1 • George's World • 25
2 • When Science Meets Faith • 71
3 • A Design For Life: George's Advice to Young People • 99
4 • The War Poet • 121
5 • Life in the Great Western Railway • 153
6 • The Life of Charles Bradlaugh • 191
7 • Henry Day and Even Swindon School • 203
8 • A Red-Letter Day • 217
9 • George's Fables • 225
10 • George Hobbs and the Spirit World • 245
11 • Heaven(s) Above • 275
12 • Science Fiction and the Paranormal • 285
13 • The World of Mrs Crabthorn • 353
14 • Selected Short Stories • 385
Appendix A: List of Works • 417
Appendix B: Glossary • 423
Appendix C: Bibliography • 424

Acknowledgements

We would like to extend a big thank-you to the following people and organisations for their help and support in relation to this book:

Peter Field, Tim Field, Donald Day, all of our former colleagues at Swindon Heritage (including Frances Bevan, Andy Binks, Mark Sutton and Noel Beauchamp), David Colcomb, Gordon Shaw and Rodbourne Community History Group, Bob Townsend, Diane Everett, Jennie Bridges, Molly White, Lydia Ponting and Dr Julie Miller

Darryl Moody and Katherine Cole at
Local Studies, Swindon Central Library

Elaine Arthurs at STEAM Museum

Aggie Wieckowska at the Shaftesbury Centre

Wiltshire & Swindon History Centre

John Rylands Library, University of Manchester

Barrie Hudson at the *Swindon Advertiser*

Preface

Inertia is probably the last reason anyone would give for having produced a book. You'll note that I don't use the term 'written' – because somebody long gone from our midst had effectively done that bit already. His name was George Ewart Hobbs.

My sole aim, since I commenced my research in February 2018, has been to bring George and his extensive body of work back before the general public. Local history projects such as this are mostly undertaken purely for the love of the subject matter – for educational and instructional purposes and not for the pursuit of profit. That is certainly the case here.

However, let me take you back to the beginning.

In the Autumn of 2013 I had the privilege of going through a box or two of items that once belonged to my Great Grandfather, Henry Day, the first Headmaster of Even Swindon Mixed School. In amongst the various photos and personal mementos were a number of newspaper clippings from the *Swindon Advertiser*. And in amongst the yellowing clippings, were the pages of a handwritten letter addressed to Henry – signed by GE Hobbs. Upon closer inspection, it turned out that even some of the press cuttings were written by GE Hobbs as well.

Having read through the prose, it struck me at the time that this was the work of a wordsmith of no mean ability. A bit florid here and there. And stylistically a bit old fashioned by modern standards – but it came across as heartfelt, deeply sincere and somehow quite exceptional.

Within months I was starting to contribute my own articles to *Swindon Heritage* magazine, yet always at the back of my mind was the thought that I ought to start doing some research on GE Hobbs. You know, just in case there was a fascinating life story or indeed a body of work waiting to be rediscovered. Or maybe even both?

In fact, in an email to Graham Carter, editor of *Swindon Heritage* in March 2014, I wrote: 'I'd be particularly fascinated to learn more of George E Hobbs. I have a gut feeling that there is an untold story waiting to be discovered.'

Fast forward then to our final, Winter 2017 issue – a bitter-sweet moment. To make matters worse, I still hadn't got round to researching George. And given that the magazine had been the perfect vehicle for celebrating the achievements of long-forgotten Swindonians, perhaps the moment had now passed anyway...

However, following a chat with Darryl Moody in Local Studies (Swindon Central Library) the following January, I was encouraged to spend some time 'scratching that itch'. I mean, what was there to lose? At the very least, it would allow me to satisfy my curiosity and salve my guilty conscience. Who knows, I might even find that George contributed a few more bits and pieces to the local press – in which case, I could put it all together in a small monograph and leave it at that. Job done. Time to move on.

At around the same time, I was fortunate enough to make contact with Peter Field, Great Grandson of George Hobbs. It quickly became apparent that George had not only been a highly respected GWR foreman and Wesleyan Methodist lay preacher, but also a locally-published Great War poet, having produced a booklet of verse in 1915.

However, what we weren't anticipating was my subsequent discovery of a huge back catalogue of written works that had previously appeared in the local press (and other publications), most notably during the period 1914 to 1929. It comprised more poetry as well as prayers, newspaper correspondence and a multiplicity of articles – all reflecting George's diverse range of interests.

In fact, George had been incredibly prolific. Furthermore, in the process of carrying out my research, I detected his style in a number of un-named articles (particularly on religious matters) and in a number of letters under the pseudonym of 'Iconoclast'. Only latterly have I discovered that this same *nom de plume* was used by someone for whom George held great fascination – namely the noted politician and avowed atheist, Charles Bradlaugh. Coincidence? Maybe.

Yet, despite having had over 175 articles alone published in the *Advertiser* series alone, one has to question why it was that such a respected contributor had remained largely forgotten until now.

Firstly, I don't think for one second that he ever courted fame or fortune. A pious and modest man from a relatively poor family, he considered that his mission in life was to preach the Christian Gospel; and through his various writings, he felt he could share his faith as well as fables, views on topical matters, and life lessons.

However, George was no dogmatic evangelist. He was tolerant in his views and often preached to congregations in other churches. Furthermore, one can only speculate the extent to which losing two children in infancy affected him as a person and his spiritual beliefs.

It is certainly true that he felt a particular affinity with younger people (particularly through his participation in the Wesley Guild and The Band of Hope) and clearly saw his rôle as a bit of an educator, bringing to their attention loftier concepts, particularly in the subject areas of classical philosophy and mythology, Old Testament wisdom, evolution, Palaeontology, geology, astronomy and creation theory. Importantly, you'll note his frequent use of the pronoun 'we' as he attempts to take his audience with him on an exploration of new ideas and schools of thought.

Just as importantly, he wrote a fair number of pieces on the challenges of day-to-day life in Rodbourne and Swindon as well as the camaraderie he experienced in the GWR.

But he demonstrated a lighter vein to his writing as well – demonstrated by his love of colloquial humour, story telling and science fantasy, not to mention his series of articles based on imaginary conversations, many of which were with his dog, 'Tiny' (a not uncommon device for exploring difficult themes and issues).

Secondly, the vast majority of his published work appeared in newspapers. At best, the contributions that appeared in Friday's *Advertiser* in Swindon (at times published as a weekly (rather than exclusively daily) paper) would survive around the house until the following Friday. Had George's collected works appeared in a traditional book form earlier, who knows, it might have been a different story.

And finally, by the time George Ewart Hobbs passed away in 1946, over ten years had elapsed since his regular contributions to the *Advertiser* are thought to have ceased. For this reason and for all of the above, it is perhaps understandable if his name had already started to slip from the wider readership although in Rodbourne, the Methodist circuit and the GWR, he remained a highly respected and well-known member of the community to the very end.

It was our original contention that George's literary output started to decline in the middle 1920s following his promotion to foreman 'inside'. Indeed, when he was made an honorary member of the *Advertiser* editorial staff in 1929, it was not only a fitting tribute to a man of letters but, at the same time, it appeared to draw a line under his time as a regular contributor. However, our most recent research shows that his work continued to appear in the *Advertiser* until at least 1934 – but consideration of this will have to wait for another time, and perhaps another book.

Up to the present day, he was all but forgotten – but with four notable exceptions.

Firstly, having spent all of his life in Even Swindon, George is however remembered within the pages of the Rodbourne Community History Group website (www.rodbournehistory.org), for being a celebrated member of an Even Swindon family with a long association with the Percy Street Wesleyan Chapel.

Secondly, around 25 years ago, the *Advertiser* ran a story concerning a lady called Margaret Peachey, who had uncovered a copy of George's anthology of wartime poems in her father-in-law's attic.

Thirdly, George's award-winning article entitled *Permanent Way Fittings and their Manufacture* is even referenced today by some heritage rail enthusiasts as an authoritative piece on GWR track and pointwork.

And finally, I note that the Society For The History of Astronomy reference George's series of newspaper articles entitled *Other Worlds Than Our Ours* in their section on Wiltshire (co-ordinated by Anthony Kinder). See https://shasurvey.wordpress.com/england/wiltshire

A few years ago whilst in lighthearted conversation with a prominent amateur historian, I posed the question why anyone would want to get involved in the often thankless but valuable work of researching and recording local history. There came the reply; "It's because – for a brief moment – we make the people 'live' again."

Well, step up George Ewart Hobbs. It's now your turn.

I hope you end up sharing my admiration for a truly remarkable Swindonian.

Noel J Ponting
Royal Wootton Bassett
November 2019

A Note to Readers

I would like to say something about the task of transcribing George's words from early 20th century newspaper columns into a modern, digital format – something that appears (at least outwardly) straightforward enough.

The newspapers had already been transferred to microfilm, and it was simply a case of checking thousands of screen images for anything that had George's byline (extremely time-consuming, but eminently achievable). Unfortunately, in a few instances, small areas of some of the images on microfilm were unclear when first transposed, and it took some time to work out, word by word, what had originally been written.

Next, it was necessary to overcome various typesetter, compositor or general typographical errors – remembering of course that newspaper columns were not subjected to the same level of proofreading as one would have normally expected with a book. More often than not, it was just the occasional word or words that needed to be corrected or interpreted. Considerable care has been taken in this regard.

Obvious spelling mistakes have been rectified, but archaic spellings have been left alone as they are very much *of their time*. However, the switch from broadsheet column to a smaller page layout has produced numerous grammatical challenges, most significantly in the under-provision of paragraphs and commas. A pragmatic approach has been adopted here – without which George's words would not be as easily read and understood when viewed through today's lens.

Finally, please note that his body of work relating to the Great War is occasionally quite jingoistic in nature and includes slang or derogatory references to the Germans that people would find unacceptable today.

Similarly, the reader may occasionally come across sentences and phraseology that is suggestive of casual sexism, emblematic of a patriarchal society or, indeed, culturally insensitive, pompous or just plain old-fashioned. Therefore, when viewed through a latter-day lens, you'll occasionally come across some familiar tropes. It is, however, *of its time* – when Britain was a far, far different country to what we have today.

Please remember that the vast majority of George's writing is now approaching a hundred years old and, in that context, it serves to demonstrate how we were, as well as to counterpoint how far we have advanced in societal terms in the interim. Once again, much thought has gone into maintaining the integrity of George's writing in historical context.

During George's lifetime, the publication that most of his writing appeared in was variously called the *Swindon Advertiser*, the *Swindon Evening Advertiser* or simply the *Evening Advertiser*, usually dependant on whether the paper in question was published daily or weekly; for a period, there were both daily and weekly editions published, so that, on Fridays, there were two different papers for readers to choose between. To avoid confusion, all our references will henceforth be to the *Advertiser*.

PS If any researchers happen across any of George Hobbs's works that are not already recorded in the bibliography at the back of this book, then please feel free to bring them to my attention. Indeed, I would be pleased to receive news of any George-related material, be it family anecdotes, news items or other feedback. In fact, I have still not given up hope that a few reference books from his extensive, personal library might well resurface in the months and years ahead, following the publication of this book.

You are most welcome to email me on: shresearch2@gmail.com

Noel J Ponting
Royal Wootton Bassett
November 2019

A Short Biography of George Ewart Hobbs

By the latter part of the 19th century, the evolution of Even Swindon from hamlet to suburb was already well underway and, by 1890, it had actually merged with the railway town of New Swindon, then situated less than a mile away to the south-east.

Demand for homes by the ever-increasing numbers of Great Western Railway workers had already resulted in the development of Victorian, terraced, artisan housing, to both sides of Rodbourne Road. And it was to this humble yet proud community that George was born. Bordered to the south by the main line to Paddington and to the north by the Golden Valley Line to Gloucester, he was to find himself, quite literally and figuratively, on the wrong side of the tracks.

George Ewart Hobbs was born at home at 23 Henry Street, Even Swindon (subsequently renamed Hawkins Street) on January 16, 1883, the third of four children of GWR fitter and metal turner, Henry Hobbs, and his wife, Mary (née Dummer). He was baptised into the Methodist tradition on February 22, 1883, most probably at the original 'iron chapel' in Percy Street.

Henry and Mary had married on April 27, 1879, in Chittoe, near Devizes, eventually moving from their home in Chippenham to Swindon, sometime in 1882, where Henry's skills as a machine maker were in great demand.

A member of the skilled working class, who were at that time the backbone of the Liberal Party, Henry gave his son the middle name of Ewart as tribute to William Ewart Gladstone, by then into his second spell as Prime Minister. Later on, George was to inherit, from his father, both his politics and his Wesleyan faith.

By 1889 the family had moved to the other side of Rodbourne Road and were living at 1 Jersey Terrace in Jennings Street – interestingly, a street where George was to spend the whole of the rest of his life. Later that year, on October 21, he entered Even Swindon Infants School, adjacent to the Mixed School, where he was to meet with the second biggest earthly influence on his life, his headmaster, Henry Day.

Having already achieved the Seventh Standard, George left school on December 20, 1895, aged only 12. It was stated at the time that he would be going on to a Higher Grade School, but whether he did so or not is unclear.

However, what we do know is that he entered service with the Great Western Railway in Swindon on November 2, 1896, aged 13, at the grade of 'boy', on a daily wage of just 10d (around £4.77 in today's terms), and the following year he began a six-and-a-half-year apprenticeship as a turner.

With the encouragement of his father, George had already become a regular attendee at the original Wesleyan 'iron chapel' in Percy Street and, later on, was to witness the building of the new, larger brick chapel on an adjacent site, which opened in 1898. Designed by renowned Swindon architect Thomas Smith Lansdown in 1894, it was to be his last known commission; he died the following year.

Already a committed Methodist, he was also to become a prominent participant in the Band of Hope, the youth wing of the temperance movement. Apart from promoting abstinence from alcohol, its other function was as a social club for children. Meetings and events were held in the adjacent church hall, which was the original 'iron chapel', and regular excursions (often with an educational bias) took members out of town. George was later to become branch secretary.

In the meantime, the family address changed from 1 Jersey Terrace to 71 Jennings Street, possibly simply as the result of renumbering, and at the end of March 1901, George was still there with his parents.

He had also fallen passionately in love. The object of his affection was Agnes Ann Thomas, who lived just a few doors away from him, in the same street.

They were married on August 23, 1901, at Swindon Registry Office and – somewhat scandalously for the time – a daughter, Dorothy Agnes Emily Hobbs, was born, less than one month later, on September 9, 1901. Interestingly, in her latter years, Dorothy was to claim that her mild scoliosis was caused in the womb, as a result of her mother being so tightly corseted to conceal her pregnancy.

Of course, the question remains why the couple eschewed a church wedding.

Was it the shame, the cost or was it the fact that he and Agnes (who was from a High Church background) simply couldn't agree on where to tie the knot?

Given that George was still only an apprentice at the time, and his daily rate was only 2s 2d, money must have been in very short supply. Indeed, it was not until February 10, 1904 that he was formally employed as a time-served fitter and turner (in G Shop (millwrights)), and saw his rate increase to 4s 2d.

Despite this, George and his family did have a spell living independently, at 5 Jennings Street. Perhaps it was the birth of a son, Reginald, in 1906, that prompted George to move back in with his father, by now living at 79 Jennings Street.

Sadly, tragedy was soon to follow. Reginald was to die of measles and bronchopneumonia, on April 20, 1907, aged only 11 months, and today lies buried in a mass (pauper's) grave, along with other victims of infant mortality, at Radnor Street Cemetery.

In 1910, aged just 27, George was formally adopted by the Methodist Church as a lay preacher, serving the Bath Road Circuit, a calling he undertook with enthusiasm for the rest of his life. While no records survive of his actual sermons, we do know that he travelled extensively throughout the locality, visiting brethren at chapels in Clarence Street, Swindon, as well as in Purton, Shrivenham, Cricklade and Highworth, sometimes riding in a horse-drawn trap. Occasionally he would even venture as far as Wantage.

But be in no doubt: the locations that always remained closest to his heart were the chapel in Percy Street and the Telford Road Mission. Indeed, from February 3, 1930 he was a trustee of the former (and until his death) and, also in 1930, briefly a trustee of the latter (at a time when merging both trusts was being actively considered).

While holding a profound faith and a deep love of the Wesleyan doctrine, George was no religious dogmatist; nor was he constrained by sectarian orthodoxy. He was someone whose very soul was firmly rooted in the working class communities of Swindon and whose vocation lay there, too. Indeed, some of his best evangelising was said to have been proclaimed while visiting the Little London Mission, on the corner of Church Road and Little London Hill, in Old Town.

A Church of England establishment allied to Christ Church, the mission was founded in 1902 as a means of 'taking Christianity out to the people'. To quote from *The Old Lady on the Hill*, by Brian Bridgeman and Teresa Squires: 'The Mission was run almost entirely by lay members of Christ Church and one who worked there later said that it was provided for people who couldn't stand the sight of a clergyman!'

George, with his apparent lack of vanity and formality, would have felt very much at home.

Career-wise, George was promoted to chargeman on May 10, 1913, and immediately saw his daily rate rise by 4d to 5s 10d (approximating to just around £28.22 per day, in today's terms).

The advent of the Great War on August 4, 1914, and the ensuing national crisis, proved to be a catalyst for many combatants and non-combatants alike, who felt moved to commit their feelings to verse. George was no exception. While he never took up arms himself, he joined many other Home Front writers and poets whose creative output (at least in the early stages) was teeming with patriotism and the need to defend Britain's honour – only for that to eventually give way to loss, grief and the repugnance of war. All aspects of jingoism were soon replaced by the sheer bloody reality of slaughter on an industrial scale.

A family story from this period has it that George often came home from the GWR in tears, given that he was then personally involved in the production of munitions and military hardware, bound for the Western Front.

He was quick to put his pen to paper. His Great War poetry represents his first known contributions to the *Advertiser*, and while the conflict in all its many aspects did feature in many of his poems, he did venture into other subject areas too, notably love, faith and the human condition, as well as the sun and the moon.

The first poem to be published was *Britain's Response*, which appeared in the *Advertiser* on October 28, 1914, and the final one of the series was *T'was Ever Thus*, which appeared on November 3, 1916. In the meantime, Morris Bros (then owners of the newspaper) published a selection of his poems in a booklet called *The British Soldier*.

In the following January, George embarked on his next phase as a writer, that of a regular columnist, correspondent and essayist – a period that was to last for well over the next ten years.

Around this time, we learn the following from George's piece, *The Virtue of Gratitude*:

> I know what it is to fret out my heart and to contemplate the direst of all human actions when, helpless and hopeless in a London Hospital, a surgeon said to me, "Man! You are going blind!" – My eyes were spared, for which I have never ceased to be grateful.

Whether this serious eye condition was congenital, the result of an accident or even due to not using sufficient precautions while observing the sun (one of George's hobbies) is lost in time.

There is no doubt that he was particularly well-read. His daughter Dorothy would later recall that she was never able to see any wallpaper on the walls of the front room at one of the homes in Jennings Street because "they were covered, floor to ceiling, with books on shelves".

From the outset (and doubtless informed by his faith), it is apparent that George was on a particular mission to share words of moral encouragement and guidance with younger people. But it didn't stop there; he also saw himself as a bit of an educator, and there is some evidence that he was also involved with the Methodist youth movement, the Wesley Guild.

By now living at 4 Jennings Street, George and Agnes had become parents to another son, Ivor, although this was also to end in tragedy when the child died from infantile convulsions and rickets on May 27, 1919, aged only two years and eleven months.

The next significant record is his appointment as secretary of Coate Amateur Rowing Club at its first general meeting, on June 29, 1921, although at the first AGM, on April 9, 1922, he had stood down from his duties. The *Advertiser* reported:

> Mr GE Hobbs was appointed Secretary, but after doing some splendid spade work on behalf of the club, he found it impossible to continue. The committee realised that it was his endeavours at the commencement of the club's existence that paved the way for the successful season that followed.

After ten years as chargeman, George was finally appointed as a foreman in X Shop on October 22, 1923, and in doing so he became a salaried member of staff. The final accolade came on December 6, 1926, when he was appointed as foreman-in-charge.

It was already clear from some of his articles that the stars and the solar system held a particular fascination for George. And so, in the guise of both a reporter and an amateur enthusiast, he travelled up to Southport to witness the total eclipse of the sun on June 29, 1927, Southport being chosen because it was located on the central line of the path of totality. George wrote about his adventure for the paper, and the front-page article is reprinted in full in Chapter 11. Having been allowed by the GWR to join the press contingent, back in 1924, when the King and Queen visited Swindon Works, and by virtue of his countless contributions to the *Advertiser*, George was able to fulfil his long-held wish to be accepted as an established journalist. And so, by way of recognition, he was made an honorary member of the *Advertiser* editorial staff. His letter of appointment, dated June 29, 1929, is reproduced elsewhere in this book.

It is generally accepted by his family that, around this point, George started to devote more and more of his time to his church duties. Certainly, he had already reached a zenith in his writing career, earlier in the year, when his highly technical piece, *Permanent Way Fittings and their Manufacture* was published by the GWR Mechanics' Institute/Swindon Engineering Society, and George was subsequently awarded a medal for its merit.

In 1934 George and Agnes moved as a couple for one last time, from 15 Jennings Street to 13 Jennings Street. Although we reference only two newspaper contributions from George during this decade, this is not to suggest that his writing career had simply drawn to an abrupt close. Indeed, preliminary research suggests that a whole new tranche of articles from this period are waiting to be rediscovered and documented. Nevertheless, he continued with his preaching and, in what were to become his latter years, he also developed an affection for the Rodbourne Road Primitive Methodist Chapel.

At the outbreak of war in 1939, he also became an Air Raid Precautions (ARP) warden, while continuing to be a highly regarded foreman. And, from 1940, X Shop became directly responsible for the production of bomb casings for shells of 250lbs, 1,000lbs, 2,000lbs and 4,000lbs; that amounts to huge destructive power. One can well imagine that the moral turmoil he had experienced during the First World War was now amplified, many times over.

A genial and extremely conscientious man, it was reported that during the war years he had to reduce his outside activities in order to keep pace with the extra work that arose.

George died at home on December 22, 1946, aged just 63, from uraemia and chronic nephritis, more commonly known as kidney failure, an often fatal condition before the widespread use of penicillin and dialysis. It is reported that, in his final days, he cut a particularly sad figure, propped up on the sofa in his sitting room.

He left no known will. His estate of just £432 11s 4d simply passed to his wife, a sum not far short of his annual salary.

Following a funeral service on December 27, 1946, at Percy Street Wesleyan Chapel, he was buried at Radnor Street Cemetery, in Plot C3617, sharing the unmarked grave with his second son, Ivor Hedley Sidney Hobbs, and his mother-in-law, Eliza Ann Thomas.

His wife, Agnes, decided to leave Jennings Street at this point, and went to live with daughter Dorothy and her husband, Joe, at 5 Farm Cottages (to be found, today, in Barnfield Close), with Joe later bemoaning the fact that he had to support his virtually penniless mother-in-law for nearly the next 18 years!

Agnes Ann Hobbs was later buried in the same plot as her husband, when she passed away in July 1964. The lack of a gravestone or indeed of any monumental masonry whatsoever is very much in line with his modest and frugal way of life; as in death, as in life.

Nevertheless, it does somewhat beg the question as to why he hadn't accumulated more capital over his lifetime, particularly as he had been continually employed by the GWR for over 50 years and had held the position of foreman for over 23 years.

Curiously, he chose to remain a tenant throughout his married life, and furthermore, he didn't drink, smoke or gamble.

The answer may lie here: George was said to have been a very generous man throughout his life, and was known to have given away significant sums of his own money to local people in distress. Perhaps this benevolence accounted for the large numbers of people who reportedly lined the streets out of Rodbourne as his coffin made its way up to Radnor Street.

And of course, there were all those books. It's a mystery what happened to them all after his death, although his somewhat well-thumbed and battered Bible does survive. And if you, the reader, ever happen across a secondhand book that originally hailed from George's collection, then please treasure it!

Looking back, Dorothy was later to recall that her father was somewhat over-protective. Perhaps this is not surprising, given that he had lost two other children in infancy. While she always held him in high regard, there was some lingering resentment that he had vetoed her aspiration to be an actress – a job he considered rather unseemly for a respectable young girl.

What is certainly not widely known is that George suffered from the irrational fear of being buried alive (nowadays referred to as taphophobia). According to the Hobbs family, he left strict instructions that, following his death, his wrists were to be cut before being placed in the grave. His son-in-law, Joe Shailes, reportedly had the onerous duty of ensuring that this act was duly carried out.

In many ways, George Ewart Hobbs typified the spirit of Swindon between the wars. At that time it was a town full of tough, working people, bristling with vision and innovation – where a paucity of education was seen as an opportunity for self-improvement rather than as a barrier to upward mobility.

As for George's lasting advice to his daughter on the subject of faith, it was: "Go and listen to all sorts of religions. And when you have, make your own mind up about it all."

And ironically, you can't get more secular or pluralistic than that.

Above: a Band of Hope meeting or outing, c1898, with George Hobbs (detail, below) holding an open book, behind his father. The Band of Hope was part of the Temperance Movement, and aimed to teach young people about the virtues of abstinence and the dangers of alcohol. (Courtesy of Peter Field)

Above: George's daughter, Dorothy, c1920. (Courtesy of Peter Field)

Right: George's parents, Henry and Mary Hobbs, date unknown. (Courtesy of Peter Field)

George Hobbs, in Jennings Street, c1933. (Courtesy of Peter Field)

George and Agnes Hobbs, c1940. (Courtesy of Peter Field)

LONDON OFFICE
169 & 170, Fleet Street, E.C.4.
Tel.: Central 5265 (10 Lines).
MANCHESTER OFFICE:
Cromford House, Cromford Court.
Tel.: City 5930.

TELEPHONE: Swindon 215, 216.
(Private Branch Exchange).
TELEGRAMS: "Swindon 215."

SWINDON PRESS LTD.

EVENING ADVERTISER
NORTH WILTS HERALD   HLH/NN.
SWINDON ADVERTISER

THE LARGEST
GENERAL PRINTERS
IN WILTSHIRE.

Newspaper House,
SWINDON.

June 29th 1929.

George. E. Hobbs, Esq,
15. Jennings Street,
Swindon.

Dear Mr. Hobbs,

It is many years since you first became associated with the "Swindon Advertiser", and your contributions have always had a wide and appreciative circle of readers.

I think it might be rather appropriate if we could look on you in future as an honorary member of the Advertiser editorial staff.

We regard you as one of ourselves, and such an appointment would be a nice expression of our relationship.

Yours sincerely,

HLHowarth

Managing Editor.

Above: George's letter from the Advertiser. (Courtesy of Peter Field)

Left: Tim and Peter Field, the only great-grandchildren of George and Agnes Hobbs. (Courtesy of Peter Field)

Chapter 1

George's World

'The past is a foreign country; they do things differently there,' is a famous and often-used quote from LP Hartley's book, *The Go-Between*, and we make no apology for referring to it, here, in introducing this chapter.

This is, after all, a book that aims to throw light on life as it existed, specifically in Swindon, a hundred years ago, with George Hobbs as our own personal go-between and guide.

While George's humanity and sensitivity, which resonate so loudly in his writing, are timeless qualities, the everyday world that his writings provide a window on is sometimes alien to us, compared with life in the 21st century.

When you are visiting 'foreign' vistas, it can be useful to have a phrase book to hand, so in this chapter we will be taking time to think about and digest the scenes he is describing, and look more closely at what George is telling us about the era in which he lived.

Not that this was ever his intention. Among the many motives he had for writing, it is unlikely he ever imagined that one outcome would be how clearly it spoke to distant generations about his world as he perceived it, yet that is undoubtedly a major legacy.

Indeed, the more you look at his works, the more they tell us about how life was in the first third of the 20th century, in a way that the other passports to that foreign country – photographs, fiction and dusty documents – never can. And they are made all the more valuable by his clarity of writing, and his ability to get across even the most complex of ideas that ran through his obviously supple mind.

The greatest beauty of it all, especially for students of social and local history, is that, just as insightful as the big subjects George tackles, such as faith, war and the universe, are the small details he reveals, often in throwaway lines. His work is strewn with little gems, so the message from this chapter is: here are a few, and keep your eyes peeled for others in subsequent chapters.

Mind your language

Just before we leave the metaphor of foreign countries behind us, it is worth looking at the language that George uses in his writings, because parts of it seem like a foreign one to us.

Examples of this can be found liberally cast throughout his writing, so we shall only dwell on a few examples.

He talks about *swank*, for example, a word for self-confident arrogance that has gone out of fashion, and which we probably don't have a suitable replacement for, today; it's a gentler version of what we would now describe as *cockiness*.

Other phrases are used in the apparently full expectation that they will be understood by his readers, and some of these come as a surprise to us. When he was writing for the *Advertiser*, George would have observed the unwritten rule governing all writing for local papers, which is that one's vocabulary should never be too high-brow for average readers, nor have them reaching for their dictionaries. So when he uses a term such as *sub rosa*, for instance (which means *in confidence*), we can assume his readers understood it – and as most of us wouldn't we can conclude either that 20th century newspaper readers had a vocabulary and literacy that was generally superior to their 21st century counterparts, or they were better read. And that's ironic because their formal education was comparatively brief, George himself having left school at the tender age of 12.

Of the words and phrases that George chooses that are clearly now past their sell-by date, some have lost much more in translation than others. *Meed*, for example, has gone completely off the radar, the word simply having been replaced by *share*, as in 'the teaching staff must also receive their meed of praise'.

But if we need Google to confirm what *meed* meant, other linguistic curiosities, such as *on the fuddle* (boozing), are easier to guess at, even if they might no longer be commonplace. The same goes for *a-jawing*, meaning verbal criticism, which was apparently reserved for when the criticism was closely related to *nagging* (a word, incidentally, that does not appear in George's works). He also uses *I'll be bound* quite naturally, although, to us, it would now sound like mockery.

Something that is very clear is how language, in George's world, defined class or perhaps intelligence – or both at the same time. This is particularly evident in his comic writing, where he uses dialogue to both define and emphasise character. If it was good enough for Thomas Hardy, it was good enough for George Hobbs, so we get *'e was fifty last tater plantin'*, *'e ain't in hemployment*, and *'e's on the Labour* (being paid unemployment benefit). Funny how the uneducated, in fiction, can't make up their mind whether to use an H or not, and have letters dropping off both ends of words!

To be fair, George is probably accurate in his transcription of the Swindon accent – which certainly was a discreet species, back then, even if it is now mostly endangered or even extinct – and the bad habits that many local folk would have fallen into, particularly regarding pronunciation.

The main mouthpiece for all this is George's main comic character, Mrs Crabthorn. While we are not surprised to find her getting on the train and heading for the Dorset resort of *Waymuff*, she isn't always so predictable, using *'oman* instead of *woman*. Where, in the history of Swindon dialect, that W was lost, we cannot say, although it has undoubtedly come back again in the century that has passed since.

A more subtle signpost to changing language comes in an article in which George eavesdrops on the conversation of some young children. When they talk about what they would do with a hundred pounds – then a vast sum of money that was difficult for an adult to comprehend, let alone a child – one of them says: 'I'd like to buy a flying machine and fly in the air. I'd like to be a pilot.' It is 1921, fully eighteen years since the Wright Brothers got airborne, and *pilot* has passed into common parlance (or at least been transposed from its maritime origins). However, what every child in the world would soon know as *an aeroplane* is still, in George's world, *a flying machine*. Just as the *aeroplane* is destined to be replaced, in due course, by *airplane* (thanks to Americanisation and modern technology entering *airplane mode*), so George is a witness to a language that is forever evolving.

In some cases we have to say it is a change for the worse, because some of George's phrases are nothing if not elegant. In one of his science fiction stories, for example, a character says he *found the problem very simple of solution*.

A curiosity of George's language is the way he slips into a kind of Gospelspeak when the question of religion arises in – of all places – one of his science fiction stories, *A Visit to the Moon*. The alien inhabitants of the moon, called Lunarians, mistake Christopher Jackson, who has built the spaceship and travelled to the moon, as some kind of deity, and George imagines this will cause them to speak in tongues not heard since Biblical times. So they use *thine* and *thee*, plus other phrases from Scripture – and it is catching, because Jackson reports that he hastened "to show them I was one like unto themselves". At least Jackson also reverts to less ecclesiastical language, telling us that he is *fagged*, meaning exhausted.

Some of George's words have been affected by changed spellings, such as *phantasy*, while others have shifted meanings or contexts.

In his comic advice to would-be young lovers, *To Seekers After Trouble*, George refers to a woman's *colour*, which we might now assume to be a reference to race. However, coming from a time when people of different *skin* colours would have been unknown or at least extremely rare in Swindon, George is able to use the term with full confidence that his readers will understand it to mean *hair* colour.

Lack of exposure to multi-culturalism and an old-fashioned insensibility to racial issues explain why there are a couple of uses of language in George's writing that grate on modern eyes and ears. They don't appear in any of the following transcripts, and neither are we going to dwell on them here, for the reasons that their prejudice reflects less sensitive times and *doesn't* reflect George's true character. Indeed, to use a typically cute George Hobbs phrase to describe something of comparative unimportance, we might say they are *but of small moment*. Anyway, there are plenty of other examples of what we might even call *Georgehobbsisms*, which simultaneously demonstrate his ability to produce attractive turns of phrase and the positivity of his spirit – of which the best example is possibly:

> It is rare that I find myself without an appetite for something. At all times I strive to profitably "buy up the moments as they pass".

With a similarly pleasing ring to it is a phrase George uses in one of his *Pen Pictures of the Pulpit* (see Chapter 2), where the three friends of Job are said to criticise him *to the top of their best*.

So as we end this brief look at the language of George Hobbs, we hope you will do your best to spot and enjoy the many other examples of his craft you will find in his writings, which is a rather less pleasing way of encouraging you to buy up the moments as they pass, to the top of your best.

The trouble with kids

Every new generation of community elders likes to think it is experiencing unique and unprecedented problems with anti-social behaviour at the hands of youths, and probably also that if only we could resort to the same two panaceas of days gone by – either a 'clip round the ear' or the presence of a bobby on the beat – then we could go back to living in Shangri-la.

The reality, of course, is that the dismay among older folk about the over-exuberance of youth is nothing new, and it was something that George and his contemporaries also had to contend with.

We know this because he penned a letter to the *Advertiser* in 1916, complaining about the breaking of windows at his church. However, in writing it he probably succeeded in creating the politest, most hopeful letter of appeal to young people to behave ever seen in the whole history of complaints about unruly children, telling us much about his character, in the process, as well as the town's problems with anti-social behaviour at the time. Notice, in particular, how he is anxious about lads 'sneaking upon another', even if it was to provide the answer to the problem, and neither does he want to give any of the perpetrators a criminal record. Sadly, we don't know whether his charming approach paid off or not, but we can certainly admire his efforts:

> Sir,
>
> May I, through the courtesy of your columns, issue an appeal to the parents of lads living in the Rodbourne and Telford Road districts?
>
> We have, at Telford Road, a Wesleyan Mission Church... which, on its north side, there is a right of way. The windows of our chapel are not of plain square glass, but coloured and diamond in shape, being held in place by lead joints.
>
> This being so, it can readily be seen, should any of the windows be broken, it means a large expense in repairs.
>
> It is known, without fear of contradiction, that some of the windows have been broken deliberately by catapult, and by stones thrown by hand. But up to present it has been impossible to immediately lay hands upon the lads.
>
> It is not our wish to offer a reward for detection because we believe this may possibly lead to one lad sneaking upon another – and this is detestable and unwanted. Neither do we wish to place this matter in the hands of the police, so that prosecutions may follow.
>
> We have appealed to the lads of our Sunday School, but we believe the appeal needs a wider range and publicity.
>
> The stone throwing is not only expensive and wrong, but it is also dangerous. Only last week the caretaker was narrowly missed by a stone coming through the window, and we think it is time for something to be done, so that it may prevent unnecessary expense and danger.
>
> We would, therefore, appeal to the parents of lads, asking them to point

out the inconvenience, expense and danger attached to throwing stones near dwelling houses and public buildings.

Thanking you in anticipation.

Yours sincerely,

George E Hobbs

Information technology

One specific thing we learn from George's writing is there was a shortage of paper during the First World War, causing real problems with the dissemination of information, and it also highlights or hints at a range of other problems on the *Home Front* between 1914 and 1918. He writes about at last having 'permission' from the editor of the *Advertiser* to write a series of articles exclusively for young people, and how he had been prevented from doing so, previously, by 'the lack of space owing to the shortage of paper'.

At the end of another of his articles, called *For Young People*, George inadvertently throws light on the way he and his contemporaries processed and stored information.

Newspapers were the primary source of all information, not just current affairs, and although Swindon was blessed with a magnificent library in the railway workers' Mechanics' Institute, including reading rooms in which a range of daily papers were available, they bought their own copies to take home – not just to read, but also to keep. It was the age of the scrapbook, when many people dutifully took cuttings to build into their own version of a Wikipedia entry on a favourite subject.

So he thoughtfully advises readers that the article he has written is part of a series, and says that 'if you are interested in the series, you can cut it out and keep it by you, for future reference', adding:

> Of course, if you are in the habit of sending the "Advertiser" abroad to friends, don't cut it out, for there is nothing worse for one to try and read than a mutilated newspaper. Get another paper so that you can keep the column by you as your own.

This all highlights the long tradition in Swindon – which continues to this day – of friends, families and neighbours sharing and circulating copies of the *Advertiser*, which means its readership has always been far in excess of that suggested by sales. We can only imagine what George would have made of later generations adapting the idea of pooling information by sharing posts on Facebook, photos on Instagram, and retweets on Twitter!

Heroic failure

It's history to us, but a key event in George's life was Captain Scott's attempt to conquer the South Pole, which ended in March 1912 with the death of all four members of the party. George revived the story in his book, *The British Solider and Other Poems, 1914-15*, drawing a parallel between 'the dangers each must face', and the increasingly desperate war. He wrote:

> With weary march and cold extreme,
> Yet in their hearts is joy extreme,
> The Southern Pole is reached!
> The battle they have fought and won,
> The task assigned commenced and done,
> with honour unimpeachable.

Today, Scott's expedition is considered the archetypal 'heroic failure', because he was beaten to the Pole by Roald Amundsen, and perished on the return journey. Yet George's poem reveals that the contemporary view was somewhat different, to the extent that he is able to use it to build sentimentality around a battle that was 'won'.

Perhaps the irony is that there is only one 'heroic failure' in British history that transcends Scott's demise, and that was yet to come: the evacuation of Dunkirk, during the Second World War, which would follow in 1940, in George's latter years.

George's take on Scott's expedition might even suggest that – during a time when patriotism based on the British Empire and the seeming invincibility of the country was still a powerful force – the concept of the 'heroic failure' may not have properly existed.

The Christmas spirit

If we thought that what might be called 'Christmas fatigue' is a new thing, then an exchange of letters to the *Advertiser* in 1922 puts us straight. Apart from reminding us how common door-to-door carol singing would have been, compared with today, it tells us that, even back then, some people were finding some aspects of the Festive Season were too much. The letter that George would respond to read:

> Sir, – Now that Christmas is drawing near, we have to endure the practice of so-called "carol singing," with frequent knocks at the door. Many of the

familiar hymns we enjoyed in years gone by have now become objectionable by the frequency of their repetition and the manner in which they are sung or bawled.

Are there no regulations which can put an end to this annoyance, which in itself is now mostly a form of begging! Everyone welcomes a well-trained choir or band and is willing to give when carols are reverently and musically rendered for charitable purposes. For such I would suggest that an authorised permit be secured as in the case of street collections, and no other allowed.

At the time of writing this protest, various small couples have followed each other, parties in opposition, singing one against the other, starting and re-starting, and so it goes on all the evening and all the week.

Yours etc.,

A Lover of Music

George replies:

Sir, – I was rather interested in the letter of "A Lover of Music", which appeared in your Thursday's issue, in reference to the frequency and disharmony of youthful "buskers". As Mike said when his friend shot him instead of the rabbit, it is "Doocedly annoying".

But could I prevail upon "A Lover of Music" to try and remember two things. First, that carol singing is a time-honoured and seasonable institution; and secondly, to remember the days of childhood.

Let me assume the writer to be a man. Can he forget the delight that was his when he too made one of a little party of carol singers, and received the few coppers that was his lot. He, like the youngsters who entertain (or annoy us) may have "bawled" just as loudly. And perhaps, even in those unenlightened days some person who was distressed by his singing may have written to the then Editor of the Advertiser about it. I do not know of course, as I have no files of the Advertiser by me.

I often feel just as annoyed as "A Lover of Music" appears to be. But when my legs grow tired of walking to and from the door to tell them to come nearer Friday, and when my ears are all a-jangle with the multiplicity of discordant sounds called music, I say to myself: "That's George grown young again."

And what is more entertaining to tired nerves than this: "Shut up yer noise, our Sam, you won't sing long with us. Poke up the light a bit. I can't see the words. Now then; ready? 'Ark the 'erald... Shut up Jack, you can't sing alto! Come on the treble 'long with me. Now then, again! Good King... that ain't it! It's 'Ark the 'erald hangels sing! Alright, go away then, sneak! I'll sing with myself!"

And then quite unabashed the youthful entertainers bang at the door, and ask for "a penny for singing so well". Their whole repertoire is not very extensive – except in patter and personally abusive dialogue. Still, they are following the Christmas custom, time-honoured and seasonable.

I offer this advice in quite a brotherly spirit. If "A Lover of Music" should get annoyed again, let me advise him to do as I did when the pup howled all night. Go to bed and cover his head up with the bed clothes. Then he won't hear anything to annoy him.

Let us try and be happy, even when our ears are distressed by "music".

Yours etc.,

GEH

So: bah, humbug to you!

Hey, Mister!

In April 1918, George paid tribute to the late Mr TR Bray, reporting the unveiling of a memorial tablet to the former Swindon draper who had been the driving force behind the establishment of the Wesleyan Mission Church in Telford Road.

This is, of course, a reminder of times when the establishment of new places of worship was common in Swindon, but the article also tells us more about the times: formality and the importance of etiquette.

It is notable that at no point in the article does George tell us the Christian name of Mr Bray, and, indeed, of the half dozen other people mentioned, we learn of the first name of only one – and only then, probably, to ensure architect Mr George Davies is not confused with any other person by the comparatively common name of Davies or Davis.

George's reports of other solemn and/or formal occasions in his writings also omit first names, even if there is a personal element to the proceedings.

By the way: Telford Road can no longer be found on maps of Swindon since it was later renamed Cheney Manor Road, and the former church is now a private dwelling.

A Day to remember

When George was invited to the annual prize-giving ceremony at his former school, Even Swindon, in August 1919, he felt compelled to accept, writing: 'I am sincere when I say I would not have missed it for a great deal.'

We should feel glad that he attended, because his report on the occasion reveals a surprising amount of information about social life in Swindon at the time, and more besides, including the kind of person George was.

It would be the last such event presided over by headmaster Henry Day, whom George highly respected, and whose influence we look at in more detail in Chapter 7.

He points out that the event was attended by 'a fair sprinkling of mothers' of the children, and even 'I fancy, one or two of their fathers'. Clearly this is not a time when fathers were expected to take such a close interest in the scholarly achievements of schoolchildren.

Henry Day's speech began with a recollection of the time when he received a schoolboy prize of his own, becoming 'the proud possessor of a full-sized guinea cricket bat'. Then he recalls the time when prize-giving at the school was first established, which would have been around 1880:

> In those days prize-giving was a problem of some magnitude; for as no money was granted for this purpose, the purchase money had to be raised by means of concerts.

This tells us that giving prizes was, in the late 19th century, something of an innovation, although, by the 1920s and 1930s, many (and probably most) schools had such a scheme. Then George adds something surprising, telling us:

> And as no books could be bought in Swindon, he [Henry Day] had to journey to Bristol in order to select and purchase them.

Perhaps more than any other single piece of information in the whole of George's writing, this tells us that whatever we thought we knew about the past, it isn't necessarily true, and the only reliable source is what the era's contemporaries tell us.

That's because we might have assumed that books would be easy to come by in Swindon during this period, particularly as the town had a reputation for its railwaymen being relatively enlightened and educated, compared with other industrial workers in Britain. It was, after all, home to the Mechanics' Institute, which was effectively the first public library in Britain. But here George is telling us that there is nowhere to buy books in Swindon.

Ironically, the existence of an easily accessible library in the town may actually have been the key reason that made a bookshop unviable (why buy expensive books when you can borrow them?). Or were books too much of a luxury for many to consider buying? Whatever the reason, it is surprising that Swindon didn't have at least one outlet dealing in new books, c1880.

We do know, however, that by George's time, book ownership had become more commonplace, since the front room of his home at 4 Jennings Street was remembered, by later family members, for having been turned into a small private library. 'Hammerman poet' Alfred Williams (1877-1930), to whom other parallels have been and will be drawn, also built up a significant private library in his home, a portion of which still exists and is currently held at the Central Library in Swindon.

In his report, George also notes another change:

> Very powerfully did Mr Day remind the children of the glorious heritage into which they have come – that of free education; telling them of the days (which I can remember) when on Monday mornings, 3d and 2d [1p] had to be taken to school by the respective members of families.

A colleague of Mr Day also gives us an insight into corporal punishment, after revealing how he had been punished during his school days, and again our assumptions are probably challenged. He reports:

> The punishment was not administered in a vertical position and upon the hands, but the posture was horizontal and upon a more painful part of the anatomy. And the young folk, evidently visualising the somewhat painful episode, roared in sheer delight.

So, by 1919, bending over to receive 'six of the best' had become outdated enough to have become an anachronism, and there was even the suggestion that it was somewhat barbaric, contradicting what we might think we 'know' about discipline in the first part of the 20th century. At the same time, however, we also discover that punishing children by hitting them on the palm of the hand with a cane was, in George's era, still quite acceptable, and it is surprising to find that even Henry Day did it.

We know this had been the punishment because, in a letter to Henry Day in the same year, George recalled the time when the headmaster gave him 'six with the cane – three on each hand'. This was apparently a punishment for lying, although George always protested his innocence!

Although we might be surprised that an enlightened and even visionary teacher like Day would resort to corporal punishment, perhaps there is a clue here that all was not necessarily what it seemed.

The comparison between the barbaric caning of the buttocks and the supposedly much less painful rapping of hands doesn't add up. Properly administered, surely a blow from a cane on hands would be just as painful. So it would be nice to think – and not illogical – that Henry Day's idea of corporal punishment not only fell well short of the humiliation of 'horizontal' caning, but was perhaps replaced by a largely symbolic light rap on the hands. Indeed, George points out that Day's methods of obtaining the best from pupils 'had ever been upon the lines of moral suasion; never upon threats of punishment', (which must have been unusual for the time). He was, after all, a man who instigated prize-giving and delighted in it, so is clearly a man who believes in carrots rather than sticks. So why, then, was he an advocate of rapping children on their hands?

Any corporal punishment that was meted out was perhaps based on its effectiveness in instilling anticipation and expectation, rather than any value from its execution, but this wasn't necessarily thought by the general public to be the most effective method of instilling discipline. In an age when parents and society as a whole seemed to put their faith in the beating of children (in the home as well as school), perhaps Henry Day only went through the motions when he was forced to mete it out. That way he would satisfy everyone's expectations, including parents, but he always has the option of doing it softly if he really has to administer strokes with the cane on boys' hands.

Also in the report of the prize-giving, George notes that prizes 'are now given for work done and not so much for attendance', which also tells us something about the struggle to get children to attend school in the past.

Also present during the ceremony was 'our old friend Mr Reuben George', whom George reserves some praise for. He would become Mayor in 1921, and is a key figure in Swindon's history, having been the effective 'father' of the Labour Party in the town, but his personal popularity does not seem to have been affected by any political opposition he might have encountered. There is another parallel with Alfred Williams here because the South Marston poet was a genuinely close friend of Reuben George; however, when he is referred to as an 'old friend' by our George, it may or may not mean they were actually closely acquainted.

When George finally comes to what he describes as the 'thrill of the afternoon', the retiring headmaster is praised and presented with his retirement gift – or rather, in the polite formality of the day, he is 'asked… to accept this token of [the staff's] esteem'. His gift is an easy chair, complete with a commemorative brass plaque, and an 'illuminated address': evidence of the formality with which these occasions were suffused, even amid genuine warmth for the man retiring.

George is still not finished with providing a window into his world, and he ends the article by informing us that the occasion was ended by the singing of the National Anthem, obviously a routine way to end all such events.

The last word goes to Coun AJ Gilbert, who kindly supplied the frame for the illuminated address, and who – in case there is any doubt – tells us that it was 'a fact' that Mr Day 'is a true type of an English gentleman'. And the same surely applies to George Hobbs; if you haven't already warmed to his generosity of spirit, then this passage from the report of Henry Day's retirement should clinch it:

> Mr Butler found time to congratulate each prize-winner upon the receipt of their prize. I am glad he did this, for… the child with a second or third prize has worked probably as assiduously as the child who was fortunate enough to take a first prize. While we bow to genius, we must not forget to take off our hats to the conscientious plodder. If any of the young folk should read this article, prize-winners or non prize-winners, let me say to them: Work, not so much for prizes – gratifying as the receipt of them may be – but work so that you may lay the foundation of such usefulness as will tend to add to the sum total of happiness in your day and generation.

Trippers and Mrs Crabthorn

Anyone who develops an interest in Swindon's heritage and starts to read about it will eventually – probably sooner, rather than later – come upon references to an annual event that dominated generations of life in the town, and which helped to define most of its glory days as a railway town.

Trip: it started as a day's excursion for railwaymen and their families, developed into a week's and then two weeks' summer holiday, and was still being called 'Trip fortnight' in more modern times, when it was rather more of a expedient factory shutdown than the fiesta it had been in earlier days.

Whole books have been written on the subject because Trip became not merely part of the town's culture, but almost a state of mind, the key factor being the escapism it provided for the whole workforce and their long-suffering families, for a tiny portion of the year.

Swindon folk looked forward to Trip for months, and those families that didn't plan carefully and save up for the extravagance of holiday accommodation and seaside treats could come home, when it was all over, to debts that might not be cleared until Christmas.

So it's no surprise that Trip is referenced, several times, in the writings of George Hobbs.

One comic sketch, called *Trip Eve and Trip Day*, written in 1920, taps into the excitement surrounding the event, as George creates a comedy sketch around the routine, on the eve of Trip, of a mother washing each of her children, in turn, in the family washtub. The central character is Mrs

Crabthorn, a fictional creation who appears in several other comic articles. This one begins by noting that the father has already gone absent without leave:

> Where's your father I'd like to know! Round at the Blue Nose, I'll be bound. It's a blue nose he'll be getting, and a thick ear in the bargain; leaving me to clean boots as well as bath you lot. Trip to-morrow and all.

We must not be too keen to read too much into what is, after all, a fanciful comic scene, but there does seem to be some indication, here, of a somewhat darker side that was underlying domestic life in Swindon in 1920.

For a start, although talk of *blue noses* and *thick ears* might seem like harmless banter, it surely reveals a violent aspect to the domestic scene that far fewer of us, thankfully, are familiar with today. We should not forget that this is an era when a man was expected to be master of his own home, and there seemed to be few limits on how extreme the methods were that he might choose to emphasise his supposed superiority.

And isn't this sketch also revealing a wife who needs to be able to give as good as she gets, including by returning violence?

Mrs Crabthorn v the fairer sex

As comical as Mrs Crabthorn is intended to be, the revealing sketch, above, suggests an undercurrent of conflict and even violence, and there are other pointers to all not being well in the Crabthorn battle of the sexes.

In another comic sketch, this time about Mrs Crabthorn completing the 1921 census, it is made clear that although the man was, by law, automatically the head of a household, some women begged to differ:

> Me and John 'ave decided, long ago, who was the 'ead of our 'ouse. An' I can tell yer it ain't John.

What is clear is that the wife can expect no help from the husband in the running of the household and the bringing up of the children, not even with the logistical challenges of Trip thrust upon the household.

The Blue Nose may be a fictional pub, but the absent father's attitude to Trip is real enough. Those debts that some families accrued because of Trip were often just a product of bad planning or the struggle of some families to scrape together enough money for the annual treat. However, for some Swindon men, Trip meant not the chance to take part in a memorable family holiday, but an excuse to spend much of the time in the pub.

The following extract is also rather telling:

'That you, John? Nice time I've got to look forward to to-morrow, an' you started on the fuddle a'ready – only went to have a drink? You was born wrong, John. You ought to have been a whale… if you was a whale the new earth would be 'ere 'fore time, for there'd be no sea. You'd guzzle it all up. Yer name ought to be "blotting pad" for you soak up everything wet.

"Didn't talk like this 'fore we were married?" No, an' I didn't have ten kids and a porous husband 'fore I married, either.'

This underlines that one aspect of Trip that isn't often considered by historians is the social challenge that Swindon's working men must have felt at the prospect of a week or two in the company of their families. These were men who worked long hours and had relatively little involvement in their children's upbringing, compared with what is usual today, and we should not underestimate the challenge and even the pressure they must have faced when suddenly expected to bond with a family, over a week or two, when they were much more used to the company of their almost exclusively male workmates. Given the alien situation they were confronted with, we might even sympathise a little with their desire to run off to the pub and escape two weeks in the company of Mrs Crabthorn!

By the time the family get on the platform, next morning, the joke is about negotiating the huge crowds – the majority of Swindonians were all at the station simultaneously, boarding their trains – and making sure they get on the right train; the Crabthorns inadvertently get on one bound for Weston-super-Mare instead, although their preference is for Weymouth.

Trip also thrust parents into the logistical challenge of marshalling large numbers of excited children on journeys and in unfamiliar accommodation; George's comic family includes no fewer than 'ten kids', but that's nothing unusual for the period.

Boarding the train, the father's reluctance or inability to help earns him another ear-bashing from the wife, who tells him to 'Pull yer 'ands out of yer pocket and give the kids a leg up', and this provides us with yet another insight into domestic conflict, as the father complains about being criticised by his wife in public. 'Too quiet I am,' counters the wife, 'an' I gets put on for it.' Clearly, men are not only supposed to be masters of their own home, but need to be *seen* to be masters. When they find a compartment on the train and discover a 'courtin' couple' in there, the father is reluctant to enter, but the wife has other ideas:

'Let the turtle doves see this little lot, an' let them 'ear you a-jawing me, then they might reconsider gettin' spliced.'

And, just to make sure the young woman knows what she could be letting herself in for, the wife turns to her and says:

> 'Used to call me his own damsel… An' he used to kiss me in the tunnel like yer young man kissed you in the last one… An' now look what 'olding 'ands and kissing's done, honey. Ten of 'em and a blotting pad for a husband.'

The article ends with Mrs Crabthorn having been shown to be someone whom we shouldn't necessarily give our full sympathy, despite her husband's liking for a drink or two, but rather a nag or busybody. The implication seems to be that the only thing worse than a weak husband was an overbearing wife. She has apparently overstepped the mark with her public criticism of her husband, with the suggestion that she is as much villain as victim.

Knowing what we do about George's character, including suggestions that he approved of radical (for the time) ideas about female emancipation, we should not assume that he has any axe to grind about feminism, women's changing roles in society or their attitude to men.

However, it is noticeable that the women in his writings are somewhat two-dimensional, and are drawn from one extreme or the other. They are generally either *larger-than-life* – and they don't come any larger (in various respects) than Mrs Crabthorn – or the sweet, innocent, dainty, vulnerable creatures at the other end of the scale, albeit often with other redeeming qualities.

The latter group form the majority of his female characters, and probably reflect an era that had a *speak-when-you-are-spoken-to* approach to women; like children, they were presumably expected to be seen and not heard. What is perhaps most curious, for us, considering we live in a time when women are cast as being too talkative and accused of chattering too much, is that George suggests the women in his world were rather the opposite.

During his comic series *To Seekers After Trouble*, he ponders the ideal suitors for men who are loquacious (what the dictionary defines as 'tending to talk a great deal'):

> We are told that like attracts like, and upon this dictum tall men should select tall women. Fair men, fair women. Loquacious men should select talkative women – though I very much doubt if one could be found. Silent and reserved men should select silent and reserved women. These are much more numerous.

So there we have it from the pen of George Hobbs: in his time, women really were seen and not heard!

We haven't seen the last of Mrs Crabthorn, because we will devote a whole chapter to her adventures (or rather *mis*adventures), but it is worth ending this brief look at women in the early 20th century by highlighting George's introduction of her to *Advertiser* readers – partly because we wonder whether a modern writer would get away with it today, but also because it is as masterful a character description as you may find from the pen of any writer in English literature:

> Mrs Crabthorn is an elf-like creature of sixteen stone burden, a head taller than myself, and built upon the lines of a thirty-six gallon cask. Whether she is patriotic upon principle or compulsion I cannot say: but certainly there is no "waste" about her. Not only so (forgive me, dear Mrs Crabthorn) but I feel certain that John – that is her husband, of whom more anon – must have courted her in the dark; never taking the precaution of providing himself with a lantern.
>
> Of course, I quite realise there is no blame attached to Mrs Crabthorn in regard to her generous outlines – or her face. I believe in giving censure where censure is due. Dame Nature was the culprit, and she must have been either cross-eyed or had a momentary lapse when she gave Mrs Crabthorn her figurehead.

Trip revisited

It is often noted that Swindon became a 'ghost town' during Trip – because the overwhelming majority of men were employed by the GWR, and would have been expected to go away during the holiday.

'The whistle blows and Swindon, the once gay town, is left deserted, desolate and sad,' confirms George, but that is not the whole picture:

> But no! Swindon was not quite deserted. There were a few left behind. And some of the few decided, previous to the Trip, to relieve the monotony by playing a cricket match.

We aren't sure why George stays at home instead of going away on Trip, but it is probably because, by this stage (1921/2), his only surviving child, his daughter, has grown up, so the 'family' has been reduced to just George and his wife. And Trip is predominantly an event for families. It's also logical to assume that the hordes of Trippers also excluded single men, since in the cricket matches that takes place while the rest of the town is on Trip, George is joined by enough men from G Shop to make up two full teams, who quaintly call themselves the *Players* and the *Gentlemen*.

George naturally adds some fiction into the story for the sake of humour, but ends the article in typically positive mode:

> One is happy to record that the real good fellowship exhibited during the match made the evening worthwhile.

Meet the family

Although we may not be surprised to find that large families were the order of the day during his era, George's references to numerous children still have something else to tell us about lifestyles.

We return, yet again, to Mrs Crabthorn, who acquired no less than a dozen children by the time she was forced to fill in the 1921 census. She has so many, in fact, that 'I've forgot 'ow many there is,' and then struggles to recall all their names. Ironically, George also seems to lose count, at times, and the true size of the Crabthorn brood is never confirmed. Ebenezer (Eby for short), for instance, doesn't appear on the 1921 census, but plays supporting roles in some Mrs Crabthorn sketches.

When she finally gets down to listing the children for the census, it is an indication of the process of naming of children in the period; we get Willy, 'Enry, Florrie, 'Erzikia, Sally, 'Erbert, Samuel and Gertrude, and a couple ('Oratio and Grace Darlin') who were named according to the common custom of recalling famous figures from history. As Mrs Crabthorn explains:

> 'Other people gives names like it to their nippers. 'Ow about the Bower War? I knows a chap called Spion Kop, an' a 'oman named Preetoria.'

Most of the children she lists come with a second (middle) name thrown in for good measure, showing us how these were considered a significant part of people's identities; indeed, it was not uncommon for people to be referred to by second names, particularly within families, whereas most of us ignore our middle names today. Even George Hobbs, himself, was at pains to sign himself, at the bottom of articles, with his middle name, Ewart, or at least the initial.

The courting years

Courtship is an ever-changing ritual – how many people even still use the term 'courting'? – and it defines generations as much as any other aspect of our lifestyles. Although the birth of his first child followed somewhat quickly after his own marriage, George nevertheless comes from an era in which purity, innocence and sheer sugary sweetness predominated – and if we were expecting some of that in his writings, we are not disappointed.

He tells us about sweethearts ('two turtle doves') on a train, and how they wait until they pass through a tunnel before stealing kisses; the meeting of would-be lovers in *Soul Mates*, a short story, is a classic study of romantic etiquette; and he has comical advice for would-be wooers in the brilliantly written *To Seekers After Trouble*.

On a potentially more saucy and maybe even sordid note, however, one of the terms he used there and elsewhere is *glad eye*, which is an arcane term that effectively means *consent*, and presumably *sexual* consent. We might be more open about discussing such subjects today, but it seems significant that George is able to summarise attitudes at the time and also sweep the subject under a moral carpet with the use of two short words! And, just in case we forget the formality of the courtship rituals, George reminds us that a now-obsolete phrase was in common parlance at the time (or at least easily understood by *Advertiser* readers), when he writes about a young man looking for a partner and on the verge of proposal, as *pressing his suit*. How sweet!

Newlywed brides, meanwhile, had a going away dress, bought and worn especially for the occasion, which we learn when one of the characters in George's story, *Doctor Nickols*, gets married. So it was clearly a common tradition at the time, seen as a key moment on a woman's journey from being a spinster to becoming a wife.

George's best romantic literary efforts are arguably in an article called *Eavesdropping & A Lesson*, in which he treats us to a description about young girls growing up that is almost poetry, would make Thomas Hardy proud, and reminds us that the author is nothing if not a natural-born writer:

> A few years pass in rapid succession and the baby girl has now the dignity of the prefix "Miss". Young men, fearing that the sun will shrivel her up, or the rain will drown her, or that she will get run over, or vanish like a ghost, see her safely to her gate – and only to her gate. But one of the knights errant is a "special", and he, with that sure confidence associated with "specials", pushes the gate wide open and enters the sacred portals of her home.

Beautiful!

Beware of charlatans

There was a curious letter to the *Advertiser* in which George wrote about 'the wonderful discoveries of Mr FA Mitchell-Hedges, FLS, FRGS, who has just returned from the hinterland of Panama'.

It demonstrates his interest in archaeology and science, and perhaps a general popular interest in exploration, although he seems to smell a rat when commenting on Mitchell-Hedges' apparent discovery of evidence that 'huge animals of the Jurassic period, long thought to be extinct for thousands of years, still roam the earth', and links these supposed facts with Sir Arthur Conan Doyle's fantasy, *The Lost World*, which would become the inspiration for *Jurassic Park*.

He then goes on to consider the origins of man, referring back to his own series of *Creation Narratives*, while considering comments about the Mitchell-Hedges discoveries by an officer of the British Museum.

George was right to be sceptical about Mitchell-Hedges, who was latterly likened to Indiana Jones, but subsequently shown to be a charlatan when the crystal skull he apparently 'discovered' in the 1920s turned out to be one he bought at an auction.

The 21st century is not without its charlatans, but George's treatment of the Mitchell-Hedges episode suggests that, when they appeared in his era, and even though it was more difficult to gain access to hard facts, they were subjected to greater scrutiny than they are today. Under the microscope of people such as George Hobbs, at least, they were evidently treated with the necessary scepticism. However, the tendency for fanciful stories, wild claims and crackpot notions to be temporarily taken up by a gullible public seems to be a feature of life in George's time; perhaps they are a precursor to a modern world in which some people are disposed to believe ludicrous conspiracy theories. George reports on these phenomena, but makes it clear enough that, being rather more forensic in his thinking, he was not taken in by the hype.

Likewise when the imminent end of the world was forecast in 1919 – by not one but two theologians, in two separate theories. A matter that was clearly one of intense speculation naturally drew the attention of George, who noted the public 'panic', and with the human race apparently days from disaster, he addressed the question in the middle of December 1919, in an article headed, simply, *The End of the World*.

Church of England preacher and evangelical thinker Rev Hanmer Webb-Peploe had drawn on records 'from the Pyramids' to show that Armageddon was due by the end of the year, but then 'a friend' of Webb-Peploe somewhat downplayed the forecast to predict not so much an ending as a beginning: the dawn of 'the New Age', which, it transpired, was 'the Golden Age' after the second coming of Christ.

Also in the public eye was Professor Albert F Porta, an Italian who had made a name for himself as a weather forecaster in newspapers across the United States. In the summer of 1919 Porta began issuing warnings about storms, eruptions and earthquakes that would befall the country, caused by the alignment of the planets. The chaos would begin on December 17 and end four days later.

The forecast became a worldwide phenomenon because it was apparently based on the calculations of an eminent scientist, and had made its way across the Atlantic to Swindon by early December.

In the United States, Canada, Britain, France and beyond, people prepared themselves for the worst. In Oklahoma, miners refused to go to work for fear of being buried alive, and, in New York, one woman took her own life rather than be killed in the cataclysm.

In Swindon, where disaster hadn't struck by December 19, George wrote that 'by the time the last editions of the evening papers are out tonight, the joke will have become wearisome,' but, being a believer in science himself, he seemed obliged to defend Professor Porta.

He pointed out that the professor hadn't actually predicted the end of the world, but 'the most terrific weather cataclysm' and there was 'no mention of Great Britain taking part in this cataclysm or of the end of the world'.

What George didn't know was that Porta was yet another charlatan. Although his name had been associated with the University of Michigan, and across the world it was assumed that he was Professor of Astronomy there, he wasn't. Indeed, he was a Professor of Civil Engineering elsewhere. It transpired that he had never actually set foot in the University of Michigan.

The whole matter tells us something about the power of newspapers at the time, because Porta's predictions in America and Webb-Peploe's, closer to home, spread like wildfire, both fantasies propelled by the apparent eminence of their originators.

And if the people of anywhere in general and Swindon in particular ever needed persuading that the end of the world was nigh, then 1919 was probably the ripest time to plant the seed. Following the horror of the First World War and amidst a Spanish flu epidemic that was claiming even more lives than the war, it was perhaps not unreasonable to suspect that there were forces afoot that would finish the job.

George, at least, remained calm. He was in no doubt that the world would, one day, come to an end, but could find no evidence that it was imminent.

He undoubtedly relished the distraction, saying, somewhat sarcastically, that it was 'rare that the thoughts of men can be diverted from football, Premium Bonds, Income Tax and other little items that make life so enjoyable'.

And soon both he and the Swindon public had another distraction to occupy their minds and newspaper columns, which George called *The Marconi Sensation*. 'The world and his wife,' he states, 'are standing with bated breath before the curtain that veils the mysterious and the unknown,' he writes, about a phenomenon we look at in more detail in Chapter 11, and which helped to inspire him to write the science fiction story *The Mysterious Message* (see Chapter 12).

In hindsight, Webb-Peploe's predictions of 'a New Age' weren't necessarily so far off the mark, because, despite the war, the flu and premonitions of the end of the world, it must, indeed, have looked to be at the dawn of something in 1920, and George sensed it; we can sense it, too, in many of his works.

Some light entertainment

We will offer some speculation about the inspiration for George's fictional writings in the following chapters, but in the meantime it is worth considering what kind of entertainments he and his contemporaries would have enjoyed – and a few clues have been dropped into his writings. We discover, for instance, that while western movies enjoyed their heyday among British children growing up close to the Second World War, 'cowboys and Indians' were firm favourites much earlier, both as movies, but also in literary form. This extract is from a Mrs Crabthorn sketch in July 1920:

> It was enough to startle an unimaginative person; but Eby is a great reader of Indian stories. At this very moment he was dreaming that a Sioux war party, under their chief "Red Cloud", were attacking the stockade of the palefaces.

Actually, the genre would fall out of favour with cinema audiences after the spread of 'talkies' in the late 1920s, before enjoying a revival in the late 1930s, but what George's throwaway lines about their origins tell us – through the medium of Mrs Crabthorn, of all people – is that not only have the movies already made their mark, but the massive influence of American culture on our own, which is a feature of British life today, had already begun.

And the influence of cinema even extends to George. While we might have expected him to fill his spare time with more cerebral pursuits, and while it would also be reasonable to think that his faith might have convinced him such things were frivolous distractions, he informs us otherwise, albeit with the caveat of *everything in moderation*:

> I am a great believer in amusement, whether it is football, cricket or any other legitimate sport – or, if you like, the picture palace. I often go there myself, and I do not remember that I ever wished I had stopped away. Yet if all our relaxation is occupied with amusement, then I do not think our lives will be benefitted a great deal thereby.

So cinemagoing has become commonplace, even by the time that George wrote that, way back in January 1917. Charlie Chaplin and the Keystone Cops had arrived on the scene by then, but a measure of how early it was in the history of cinema is that some of the giants of silent movies still remembered today – Buster Keaton, Harold Lloyd, Greta Garbo – were, as yet, unknown. Note that this is also when Britain was still at war, suggesting the conflict had limited (if any) effect on cinemas and other entertainments.

Also notice, by the way, George's reference to 'legitimate sport', suggesting there was an interest in more dubious types – presumably those that existed to feed an illegal gambling industry, and which would have been a complete anathema to George.

Thoughts of war

The First World War is a complex conundrum for historians to unravel, and George provides lots of insights into contemporary attitudes towards it, so that anyone trying to understand the mood in Swindon and the rest of Britain when war was declared in August 1914 should read his 'war poetry' (see Chapter 4) as a starting point.

It is far removed from the output of poets like Wilfred Owen, Edward Thomas, Rupert Brooke and Siegfried Sassoon, who actually witnessed action, but it does give us a window into the complex situation on 'the home front' (a phrase we might use today, but which isn't used by George), as well as attitudes towards the war that we may find surprising.

Indeed, when one also takes into account all his other writings that reference the war, George provides an interesting picture of a public that, even at the height of the conflict, is not necessarily as united behind the war effort as we might expect, particularly when compared with what we know about the greater unity of Britain during the Second World War.

We learn from him that the idea of a home front – what George dubbed 'equality of sacrifice' – was still evolving when the First World War ended. Thanks to George's writing, in fact, we find that, if anything, there may have been more unity *after* the war, than *during* it, although it seems that people became more united by resentment. This was even felt by apparently mild-mannered characters like George, and it was strong enough to surface even when he was writing comical sketches about Mrs Crabthorn, and even when nearly two years had elapsed since the Armistice.

Part of the resentment was aimed at those who had taken advantage of shortages during the war:

I followed her in with feelings similar to what a profiteer will have, when, at the crack of doom, the gentleman with the trident and toil invites him into his well-heated den.

But the Germans hadn't been forgiven, either, with George suggesting he supports the imposition of heavy reparations on former enemies, a policy which eventually became a major factor in the rise of the Nazis in the 1930s:

> I have concluded my visits to Mrs Crabthorn and I am free to confess that happiness is once more mine. No inducement short of the amount
> Germany owes the allies will take me there again.

George's writings during the war made it clear that the conflict itself was far from the only thing on people's minds, and there was a very real feeling that everything would collapse because of growing support for Home Rule in Ireland, trade union unrest, and other clouds on the horizon. The possibility that the Amalgamated Society of Engineers (ASE), a trade union, would call for its members to withdraw their labour alarmed George enough to write a letter to the *Advertiser*. Published early in 1918, soon after the Russian Revolution, it seems to show there were genuine fears that the same could happen in Britain, despite the war. His letter begins:

> Sir, – It would be the merest commonplace to say that the times in which we are living are serious. The very air seems surcharged with potent factors of destruction. Rumours and innuendos are flying round section to section that one may not be considered pessimistic if one becomes apprehensive of the immediate future.
>
> In a humble way, I wish not to aggravate, but to try and palliate the situation, that the air surrounding our various trade organisations may be cleared of this poisonous and irritating influence.

And ends:

> There is talk of downing tools. As Englishmen, such a suggestion cannot be tolerated. Other means may be found, but not this! Do you know, or have you considered, what this would mean?
>
> Thousands of our members are yielding their all in France and elsewhere. Would you allow them to get murdered without a chance of effective defence? This is what it would amount to if the ASE and kindred trades carry out their threat.
>
> It is a suicidal suggestion, and no one worthy of the name of Englishman or Britisher would dream of such a thing.
>
> As a member of the ASE, I would refuse to down tools under any circumstances that would jeopardise the lives of those brave men who are fighting.

What about the workers?

The same conflicts and dilemmas that his contemporary and fellow writer Alfred Williams struggled with, in regard to industrial relations and the growth of socialism, are also evident in George's works. As we have seen, unrest during the war prompted him to write a letter, about potential industrial action, to the *Advertiser*, but he also brought the subject up in his columns in the paper, notably in one of his *Pen Pictures of the Pulpit*, in 1924. Although drawn to trade unionism and interested in socialism, like Williams, George ultimately steps back from supporting changes that are going to upset the political and social order, and for George, the question of faith only complicates the issue.

In the following extract from the article, George tries to put his thoughts in order, and advocates workers labouring for *the common weal* (to quote another one of his charming phrases) to also strive for greater fulfillment, beyond the workplace: yet another echo of Alfred Williams. But stand by for a final sentence that puts everything in perspective for us:

> A wage slave is one who works for money and with no higher thought. Such try to get inspiration by getting as far away from toil as possible. They do not intend to do too much. Toil to these is nothing but monotony and drudgery.
>
> The worker should escape from the thought of mechanical routine to the larger thought. The inventor, the genius, and the worker, are all parts of a whole and each and all should labour together for the common weal.
>
> The highest sanction had been given to toil. The "Light of the World" had been a toiler. He had been a son in the home and a youth in the workshop and in His parables he revealed His sympathy for every helpful section of the social order.
>
> Is it possible to "crown labour with true wealth," to realise the true dignity of toil, that we should labour for the good of our fellows? The answer cannot be given on a Sunday evening. It can be given from Monday morning to Saturday noon.

So, whatever our opinions on the issue of workers and their rights might be today, we need to bear in mind just how different George's world was to ours, because if we need to understand how work was central to the lives of Swindon and its railwaymen, George informs us that the working week was still five-and-a-half days long, he and his workmates even being obliged to work on Saturday mornings.

And when he alludes to the need for personal knowledge and enlightenment, remember that this was also an era when children received a comparatively short education, as one of George's articles in a series called *For Young People*, published in 1917, underlines:

> I want to write something... that those who are in the upper standards of our schools, and those who may have left school and are up in their teens, may find something interesting to read and talk about.

It's a reminder from someone who himself left school when he was only 12, that whereas the vast majority of today's teenagers are still at school, in George's era the 'teens' have already gone off to work.

Together, the references to the working week and the school leaving age, might be throwaway lines for George, but for us they not only colour in the picture, but emphasise that his aspirations and achievements in his life outside his work were all the more remarkable because of limitations on leisure time and education – making him all the more worthy of a book like this!

Death from the air

Just as Alfred Williams did, so George selected specific incidents from the news of the First World War as subjects for his poetry, realising their potential to be fuel for another rallying cry, and he wrote one called *The Air Raid of Jan 31st 1916* that dealt with the new horror of death on civilians, wrought from the air by Zeppelins.

It emphasises that while bombs falling on civilians would become a key feature of the Second World War, the same fears were also common in the First World War.

George saw it as a cowardly tactic, not least because some of the victims were female. In all, 61 British civilians died on the night in question, in a raid by nine airships that was meant for Liverpool, but hit three Black Country towns instead. Two pilots, sent up to locate the airships, died when their aeroplane crashed, and at least 16 Zeppelin crew members died as a result of Dutch groundfire. Why George chose this particular action to write about is unclear: air raids had begun as soon as the war had started in 1914; became a specific tactic over Britain in 1915; and killed more than five hundred people over the duration of the war.

The threat clearly had a great effect on the population, as George's poem illustrates, even though there is no record of an attack over Swindon. However, there is a local connection because Reginald 'Rex' Warneford, who lived for a time at the family home in Highworth, became the first pilot to bring down a

Zeppelin in June 1915, an action that earned him the Victoria Cross. Warneford, sadly, was killed in a flying accident, days later.

A dog's life

The curious arrival in George's story of his dog, Tiny, throws light on attitudes towards pets, a hundred years ago. Bearing in mind that this is wartime, with problems of food shortages and increased economic pressures, we might be surprised to find that people were still willing or able to have pets. In one of his fables, George explains to Tiny about the serious problems of not just the supply but also the cost of food, and eventually comes round to the dilemma of choosing to feed dogs when people might be going hungry. In a shocking turn (although we don't learn how likely it is) we discover that some are starting to advocate the slaughter of dogs as a result:

> "There are humans today who are advocating the decease of such as you. I imagine them to be folk who have little or no love for dogs, and who certainly do not stop to consider what the result would be should a wholesale and ruthless destruction of dogs take place. But the time may come when even this drastic suggestion may be put into actuality and..."

Back to the future

In Chapter 12 we will take a more detailed look at George's ideas of what the future might bring, looking at his science fiction writings, but his other works also give us glimpses into his fertile mind, and suggest how open the public, in general, must also have been to crystal ball-gazing.

Yet again, it's Mrs Crabthorn who is the vehicle for one surprising flight of fantasy in his works, in two tales about her purchase of a robot. George wrote these in 1923, only three years after the word first entered the language. The stories tell of a robot bought to do household chores, George perhaps imagining that they would soon become commonplace in domestic life.

His other speculations about future technologies include ideas for rocket science, as he dreams of space travel and imagines that electro-magnetism will provide the propulsion (also imagining it would drive boats), but grossly overestimates the time that will be required to reach the moon (33 days), as well as guessing wrongly about what the astronauts might find when they get there. George, by the way, describes what we would call the *far side* of the moon, as the *night side*. His hero in *A Visit to the Moon* doesn't get to see it, and one wonders whether even George could have imagined that, long before the century was over, astronauts of the Apollo missions would.

Indeed, for all his creativity, which must have gone well beyond the dreams of most of his peers, there is still a limit to how far George's imagination will carry him. It gets him as far as the moon, but not Mars – because, when that planet appears in his science fiction, it is all about observations of its surface, with the possibility of spacecraft making the journey there seemingly too ridiculous even for him to contemplate.

Although George may not have foreseen travel to Mars, he did, nevertheless, imagine there would be space food, in his story *A Visit to the Moon*:

> My food and drink were made in concentrated form, and though I took what I considered to be a twelve months supply, the whole occupied a space of but six cubic feet.

There is also an ironic coincidence in *The Mysterious Message*, in which Professor Fellows reveals that there is a previously undiscovered planet between the sun and Mercury, which George names as Vulcan, which the creators of *Star Trek* would later name the home planet of Mr Spock.

Domestic life

Arguably the most fascinating aspect of all of George Hobbs's writing is the insight it affords us into what domestic life was really like, a hundred years ago. What was, at the time, a mission to alternately entertain and educate his readers, is now a rare legacy in that it enables us to be transported right into the home of someone from the era.

Even when he is talking about a heavy casting at the Swindon Railway Works foundry (see Chapter 5), for instance, we are reminded that blancmange was a common dessert on the table of people like George, and they would go to the trouble – and it was a trouble, in an age before convenience foods – of serving it in a serrated or '"fancy" mould'.

Elsewhere, George tells us that men like him washed – not in a sink, as we might imagine – but in a bowl, using water that had been boiled on the fire.

Snapshots of real life arrive like this, throughout his writing.

While talking about the problems caused by inflation during the First World War, George tells us that 'even a rabbit is spoken of as "a little dear"'. From this we learn not only that rabbit was commonly eaten in the first quarter of the 20th century. It also tells us that, in Swindon, people were likely (possibly *more* likely) to buy one from the butcher, when we might have expected them to hunt or rear one, instead. We also learn that rabbit was not a staple of people's diets, but rather considered a cheap substitute for other meats.

We even find out about the writer's writing process, and discover that his articles are written in pencil, which provides yet another parallel with fellow writer Alfred Williams, who did not acquire a typewriter until his latter days. George also eventually acquired a typewriter, and although there is also evidence that he used a pen when writing formally or finally, it does seem that a pencil and a rubber were more convenient tools if you were a wordsmith unlucky enough to be born into an era long before cut, copy and paste, and CTL-Z were invented!

Another aspect of George's life that we are far removed from, thanks to our 21st century standpoint, is the practice of people sharing household basics. Whereas "borrowing a cup of sugar" would be an anachronism, now that neighbours rarely borrow anything from each other, through Mrs Crabthorn's antics George informs us that it was still common in his era:

> 'What's that Billy Johnson? Yer mother wants to borrow the bath? Well tell her she can't have it then. She's a'ready got my frying pan, tell her to bath you in that...'

It is fitting that we should end this chapter by looking at a four-part series of articles that George wrote in 1921, which provide the most concentrated insight into domestic life. If you wanted a glimpse into a day in the life of George Hobbs, this is it, and never mind that it is wrapped up in a situation comedy based on an apparent challenge he has accepted from his wife to do her work for a day. Called *A Day's Efforts and Its Results*, it is the perennial *Battle of the Sexes*, except that phrase hadn't yet passed into common understanding. And don't be surprised to find that George fails miserably.

Look beyond the slapstick and you can find a vivid picture of an everyday working-class home of the period, and if you look even deeper, you can see hints of much broader (and perennial) issues, such as the roles of men and women, inequality, and the influence that the Bible still had on the issue. Ironically, while it is, on the surface, a comic admission of Man's inferiority to Woman when faced with domestic chores, it also serves to (perhaps inadvertently) reinforce the idea that still dominated George's era, which was that a woman's place was in the home.

But this entertaining escapade also has much else to tell us about the way people lived in George's time.

For a start, there are clear indications of how the approach to food has changed over the last century. In George's world, meals arrive according to a strict timetable, and there are four of them. In an age when some of us skip breakfast, and (even if we don't) are unlikely to sit down with others to eat one, we are even more unlikely to do what George did, later in the day, and have a formal supper. And snacking, as we know it, hadn't been invented!

Even by naming the meals, he tells us something about the culture of working-class Swindon in the early 20th century, because the mid-day meal is 'dinner'; just like snacking, 'lunch' doesn't seem to have been invented yet!

George's experiment in role reversal, by the way, presumably came at the weekend, and probably on a Sunday. On working days, which routinely included Saturday mornings in 1921, he would have clocked in at work by 7.30am.

Breakfast turns into a disaster, mostly because the preparations, the timing and the operation are quite complex, but also because George obviously doesn't have the benefit of today's convenient kitchen gadgets. Before cooking can commence, for example, he has to 'light the gas, set light to all the wood I can find and hang the kettle upon the top'. Evidently, water is boiled over the fire, not on the cooker, which was probably what we would now call a range.

Even before these preparations could begin, George had to find his way downstairs, and informs us that he requires a candle for this; electricity was widely available in parts of Swindon by 1921, but apparently not in the Hobbs household.

Falling down the stairs, George talks of a 'rift within the lute': a now obsolete term his readers must have instantly understood the meaning of (an apparently minor piece of damage, likely to have fatal consequences).

Then he comes face-to-face with something that we are just as unlikely to encounter in a domestic situation in the 21st century: 'a wild, ferocious bull cockroach'.

While cooking breakfast, he tells us that he had to formally lay the table, before revealing that: 'being in an affluent position, [I] made preparations for boiling the eggs (eggs for breakfast denotes wealth).' So a simple egg is not just a sign of affluence, but actually wealth, and it sounds like an apology from George to the majority of his readers. Although many of them would have been highly skilled, most would still have lived a more austere life, compared with him, since he was a foreman. So it's no wonder that, when the eggs end up on the floor, George 'gazed almost with tears in my eyes, upon the ruined breakfast'.

The farce continues with policemen arriving at the door, whom George describes as 'two mighty sons of Anak'. This is a Biblical reference to a race of giants that is unknown to the majority of us today, and in using it he is not only telling us much about his own faith and knowledge of the Bible, but also revealing that he can safely use such a reference and trust that his readers will understand it.

The police inform George that his chimney is 'on fire'. This was not an uncommon occurrence with coal fires, where residue – mainly soot – in the chimney would catch fire. It was usually caused by insufficient sweeping, but sometimes also bad luck, and the symptoms were often more visible outside the property than inside. George's comic tale also informs us that allowing a chimney to catch fire was, actually, an offence, carrying a fine of half-a-crown (12.5p).

Even a joke that George has with the policeman, about it not being *his* chimney, but rather his landlord's, tells us something profound about his life.

His home – 4 Jennings Street, Rodbourne, Swindon – was almost as humble as terraced houses could be, a bona fide two-up, two-down. Yet it is clearly all that George can afford, despite being a foreman. And now we discover that he doesn't own the property, either.

Next, he manages to break a cup, which falls to the floor and unluckily misses what he calls the 'collision mat', apparently one designed to provide a soft landing in a kitchen that would otherwise have been hard-floored, probably with linoleum. This requires him to repair the broken cup; his era was not one where crockery could simply be replaced, and he didn't have the luxury of owning spares.

Before he can move on to dinner, George discovers there are other domestic tasks to perform, since it is 'washing day'. Long before working people had machines to aid them, the washing of clothes was such an undertaking that housewives generally put aside a chosen day each week for it. George explains that this involves filling a 'copper' with water, and placing it on the fire, clearly the main source of energy in the house, even though gas is laid on to a cooker.

Undeterred by the challenge, and driven by some patriotic pride of triumph over adversity (which we might now call the 'Dunkirk spirit'), George decides: 'so being a Briton I determined to show all and sundry what I was capable of doing when put to the test'.

Unsurprisingly, his attempts at dinner are just as disastrous as the botched breakfast, his aim being to cook and serve 'baked herrings with potatoes and fried tomatoes'. Herring was a staple of meals across the country during this period. Mostly fished in the North Sea, they were a good source of vitamins and protein, and – more significantly – cheap, until over-fishing led the industry into almost terminal decline. The cooking process began with taking a whole herring and removing its head and tail, then gutting, but George makes the mistake of leaving the fish on a plate while he goes upstairs to carry out other chores: washing the floors – again, hard floors, probably with mats, but not carpets – cleaning the windows, and dusting 'the Dresden': probably a reference to their 'best' crockery and ornaments, since Dresden is a type of porcelain, mostly associated with decorative plates and pairs of urns.

Needless to say, the potatoes burned and 'some marauding feline... actually stood in the tomatoes' to get to the herring 'and dined without receiving an invitation', so George has to resort to buying fish and chips as a replacement; telling us that, despite everything else, at least he has arrived in an era of takeaway meals.

The items on the menu for tea, which was due to be delivered at precisely 4.30pm, might be something of a surprise to modern eyes, compared with the simplicity and frugality of the other meals, and this demonstrates that, however poor George's lifestyle might otherwise seem, tea was considered an opportunity to indulge oneself.

He opts for 'sliced bananas, covered with custard, and a nicely browned currant cake, covered with almond icing'. A tropical and exotic fruit like a banana might seem to be an anomaly in the diet of working people in Britain in the early 20th century. However, whereas the bulk of Britain's banana imports now come from Latin America, a primary source, back then, were Caribbean islands like Jamaica (which was still a British colony and didn't win independence until 1962).

With three disastrous meals under his belt, it's hardly surprising that poor George fails miserably when he attempts to deliver the fourth. Supper, or at least the formal act of sitting down to eat a meal, comparatively late in the evening, has largely gone out of fashion since George Hobbs attempted to prepare his. When one bears in mind that an early start was required for work, the next day, and that 9pm was significantly closer to bedtime than it might be for most people today, supper is even more interesting. Clearly, people of George's era were used to going to bed with full stomachs! In this respect, his choice of sprats, fried in boiling dripping, is even more surprising!

Finally we come to looking at transcriptions of full articles themselves, but it's worth reiterating what was written at the start of this chapter – because, alongside the pleasure of reading George's works, there is the joy of discovery. His pen-pictures tell us far more about the life he led than photographs ever can, and it is fitting that we start with a pen-picture that does what old photographs of Swindon rarely did, which was to point the viewfinder towards the inside of homes, and at supposedly ordinary things.

See what else you can spot from the following story. Everything else that follows in this book is also George drawing back the curtains on a window on a vista that is now foreign to us.

A Day's Effort & Its Results [1]
Amusing Article by George E Hobbs
(First published: February 4, 1921)

The bitterest experience that can happen to a mere man is when he is proved incapable of performing something he has boastfully asserted he could easily do. I have passed through such an experience, and believing it may prove of interest to my fellow boasters, I hereby sorrowfully place it upon record.

It all came about through a deep conviction I hold, namely: the superiority of Man over Woman. I have always believed the Biblical story in which is recorded that woman came after man – a long way "after" too, at that. But I am not rude enough to agree with a bachelor friend, who feelingly suggested "she has been after him ever since". Woman is "after" man only in the comparative sense; never in the matrimonial sense. Certainly not!

If any fair reader doubts my assertion as to the superiority of man over woman, let her engage in a throwing contest with a man (personally I am not available).

The man invariably will go somewhere near the mark aimed at; while the woman will as invariably hit some object nearly at right angles to her aim. I was once the unfortunate object at right angles to a lady's aim – so I know. But that sounds like boasting again, and I have a very painful experience to record.

My Waterloo

I was informed that work appertaining to domestic life was of such a character, no man could carry out its duties successfully – even for one day. "Poof!" I replied airily, "I could do it on my head" – and that was the beginning of my Waterloo.

I was to try for one day only and to be fair, work to a timetable: Breakfast 7.30am; dinner 12.30pm; tea 4.30pm, and supper at 9.00pm. If only I could have foreseen what would happen, I should have swallowed my pride, admitted my incapacity, and retired as gracefully as circumstances permitted.

Unfortunately I quite forgot to set the alarm overnight, with the result I did not awake until 7.10am – and breakfast was to be upon the table by 7.30am. Out of bed I sprang, and evidently sprang too far, for my head came into violent contact with the wall and I found myself sitting upon the bed vaguely striving to establish the identity of the villain who had hit me. When my senses admitted coherency, I hurriedly dressed and, taking the candle to light the way, proceeded down the stairs.

I have written "proceeded" but "projected" would be the truer word. The top stair rod had mysteriously detached itself from the holders during the night and, of course, I stepped upon it.

I was always under the impression there were twelve steps to the staircase, but upon this occasion I counted only two: one at the top when I said "Oh!" and one at the bottom when I said something else.

Naturally the candle and matches accompanied me in my spiral dive down the stairs, but the bottom steps proved to be the "rift within the lute"* and a forcible separation was the result. I found the matches at last, but not until I had found two tin-tacks, calmly reposing upon their heads; and something which resented capture every bit as much as I resented capturing it. It was a wild, ferocious bull cockroach, which to my slightly excited senses seemed to me to be as big, well, quite as big as a cow cockroach.

"Outlook" Becomes "Blue"

It was now rapidly approaching 7.20am and I was getting anxious. It was the work of a moment to light the gas, set light to all the wood I could find and hang the kettle upon the top. Then I had the table laid, and being in an affluent position, made preparations for boiling the eggs.

The water came to the boil beautifully and I was just about to place the eggs carefully into the saucepan when a terrible rat-tat came to the front door. Down went the eggs with a woeful crash upon the floor, and I gazed almost with tears in my eyes, upon the ruined breakfast. But somebody had to go through it, and I went to the door determined to take it out of whoever it was had caused me to lose my breakfast, and nearly lose my reputation as well.

I opened the door with hot words upon my lips, but my courage sank to zero when I saw who my visitors were. Two mighty sons of Anak stood there, each dressed in the majesty of the law. Visions of murder, bigamy and a muzzle-less dog flashed through my mind.

"Your chimney's on fire!" said the officer in charge of the squad.

"Oh!" I replied, relieved to such an extent that I could afford to be facetious. "You're wrong, it isn't my chimney."

"Yes it is," contradicted the officer, ordering the squad to form fours and surround the house.

"But it is not," said I emphatically, "it belongs to the landlord."

"That's the same thing," he thundered menacingly. "At any rate the chimney you are responsible for is on fire."

"Pardon me," I replied courteously, "but you are wrong again. It is not the chimney but the soot that is on fire."

This was evidently more than he could stand, for he wirelessed the squad back to the base, formed him up, dressed him by the right, and then placing himself at the head of the column, marched into the house.

Out of the Frying Pan

And what a sight met my view when we all arrived into the kitchen. I had quite forgotten the kettle in my interesting interview with the police force. The handle and the spout had evidently had words with the body of the kettle and had parted company. Both were in the fire, and even as I watched the bottom of the kettle also dissolved partnership.

"You're evidently in the cart this morning," said the squad feelingly.

"Yes," I replied sadly, "but don't interrupt while I total up the casualties."

Sorrowfully I made up my accounts. On the debit side were: A lump on my head, a pain where I sit down, three smashed eggs – still lying upon the floor, the kettle in pieces upon the fire, and half-a-crown for the fire in the chimney. And I could not place upon the credit side "one successful breakfast".

Never mind. I'm a cheerful soul, and I still had a chance of winning back my reputation. There was dinner, tea and supper yet to come.

*An apparently minor piece of damage, likely to have fatal consequences

---

A Day's Effort & Its Results
"The Second Chapter"
By George E Hobbs
(First published: February 11, 1921)

There is nothing so calculated to upset one's temperamental equilibrium as a smile of derision or a contempt. It is all the more irritating when it is not deserved. I know that a breakfast of buttered bread and cold cater is not very appetising, but what could I do against an inexorable fate? The fact that I was covered with bruises, with a new kettle to buy and half-a-crown to fork out in order to palliate an offended bye-law ought to have prevented further indignities to my feelings. But no: The smile of derision became more pronounced as the luscious meal advanced. Then the tin hat was put on with vengeance.

"How do you think you are getting on?" asked the smiling one, sweetly. "Progressing backwards are you not? Don't you think you had better give up and – " "No!" I roared, rearing up on my hind legs. "You clear out as soon as you have finished breakfast and don't come in again until 12.15. I will show you then what I am capable of doing."

"All right," came the answer; then, with a broader smile: "You won't forget the washing?" "Washing?" I queried blankly. "What washing?"

My Own Selection

"This is washing day," replied my amiable partner. "You selected the day yourself, and you said you could do ALL the work associated with domestic life on your head. I'd just love to stay here and watch," she concluded, insinuatingly moving towards the street door, "but never mind. I'll be in at the death."

It was no use remonstrating; so being a Briton I determined to show all and sundry what I was capable of doing when put to the test.

Luckily the breakfast things demanded very little attention; though I took the precaution of placing a nice soft mat in a convenient position in case any portion of the delicate breakfast service slipped. One cup only proved refractory. It slipped through my fingers and in trying to catch it I knocked it clear off the collision mat, with disastrous results. I pieced it together with such exquisite skill a cubist would be driven into raptures could he but see it. If it is not quite its original shape, at least it is better than some folk's arguments – it will hold water.

My next job was to fill the receptacle provided in all modern dwelling houses for wash days. I do not wish to use the name I know it by or folk will think I am vindictive over the chimney catching fire. "Filling the copper" does not sound polite in the circumstances, so I shall not use it. Having filled the aforesaid receptacle with water I lit the fire beneath, intending to prepare for dinner while the water was coming to the boil.

A Sudden Exit

Of course it was nothing but natural the flue should be stopped up, but how to clear it caused me to lose a great deal of mental energy. At last I remembered. In a newspaper column set apart to help those in distress I read once that gunpowder was a good thing to clear a flue closed by soot. I could not remember, however, the amount one should use. At last I decided upon the amount, and then added a little more to be on the safe side.

As I sat in the backyard gazing up at the fleecy clouds sailing by and ruminating upon the strange vicissitudes of life, my thoughts reached concrete shape in a sign of thankfulness. How glad I was that the back door had been open. I am sure than my sudden exodus into the wilderness would have been of a much more painful character if I had gone through the door instead of the doorway.

The two sleeves of my shirt were missing, as well as a hat which I was sorry to lose. Still it might have been my head, and that would have been worse than losing a hat; though folk have said rude things about my head. I must have been slightly discoloured too: for a neighbour passing at the time, thinking I was the coalman, said: "I'm glad to see you. I was nearly out. Four please."

But all sorrow at personal discomfort vanished when I saw the state of the boiler. How true it is that every poison has its antidote, and every trial its compensations. The boiler was in the same position as I had been when I first landed in the back yard – upside down. But unlike me it had failed to right itself. "Washing's over for to-day at least," said I joyfully. "And now for dinner."

I decided upon fish. Baked herrings with potatoes and fried tomatoes. I know my work and set about it in a businesslike manner.

The Banquet

Upon the order "one", I grasped the herring in the left hand, holding it firmly to prevent it kicking, and severed its fo'c'sle head. Reversing I did the same service to the steering gear. Upon the order "two", I opened the herring fore and aft and removed the turbines which I found amidship. Four of these denizens of the deep I served in like manner, and laid them upon a plate, ready for baking. As it was rather early for dinner I placed the fish in a cool place, peeled the potatoes and put them on at a slow boil, and sliced the tomatoes, ready for their introduction to the frying pan.

All was progressing splendidly. My chest filled with pride as I contemplated the praise which would be my due when this appetising repast was partaken of.

Upstairs I went in high glee; washed the floors, dusted the Dresden, and cleaned the windows. Then downstairs again to complete the dinner.

Upon reaching the kitchen a peculiar odour assailed my nostrils. What did it portend? Surely my good luck was not about to desert me. I went to investigate, and what I saw was enough to break the heart of a giant.

The gas company must have supplied extra quality gas upon this occasion, and I had not allowed for such an unlooked contingency. The gas flame must have been quite above zero for it had not only evaporated all the water in the saucepan, but had cracked its appendix and burned the "spuds" to a cinder.

"Never mind," I cogitated cheerfully. "We still have the herrings and tomatoes."

But we hadn't! Some marauding feline had entered the open door and dined without receiving an invitation. If it was a Tom cat he was no gentleman, and if it was his wife she was no lady. Whichever it was did not know their manners; for he or she had actually stood in the sliced tomatoes and cleared the herrings to the very bones.

Sadly I lowered the colours to half-mast and went out to purchase some fish and chips. On the door step I met the wife. "I've come back for dinner," said she cheerfully. "Yes," I answered, "and I'll come back too when I've got it."

A Day's Effort & Its Results
"The Third Chapter"
By George E Hobbs
(First published: February 18, 1921)

Some time ago I stood upon a football field watching a match fraught with great issues. Half-time arrived with the score two-nil against my favourite team – and apparently the match was lost. In the second half, however, the home team seemed wonderfully rejuvenated. They played inspired football and drew two each.

I thought of that wonderful match and it inspired me. Half-time – to be precise, 12.30 p.m. – I was two down. But I was a long way from being beaten. I, too, would rejuvenate. To use Samson's explicit as a metaphor, I would take hold of the pillars of success and bring death and destruction upon the contempt in which I was held.

The calm way with which my wife took the dinner of fish and chips quite surprised me. In fact it made me suspicious. Then I learned she had anticipated a fiasco and dined out.

That "anticipated" nearly caused me to see red. It revealed a lack of faith in my capabilities; a want of confidence in my undoubted superiority. What annoyed me, too, was the fact she was more concerned about the demolished boiler than my painfully sudden journey into the backyard. And then to add to my torture she began to ask questions of a satirical nature. Which did I consider was the more painful: contact with the force which began my meteoric flight, or contact with the backyard wall which ended it? Was my flight semi-circular, parabolic, or was it in a straight line? Did my general bearing suggest dignity or dishevelment when sitting upon the cold, cold ground? etc., etc.

It is a tribute to my self command that no unseemly retort escaped my lips. But then that is my usual attitude. While the record is declaiming its precious subject matter, I think furiously. But when the needle is removed for want of breath I forget the neat little retort I had been nursing. Suddenly I remember, but before it is uttered another record is in service, and I am silenced.

Upon this occasion I waited my opportunity. Respiration was becoming enfeebled; so I knew an air pocket was in the vicinity. When it came I seized my chance and said with my accustomed courtesy: "Don't let me see you again until 4.30 p.m., and then you will have the surprise of your life," – she did, but I didn't mean it that way – "One thing I would ask. As I intend having something nice for tea, please do not take tea out." Alas for woman's subtlety! I sometimes wonder whether it was the woman tempted the serpent instead of the serpent the woman. My wife respected my wish. She did not take tea out, she took coffee instead.

The Real Business

It took but a few moments to dispose of the dinner things, and then the real business of the afternoon commenced.

For tea I intended to have sliced bananas covered with custard, and a nicely browned currant cake covered with almond icing.

I must here make the confession that sometimes I suffer from fits of abstraction: Therefore absentmindedness must be the excuse for my first error. Subconsciously I must have been thinking of my usual labours; for after removing the skins of four bananas I placed one upon a chair with the intention of holding it with my foot while I back-sawed it through to the marks. Applied pressure on the precious fruit brought back my wandering thoughts, and I sliced the other three in a rational and becoming manner. Then I made the custard, sweetened it with some castor sugar I found, and poured the semi-solid mixture, steaming hot, upon the bananas. I then placed it in a cool place to set for tea. I was really proud of that custard for it represented my first success in the culinary art. And now for the cake.

My first trouble came at once. I could not find the basin in which to mix the ingredients. I do not suggest it was hidden deliberately, but the fact remains it could not be found. Necessity, however, being the mother of invention, I soon found something I could use. I scoured and rinsed the bowl I wash in, arguing that what the eye sees not the heart grieves not for. I found, so far as I was concerned, it made an ideal mixer.

Holding the bag of flour in my hand I counted the various ingredients to see if I had all I wanted. I counted aloud, with my hand rising and falling in unison with my voice. One – marge; two – currants; three – milk – and flop went the flour on the floor. With the aid of the brush, used for sweeping in the fire grate, and the fire shovel, I soon had the flour picked up from the floor, and to avoid further trouble I put it in the bowl as it was. Of course it did not look quite like flour ought to look, but no one would know when it was baked.

Needed kneading

Into the slightly discoloured flour I put currants, marge, allspice and milk, and commenced to knead. I needed to knead, too, for I found the mixture very stiff indeed. Still, a little more milk helped, and then I found it was too wet. More flour, too stiff. More milk, too wet. So I continued until all the milk and half of another bag of flour was consumed. Then I added water and more flour and still could not obtain the right proportions. The bowl was now filled to the brim. The marge wept for sheer loneliness, and the currants had long since lost their identity in the overwhelming mass of milk and flour.

Then I was struck with a bright idea. Instead of a cake I would call it a pudding, and boil it. I ought, of course, to have put it in a basin and tied a cloth over the top, but I was not so well versed in puddings as I was in cake. I tipped the whole of that ugly looking mass into a cloth, tied it up and put it in a saucepan to boil.

No words can adequately express my horror when I saw the result of my labours. The cloth had burst in the saucepan, and if I dared I would have served it up as pea soup. It is now resting in a deep and sheltered grave, and when I see it in my dreams it nearly produces the ague.

With pride I turned to the bananas and custard. Here, at least, I had succeeded. One taste, and I stood almost petrified. I had mistaken the salt for castor sugar.

The time is 4.10 p.m. Twenty minutes to tea time. I have just buried the custard and bananas side by side with the cake-pudding, and all that remains for tea is just bread and tea. I had used all the marge in the cake-pudding – and now I wait for the footsteps I dread to hear.

A Day's Effort & Its Results
"The Fourth Chapter"
By George E Hobbs
(First published: March 4, 1921)

It was my intention to ring down the curtain upon this present series, particularly upon that part which concerned my culinary abilities. But folk are not content that I should. Constantly I am asked: "What was the fate of the supper?"

"Fate," I would point out to those concerned, is a unfortunate word to use. It suggests pre-judgement; an adverse verdict given before the prisoner is arraigned. Still, I must not be too fastidious over methods; for that is the usual attitude towards old offenders.

"The prisoner pleads 'not guilty' your worship. But there are three previous convictions recorded against him for similar crimes," says the custodian of law and order. "Three previous convictions?" exclaims his worship, aghast. "Then of course he is guilty in this case also. "Twenty-one days without the option!" – and so it goes on.

Previous Convictions

There were three previous convictions recorded against myself – breakfast, dinner and tea; so of course I was guilty in regard to supper. That is why my friends used the word "fate", insinuating I had failed again. In this they were wrong, which statement I will qualify anon.

First, however, I wish to utter a warning. There are folk who have penetrated far, far beyond the "fate" stage. Their remarks upon my efforts with the breakfast, dinner and tea have been so flagrantly abusive that had I been of a quarrelsome disposition, undertakers would now be working overtime. I merely mention this as a preliminary caution. There is a limit to my endurance, and I do not wish to waste half the week attending inquests.

But my chief reason for wishing to ring down the curtain prematurely upon this series is that I wish to save other men from making asses of themselves. While still adhering tenaciously to man's superiority over woman, I say it now cautiously and inaudibly. Others, however, have not learnt my discretion, and foolishly have declared to their wives they could not only do better than myself, but make a good job of it in the bargain. Several have been dared by their spouses to try it, and the offer has been accepted. My only hope is that all the trials will be conducted on the same day. If so I can see I am in for a glorious time. I shall arrange for a day off: visit each in turn, notebook in hand, and record my impressions – that is if impressions are not recorded upon me first.

The Final Dash

But now to return to the narration of my final dash for culinary honours – to the supper, the fate of which my friends are anxious to learn.

Five o'clock saw my wife again outward bound upon a mission of mercy. That mission was to leave me alone so that, unassisted, I could achieve a great triumph. And let it be blazoned throughout the two hemispheres I succeeded in winning through.

In justice to truth I must admit I encountered difficulties. But that is not the point. My success lay in the fact that I succeeded in getting an appetising supper.

As soon as the coast was clear I slipped out and purchased some sprats. These I knew were very appetising when lightly swilled and drained in a colander, dipped in flour and fried in a pan of boiling dripping. I purchased sufficient to compensate any losses enroute to the table. It was well that I did so, as the sequel will show.

My first trouble came from an unexpected quarter, and occurred before I reached home with my precious burden.

If folk must have dogs on a lead at night they should be compelled to shorten the lead so that the dog runs to heel. Naturally, when I saw approaching me through the gloom a young lady and a little white dog on opposite sides of the path, I did not dream there was a lead between them. I was in a hurry, so were they; with the result I fouled the lead and fell. With a muttered apology the young lady passed on, leaving the sprats and me somewhat mixed upon the ground. Hastily I picked up my flotilla of submarines and made tracks for home, which I am glad to say I reached safely.

Fire and Gas

It did not take me long to swill and drain the sprats, and prepare the frying pan to receive them. The first panful I fried over the fire, but not the second. I will tell the reader why I changed from the fire to the gas ring. Being that the chimney had caught fire in the morning – I have already recorded this painful incident – I naturally thought there would be no more soot to come down. In this I was mistaken; for no sooner had I had the first panful of sprats nicely browned than they became "un-nicely" black. Down came the soot and smote amain my fishes in the pan. So I had to throw my first consignment away.

After cleaning out the pan I transferred to the gas ring to try my luck there. I filled up the pan with sprats and I saw to my unspeakable joy they were turning a lovely brown. One more sprat I put in, and that one proved my undoing so far as that panful was concerned. Just as I was placing it carefully in the pan a vicious splash of boiling dripping struck my hand in a tender spot. "Oh!" I shouted, flicking my fingers in agony. Evidently, I flicked too hard for the next thing I saw was the pan and sprats in the coal bucket, standing near. My third attempt was better, and, though there were not so many sprats for supper as I intended, yet we sat down to an enjoyable meal – of a few nicely browned sprats.

Thus ended a most momentous day for me. I had won in the last event and therefore am worthy of a hearty "Well done".

I was "well done", so never again for me.

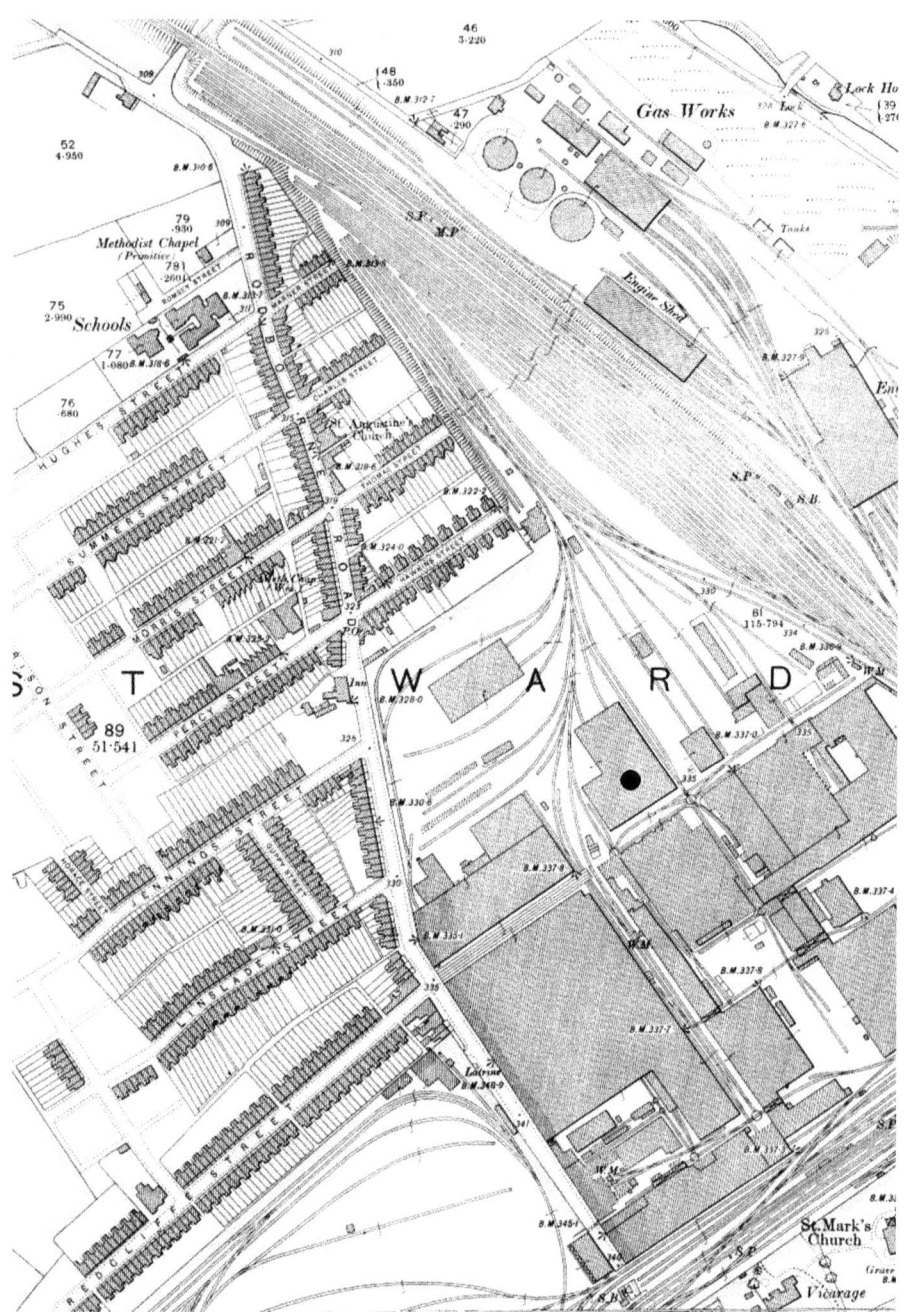

An early 20th century OS map of Rodbourne, featuring key locations in George's life, including Jennings Street (number 4 is in the terrace closest to the junction with Rodbourne Road); the chapel in Percy Street, here with the earlier 'iron chapel' still adjacent; the Methodist Chapel and Even Swindon School, towards the top; and X Shop in the Railway Works, where he was a foreman (which we have marked with ●).

Worshippers from the Percy Street Chapel arrive at Cheddar by charabanc during an outing in the summer of 1922. George himself doesn't seem to be on board. (Courtesy of The Swindon Society)

The Palladium, in Jennings Street, soon after it opened. The building still stands, opposite number 4, where George lived for some years. He admitted to being a regular cinemagoer in an article published in 1917, but this was eleven years before the Palladium was built in 1928; note that the land is unoccupied on the map, opposite. It closed as a cinema in 1958. (Courtesy of Rodbourne Community History Group)

An aerial view of Rodbourne, looking south-east, in 1924. Jennings Street School (now the site of a community centre) is on the far right. At this time Swindon's Railway Works was at its height, and A Shop (in the background, across from the park) was the biggest covered workshop in Europe. (Courtesy of The Swindon Society)

Chapter 2

When Science Meets Faith

Life must have been relatively straightforward for the God-fearing Victorians, but the more enlightened generations of the early 20th century faced rather more of a test of their faith.

George Hobbs was no exception as his natural and clearly rather sincere beliefs were challenged on three fronts. For a start, there was watching the unfolding horrors of the First World War and wondering whether one might now be living in a godless world; then, in the mind of a man who embraced science and some modern thinking, there was the unresolved question of evolution and how this could be squared with the Biblical version of creation; finally there was George's personal tragedy, the loss of two of his children in infancy, a sadly not uncommon outcome for many parents of the era.

Although George's writings reveal a man who is more than willing to wrestle with possibilities to find a way to reconcile his religious beliefs with his scientific curiosity and knowledge, it would be quite wrong to call this a 'struggle', because his faith is never in question. Far from it.

In *The Triumph of Love*, a poem written in November 1915, George talks of God as 'my lover', and in another, from March 1916, called *In Faith*, he argues that faith can be used to overcome the challenges of war:

> But human sense is ofttimes wrong,
> For when it says "Impossible,"
> A simple faith, sublime and strong,
> Will turn it to "Possible."

In *Trust*, he tackles, head-on, the question of continuing faith in a world seemingly tearing itself apart in the First World War, beginning by asking God

'How canst Thou lie there sleeping, with death and danger nigh?', but concluding that 'God is still the Pilot'.

The theme is the same in *To The Despondent One*, a long poem that was originally published in the *Advertiser* in three parts. 'What! No God? did you say brother...?' asks George, as he attempts to reassure readers that despite the continuing war, 'God is Love, and He will never/Cease to love the world, and you.'

In these wartime poems, George clearly sees his role as trying to raise morale, often suggesting faith as a potential source of strength in such dark times, and harking back to happier times, so while the earlier poems look to patriotism as an uplifting device, later ones tend to give way to sentimentality and optimism.

Sometimes he speaks purely of love, and when he does, it seems to come arm-in-arm with faith, George clearly wishing his readers could see them as twin beacons in desperate times. One poignant poem (*Love Fills The Void*) is about an unnamed woman who lost her husband in the war, but discovered she was pregnant, and gave birth to a daughter. 'Love fills the void,' says George, forever positive, and it's probable that this poem was based on someone he knew personally.

But even George struggles as the war continues and becomes ever more desperate. In *My Need*, he admits: 'I need a hope to ease my heart's distress.' Eventually, he is forced to concede that 'death reigns' in one poem, and although it is called *The Desert Shall Rejoice and Blossom as the Rose*, it doesn't actually offer much hope for an end to a wind that 'blows fitful, blasting and hot'. Perhaps there would be no heaven, after all, to overcome the hell?

But it is a rare island of pessimism in a sea of optimism, because even when George writes a poignant tribute to fellow preacher, Lance-Corporal George Gee, who was killed in action in June 1915, the message of this poem is that they will meet again and 'clasp again each other's hand'.

George is also forced to consider his faith in relation to the greatest question of the age: the origin of man.

When he writes about it in 1917, it was already half a century since Charles Darwin shook the foundations of religion and personal faith with his book, *The Origin of Species*, but it had effectively taken that long for many men and women of faith to confront the ultimate dichotomy of evolution versus creationism. George Hobbs is the perfect embodiment of someone trying to come to terms with being a man of faith, while, at the same time, being a man of reason.

It is curious that he uses his 1917 series, *For Young People* (see Chapter 3), to try to unravel his own thoughts on the subject of the origins of the world, and therefore Man. He begins by offering three potential answers:

(1) Either the world must have existed from eternity the same;
(2) Or it was formed by chance at some unassigned period out of pre-existing materials;
(3) Or it was created by an omnipotent and intelligent Being.

After quickly ruling out the first option, he turns to the two other possibilities. Quoting extensively from Dr Alfred Russell Wallace, a contemporary of Darwin who had similar theories about the origins of life, George argues that the delicate balance and 'the wonderful precision' of the natural world could not be entirely a result of chance, thus ruling out the second of the three possibilities put forward.

This leaves us with the third option of the world having been brought into existence by an intelligent being. There was clear evidence, George suggested, of 'firmly impressed thought, design, plan'. However, if it seems like we are in the home straight and on the verge of finding out how George reconciles these apparently conflicting ideas, we aren't. We are just getting started.

In his consideration of the creation, George gets sidetracked by considering the deities and religious systems of Ancient Egypt, which were already beginning to grip the public's imagination; Howard Carter's famous discovery of Tutankhamun's tomb was still five years away, but the project to find it was now two years old. George demonstrates a similar considerable knowledge of the beliefs and practices of Assyrians and the Babylonians and even the Japanese, and various other cultures and races, including more modern ones, as he considers how these cultures approached the subject of religion and how they explained how the earth and life came about.

It all amounts to a long and somewhat convoluted theological study, more concerned with Scripture and Man's other interpretations than tackling the real issue of creation, but perhaps this tells us much about the approach to religion at the time.

George's direct knowledge or experience of other religions is not typical, but otherwise he reflects a Britain that was, after all, still steadfastly Christian and, indeed, Anglican, which seems to be reflected by his pre-occupation with the nuts and bolts of faith and worship, including the Biblical account of creation.

But he is a man of science, remember, so George uses science – as far as it goes – to consider the origins of man. Not surprisingly, he turns to the fossil record, since it was the main source of data in his time, long before the subject was revolutionised by microbiological evidence and, since the 1970s, the emergence of genetic science through DNA. George's estimation that the emergence of Homo sapiens took place at around 100,000 years ago is, therefore somewhat wide of the mark – today experts think it was 300,000 years – but his error is understandable.

It is worth stopping here, by the way, to observe that here is an ordinary Swindon railwayman (albeit a foreman) who is not only interested in the subject, but shows himself to be very learned, even though he has had no formal or full-time education in such matters. And despite having limited free time. How did men like George find time – for instance – to travel to Bristol Museum (as he reveals in his writings) in order to see its geological room?

Even before he starts to pursue questions of faith, however, George has to give himself permission, and he shows he is not unaware of the great irony that exists in his curiosity. After all, it was the established church that had stood in the way of true enlightenment for centuries. People like him would once have been considered heretics if they sought answers to the mysteries of space that were out of step with what the Bible and other theologies taught, but: 'Happily we live in days where individual opinions no longer render men liable to the tortures; and truth or imagination can be expressed without fear of wrack or scourge.'

Not that George's (and others') search for enlightenment were necessarily welcomed by his contemporaries. The views of more conservative elements of society, and particularly inside the Church, are, it seems, still a factor.

There is evidence that George still feels that discussing such questions openly is going to ruffle the feathers of some of his readers, because he talks in terms of having to 'excuse' his curiosity, and alluding to 'offence' and 'forgiveness', pointing out:

> There are not a few good people who think it wrong for finite beings to probe the infinite. Mysteries, we are told, are best left alone; no good will come in trying to search out that which it is not intended for us to know.

A statement he makes in the lead-up to his theories about creation is also revealing:

> I think that in the minds of some good people, there is a secret fear at the revelation that may ensue as to the result of intensive research. But why the fear? Can man disprove God?... Thank God the day has happily gone when progressive thinkers are consigned to hell.

Even as far into the argument as article 13 of *The Story of the Creation*, George is still looking over his shoulder:

> I think no harm will be done if we embrace the means at our disposal to conduct an investigation into the results of scientific and philosophic research, that we may know something of the conditions that must have

> prevailed when life dawned upon the earth. Let us conduct our
> investigations without fear, but with true humility at the greatness of the
> task.

Fortunately, George clearly doesn't believe in this outdated *ours is not to reason why* approach, and goes a step further, arguing not only that Man should make use of his brain so that it doesn't become redundant, but that it is ultimately his duty to do so, and that that duty was given to him by God.

And so, at last, we are finally coming to George's theory about creation and evolution:

> I humbly submit my deductions, that man was truly developed as he was
> created; he was as truly created as he was formed; and he was as truly
> formed as he was created and developed. Let me explain.

The explanation begins with what George considers a fallacy: the idea that God literally created Man in His image. It is, he said, Man's soul that simultaneously makes him like God and different from the animals, who don't possess one. By 'soul' he means 'a spirit', and by this he means 'reason, conscience and will'. Yet ('and modern research has proved it so') 'we can reasonably say that Man was formed from the dust of the ground', and to the theory of evolution 'we must yield our consent'.

So, once he has spent a little time dispelling a misconception that was popular at the time, that Man was *descended* from apes, rather than *related* to them, George admits that there is no denying Darwin, and even that there has to be a question mark over the idea of a single creation found in the Book of Genesis:

> That some explanation must be given for variety of species is patent to the
> most shallow of thinkers, and if some explanation must be assigned, what
> better than to yield our consent to the hypothesis most in harmony with
> reason? No real thinker of today would give the chance theory a second
> thought, because it is both illogical and unnatural. The theory held for so
> long – that of a separate creation – is scarcely more tenable, especially when
> we remember the eternal existence of the creator and the absence of a
> motive for creative speed. It savours of magic, and is altogether unlike the
> understood character of God. To my mind, those who persist in declaring a
> separate creation, with the idea of showing the greatness, the omnipotence
> of God, really declare his dignity as less rather than greater. If He is the God
> that we conceive him to be – omnipresent, and omniscient – chance must
> go by the board. And if He has the nobleness of Omnipotence, then magic,
> or spectacular display is beneath His august dignity.

Then, at last, he finally provides us with his solution to the conundrum of an evolved being also being cast in the image of his maker:

> I believe that with the full organic development of man there came a special creative act on the part of God, yielding to man reason, conscience and will, and thereby creating man in His own divine image. From this moment, man became what God intended him to be – a creature capable of reciprocating love; a creature of thought; of choice – a being who could intelligently hold communion with God.

Furthermore, George argues that the 'spark' that brings life and is extinguished by death also reveals the hand of God:

> In regard to the basis of sentient life – the mysterious spark that vitalises the physical, and escapes at death – it is reasonable to believe, in fact it is the only explanation, that it was due to a special creative act on the part of the Creator. It is conceivable that this secret must for ever be impossible to the knowledge of man.

Article 18, the final one of the series, includes a handy summary of George's theory, just in case we hadn't got it:

> Taking the inspired creation poem of the Bible to be my foundation, and the results of modern scientific research and deductions to be the material with which I build, I hereby erect my temple of belief.
> i) I believe that all physical structures are the development of lower and simpler forms of life; that in regard to man, at a definite epoch in the history of the world, a male and a female being of the same order stood out above the rest of animate life, possessing by development an upright posture, and with the formulation of the larynx thereby permitting articulate speech; and having the indisputable mark of birth upon them.
> ii) I believe that the physical structure of man is truly formed from the dust of the earth, composed in scientific language of elemental atoms similar to those that compose the material earth.
> iii) I believe that with the full organic development of man there came a special creative act on the part of God, yielding to man: reason, conscience and will, and thereby creating man in His own divine image. From this moment, man became what God intended him to be – a creature capable of reciprocating love; a creature of thought; of choice – a being who could intelligently hold communion with his God.

Naturally, it is up to us to draw our own conclusions about George's theory, but less important than whether he is right or wrong (or if we will ever find out) is the extraordinary lengths he has been prepared to go to in order to ask the question and try to find an answer.

We should not lose sight of the fact that, over many hundreds of words and a whole series of articles, in the pages of a local newspaper in an industrial town, its columns have been given over to a humble railway worker, and the reader has been taken on a journey concerned with advanced anthropology, geology, history, archaeology, philosophy and theology, and all during an era when we might otherwise have expected reports of paper shortages, petty crimes and the latest news from the Western Front.

Once again, George has reminded us that what they might have lacked in scientific knowledge, compared with today, he and his contemporaries made up for with a curiosity and a willingness to get to the truth, no matter how uncomfortable the journey and the conclusions might prove.

Not that George's curiosity was confined to the origins of Man. Other theological questions and other aspects of his deeply-held faith also permeated through his pen, in all of its rich abundance. Sometimes it had a softer approach, in the form of his modern-day fables (see Chapter 9) or pieces extolling the virtues of moral rectitude and the performing of unilateral acts of charity for the good of the wider community.

But, in the case of his series of ten articles entitled *Pen Pictures of the Pulpit*, together with the single article *Pen Picture of a Mission Service*, it was more evangelical – and unapologetically so, at that. But always revealing.

The 'pen pictures' take the form of reportage, and for the most part are a weekly account in the *Advertiser* of a cycle of sermons given, amongst others, by the Reverend WA Prunell OBE, at the Wesleyan Church in Faringdon Road (nowadays The Platform, and before that, the Railway Museum). George writes:

> I am reminded of a remark passed by a friend that "these things should be left to religious journals" – to which I instantly retorted that narrowness was not, after all, the prerogative of religionists.
>
> A live newspaper caters for all the legitimate aspirations of the public. Hence, partisans of sport, theatre goers, businessmen, politicians all find something to their individual taste outside the interesting general news which is supplied. And under the broadminded policy of the Editor, religionists are not exceptions to this general rule.
>
> Therefore, I take delight and count it an honour in writing for a week or two of sermons I am privileged to hear.

We have not sought to reproduce all of the individual articles in their entirety (for those who would wish to find out more or do further reading around each subject, there is a bibliography at the back of this book to facilitate the finding of the actual newspaper column in question).

Instead, we have selected six that serve to provide a flavour of Methodist services in the immediate post Great War period, as well as an insight into some of the day-to-day affairs at the churches that George held so dear. And some of the existential challenges, too.

It will come as no surprise that George takes the opportunity to expand on some of the themes himself, drawing on his own knowledge of Scripture and his love of metaphor and simile.

All this, of course, is set against the background of a changing world – not to mention a general public for whom church attendance was beginning to lose its attraction (although Methodism in Britain saw a brief resurgence between 1921 and 1927).

Topics include the post-war economic slump (and consequential industrial unrest), love of one's fellow man as the preferred route to personal fulfilment, the need for idealism as a means of promoting social cohesion, and personal suffering as a path to character enhancement, as well as faith and temperance.

On one level you could well argue that George was what we might refer to as a 'big tent' preacher, who sought to reach out to many other believers from the protestant or non-conformist traditions. But here he is, in this series, very much 'at home', recording sermons from preachers from within Methodist places of worship.

Before considering the first transcriptions of George's articles, it is worth pausing to consider what remains, today, of the four locations with which he was most closely associated during his time as a preacher.

The Percy Street Wesleyan Church held its final service in 1956, and later that same year, on June 19, it was sold to Bayworth Properties Ltd, a sister company of Thorn TV Rental Ltd and Rentaset Ltd. While the facade was extensively remodelled, much of the rest of the building (at least from the outside) remains largely as it was. Originally converted for commercial use in the 1960s by Radio Relay, it now comprises office accommodation. You can get a good view of the rear from the Morris Street car park.

The Church of England Little London Mission fell into disrepair during the Second World War, eventually closing in 1949. Four years later it was sold to a local builder and used as a store. At the time of writing, the Pope Bros site at 13 Cricklade Street is vacant and awaiting redevelopment.

The Rodbourne Road Primitive Methodist Chapel opened in March 1901. It held its last service on January 5, 2003, and was demolished shortly thereafter. However, the more modern hall, which was adjacent to the old Victorian chapel, was subsequently converted to become the new chapel.

The former Telford Road Wesleyan Mission Chapel was finally sold off by the church in 1953, having struggled for much of its existence since it opened in 1901. Indeed, this may well account for the fact that George's booklet of poems, published in 1915, included the following line on the inside front cover:

> I am presenting this book to the Public with the distinct object that all profits will go towards the support of the Telford Road Wesleyan Mission Church.

So, while some of his religious writing reports the sermons of other preachers, there is much that is concerned with his own personal views, and it is fitting that we begin with a hitherto unpublished piece that not only sees George share some of those views, but also seems to be the closest we will ever have to one of his own sermons.

The Virtue of Gratitude
By George E Hobbs
(Not previously published)

It is a truism that human folk are slavishly self-sufficient until faced by trouble. When trouble looms upon the horizon, then, like the drowning men, they clutch at any straw floating in the vicinity. And such are the vagaries of human conduct that when the trouble has been safely and satisfactorily negotiated – by means of the help sought and given – the helper is consistently ignored.

In that lovely library of books, the Bible, the common lot of "helpers" is recorded in words of great pathos. Says the Psalmist:- "Mine own familiar friend has lifted up his heel against me." In other words, in one short sentence the Psalmist records that he has given help to a friend and has been rewarded by a kick.

Often has the story been told of folk who have risen from lowly surroundings to heights of affluence and power. In their climb upwards they have been given, gratuitously, the backs of others upon which to stand. And when, in process of time, their goal has been reached; when fame, and power, and wealth are theirs, they not only,
> Forget the dung-hill from which they grew,
> And think themselves the Lord knows who.

But they consistently forget the backs upon which they have stood. Backs that uncomplainingly have borne them upwards. In some cases it has been the old mother & dad; in other cases, friends. It matters not who – they are forgotten.

We are told that no difference exists between the multitude of vices of which human beings are the heirs; that, "If we offend in one point we are guilty of all". Even so, I find myself differentiating, for in my judgement ingratitude is the worst of all vices.

As one looks out upon life today one wonders, and have often wondered, how God looks upon the present state of world affairs. Reams of paper have been used, and millions of words spoken, all giving the writer's or speaker's views of what they imagine God's reactions to be to this hell upon earth. However perfect the literary effort, however flawless the diction, they all leave me unimpressed and unsatisfied.

To say that this horrible shambles is a "moulding" process in the plan of the Eternal mind is, to me, not merely meaningless, but grotesque, even libellous. That God could formulate such a plan in which He deliberately ordained perfection through suffering too awful to contemplate cannot be logical or true. Rather would I forsake any idea of God and pin my faith to blind fate than believe in any such postulation. But I do not believe in such an hypothesis. I have a higher conception of the Deity than that.

Even before man became man the Divine Will planned out his stature. It was a standard like unto His own nature, lofty, true and good. In fulfilling that planning the Divine Will came to the human soul like the soft south wind, gentle, and healthful. Never was it harsh or forced, but guiding, wooing, brooding. It came, "in semblance of a dove, with sheltering wings outspread".

And it came upon every normal man and woman.

In order that man should be strong and virile, certain powers were given him. These powers were to be the hall mark of his manhood. The beasts of the field were conditioned by instinct. Man was to condition himself by his own choice. The Divine Will planned and guided, man could follow if he so willed. The choice to acquiesce or refuse was to be man's prerogative alone.

As we scan the ages we see man's reaction to the Divine planning. Too often that reaction may be summed up in the pathetic words of the Christ as He stood gazing upon the multitude of the Holy City. Said He:- "How often would I have gathered there as a hen gathereth her brood under her wing – BUT YE WOULD NOT!"

And yet, through all the perversity, the waywardness, the selfishness of man, God has been true to His original planning. Ceaselessly has He wooed man to the highest and best. And ever has He given to man the Best of which His great heart and knowledge is capable. That best is appreciated but only by its loss.

I know what it is to fret out my heart and to contemplate the direst of all human actions when, helpless and hopeless in a London Hospital, a surgeon said to me, "Man! You are going blind!" – My eyes were spared, for which I have never ceased to be grateful.

The generality of folk have eyes to see the glories of nature, tree & flower, flowing stream and lofty hill, the night sky with all its wonderful inspiration. They have ears to hear the song of birds, the music of little children's voices. They have powers with infinite possibilities. Powers, which may transpose the commonplace into things of loveliness and joy. Above all, deep-seated in every human heart, are they springs of capacity for Divine intercourse – literally, communion with the Great Eternal Mind. All these are the possession of man if he so wills. Yet, such is the perversity of human thinking that God is ignored in times of prosperity and sought only in times of peril and intense trouble. Never is gratitude expressed for all the lovely things of life. Just a howl or terror and a cry for help.

And God, infinitely patient with His stubborn children, yet knowing the frail value of human fidelity, sends out that help. And when the trouble is safely and satisfactorily negotiated, the source of help is forgotten. Not one single expression of gratitude, even for the safe escape from trouble, just forgetfulness and silence.

In this hour of dire need, when troubles press heavily upon the world, can we not remember the Great Source of our help? God is still the Father, and He waits, so patiently, for some sign that He is needed. But He cannot force Himself where He is not wanted. Just as He is "wished" for; just as He is sought, so will He answer with impregnable assistance. And in that seeking after Him let gratitude be expressed, in word and by deed, for all past help.

Believe me, no help can come to a world so utterly given over to evil things, unless it is sought through the desire and choice of man. When man desires God, when man chooses God, then will dawn the New Earth, wherein dwelleth Righteousness.

Pen Pictures of the Pulpit (1)
Universal Unrest – Solution and Consolation
By George E Hobbs
(First published: September 3, 1920)

In the years that are gone, before this earth of ours assumed its present beauteous form of rolling hills and luscious vales, of singing streams and awe-inspiring oceans, there were cosmic convulsions of such awful intensities to shake our globe to its very centre. Presently, in the ordered time of the Great Architect, there came a gradual diminution of these upheavals, which finally were hushed in the gentle lap of a cooled ocean and the tuneful song of the soft south wind.

From a colourless, shapeless, heaving mass there came order, beauty, serenity. We may say without being accused of running into fanciful speculation that the present beauty of the earth could not have been but for awful cosmic convulsions.

Today the peoples of the earth are passing through what one may term the "cosmic convulsion" period; a period of universal unrest. The race is being stirred to its very depths, and that which one believed to be stable and rigid – human principles – is proving its instability in a thousand inglorious ways.

The beauty of the earth came because of the yielding passivity of its elemental constituents to supreme law. The beauty of a regenerated society can only come through an intelligent acquiescence, not to a worn-out dogma or musty creed, but to the loving and [word not clear] invitation of a personality.

"These shall go away into everlasting punishment," the picture of a torture-loving God is laid aside in the museum of antiquities and one stands enthralled before a visualised figure who, with open arms, says: "Come unto me and I will give you rest."

Such were the thoughts that passed through my mind as I sat and listened to a wonderfully inspiring sermon preached by the Rev. W. A. Prunell O.B.E., at the Faringdon Street Wesleyan Church on Sunday evening last.

The sermon was a sequel to the previous Sunday evening's discourse, in which the rev. gentleman treated of the "causes" of the world's unrest.

In introducing the sequel, Mr. Prunell was bold enough to use the definite article. And one is constrained to observe that definiteness is the great need of present day leadership, whether in religion or politics, or in any department of life wherein great issues are at stake.

Not "a" but "the" solution to the world's unrest was treated of. And the text was taken from St. Matt, 11th chapter, and the 28th and 29th verses. "Come unto me and I will give you rest." "Take my yoke upon you – and ye shall find rest." The first is a rest given through obedience; the second is a rest found through service.

Superficial thinkers would have us believe that the world's unrest is due to material causes. The new self-consciousness is believed be the avenue that leads to the great panacea. Men are placing a higher value upon their services, and in higher wages and better conditions men see from the valley the bright-tipped mountain peak that bespeaks the break of a glorious dawn.

Very sympathetically Mr. Prunell dealt with this aspect of a profound problem. There is a need for a higher valuation and a more congenial environment, but if the spring is poisoned at its source it is of small value to try and purify the surface water.

In carefully selected terms, the purification of the upper water was abandoned and we were taken to the fundamental source of the trouble. Material causes were of a temporary character. The permanent basic trouble is soul unrest. Strip humanity of its wild clamour for power and position, and its hysterical demand for riches and pleasure, and underneath there is the ceaseless pulsation of soul unrest.

Self-consciousness within limits may be a good thing, but there is ever the danger present that it may develop into a circle with self at the centre and self at the circumference.

Mr. Prunell quoted the parable of the rich man whom one may style as being psychically egotistical. He advised his soul to rest satisfied because of "my" superabundance. But an unseen witness pronounces his doom:

"Thou fool! This night thy soul shall be required of thee. He was a fool because he thought his soul unrest could be appeased by material prosperity. He was circumscribed by self and, to quote the simile used: 'A selfish man is like a hedgehog rolled up the wrong way, constantly pricking itself.'"

But where lies the solution to soul unrest?

Does it lie in observances or ritual? Is the solution to be found in organisation – the bugbear of modern church life? No so. Soul unrest can never be appeased by these things. It has an objective setting and really is a quest for life, the fullness of which can never be realised by any external paraphernalia. It can only be satisfied by an indwelling from the mighty fount of life. Self-expression must give place to God-expression and self-consciousness must be superseded by God-consciousness.

But the noise and bustle of life so often prevents the unrestful from discovering the unseen source of rest. Mr. Prunell illustrated this point by a very pretty simile. A short time ago he was visiting a large flour mill. The source of power was hidden, but presently the noise of the machinery ceased and he heard the trickling running water. The ensuing silence had revealed the source of power: it was a water-driven mill.

"Hush! Listen! A voice of exquisite tenderness is calling." It is the voice of one who has called down through the ages. He sees the agony of the once pure flower, now befouled by the grime of life. He sees the anguish of the mother as she clasps her dying darling to her breast. He hears the groans of the toiler as he is ruthlessly cast aside from the wheels of industry, and with arms outstretched to the world says:

"Come unto Me. All ye that labour and are heavy laden, and I will give you rest. Take my yoke upon you – and ye shall find rest unto your souls. The rest of obedience. The rest of service."

Pen Pictures of the Pulpit (2)
A Discourse on Knowledge v Love Dissected
By George E Hobbs
(First published: September 10, 1920)

"Knowledge versus Love," was the title of a discourse delivered by the Rev. D. P. Fuge at the Wesleyan Church, Faringdon Street, on Sunday morning last. The occasion was the Sunday school anniversary, and one feels bound to confess the whole of the day's services were delightfully refreshing and instructive.

The preacher's text was taken from St. Paul's First Letter to the Corinthians, the 8th chap., and the latter part of the first verse: "Knowledge puffeth up, but Love edifieth."

The subject resolved itself into an investigation of the respective merits of knowledge, or more correctly, academic learning and the attribute of love, as a means by which the great mass of the people are to be won for the highest and best. The subject is timely and should prove of vast interest to active church workers, ministerial and lay; for herein is suggested the possible cause why queues at church doors are conspicuous by their absence.

We can imagine, said the rev. gentleman, the atmosphere of a debating class in which great subjects are under review. Knowledge versus Love is the subject. Which is the more powerful factor for good? Knowledge is power. It is depicted as a lamp guiding the feet to solid paths, or as a lighthouse throwing its beneficent beams upon haunting problems and lifting somewhat the veil that obscures.

Before the vote is taken one realises that the preponderance of opinion is upon the side of knowledge, when the wise old man in the chair sums up. He has taken careful cognisance of the attitude of the class, and he sees they are worshipping not at the shrine of the highest knowledge but at the shrine of academic learning. Behind him he has a whole life's experience and he knows the pitfalls that await those to whom academic learning is the be all and end all of life. He sums up briefly but forcefully. He quotes the words of St Paul: "Knowledge puffeth up, but Love buildeth up."

Ignorance No Virtue

But if knowledge puffeth up, there is no suggestion that ignorance is a virtue. Ignorance is a mighty power for evil. A great divine was once asked if he really believed in a devil. His reply was: "Yes, I believe in three – one at each end of the stick and one in the middle. The devil of the rich is gluttony, the devil of the poor, starvation, and the devil in the middle is ignorance. Ignorance is the worst devil of all.

At one time our lads were cruelly ignorant towards frogs and birds. But now, nature studies were inculcated in our schools and cruelty is vanishing. Ignorance goes down the coal pit and an appalling disaster occurs. It goes into the signal cabin and ruin and wreckage follow. It goes into the chemist's shop and folk are poisoned.

And what deadly evils follow when ignorance attends in the social and religious realms. It foments class hatred, and is the great menacing bulwark against progress and development. It hurled the souls of a martyred host in eternity, and was the primal factor responsible for crucifying the Christ upon the Cross. So deadly is ignorance that knowledge must be magnified.

Apparently then, by deductive argument, knowledge is the greater factor towards the development of the highest and best. Yet stay! One illustration may disprove the claim. Matthew Arnold – poet, critic and educationalist – who lived from 1822 to 1888, was anxious to be an apostle of light. He was truly a great man, yet he exercised very little influence in the direction he wished. Why was it?

It was because academic learning blocked up the avenue to the highest usefulness. His division of English society into Barbarians, Philistines, and Populace – the latter referring to the working classes – savours somewhat of pedantic superiority. And such methods in one who wishes to influence for the best must prove abortive.

The Secret

Academic learning is a menace that often protrudes itself upon theologian, preacher and reformer. And reformation that is attempted from the pedestal must prove non-effective.

The Christ had all knowledge: yet it was not His wonderful knowledge that was His chief charm. It was the fact He stooped to lift humanity to higher ideals and nobler aspirations. And preachers and leaders of men who would influence for good must come down from the pedestal and humbly graduate in the school of love. That is the secret of successful reformation for "though I have all knowledge, and have not love, I am nothing."

"Knowledge puffeth up." Like a child's toy blown up it soon bursts, but "Love edifieth." It builds up. The process may be slow but it is effective.

A definition of love may prove a difficulty, but its operations can be seen and understood. A soldier in the trench sees a comrade fall in No Man's Land. Heedless of the flying bullets, he clears the parapet and brings back his wounded comrade into safety. That is love. Love causes the mother to forget weariness and fatigue as night after night and day after day she watches and cares for her sick child. Love causes the physician to go into a leper colony until he himself dies a leper.

In conclusion, we had two pictures presented of a character out of Dickens's "Christmas Carol". Scrooge was the character, and in the first picture we saw him as a soured old miser, hating Christmas on principle. In the next picture, we saw a complete transformation. The soured old miser was now a happy, joyous dispenser of good things, spreading gladness wherever he went.

How came so great a change? Only one cause: He had learned to love!

Knowledge is great and its possession is desirable, but Love is greater; for it woos to the highest and best.

Pen Pictures of the Pulpit (4)
The World and Its Need of the Visionaries
By George E Hobbs
(First published: September 24, 1920)

The world cannot do without its visionaries, its dreamers and its idealists. The materialist, steeped in that which he can touch or see, accuse such as being metaphysicians, with airy fancies that will no more materialise than the phantom castles in Spain.

But the materialist will surely remember that the solid mechanism which he handles was first of all a visioned ideal; passing through the vaporous stage of inception, on to the liquid stage of assembly, thence to the solid stage of completion.

And the materialist will also remember that advancing civilisation has passed, or is passing through a similar process. If there is any virtue in our present state of civilisation it is not due to a mechanical evolution, but first to visionaries who saw an ideal infusing their fellows with a desire for the consummation of that ideal until it solidified and became realised.

To the minds of those who live only for the present, some ideals are grotesque and impossible of realisation. Others are content to reiterate: "The time is not opportune. This can only be realised in the remote future." Both ways of thinking are bad, and the activities of each school of thought towards a higher life reaches the same totality – which equals nothing.

Ideals are sometimes received with little enthusiasm because of their revolutionary character and apparent unworkability. But if they are true ideals, and declared with boldness and confidence – however much at variance they may seem to be with practicability – consummation must be achieved in process of time; and the "process of time" is governed by the sympathy or lack of sympathy with which it is received.

These fragmentary thoughts are the outcome of a remarkably forceful sermon preached by the Rev. W. A. Prunell, O.B.E, at the Farringdon street Wesleyan Church on Sunday evening last.

For text Mr. Prunell took a stanza of beautiful old world poetry, which the Revised Version of the Bible gives in the 21st chapter of Numbers:

> "Spring up, O well; sing ye unto it;
> The well which the princes digged,
> Which the nobles of the people delved,
> With the sceptre and with their stayes."

The story is set in the morning of human history, and this portion of ancient literature depicts a scene in the daily routine of the people who lived in those far off days.

The duty of drawing water from the wells was performed by the daughters of the people. It was a work of drudgery; a monotonous daily sameness, and no relief came by way of change. And yet the toilers sang – not as the sailor who sings to give rhythmic expression to every movement – but the joyous song of a free spirit untrammelled by the clogging effect of daily monotony.

In New Testament times the work was still performed by the daughters of the people, but the song had ceased. When the Samaritan woman heard the mystic words of the Christ she asked that the "water of life" may be given her, that the drudgery and monotony may cease. One can scarcely wonder at the difference between the two pictures, for this woman was a type of the age in which she lived. The non-use of spiritual faculties rendered flight above environment relatively impossible.

But to come back to the first picture. The daily journey to and from the well. The same daily act performed. The same faces met with drudgery and monotony yet they sang as they toiled. They sang in harmony with the gurgling waters beneath.

The song was prompted by the fact that it recalled to them the ancient dignity of a great past. It was the princes and the nobles who had digged the well. It recalled the ideal of a golden age, when all classes worked in sympathetic harmony for the common weal.

The thought of the past brings to the present a nobler dignity. The thought of monotonous drudgery was superseded by a greater thought – they were in the line of succession of invention and genius. Nay, further, they identified themselves with the inventor and the genius, for they were ministers administering to a common life. With such a rich and exalted conception of their labour, monotony fled and drudgery was merged into the purest altruism.

If the subject had been terminated at this point it would have been like a disappointing instalment of a serial. With strikes and rumours of strikes covering in the air; and with the possibility – being a "parson" – of being misunderstood. Mr. Prunell applied the ideal of the story to present day life. He had heard men say they were not going to be "wage slaves," and he trusted they would not. A wage slave is one who works for money and with no higher thought. Such try to get inspiration by getting as far away from toil as possible. They do not intend to do too much. Toil to these is nothing but monotony and drudgery.

The worker should escape from the thought of mechanical routine to the larger thought. The inventor, the genius, and the worker, are all parts of a whole and each and all should labour together for the common weal.

The highest sanction had been given to toil. The "Light of the World" had been a toiler. He had been a son in the home and a youth in the workshop and in His parables he revealed His sympathy for every helpful section of the social order.

Is it possible to "crown labour with true wealth," to realise the true dignity of toil, that we should labour for the good of our fellows? The answer cannot be given on a Sunday evening. It can be given from Monday morning to Saturday noon.

Pen Pictures of the Pulpit (8)
The Problem of Suffering
By George E Hobbs
(First published: June 24, 1921)

A very able and striking sermon was preached on Sunday morning last by the Rev CW Martin at Wesley Church, Faringdon Street. The subject was one around which controversy has raged for thousands of years, and one to which there is still a deal of mystery.

The rev gentleman dealt with the problem of suffering, basing his discourse upon the suffering and privations of one who "was perfect and upright, and one that feared God and eschewed evil" – Job.

The mystery of suffering is a subject the superficial thinker would be foolish to dilate upon. Profound thought must be exercised if beneficent light is to be thrown upon it. And Mr Martin's discourse revealed that profound thought has been exercised to the help of the those who were privileged to listen to him.

It its not my purpose to record the sermon verbatim but rather to attempt a brief survey of some of the points raised.

Modern students have long since ceased to literalise certain portions of the Bible. This in no [way] detracts from the sublime teaching. In many cases it enhances its beauty and permits a thoughtful mind to delve into treasures.

Whereas a literal rendering would confuse by its distorted and exaggerated imagery, and the beauty of its teaching be lost.

It was therefore with no surprise (certainly with no regrets), we heard that the Book of Job should not be taken as literal history. It should be taken as an allegory, a dramatic poem based in all probability upon a tradition of the Hebrews.

It possibly was true that "There was a man in the land of Ug, whose name was Job" and that he suffered loss and sickness, and the author takes hold of the dry skeleton of the tradition and clothes it in sumptuous apparel – the apparel of noble language and majestic sentiment.

But the author is an artist. Merely to decorate does not satisfy him. Hence he vitalises the tradition with a pulsating life. It develops, it grows, it inspires, it teaches; in fact, so wondrous is its life that it lifts the veil and we are permitted to understand somewhat of the problem of suffering.

Hunting a Fallacy

In the author's day the prevailing idea was that personal calamity and suffering was caused solely by personal wrong-doing, and personal prosperity was the result of personal goodness. But the author has given profound thought to this supposed truth, and his meditation has led him to become not merely a doubter but a zealot to prove its fallacy. His keen perception of human affairs has shown to him that sometimes the unscrupulous one became prosperous and the honest one a pauper.

Sometimes the abstemious one became stricken with terrible sickness and the riotous one escaped plague and pestilence, and enjoyed normal health.

And so in sublime language; in metaphor and simile of wondrous beauty, the author inspires his characters to debate the problem of suffering.

The three friends of Job who came to commiserate with him forget compassion and criticise Job to the top of their best. They walk easily along the well-worn track of Hebrew thought. Job had been prosperous – therefore good. Now, bereaved of his children, stripped of his wealth, despised by his wife, stricken with a loathsome disease, an outcast in the ash-heap – the garbage den of the city – he must be evil.

After the three friends of Job had done their best – or their worst – in showing him how evil he must have been, and rendering Job much more mystified than before they came, a new speaker is introduced in the person of Elihu.

First with respectful attention, and then with ever-growing disgust, Elihu listens to the speeches of Job's three friends. He noted that the first round of speeches were circular in their orbit.

They ended just where they began. The second and third cycle of speeches meet with the same fate, and Elihu is constrained to believe that "great men" are sometimes bankrupt of progressive thought. With kindling wrath, Elihu plunges into the debate, and with biting sarcasm spares not "the men of years". He shows them the falsity of their argument, and strives to lead them to a better understanding of the problem of suffering.

And so, carefully and thoughtfully, Mr Martin enunciated his deductions from this wonderful dramatic poem.

All Suffering Not Penal

Wrong-doing must sooner or later, in some way or another, bring in its train suffering. But all suffering is not penal. He [Job] protested his innocence and his integrity was finally vindicated. In the all-wisdom of God, sometimes it is necessary for the perfecting of character, for one to have to pass through the furnace of affliction. The Christ was "perfected through suffering" and sometimes it is needful that it should become a human experience. At such times the experience is painful, a mystery in [its] very truth.

It is a mystery to the sufferer because at the time it is impossible to see its relationship to necessity. It needs detachment from oneself – a very difficult but not impossible proposition – [for] in many cases, [it requires] the width of years before the relationship is seen or understood.

In the valley, said Mr Martin, one can scarcely appreciate the rugged grandeur of the surrounding hills. It is only as one stands upon an adjacent promontory that one can appreciate the surrounding beauty, and judge the relationship of the hill to the valley.

Friends of sympathy may become critical dogmatisers – I felt that a much stronger word could have been used than "may", for criticism is far easier than practical sympathy – but truth will vindicate its own.

I could not help thinking of some who in the agony of bereavement and sorrow have argued along similar lines to that of Job. "What wrong have I performed that I should be so punished?"

The answer seems to be that the suffering is not punishment for wrong-doing. It is not chastisement, but rather a remedy whereby character is perfected.

Pen Pictures of the Pulpit (9)
Steps Leading Upwards
By George E Hobbs

(First published: July 7, 1921)

No one, I think, can look upon the spectacle of young manhood and womanhood voluntarily dedicating its powers and possibilities to some noble service without being profoundly moved. Much more is this so when that service is believed to be the highest in the whole survey of human experience.

It is wonderfully impressive to see one in declining years, after a lifetime of battling with contrary winds and vicious currents, step into the sure haven of positive service, and dedicate the last few short years of life to usefulness and unselfishness. But such service at best is emaciated and weak. It lacks the full rich blood of youth. It lacks the enthusiasm that thrives under wet blankets. It lacks the courage, the joy, the burning faith, that laughs at impossibility and cries "It shall be done!"

But when youth, sanely and comprehendingly, voluntarily dedicates its powers and possibilities to a high and noble service, that which is lacking in the weakened service of a declining life, is found here in quantities of stimulating proportions.

So one felt on Sunday morning last at Wesley Church, Faringdon street, during the service conducted by the Rev. W. A. Prunell O.B.E.

The service was significant in the fact that a number of young men and women were to be received into the full membership of the church: their allegiance to its Spiritual Head being ratified by public and voluntary attendance at the table of sacrament.

Stepping Stones

The service, therefore, was so arranged that each succeeding part was as stepping stones, ever leading upwards and onward to the culminating point of public confirmation.

I could not help thinking that a few years ago certain details of the service would have startled the worshipper into protestation. Non-conformists hated anything that flavoured of "Churchism". Their boast lay in their freedom from formality and ritual. To introduce the chanting of the Lord's prayer after the opening prayer was to court obstreperous objections at quarterly meetings, and the introducer to be stigmatised almost as a heretic.

To chant the "Te Deum" or the "Magnificat", or responses to the commandments by the congregation could not be thought of – but wiser counsel prevailed, and many of our services are richer thereby.

After the choral part of the service, Mr. Prunell delivered a short discourse from a text in St John's Gospel, Chap. 21. verses 18 and 19.

Mr. Prunell said he wished to take these words from their context and suggest that they set forth, in figures of speech, the characteristics of youth and advanced age. In fact they covered the whole period of human life upon earth. The former part of the text was typical of youth. "When thou wast young thou girdedst thyself and walkedst whither thou wouldest."

In these words one can see self-reliance and self-determination. Presumption and rashness is also suggested, for that, too, is a characteristic of youth. And although presumption and rashness often has to be paid for in the hard school of experience yet one must remember that these qualities stamp the youth as a living youth, with powers of vital activity. And there only needs sane teaching to direct these characteristics into qualities for good and useful service.

Enthusiasm of Youth

Mr. Prunell has real sympathy with the invigorating enthusiasm of youth. He would encourage rather than deter everything that made for a vigorous, healthy Christian life.

Youth in its enthusiasm delights in that which is hard and difficult. And that is why the Cross of Christ – the Cross which is the very centre of the world's effort and progress – appeal to young folk. The path of the Christian is not smooth and easy. It is hard in the extreme. It calls forth the best and the noblest efforts, and needs the highest courage and determination. It is a great thing when a young man or woman consecrates their powers to God.

The latter part of the text is typical of old age. "When thou art old another shall gird thee and carry thee whither thou wouldest not." But to each, youth and age, the command is:- "Follow Me".

Old age is the time when strength is diminished; when the powers are narrowed, and when circumstances are stronger than personal effort. Presumption and rashness have long since been mellowed into humility and strength of purpose, and though in the evening of life there is dependence upon others – for "Another shall gird thee," – and personal inclination controlled by another's will – "and carry thee whither thou wouldest not" – yet the same command is given. In youth with its powers of enthusiasm and courage; in age with its experience the command is "Follow Me!" In every step of human life the need of the Christ's companionship and help is great. And that help will never be denied to those who seek it.

Preceding the Recognition rite, Mr. Prunell gave an impressive address to those about to assume the responsibility of church membership.

"A few years ago," he said, "your parents brought you into the church as helpless babies. They, in faith, dedicated you to the service of God. You were unconscious of the great issues involved, but you were received into the congregation of Christ's flock. Your parents have carefully instilled into your minds the noble and lofty ideals of the Christ, and they have been assisted by the personal witness and instructions of your Sunday school teachers.

"To-day, of your own free choice, you are crowning what your parents did in faith. This act of yours is a public confirmation that you are admitted to the full privileges of your church."

Mr. Prunell then took by the hand in turn each one of the "recognised" members. There was about twenty young women and fifteen young men. After which nearly 100 partook of the sacrament of the Lord's supper.

Pen Picture of a Mission Service
By George E Hobbs
(First published: October 27, 1922)

Remarkable and unprecedented scenes are being witnessed nightly at Percy Street Wesleyan Chapel, Swindon where a month's mission is now in progress. The mission has set free a new slogan in the Rodbourne Road district, and is spreading to other parts of the town. The slogan ensures a dialogue, and runs thus:

"Have you heard him yet?"

"Who?"

"Why, Tom Daniels! The man who makes himself heard every night from 7.30pm to 9.30pm. and all day on Sunday." And so it goes on, but space is precious.

Having had the slogan hurled at myself, and hearing that there were special features attending this mission, I went to Percy Street Wesleyan Mission on Sunday night. Mr Tom Daniels is a firm believer in physical healing by faith.

I saw no demonstration on Sunday night of the healing art, but in an interview I had with one who has been attending the meetings, and one who has had repeated illnesses, I was informed that wonderful help had been given. The friend himself told me he had never felt better in his life. Previous to the mission his diet had to be carefully considered on account of his complaint. Now he can eat almost anything without ill effect. There are several who can subscribe to the same testimony.

On Sunday evening a large congregation gathered to hear Mr Daniels preach. That the message was appreciated was evidenced by the audible punctuations of the more fervent of the congregation – a thing that one rarely hears now even in a Methodist meeting. Whether the absence of audible responses is a sign of sedateness, shyness, or mere indifference to the message is a problem I must leave to the expert in congregational deportment.

One gets enthusiastic at a football match and is eager with "Hear! Hear!" at a political meeting, so why not? I said I would leave this knotty point to the expert, and there will I leave it.

No Great Distance

Mr Daniels took for his text Mark 12, 34: "Thou art not far from the Kingdom of God." Mr Daniels said he did not think there was any great distance between some who listened to him and Christ. They were very near to the Kingdom; in fact, on the boundary line. Only one step was needed, and he trusted they would take that one essential step that night.

To illustrate his point Mr Daniels recited an amusing experience which once befell him. He was speaking at a temperance meeting at which a manufacturer occupied the chair. After he and a friend had delivered their addresses, the chairman arose and informed the audience that though he had every sympathy for the temperance cause, he himself was not quite a teetotaller. He took very little indeed. In fact his position was he was next door to a teetotaller.

Immediately Mr Daniels' friend leapt to his feet and said: "Sir, next door's empty, will you flit?" "I'll flit tonight!" was the reply, and he became an abstainer. He was very near, but that night he took the one additional step. That was the step Mr Daniels wished his hearer to take in respect to the Kingdom of God.

Some folk can hardly be distinguished from Christians, yet deep down in their hearts they are conscious there is something lacking. The continual cry of their hearts is: "What lack I yet?" It is the one essential step of complete surrender to the highest and noblest – the surrender of the life to Christ.

Continuing, Mr Daniels said he was once preaching in a little hamlet at the foot of Snae Fell, in the Isle of Man. In this small village all were converted except two. One of these loved the little chapel so well that in order to be near it he purchased a cottage close by. One Sunday morning Mr Daniels preached from the text: "One thing have I desired, that will I seek after," and the man who had purchased the cottage attended the service.

The service made such a profound impression upon him that immediately after he sought an interview with the preacher. He told Mr Daniels that he had been taken into that particular chapel as an infant, had passed through the Sunday school, and was at that very moment a teacher in the school. Yet it had been revealed to him that morning he was not really and truly a Christian. He had not taken the step of actual and definite surrender.

Thought He Was a Christian

He thought he was a Christian simply because he regularly attended chapel and was teaching in the Sunday school, but Mr Daniels' heart-searching message had revealed to him the contrary. He, like the scribe, had been near to the Kingdom of God, but that morning he took that one necessary step and completely surrendered his life to his Master.

Mr Daniels gave other incidents of his life's experiences, some full of pathos, others in which the saving grace of humour gleamed, but all bearing upon the one point he wished to force home – the necessity of taking the one step.

Concluding his discourse, Mr Daniels made a strong appeal for the intellectual acceptance of Christ. He would like to see those who had acquired great knowledge give themselves to God. God needed today educated men and women. To the young people who were present he would say he wished them to grow in knowledge. He liked to hear them ask questions, so that their knowledge might be fuller and more complete.

I thoroughly agreed with Mr Daniels, particularly in his last statement. Yet, even as I recorded his words, my thoughts went to one whose life was completely changed because he asked a question relative to spiritual things. Poor Charles Bradlaugh! What a power he might have been in the church if it had not been for the stupidity of the Rev JG Packer. Bradlaugh desired fuller knowledge, and asked the rev gentleman a question while being prepared for confirmation. The answer was the suspension of his "most promising pupil" for three months from his duties of Sunday school teacher.

During the service a solo was beautifully rendered by Miss K Brotheridge.

Contemporary photographs of Percy Street Chapel, which was an important part of George's life, have been difficult to come by. He was almost certainly present when the photograph, above, was taken, showing the new brick chapel under construction, in the shadow of the old 'iron chapel', when George was a teenager (courtesy of The Swindon Society). The interior of this new chapel, which opened in 1898, is pictured in the postcard, opposite, top (courtesy of The Swindon Society). The only known photographs of the front of the new chapel and the interior of its iron predecessor (opposite) were provided courtesy of Bob Townsend and Diane Everett, thanks to a wedding album; Bob's parents were married there in 1932, and George may well have attended.

An architect's drawing of the facade of the Percy Street Chapel (courtesy of the Wiltshire & Swindon History Centre), and the site in 2019 (author's collection).

Above: inside the mission in Little London, Old Town, Swindon, where George sometimes preached, pictured here during Harvest Festival in 1905. (Courtesy of The Swindon Society)

Left: the building in 2019. (Author's collection)

Chapter 3

A Design For Life: George's Advice to Young People

After the complexity, controversy and convoluted approach to the clash of science and faith that featured in the previous chapter, we now come to an aspect of George's writing where he draws on his faith to provide heartfelt and sincere advice to any young people who might be reading his columns in the *Advertiser*.

There were many facets to George's life, but one of the most significant strands appears to be his mission to young people, whether it be through the Band of Hope, the Wesley Guild or via his preaching from the pulpit. Here he extols the virtues of a life of moral probity, of fidelity and of charitable giving, as distinct from his commitment to the teaching of the Gospel.

But how better to extend his reach than through the pages of the *Advertiser*? His first contribution amounted to his personal manifesto, paving the way forward for a series of articles specifically aimed at children and the younger members of the community. The first three pieces were entitled, simply enough, *For Young People*. Part one is reproduced in full, and serves as an introduction to the subject matter under discussion – namely the theories associated with the creation of the world.

Not all of the advice that George ever dispensed was theological, nor, indeed, deadly serious. After all, we already know that he possessed a reasonably developed sense of humour. This is more than evident in the four-part series entitled *To Seekers After Trouble* which you may have guessed is marriage guidance – or more accurately, mostly pre-marriage guidance. So, prepare yourself for lighthearted early-20th century advice on selection etiquette and the perils of non-verbal communication; on how to actually choose a potential partner; wooing; and the honeymoon period and beyond, followed by an 'and finally...' Well, all good advice ends with a punchy summary doesn't it? I think we're left in no doubt where George stood on the whole marriage 'thing'.

This chapter concludes with a short series of open 'letters' in reply to correspondence from a lad called Frank.

Given that George had held various positions of trust within the local community and clearly enjoyed working with young people, it wouldn't be at all surprising if he had received numerous requests for help and guidance on a whole raft of subjects over time. So while I doubt that Frank as a specific individual ever existed, I've no doubt that the name stands as a convenient archetype and represents an excellent conduit for questions of this nature.

In the first piece, *Making a Success of Life*, George recommends that one should possess the following attributes: cleanliness of mind, essential study and thoroughness in study.

And in the final letter, *Spirit to Achieve*, we're treated to some interesting background relating to the construction of the Severn Tunnel, which is used as a metaphor for the fact that one should never, ever give up. Furthermore, we're taught that the road to success is all about knowing the theory as well as the practical.

Please read and inwardly digest. There'll be questions afterwards!

For Young People (1)
By GEH
(First published: January 10, 1917)

Dear Young People,

At last I have the Editor's permission to write a series of articles exclusively for your reading. I have long wanted to do so, but the difficulty has been the lack of space owing to the shortage of paper. Things, however, seem now to be on a "war-normal" basis, and as a further reduction does not at present cast its shadow, the way opens for a commencement to be made.

This first column will be in the nature of an introduction – not altogether to lay down a hard and fast programme of subjects on which I propose to write, but to indicate briefly my object in writing.

Unhappily, we have the world – or a large portion of the world – at war. Each nation is bearing its proportionate burden, and here in England the burden is felt by each section of the community. With the coming and continuation of this gigantic struggle, there has also come a super effort to amuse. This may not be wrong in itself, because if it was all burden and no relaxation, if it was all worry and no rest, then life would be intolerable.

Even the brave fellows in the trenches that are upholding the honour of the old flag, even these have their periods of rest, frugal though they be, that they may be better fitted for a renewal of the struggle that means so much to you and me. No! It is not wrong in itself to amuse, but – and it is a big BUT – there is something greater than amusement.

There is solid reading, and solid thinking, and so if in our burden bearing and our amusement we set a time apart for solid reading and thinking, then I do not think we shall go far wrong.

I am a great believer in amusement, whether it is football, cricket or any other legitimate sport – or, if you like, the picture palace. I often go there myself, and I do not remember that I ever wished I had stopped away. Yet if all our relaxation is occupied with amusement, then I do not think our lives will be benefitted a great deal thereby.

Young men and women ought to do some solid reading and thinking, and it is with a real desire to help to this end that I write.

First then, I want to write something grippable and interesting; something that shall whet the intellectual appetite for more intellectual food; something that shall be simple and easily understood, so that those who are in the upper standards of our schools, and those who may have left school and are up in their teens, may find something interesting to read and talk about.

I hope to deal first of all with the creation of this world of ours; its probable origin and development. As I wish to deal fairly with this question during the course of our investigation, I propose giving you the various theories of its origin: mythical, religious and scientific.

There will possibly be at times a difficulty in distinguishing between the mythical and religious, because nearly all the mythical stories of creation claim a Divine revelation. That as it may be, we shall try and find out that which appeals most to our reason.

I want to avoid scientific terms as much as possible, and where necessity demands their inclusion, explanations will be given so that all may understand.

After dealing with the various stories of creation, we shall then proceed in our investigation up to the glorious, "star-bespangled" Heavens, and see if we can catch a glimpse of the mighty systems that are hidden from the non-searcher.

In our survey, which I shall try and make as extensive as possible, there will be other interesting matter which will constantly demand attention; this shall be attended to in its due order, and everything will, I trust, be found instructive and helpful to all those that shall read.

The theories of the creation of this world of ours then, will be our first study.

I remember reading somewhere that Milton has represented Adam, when rising at once in Paradise, and in the full perfection of his senses, as astonished at the glorious appearance of Nature, the Heavens, the air, the earth, his own organs and members; and led by the contemplation of them to ask whence this wonderful scene arose?

I am afraid that we of the 20th century rarely trouble ourselves to investigate the wonders of nature even far enough to ask whence and how? I suppose the true explanation lies here. We do not rise, like Adam in Paradise, in the full perfection of our facilities. The glorious fabric of the universe which is before our eyes from infancy, and gradually comprehended as the intellect expands, loses its effect upon our minds, but would strike us vastly different if all the beauty, variety and regularity of the world opened upon us at once, when the powers of the understanding were capable of appreciating them.

Though this may be true to a certain extent, yet there have been times in our lives when just as a passing thought, perhaps, we have thought of the whence and how. We have dismissed it then as being too much trouble to pursue the investigation further. The generality of us have not troubled any more about it, but thank God for the few great minds that have thought it worthwhile to make this question a life study.

All down through the ages, the schoolmen have been trying to solve this great mystery. And what has been the result of their labours? Let me try and explain. The masterminds of the ages have done in a sense just what we did when we went to school. During the lesson of arithmetic, we had to do a sum in simple addition. The items were called out one by one by the teacher, and as these were called out we put them down upon slate or paper. Sometimes we made a mistake, and then if it was upon paper we were writing, we drew a line through the wrong figures and put the right ones perhaps lower down.

This is just what has happened in the problem of the world's origin. The philosophers and scientists of the past ages called out the items one by one. Each succeeding age questioned the items that had preceded them. Soon a mistake was noted, the line of disapproval was drawn through the wrong figures and the right ones, due to new discoveries, were inserted. So the great addition sum went on: sometimes right, sometimes wrong, and even today with all our education we dare not say the sum is finished.

Truly we can say our knowledge is more complete; the findings of our philosophers and scientists are more certain and the sum is reaching towards completion; but many years must elapse ere we can say *finis*. It is possible that absolute certitude, on this great question, may never be the possession of earth's race. There are so many things that are still a profound mystery.

In the great chain of evidence, many are the links that are missing. On the other hand, we may be on the eve of great discoveries. Things long bound up in mystery may be about to open their secrets to the astonishment of the human race.

This 'by the way' (I am overrunning myself before I have scarcely commenced, and that is a bad sign): What then are the findings of the past? We live in a privileged age. We have at our backs all the accumulated findings of the past.

That which proved insurmountable to the scientists of the 10th century was like ABC to the schoolmen of the 14th and 15th century; and that which proved impenetrable to the schoolmen of the 15th century stands revealed in all its beauty to the present day student. So, we make progress – not to learn that we may selfishly enjoy – but learn so that by our industry we may put down another item for the consideration and help of those that come after us.

We have benefitted by the labours of the past – and here, let me digress a moment. When I say that we have benefitted from the labours of the past, do not think for a moment that those who delved into these mysteries had an easy time – far from it. Their studies were conducted under the most difficult of circumstances – circumstances which would turn many a student of the 20th century pale with horror.

Not only had these men crude instruments wherewith to make calculations and observations, but they also had to combat a terrible monster – in the shape of superstition. Woe betide the luckless scientist whose findings clashed with popular thought and belief, especially if he was hardy enough to publish his findings broadcast. Ridicule was the least offensive weapon used. It was more often of a much sterner character.

Let me give you one illustration, and one of many that could be cited, showing what a scientist had to face in the days that are past – and happily passed. In the year 1564 there was born in Pisa, in Italy, a baby boy who was destined to become a greater astronomer and physicist. His name was called

Galileo, and from his earliest he was fond of books and study. When only 24 years of age he was given a lectureship at Pisa University. Through his inventions and discoveries, he was looked upon with suspicion by representatives of the church, and he also came into disfavour at court. He left Pisa and went to the University at Padua, where he became professor of mathematics – this was in 1592. In 1609 he constructed a telescope on the model of that of Hans Lippershez of Middelburg in Holland.

Now began his great struggle with popular thought. With his newly constructed telescope he discovered four moons of Jupiter. To his amazement he found that the satellites of Jupiter were not stationary, but were revolving round the planet. This led him on to other discoveries; the uneven surface of the moon was demonstrated, also with his telescope he discovered sunspots. All this led up to his great discoveries.

The prevailing notion was that the earth was the centre of all motion and all activity; the sun, moon and stars were all revolving round the earth. Galileo discovered in his observations and researches that the very opposite was the truth: the moon revolved round the earth, and the moon and earth revolved round the sun. What was he to do? Dare he publish that which he knew to be true, though it was against popular belief?

Galileo decreed in his own mind that it was his duty to publish his findings to the world at large, and with faith in the truth of his discoveries, but with a little natural fear, he told out to the world what he had found. Immediately he again came under the ban of the Ecclesiastics, and in 1616 he was cited to appear before the Inquisition. The Holy Office decreed Galileo's new theory of the Solar System was philosophically absurd, and commanded him to discontinue his teaching.

In 1632 he published his "Dialogues on the Systems of the World" and because of these he was ordered at once to appear before Pope Urban VIII at Rome.

On the 21st of June 1633, Galileo was conducted in the dress of a penitent before the Judges of the Holy Inquisition to receive judgement. He was called upon to renounce and abjure as false the opinion which his whole existence had been consecrated to form and strengthen.

Galileo was now 69 years of age, and in his declining years he feared and dreaded imprisonment and there – on bended knees before his Judges – he recanted, and publicly renounced his faith. It is said that as he rose from his knees, he whispered to one of his friends standing near, "E pur si muore" – "It does move through."

It was indeed a pitiable sight. Here was a venerable old man who had enlightened Europe by his discoveries, on bended knees before an assembly of haughty, ignorant bigots, renouncing by their compulsion, those truths which nature, and by his own conscience, affirmed to be incontrovertible.

Truly it was a spectacle that cannot be thought of without indignation and abhorrence. Galileo was detained, but afterwards he was allowed to go free. When returning to Florence, he remained there in seclusion till the day of his death which occurred in the year 1642.

The Church, or at least the representatives of the Church, have not always been true to their Master. The Christ ideal is Truth, but almost in every age those who should have assisted towards the establishment of truth have been the drag-shoe to the wheel of progress.

(To be Continued)

To Seekers After Trouble (1) Instructions by George E Hobbs

(First published: April 29, 1921)

The historic advice given by Punch to those about to marry occupied very little space in the pages of that well-known journal of satire; nor does its verbal repetition expend much energy or waste much breath. One little monosyllable, which, if implicitly obeyed, would end for all time those wars and rumours of wars incidental to connubial bliss. To place a new thought upon Tennyson's well-known line, we should have:

"Earth at last a warless world, a single race, a single tongue."

"Don't!" said Punch to those about to marry. And while I am of the opinion it is wise and judicious advice, I am also conscious that it is opposed by an irresistible dynamic called "the human factor".

It is this human factor which goads unsuspecting males to leave the broad road of destruction – my mistake, I should have said the broad, pleasant road of bachelorhood – to journey along the narrow and tortuous paths which are governed and controlled by a loving spouse.

Therefore, realising that the human factor is in strong opposition to the advice given by Punch, and that most normal young men will look forward to the great "sacrifice" of marriage, I feel it incumbent upon me to help shy males who are in difficulty over this matter.

The first thing to do when a young man is seriously afflicted with matrimonial intentions is to find a girl who will have him. This is very essential and is known as the first principle in matrimonial law.

Theoretically this first principle is as clear as mud, but in practice it is far less clear. Hence the necessity of caution and clarity of vision before the breaks are eased off.

Having mastered the first principle – that a "woman in the case" is an integral item to marriage – the next step is a right selection.

I must emphasise the word "right" selection, because it should be obvious to all intending benedicts there is a wrong as well as a right selection.

"F'rinstance," as Lord Algy was in the habit of saying, a man would not only fall foul of the law, but also commit an act of indiscretion, if he selected his maternal or paternal grandmother. The lady in question may have been an excellent partner to the grandfather, now deceased, but that is no criterion – even if such a union were permissible – that she would make an excellent partner to the grandson.

Prohibited Degrees

To save a young man undue brain-lag during the period of selection he should study the law of Kindred and Affinity, wherein he will find there are degrees of relationship, to the number of thirty, of whom he must not marry. This, so to speak, narrows the circle, and sets a young man off somewhere in the vicinity of legitimate prospective partners.

Even now great care and caution needs to be exercised, for it is not considered etiquette to select another man's wife.

I am quite aware that this rule is broken even in the higher stratas of society. In fact, I am told that this game of "pinching" other men's wives is quite of daily occurrence. But I would seriously advise any young man afflicted with matrimonial proclivities not to follow such a course. It is not only bad form, but also dangerous in the extreme. The husband of the lady selected may be another Frank Moran, and it would be exceedingly painful, as well as undignified, to have to appear in public with ears large enough to flap, and eyes which would put Cherry Blossom in the shade. No, no, the circle must be again diminished.

Having excluded near relatives and other men's wives – and other young men's sweethearts, by the way, for that also is bad form and may be dangerous – we come now to the field of legitimate selection.

It is here where the young aspirant will be in the cart if he does not move with circumspection.

Under no circumstances must a novice judge hastily by outward and visible signs. That is to say: He may pass a young lady with whom he has a slight acquaintanceship, and who may come within the circle of legitimate selection. As she inclines her head in response to his raised hat she winks at him. But step warily, young man. It may not be the wink of encouragement. It possibly is a physical effort to shut out the menacing charge of a gnat fly.

If, by any chance, he should mistake the sign and wink back, under no circumstance must he look embarrassed. When the young lady expresses her indignation, let him remember the gnat fly suggestion and get that in first. At the same time let him take out his pocket handkerchief and wipe his eye.

A Detail

One warning I would give. Let him remember to apply the handkerchief to the same eye he winked with, or the deception will be exposed.

Again. I once heard of a charming young married lady who had a nervous affection of the neck. Every now and again she would unconsciously jerk back her head, and a little to one side, which, in conscious action corresponds to "Come along with me!" She and her husband went to the sea-side for the benefit of the wife's health.

Walking along the sea-front by herself – the husband was following later – she became somewhat disconcerted by seeing a young man looking at her. This brought on the nervous disorder, and as she jerked back her head, the young man, thinking it was an invitation, accepted with alacrity.

Hurrying to escape his unwelcome attention she glanced over her shoulder – and unconsciously wagged her head again. This, of course, doubly assured the young Lochinvar that the "glad eye" was his, and he went forward with accelerated speed.

At that very moment he came violently into contact with an irresistible force, in the shape of an indignant husband. And:
> So this young Lochinvar went over the top:
> 'Twas a rock underneath that caused him to stop.
> And when he awakened he looked out to sea,
> And said, "Well, I'm jiggered – who'd 'a thought it of she?"

And so young man, as I have already instructed you, never judge hastily by outward signs; for they are inclined to be rather deceptive.

Above all do not be precipitate. Wait patiently until next week. By then I shall have again sat on the lap of the gods, and further wisdom I will impart unto you. Till then, farewell, O seeker after trouble.

To Seekers After Trouble (2)
Further Instructions by George E Hobbs
(First published: May 6, 1921)

Before I dilate upon that exquisite period wherein dark days are illuminated by the forty thousand candle power light of love; days in which toothache is easily relieved by osculation and onions are rigidly excluded from daily diet. I feel it necessary to enlarge somewhat upon the advice I gave last week. And here I must ask readers who really heed advice to be a little more considerate. It is very annoying after obtaining the assistance of two policemen and an ambulance for a postman who is in the apparent throes of apoplexy on the doorstep, to find that it is merely a passing fit of hysteria through reading advice sought for upon a postcard. Please do not ask advice upon a postcard.

On the other hand, my time is so restricted I cannot wade through twelve sheets of closely written foolscap, when all that was required was: "I am a man like Zacharias, short of stature; ought I to select a tall woman?" To this correspondent I would urge that his selection should be some few inches shorter than his screed, and somewhat less cramped.

There are others, I find, who are perplexed along similar lines. Should fair men select dark women? etc, etc.

We are told that like attracts like, and upon this dictum tall men should select tall women. Fair men, fair women. Loquacious men should select talkative women – though I very much doubt if one could be found. Silent and reserved men should select silent and reserved women. These are much more numerous.

On the other hand, if we take the physical order of the universe as a pattern we find the opposite to be true. Equipoise and harmony are maintained by the action and reaction of opposing forces. Centrifugal force is opposed by centripetal force, and the solar system is maintained in perfect order and safety. Therefore, if we take celestial phenomena as a pattern, a tall man should select a short lady, and a diminutive man should select an elongated lady.

Of course, this latter would scarcely pan out satisfactorily because there are terms of endearment which, if expressed, would be slightly on the side of incongruity. Just fancy a Lilliputian Scotsman looking up (somewhere near the ceiling), into the face of his dear one, and saying in the intensity of his feelings, "My wee lassie!" And she, no less emotional, looking down into his bright, animated face replying, "My stalwart laddie!" Such a picture would frighten even Bairnsfather [a prominent cartoonist of the era].

A Stage Further

And then, to carry the picture a stage further. There may come a time when the joy bell has ceased its ringing. It may be that the clapper has fallen out of the socket, or the rim has worn off. It would be very distressing to the diminutive husband if, for some fancied misdemeanour, his elongated wife picked him up, shook him and smacked him soundly and placed him upon his feet again.

And there is yet another contingency, a contingency that is by no means improbable or remote. It is possible that the tall lady may be near-sighted and somewhat deaf. If such was the case, imagine the horror of the abbreviated senior partner, if his wife grasps him instead of their son, forcibly undresses him in spite of his gallant struggles and places him in the cradle to rock him to sleep.

No, no! The case is so complicated in which there is a big difference in altitude that I feel I cannot advise. I shall feel much more safe if I turn to opposites of a different character.

If it is true that opposites tend to domestic harmony – and that is all we poor mortals wish for – then the silent and reserved man should look out for a loquacious partner. These, as I have barely intimated, are very rare and hard to find. But if the silent one is persistent in his search, I venture to suggest that in time he will meet with ultimate success. By ultimate success, I mean so far as his search is concerned, I do not pose as a seer, and therefore I cannot look forward into the future and say definitely that such a union will be ultimately successful.

It is quite understood that these instructions are for young men. But in this case I feel it necessary to include young ladies. If the silent one of either sex should select their opposite and should eventually find that the serenity of wedded bliss is somewhat impaired by too much 'gobble', a remedy is easily procurable. The silent one should go to a chemist and purchase an anaesthetic of low power and high velocity. Uncork the bottle when the talkative one is not looking at his or her victim, and soon he or she will not be looking anywhere. A quiet peace will pervade the home, giving the silent one ample opportunity of reflecting upon the fact that so far as they are concerned the law of opposites is an "ass."

A Colour Scheme

But now we come to opposites of a different hue. "Hue" is the right word, for I mean colour. I am not sure if it is right to speak of men as "blondes" and "brunettes". I know it is right to speak so of ladies, but I am not sure if this is a happy term as applied to the male sex. At any rate for my purpose here I shall be a law unto myself and apply such a term. Therefore ought male blondes to select female brunettes, and vice versa?

Let us deal first with the dark visaged young man who is seeking a blonde as his lifelong partner. I fear I am treading upon dangerous ground and, therefore, must walk warily. Not only do fashions change with the rapidity of greased lightning, but complexions also change – at least so I am told. Great care, therefore, is needed to see that the young man in question selects the genuine article. This young man is enraptured with his opposite. He is dark, she is fair. For weeks and weeks he is constantly making up his mind to press his suit [seek out a romantic partner], and as constantly his heart fails him at the crucial moment.

Then one day, he becomes determined. Here she comes. He raises his hat and... Heavens! She is a brunette. Oh yes, she is the same young lady only, as I say, complexions change as do fashions.

And after all, what does it matter?!

If the young lady was adorable as a blonde, she is the same adorable person as a brunette. So, let the law of opposites go hang! And please remember this: there is many a fair blonde overnight who is a very dark brunette the following morning – after she has cleaned the grate. So, the colour test had better be dispensed with.

Next week – "The Wooing Period."

To Seekers After Trouble (3)
Further Instructions by George E Hobbs
(First published: May 13, 1921)

One of the commonest of mistakes a matrimonially inclined young man is apt to make is the belief that, when he has selected a young lady as the potential sharer of all his joys and the potential cause of all his troubles, the major part of his work is done. He thinks he has only to butt in and the prize is his.

In some parts of the world, as I shall presently narrate, this is the order of procedure. But this is not so in the highly civilised country that has the honour of counting among its noble sons men like... well, modesty (and the fear of engendering jealousy) forbids me to publish names.

When the disciple of Eros is satisfied he has made a wise selection, he must thoroughly understand that is but the preliminary round, so to speak; the prelude to the cataclysm which is inevitable after the shy, trembling "yes" has been spoken. Even so, we believe there is an intermediate state between mortal life and the consummation of all our aspirations, so there is an intermediate state between the period of selection and the period of realisation.

This intermediate state (some substitute "terrible" for "intermediate") is called the wooing period.

The Wooing Period

It is no use for a young man to think he can escape this period. If he would win, he must woo – though it does not always follow that he will win if he does woo. The girl may be willing to be wooed; the mother of the said damsel may be a faithful ally, but the father has other intentions.

If these circumstances should prevail and the young man finds himself thrown ignominiously out into the road three times in one week, he should not be discouraged. He must remember that perseverance is a quality most fathers admire – and try again. Under no circumstances must his indignation cause him to sidestep and allow the father to propel himself into the road. Fathers, as a rule, never forget or forgive indignities. Of course, there is no loss of dignity if the young man, hearing hostile approach, should extricate himself gracefully and retire before the ejectment order is administered. The best of generals sometimes retire before an invincible foe.

If, however, the young lady assists at the first ejectment, the young man must readily perceive this is tantamount to dismissal. In that case he will have to play through the preliminary round again. In other words, he must select elsewhere.

But let us suppose that all the circumstances point to a favourable reception of his advances. The girl does not ignore him, her brothers tease her respecting him, her father taps him for half-a-crown, and her mother gives her sage advice. All those circumstances being favourable, what is the best method for him to adopt in order to woo and win his lady love?

We often hear the advice to "learn from nature" but in this matter I do not think this should apply. For instance: Darwin tells us that among certain birds, the rock thrush of Guiana and birds-of-paradise in particular, the female bird is won by the male bird that has the most brilliant plumage, the sweetest song, and which performs the most graceful evolutions before her admiring eyes.

Follow Not Nature

Just fancy then, our young Horatio bedecking himself in such gorgeous apparel as to suggest he is the loose end of a stray rainbow. As soon as he is near the lay's bower (I mean home), he begins to whistle "Bubbles," and prance about with the elegant grace of a hippopotamus and with the persistency of a recurring decimal. What effect would it have upon the lady's mind? No, no, Horatio! An' that be your name, follow not nature I beg of you.

An easier, but not altogether satisfactory way is to buy the young lady from her parents. This is by no means an original method, so I do not claim the copyrights of the suggestion. In fact, I am told that in the highest circles there are cases on record where the personality of the man having failed to charm, a few moments' conversation with the girl's parents, and the rustle of crisp notes has worked the trick. If this was a seriously written article, I should unhesitatingly say that such a man deserves to have his notes thrust down his throat with an iron-shod ramrod, but to resume the spirit of these exquisite instructions.

In Melanesia (the name given to a series of groups of islands in the South Pacific), winning a young lady by barter is quite a common practice. If a matrimonially-inclined youth of the New Guinea islands has given the "glad eye" to a New Guinea maiden, and the glance has become reciprocal, it immediately becomes evident to the youth that the selection stage is over and the wooing period must begin. Off trots dusky John, kills and roasts a pig or two, slings them upside down upon a pole, and sends them by express messengers to his lady's dusky father. If the price is sufficient, well and good. If not, the youth must send in more pigs until the price is equal to the value of the girl's charms.

Barter

This method, of course, may work with satisfactory results in New Guinea, Fiji or in the Bismarck Archipelago, but I scarcely think I should care to recommend it in this country. Undoubtedly this method would have its advantages, with the price of bacon as it stands today. But if a youth decides to woo his lady by barter, he will influence the father with better results if he would send him a ton of good house-coal, or a tree cut up in just the right lengths for firewood. At least it is worth a trial.

There are other methods, much more effective and far less costly than wooing by barter. In some parts of Africa, the wooing youth does not give the young lady the "glad eye." He gives her something that she remembers all the rest of her life. By the law of his tribe the wooing youth is permitted to go into the forest with a cudgel and bludgeon the first presentable unmarried female he meets, and carry her off while she is still in an unconscious state. She is then considered to be his wife.

Of course, in Africa this may be considered as quite a good way, though I can quite conceive it has its disadvantages. It must be terribly sad to the amorous youth if he finds he has hit his beloved a trifle too hard, and made himself a widower at the same moment he made himself a husband.

Gentler Methods

In England, however, I do not think that such a method should be used. And although after marriage the husband may often feel he would like to bludgeon the lady of his choice good and hard, yet I would strongly recommend gentler methods during the wooing period. I would urge this from the standpoint of example.

English girls have been taught the meaning of reciprocity. If the wooing youth resorts to cudgelling before marriage, he must remember that the business end of a broom in the hands of an exasperated woman can do a lot of damage to his figurehead after marriage.

Gentler methods must be used. Methods of... but there, who ever heard of a duck being taken to a pond and taught to swim? Methods of wooing are instinctive, Horatio. Quite instinctive.

If the reader wishes to read the conclusion of this sad story, they will find the last episode in next week's Advertiser, entitled "The Period of Realisation", which being interpreted means "The Consummation of Trouble."

To Seekers After Trouble (4)
The Final Instructions: by George E Hobbs
(First published: May 20, 1921)

Those of my readers who have had the audacity and the sublime patience to read through the whole of these exquisite instructions, will remember the first of the series. I stated in the first article that the advice given by Punch to those about to marry was opposed by what is known as the human factor. As long as this old world goes joyously round, wars and rumours of war, strikes and rumours of strikes, coal in plenty or no coal at all, a glut of houses or no houses, will never prevent normal young folk from adventuring into the mystic wonderland of matrimony. The call is age-long and worldwide, and cannot be denied. It is universal in every sense of the word.

Therefore, seeing that young men will seek trouble, it was necessary that

I should sympathetically dispense advice which would guide them during the initial stages of their matrimonial venture.

As we have already noticed, the first stage entered is the period of selection; the period in which search is made for a possible partner. A suitable title for this period is: "Searching for Trouble."

Having sought and gained some sort of encouragement from the possible partner, the next stage entered by the unsuspecting seeker is the period in which he cajoles, bothers, badgers and worries the said possible partner to be "his'n". And when she is his'n then he is happy – or believes himself to be, which amounts to be the same thing.

Some sentimentalists term this period "Halcyon days", but a better description is "days of foreshadowed trouble". But, of course, the bewitched seeker does not know it. He does not even anticipate it. But then, neither did the heroic fly whose memory is perpetuated in the poem that children love to recite. Listen to its pathetic witchery:

"Will you walk into my parlour?" said the spider to the fly.

"It's the nicest little parlour that ever you did spy."

And many a poor old fly has believed the yarn and walked in. Let us remember them in silent sympathy, for they never had a chance to walk out of that parlour again.

Algy may cajole, bother, badger and worry Angelena for her "yes". But all through the ages, Arachne has never lost the art of weaving – only she knows how to conceal her web.

Lapses from Veracity

During this period young men should be warned against making wild and irrational statements.

Mr Winston Churchill has somewhat robbed these statements of their rugged surname, and given to them quite a delicate and simple designation. He calls them "terminological inexactitudes", so we will let it go at that.

It is not right for the young man to promise he will get up and do the washing before he goes to work, he will clean the house through once every week, he will give up smoking and football – and kissing other young ladies. These are terminological inexactitudes; in other words, they are untruths, and should not be indulged in.

And so we come to the final period in the matrimonial drama. The period of wedded bliss, or "trouble consummated".

Now no one can deny that a wonderful change has taken place in the general conduct of Horatio during the two periods preceding the matrimonial alliance. Horatio himself has noticed it. During the selection period it was astonishing to him how life seemed to change, and when he was suffering badly during the wooing period the transformation was, to him, utterly bewildering.

A happy bird serenading its mate as she broods over her nest was once an ideal target for the slug in his catapult. But now, he has no desire to "see if I can hit him", for there is a subtle and indescribable sympathy between the whilom slaver and the happy songster.

The bright-faced flower that once was flicked off in pure wantonness with his swinging cane is now left in perfect security, for it reminds him of her. She, like the flower, is fragrant and sweet, and he loves the little, inoffensive primrose and violet for her sake.

At one time the only "stars" he ever thought of or knew were those who displayed their charms from before the footlights. Now, in company with his "star," astronomy becomes a practical study. Away from the madding crowd, in the silence of the evening, two faces are upturned to the sapphired dome of heaven. In the ecstasy of feeling, Horatio whispers, "How beautiful does the goddess of love appear tonight? Which is that? Why Venus – over there to the East. And how bright are those... oh, thank heaven there's a cloud coming over the moon."

And so it goes on. Yes, Horatio is happy. Happy in the wonderful change that has taken place in his life. As it is the height of indelicacy to stave at unalloyed happiness (which usually takes place during the "honeymoon" period), we will draw for a moment an impenetrable veil.

And then, Horatio wakes up!

He discovers that the friend who told him two could as cheap as one was a l*** (I mean he discovers he has been told a terminological inexactitude). He discovers that the gentle girl who could say "Yes, dear," with clinging arms, can now say "Yes, my love," with a clanging broom handle.

"Where Did This Come From?"

He discovers that should a long stray hair be found upon his shoulder, careful comparison is at once instituted. If the hue should coincide with the tresses at present worn by his amiable partner, all is well. But if, in the process of comparison there is a disagreement in shades then the Riot Act is read. Not only read – it would not be so hurtful if it was merely read – but expounded, dissected, enlarged upon and finally the minutes of the previous meeting are open for discussion.

If the delinquent is happy in the procession of a mother or sister who has tresses similar to that found upon his shoulder, then the minutes are passed as read. If no near relative is available then Horatio must give in, throw himself upon the mercy of the court and take his punishment like a man.

He will discover... But why continue? If I were to write of all he discovers I should fill all the columns of the Advertiser, so I must desist.

But one final word, Horatio. For all the pretended satire poured upon the marriage state, it is the ideal existence for normal folk. If mutual trust, confidence and love is given then the only discovery each will make is that of complete happiness.

Married life is a compact of complete trust between two intelligent beings. Each bears a responsibility in that compact, and when two beings determine that their wedded life shall be a success, it will be a success. It greatly depends upon the strength of the determination.

[PS: George and Agnes were married for 45 years, ending with his premature death at the age of 63.]

Making a Success of Life
Mr GE Hobbs' Letters to a Young Lad
(First published: November 24, 1922)

My Dear Frank, My late schoolmaster once asked me if I would undertake to write a story depicting the life of a lad working in a large factory during the years of his apprenticeship. I informed him I would do so at the first favourable opportunity. In fact, I was about to write such a story when your letter reached me.

After carefully perusing its contents I am convinced the story must be delayed for a time because, as your letter demands immediate attention, the compiling of my answer will engage my most serious thought. I must confess your concluding request somewhat disconcerted me. You ask that all answers to your letters shall be published in the Swindon Advertiser. This, of course, is a matter entirely for the editor to decide. And if this reply should be published, you will quite understand it is by the kindness of the editor.

Let me say first of all, I am glad you have been so like your name in stating the problems confronting you. It not only indicates a real desire to get at grips with those difficulties, but also a real desire to master them. Its very frankness will help me in my reply to you. There are definite questions and they demand definite answers.

To sum up your request in one sentence, you wish to know how to make a success of life or, to use your own words: "How can I make good after serving my apprenticeship?" To give a general answer to this general question I must reply: You will experience a great difficulty in making good after your apprenticeship if you do not attempt making good during that time. A simple and well known illustration will serve.

Stability of the Structure

The stability of any structure depends almost entirely upon its foundation. A masterman, having a building, or a bridge, or any structure to erect will be almost sleepless while the foundation is being prepared and complete. Presently it is finished to his entire satisfaction, and the structure itself begins.

Under his supervision, the most exquisite work is wrought and men, passing by, call him a genius. He is proud of his work, not because of what men say, but because he knows his structure is solid and secure; and will stand the test of time.

The foundation is hidden, and men praise him for the superstructure; but he knows that his structure would have collapsed even before it was completed if it had not been for that good, careful foundation.

So that I would urge you to begin making good now, for it is now that you are digging the soil and preparing the foundation of your life.

The foundation then, being of primary importance, the first thing to consider is what material must be used to form and lay it securely. Here are the ingredients in their order of importance:

Cleanliness of mind

Essential study

Thoroughness in study

Now, Frank. Let us face facts. We shall be all the better equipped if we do so.

I gather from your letter you have come into contact with a remarkable man whose standard of life is not quite that which I have tabulated above. And, to use your own words, "He is successful in all he undertakes."

I shall not attempt a denial of such a possibility. There are folk who have made a distinct impression upon the world without taking much note of the above ingredients. A combination of circumstances outside of themselves, has made them what I may term "ready made geniuses".

The energy of their brain is taxed only nominally when confronted by a problem, and seemingly, however complex that problem may be, details of construction are quickly understood. But with all due respect to these folk, there is very little virtue accruing to them for that which they achieve. This may seem very strange to you, but I will try and make it clear.

The most precise of geometricians could scarcely improve upon the construction of the hexagon which goes to form a honey-cell. But the brain of the bee is not worried over its construction. It works by instinct and not by acquired knowledge. Consequently, although the symmetrical beauty of the cell calls forth admiration, there is no virtue ascribed to the bee for the work done.

It would be the height of folly for me to force this comparison to the extreme, but I would force it far enough to prevent you making the mistake of taking the abnormal for the normal; the instinctive for that which is acquired.

The man whom you have met is abnormal and there is more of the "bee-instinct" about his accomplishments than there is of the virtuous achievement of acquired knowledge.

A Clear, Healthy Brain

If the normal youth is to succeed in the vocation he has taken up as his life's work, he must first of all of necessity have a clear, healthy brain. And a clear, healthy brain is not possible when the mind is unclean. A clean mind is the first essential to success. You tell me of the conversation of certain men around you, and of the bestial sketches you have been compelled to see in certain places. Unfortunately this is lamentably true. But without labouring the point, they need have no terrors for you – if you keep your mind clean.

There is an old saying which reads something like: "You cannot prevent birds alighting on your head, but you can prevent them building their nests there."

So, though you cannot close your ears or shut your eyes to these things, you can prevent the poison from lodgement in your mind. And the way to prevent lodgement is to cultivate positive thinking along clean lines.

I must close now, but will write you again.

Your sincere friend,
George E Hobbs

Spirit To Achieve
By GE Hobbs
(First published: December 15, 1922)

In continuation of his "Letters to a Young Lad," Mr George E Hobbs writes:
My Dear Frank – I am in receipt of your reply for which I thank you. I am

glad to know you have determined to do your best in the struggle to achieve. Perhaps it is traversing the ground over which we have already passed, but let me say it is just that spirit I want you to possess. The spirit which in the face of difficulty is dauntless and unafraid. The spirit which cries, "I can and I will!"

I remember reading somewhere of the tremendous difficulties encountered by Mr TA Walker, the contractor who constructed the Severn Tunnel; and how, by sheer determination, he overcame those difficulties.

I believe the work upon the tunnel was commenced in the year 1880. In the first two years, the progress was so slow that it cost on an average £17,000 per month in its construction. In 1883, better progress was reported, when suddenly the great spring burst, flooding the works at the rate of 27,000 gallons of water per minute. The machinery at Mr Walker's disposal was capable of dealing with only 16 gallons per minute, and to increase the troubles, the contractor was already £100,000 in debt upon the undertaking.

It was an appalling situation, and one calculated to break a less stout will than his. With heroic zeal, he increased his plant at a cost of £16,000 and eventually, with the assistance of his sympathetic staff and the extraordinary efforts of Lambert (the diver), the water was apparently subdued.

Again the great spring flowed, and again it was subdued until the year 1886 the tunnel was ready for inspection.

It is the spirit to achieve that is needed, and I am glad you have determined to achieve.

In respect to the second ingredient in the foundation of success – "essential study" – I scarce need advise you here. The engineering course for students during successive years is not only tabulated upon posters in the factory, but advice is given in this connection by the Principal at the Technical School. I therefore come to the third – and last – of the foundation ingredients – "thoroughness in study".

What a wonderful thing is knowledge. To be able to say "I know!" convincingly, and qualify it with a practical demonstration. Of course, Frank, all things cannot be so demonstrated. Knowledge is a serial story in which "to be continued" must ever appear, and "Finis" is never encountered.

Even though you should become the greatest philosopher or scientist the world has seen, "to be continued" would still hold good. You would still have to utter Sir Isaac Newton's dying words when he said, "I have only just touched the 'fringe of knowledge.'"

But there are things you can know and things you must know if you are to achieve success in your life's work. And these essential things can be known by you if you are but thorough in your studies. Thoroughness with less capabilities is much more likely to achieve success than looseness of study with greater capabilities. It is the thorough plodder who wins every time, and who may include the positive "I know" in their vocabulary.

I am told by teachers of music that one of the greatest difficulties they have to encounter is to keep their pupils from "tunes" until the scales and exercises are mastered. I suppose that there is a fascination about playing a tuneful air which scales and exercises do not possess. And the tuneful airs are murdered in consequence of pandering to that fascination. To use again my metaphor of the foundation: the building cannot be secure if the foundation is faulty.

If you are not thorough in your methods, Frank, you will make the same fatal error. A strange fascination invariably lurks two chapters ahead of your immediate study. But let me seriously advise you never turn to page two until you have mastered page one. It does not matter in the least if you are a little longer in grasping the contents of page one. The essential thing is not speed but assimilation. Let the contents of page one be yours in its entirety, and then, with perfect confidence, you can turn to page two.

When I write of "studies" and "pages" I want you to understand I refer equally to theory and practice. It is as needful for you to become a practical craftsman, as it is to be an expert in theory. To illustrate simply:

It is one thing to be able to calculate, by the speed of travel and density of cut, how long it will take to complete a job in the lathe; but it is another matter to be able to do the job so that it will serve the purpose for which it was intended. It is one thing to be able to calculate that an injector, with a given millimetre bore and with its appendages in true alignment and proportion, will feed a given number of gallons of water per hour into a boiler.

But, it is another matter to take injector castings and machine them so that the finished article shall do as required.

Therefore, Frank, it is essential for you to be as thorough in the practical as in the theoretical.

With this I close. Wishing you all the success possible in your life's work.

Your sincere friend,

George E Hobbs

Chapter 4

The War Poet

George's canon of poems and a few prayers is an extensive one, and something that represents his first known contributions to the *Advertiser*.

The first poem to appear was *Britain's Response*, on October 30, 1914, and strongly suggests that this phase of his life as a writer of verse was prompted by the recent declaration of war on Germany, on August 4.

Many of the poems were informed by the conflict and by George's deep love of his faith. However, a few also provide a window on his family and private life.

The war poetry mostly deals with the themes of patriotism, honour, revenge, love and loss – not uncommon tropes in the circumstances. However, what makes it more notable is that his sub-jingoist sentiments were those of a committed Christian for whom 'Thou Shalt Not Kill' was one of the Ten Commandments. In spite of this, George clearly felt that this was a 'just' war and that those who took part on the allied side would be forgiven on the basis that it was a fight between good and evil.

Despite being only 31 years of age by the time war was declared, George never went on to do military service himself. Great-grandson Peter Field recalled: "My grandmother told me that he was not allowed to join up because his expertise in the factory was required in terms of engineering related to the war effort. She told me that he got very upset when he came home from work sometimes, during that time, because of what he was helping to produce to be sent to France, in terms of its destructive power."

The GWR Works certainly played a major role in relation to the war effort. The day after war was declared, the British government took over control of the nation's railways, and immediately placed day-to-day management in the hands of a Railway Executive Committee. At Swindon, resources were directed towards producing additional locomotives for shipment overseas, as well as the conversion of carriages into hospital trains and the production/conversion of wagons sufficiently high-sided for the conveyance of horses.

A few years later, the GWR was to report that 'immense quantities of munitions were made in the Great Western Works, including the complete manufacture of guns, shells, fuses, bombs etc., together with parts for submarines, paravanes, howitzers and mines. A large quantity of Toluol was also produced for use in the manufacture of the TNT explosive. Great Western engines, ambulance trains and wagons were a familiar sight in all fields of operations abroad. Some of the engines are still at Salonika and some, alas, are at the bottom of the sea.'

But it didn't end with this. As www.swindonweb.com reports:

> The factory turned out an average of 2,500 six-inch-long shells, every week, over a two-year period; a total of nearly 500,000 fuses for explosives; no less than five million cartridge cases – and also some of the guns to fire them. A complete manufacturing line was installed to make anti-aircraft guns, while 4.5-inch howitzer and 60-pounder guns were also turned out, along with 338 field carriages, including 40 large naval guns, and hundreds of thousands of other weapon parts.

Perhaps the above provides an insight into why George, from time to time, was plunged into emotional turmoil.

He had stated in April 1915 that he was 'debarred from going out there to fight himself' when, as a time-served fitter and turner, he was clearly considered too important to the overall war-effort within the works to be allowed to join the colours. In any case, George's trade union, The Amalgamated Society of Engineers, helped to secure exemption from conscription for craft union members in late 1916.

It wasn't long before Morris Bros, the three sons of the founder and owner of the *Advertiser*, produced a booklet of George's poems entitled *The British Soldier*, which contained 24 poems, 23 of which had appeared in the paper during the period October 1914 to July 1915.

But George was a far more prolific poet than this. Thus far, a further 21 poems have been rediscovered, including one that was found in a private archive and which has not knowingly appeared in print before. And not forgetting two prayers, both of which are reproduced below.

Much can be described as heavily rhythmic Georgian Romantic conventional verse, heavily laden with sentimentality and patriotism, containing idealised views on relationships and, in particular, with regard to Britain and the Empire's role as the bastion of all that was good.

By November 1916, George's rich vein of original poetry ended, although we should mention that two more appeared in the press in 1922, and a further two in 1923. However, given that his long series of newspaper articles commenced in early January 1917, it's hard not to think that poetry simply didn't allow him a big enough platform to expand on his burgeoning thoughts, beliefs and opinions.

We know that the booklet of verse was well-received and that 750 copies were sold – no mean achievement when you come to think of it. Furthermore, George even came to the attention of Swindon's greatest-ever poet. In his letter to Henry Day dated February 21, 1916, he writes: 'I may say Mr Alfred Williams has sent me a very kind letter on my contributions to the Swindon Advertiser.'

The following therefore comprise only a representative sample of his poetic output. We like to think that this selection includes some of his most significant contributions in terms of their style, content or accessibility.

Britain's Response
(First published: October 31, 1914)

An overly sentimental and self-indulgent piece, comprising a four-line stanza with rhyming couplets. It deals with an elevated and romantic sense of honour which frames the story of Britain's call to arms in defence of Belgium. Rhetorical in tone, it contains a number of archaic contractions. Stylistically, it is emblematic of the work of Rupert Brooke and Laurence Binyon.

> The war clouds had gathered over Britain's fair Isle,
> Full heavy with import, and men ceased to smile:
> A grave situation – a treaty ignored;
> A nation's fair honour by craft had been lowered.
>
> The war clouds that gathered had burst with the weight
> Of Belgium's sore anguish – a neighbouring State.
> Her people were peaceful, no quarrel they sought
> But then in the vortex completely were caught

The teeth of the mastiff were fixed in its prey:
Brutality, latent burst forth in full sway,
Cared they not for honour? No, not if it came
In the way of progress to victory and fame.

But fame worth the winning will never ignore
The rights of the weaker, the lives of the poor:
The honour of Prussia is stained with this crime
Their troth lightly broken – the end, to save time.

The cry of oppression by Britain is heard:
On parchment was written her strong plighted word
Would Britain refrain, by fears overpressed?
Or would she respond and aid the distressed?

Britain has spoken and over the land,
The bugles have sounded with sharp, clear command
To arms! they are calling – go sharpen the sword
For Britain counts honour, no less than her word.
The troubles domestic, so strong to divide;
In national danger were thrust on one side;
And Britain stood solid for honour to fight:
Her word that is plighted she never can slight.

And far o'er the Empire the cry did resound:
The Children of Britain can always be found
To fight 'gainst oppression, whatever the cost:
So armed they for Belgium; no time must be lost.

From Ind. came contingents; and Afric's brave sons
Both eager for breaking the might of the Huns;
From far Australia, and Canada, too,
All solid for Britain, courageous and true.

Yes, Britain has answered, in the only way
To check the advancement of cruelty's sway;
And rue shall the Germans their dishonoured faith;
Their country o'ershadowed by disaster's wraith.

O! God of the Battles to Thee now we cry,
Our forces to strengthen, and each brave Ally:
They fight all for justice 'gainst tyranny strong:
God give them the vict'ry! – they fight against wrong.

No Conscription!
(First published: November 13, 1914)

A quatrain with alternating lines of rhyme. While conscription was not introduced by statute until March 2, 1916, this poem stresses the importance of the new liberalism of individual choice and, given that it was first published in the autumn of 1914, it is an early example of this assertion. Furthermore, it seeks to emphasise the notion of the individual having a direct line to God.

No conscription! no conscription!:
England e'er must stand to lose,
If her sons, without exception,
Cannot, of their freewill, choose
No conscription! no conscription!:
'Tis a curse we all must fear.
We enjoy emancipation:
Be our watchword, 'Volunteer!'

No conscription! no conscription!:
Continental systems make,
Freedom's boast a contradiction:
Spurn the thought, for freedom's sake!

No conscription! no conscription!:
Not while Britain's sons respond
Nobly to persuasive diction,
Leaving home and friendships fond.

No conscription! no conscription!:
Others wanted? – They will come;
Freely? Yes, without compulsion,
To the Front or 'fending home.

> No conscription! no conscription!:
> No! – But if one conscript's made,
> Then will freedom, with the nation
> Pass into the night of shade.

Don't Criticise!
(First published: December 5, 1914)

This poem employs a form of versification where adherence to the rhyming structure appears to take precedence over the deadly serious subject matter. Here, George calls on the British public to be more understanding with Winston Churchill and the Royal Navy High Command in relation to their perceived reluctance to take on the German fleet. The Royal Navy had already sustained numerous losses, including that of HMS Audacious off the north coast of Ireland on October 27, 1914, of HMS Aboukir in the North Sea on September 22, and of HMS Good Hope and HMS Monmouth off Coronel, Chile, on November 1. Anxiety was further heightened following the bombardment of Great Yarmouth by the Imperial German Navy on November 3. Consequently, the British public were becoming increasingly demoralised by Admiral Jellicoe's cautious approach – yet George urges patience and gently reminds readers that the Royal Navy was already heavily deployed in protecting merchant shipping, as well as the troopships bringing in soldiers from all over the Empire.

> When you sit at home in comfort, or you walk along the street,
> When you talk to your companion of the gallant British Fleet,
> When you ask of what they're doing, in a criticising way,
> Just give answers to these questions ere another word you say.
>
> When the Germans in a hurry sought an open road to France,
> Crushing Belgium in their progress, with huge cannon, sword and lance;
> When the Government of Britain saw their duty was to fight –
> Who piloted the transport ships in the dark and silent night?
>
> When from Empire's farthest bound'ry many sons of Britain came
> To fight against an enemy that had clothed herself with shame
> Full many leagues must be o'erpassed ere they reached the fighting line,
> And every soldier that embarked landed safely, fit and fine.

When you think of all the boasting from the Kaiser's foolish lips,
    Of invasion and destruction, aided by his battleships;
Yet something stops his many schemes, from fruition they are stayed-
Can you name this little factor, why these schemes are still delayed?

(We will give our soldiers credit – may God bless them every one!
From the Continental coastline they have kept the boastful Hun.
But should that coastline be exposed, and its towns in Prussia's grip,
    There is still a potent factor in each British battleship.)

When you sit to have your breakfast, or your dinner, or your tea,
Much of what you eat, my brother, comes from lands across the sea.
    Can you do a little thinking, and inform me, if you can,
    How that food can reach you safely, leaving out the sailorman?

When you think of men unceasing, through the day and through the night,
    At their stations stay unwearied, ever waiting for the fight;
When you think of this, my brother, hush your criticising voice-
Give Churchill, Jellico, Fisher praise unstinted for their choice!

Commander Holbrook & The B11
(First published: December 23, 1914)

Once again: a straightforward rhyming couplet, written in an elevated patriotic and conversational style – yet, on this occasion, containing elements of common dialogue between the crew and their commander. On an historical note, it recounts the story of the daring raid in the Dardanelles on December 13, 1914, in which the Royal Navy submarine, B11, commanded by Lt Norman Holbrook, passed through five rows of mines before sinking the Ottoman battleship, Mesûdiye. Lt Holbrook was subsequently awarded the Victoria Cross for this courageous action – the first time such a decoration was given to someone in the submarine service.

    Come list, ye sons of Britain, to a tale I will unfold,
    A tale of British courage, true and faithful, shall be told.
    No thought of empty boasting – 'tis on solid truth I lean
    About Commander Holbrook and his British submarine.

The scene of this brave action, where the B11 went
Right down beneath the water, on its deadly mission bent,
Was the far-famed Dardanelles, strewn with many a floating mine,
And currents that would baffle eight commanders out of nine.

But there the young Commander thought his duty was to go,
His mental calculations drove out all thoughts of "No!"
When duty called he answered, let the cost be what it may,
And if his crew were willing, who would dare to say him nay?

His crew were British Seamen, and they answered quick and clear,
"Just give your orders now, sir; we are willing, never fear!"
He gave the order promptly: "Make all ready now to dive!"
Each man flew to his station, each with heart and brain alive.

Down sank the B11, 'neath the rough Ægean Sea,
Its young Commander steering. First his course was danger free;
But soon a fearsome danger came before his startled view,
For mine-fields here lay scattered, and their mighty force he knew.

But careful and undaunted did Commander Holbrook steer,
Between those deadly mine-fields, and the crew gave such a cheer!
Each loved their brave young Captain, and for him they all would dare,
To do their duty nobly, and with him the dangers share.

Then spoke the young Commander, with the helm firm in his grip,
"Torpedo men, make ready; train on yonder Turkish ship;
Your aim make true and faithful, and for Britain strike a blow!"
It was done – the Turkish warship slowly sinking down below.

But now another danger faced these dauntless heroes bold:
The fort guns came in action, and their message to them told
That they were now discovered, quick their journey must retrace:
Each felt in that grim moment 'twas 'twixt life and death a race.

With dangers all around them, yet these heroes, undismayed,
Stood fast each to his station, though at times they were delayed.
Yet in the end they triumphed, British pluck had told again,
And the memory of this deed Britain's sons will e'er retain.

The Last Goodbye
(First published: December 28, 1914)

This is a rather tragic story of love and loss – heavily sentimental, but quite typical of much of George's oeuvre. Unusually, this is the only one where he seeks a tune to fit the three eight-line verses and two four-line choruses. Perhaps, over one hundred years later, this can still be achieved.

The Author is desirous of finding a tune for the following lines.
Can any reader supply this?

Two lovers stood in leafy shade:
A stalwart lad, a charming maid;
No thought of time, no thought beside
That each was by the other's side.
To-morrow's sun will see him go
From her away, to face the foe!
And as he bends to kiss good-bye,
He whispers, "Sweetheart, do not cry!"
CHORUS: "I'll think of you when far away;
My sweetheart true, for you I pray
The hour is sad, for we must part:
Kiss me once more, my own sweetheart!"

The ship sailed fair across the sea,
Safe-guarded by the King's navee:
On board that ship the lover stood,
And thought of her, so fair and good.
Her love had been his guiding star,
Like Pole-star guides the ships from far;
And as he thinks, he heaves a sigh,
Then whispers gently, "Dear, good-bye!"

But now a change comes o'er the scene:
No time has he of love to dream:
The bugle calls, a sharp command,
As shot and shell scream o'er the land!
The lover grasps his trusty sword:
But, ere he gives his men the word,
A cruel shot has pierced his brain:
He'll ne'er on earth see her again!

CHORUS – (For last verse only):

And thro' her pain there beams a light:
His death came not in wanton flight.
In honour's cause his life was given:
He dwells in peace with God in Heaven.

The British Soldier
(First published: January 2, 1915)

This, the title poem of the booklet published in 1915, embodies an heroic sense of loss.

Out in the trenches throughout the day,
Standing in water and softened clay,
Fighting for honour in foreign land,
The British soldier makes firm his stand.
His not to question the reason why,
Bravely resolving to do or die,
Thinking of loved ones! Aye, it inspires,
Enthusing courage that never tires.

Out in the trenches throughout the night,
In hours of darkness still he must fight;
Weary, exhausted, yet undismayed –
Still with a dauntless courage arrayed.

Now comes cessation of fearful strife,
Staying the carnage of precious life;
The foe has retired, they cannot stand
'Gainst the pride and strength of Britain's land.

Sleeping and resting as best he can –
No downy pillow for this brave man;
His mattress must be the softened clay,
As he rests at night, or through the day.

Now he is resting; but not for long –
Soon will the cannon renew its song;
From solo 'twill swell to chorus loud –
From sunshine of rest to turmoil's cloud.

Yes, this is his life by day and night,
Fighting for honour, for truth, and right;
Wounded, disabled, yielding his life
In the bitter clash of battle strife.

Will Britain forget in days ahead
The limbs that are lost, the gallant dead?
Shall widows and bairns and helpless men
Be turned to their own resources then?

Let Britain keep fresh each noble deed,
And proudly respond to each their need,
For their needs must be a nation's care –
Let Britain to all be just and fair.

Love Fills The Void
(First published: March 26, 1915)

This is a heart-rending piece, written in the female voice about the loss of a soldier-husband on the battlefield, and the wife's consequent flirtation with suicide. The preamble purposely excludes the surname of the woman, whose bereavement forms the subject matter of this eight-verse poem. However, it strongly suggests that this particular woman was well-known to George, rather than being an entirely fictional character.

(Mrs _____, whose husband was killed in battle,
has given birth to a daughter).

Take now my life, for life has ceased its charm,
Naught is there now for me on earth to live;
Spirit of Death – from thee I fear no harm,
For from thine hand re-union thou wilt give.

He that I loved, and loved with passion strong,
Lies 'neath the sod of Belgium's stricken land:
Life will to me be meaningless and long,
If 'tis unblessed by his devoted hand.

Ah, let me think, ere yet I sink to rest,
Of gladsome days when honeyed paths we trod;
Our vows were true, we gave to each the best:
Vowed each before the altar of our God.

Yes, we were one! Less cannot live alone!
O cruel shot that laid my husband low!
Naught on this earth can ere for him atone:
Cease, earth-born life, cease now thy useless flow!

What is this new, this strange delightful sense
Steals o'er my soul and calms my troubled breast?
Spirit of Death – call not my soul from hence
Till I have proved what means this new-found rest!

O, Baby mine! I feel thy gentle breath,
Like morning dew, refreshing, calm and sweet;
Easing my pain and calling me from death:
E'en calling me a mother's life to greet.

Come Baby mine! Come closer, closer yet:
Chaos is bridged by thy entrancing form;
Divinest love my lonely soul has met,
Bringing me peace from sorrow's cruel storm!

Yes, I must live – my baby needs my care:
Angels of God, protect me now from death!
For her dear life has come my heart to share:
I plead for life, I plead with every breath.

O God Bless The Mourners
(First published: April 16, 1915)

As far as is known, this is the only acrostic prayer (or poem, for that matter) written by George; a prayer whereby the first letter of each line spells out a separate word or phrase – in this case, the title. Little did the general public know, in 1915, how the losses would multiply in 1916 and beyond.

A Prayer

      O God of pity, God of Love
Grant now Thine help, from Heav'n above;
      O Let Thy mercy freely flow
   Down to these hearts so sad and low.
   Before Thine altar, Lord, they stand,
   Larger doth grow the strickened band;
     E'en as they're waiting, give relief:
   Sustain them in their poignant grief.
   See they are helpless, gracious Lord;
   They cannot speak one broken word;
   Heavy with sorrow's grievous load,
    Exhausted on life's rugged road.
     Mighty in pity as Thou art,
   O hear the throb of each sad heart!
   Unite thy weakness to Thy might,
   Redeeming them from darksome Night.
   Nought are we pleading, only this:
    Even for those in grief's abyss –
    Reveal Thy mercy to them, Lord;
Speak now one gracious, healing word.

I Will Repay

(First published: May 14, 1915)

This poem is highly religious and rhetorical, delivered as if from the pulpit. Although not mentioned by name, it is hard to imagine that this is not about the RMS Lusitania, which was sunk by the German submarine U-20, off the southern coast of Ireland, on May 7, 1915, with the loss of 1,198 lives, including many civilians. Among them was 30-year-old Swindonian, Maud Chirgwin, the wife of a railway stores clerk, and their eight-month-old son, Richard. They were travelling from Cuba, bound for Liverpool. The sinking escalated the entry of the United States into the war.

   Have you no pity, no pity, I ask?
   Do you find joy in your devilish task?
What were your feelings, when, standing aback,
 The proud ship came sailing, right in your track?

Exultant, inflamed with passionate spleen,
Waiting to hurl, in your curs'd submarine.
A message of Death, to hundreds of souls:
A deed that could only be done by ghouls.
Captained by Satan, and manned by his crew
Of fiends incarnate, for each of you knew
That innocent bairns, and helpless old age
Would sink 'neath the wave, thro' your hellish rage.
Your judgement I leave to the care of Him
Who gave to the world the message so grim:
"Who causeth a child to suffer or fall,
Must answer to Me, when his name I call".

True Love – Life's Greatest Blessing
(First published: June 18, 1915)

Upon reading this unapologetically sentimental ballad, it's natural to think that this is a love song from George to Agnes. Indeed, it's unimaginable that he would/could write so longingly to any other woman. Furthermore, he makes clear reference to days of sorrow and their 'dear dead' – most probably in memoriam to their son, Reginald, who had died in infancy. However, where it does depart from being strictly autobiographical is the specific mention of a church wedding – when of course they took part in a Registry Office ceremony only. Stylistically, it is reminiscent of Alfred Williams's 1913 poem, *If Love Came Unbidden*.

List to me, dearest,
Fairest and nearest
List as I sing the old love song again;
Here in the moonlight,
Under the starlight,
Memory's stirred by its haunting refrain.

How I remember
That glad September,
E'en as we wandered through meadow and dell,
Spirits seemed o'er us,
Chanting the chorus
"Love" is the message that each of them tell.

Beaming with gladness,
Banishing sadness,
Fond were the tokens that you and I gave;
Vowing that ever
Nothing should sever
Love-bonds that bound us more strong than the grave.

Life never brighter,
Heart never lighter,
When at the altar you stood by my side;
Bravely confessing
Love's purest blessing,
Leaving the church as my bonnie sweet bride.
Not always flowers,
Garlands and bowers
Birds have not always sang carols overhead;
Flowers have faded
Sorrow's stream waded,
E'en as we gathered around our dear dead.

Yet with the sorrows
Came brighter morrows,
Cheered by the presence of love deep and true;
Darkness was banished,
Irksomeness vanished,
"Love" was the secret, as each of us knew.

Come then, my dearest,
Fairest and nearest,
List as I sing the old love song again.
Angels are o'er us,
Chanting the chorus,
"Love" is their message, and "Love" the refrain.

Where Dwelleth Peace?
(First published: June 30, 1915)

Here, George extols the virtues of the heavens and the natural environment as a spiritual haven from the strife of the Great War. Typical of the true Romantic tradition, it is said to have echoes of Wordsworth.

Where dwelleth peace?
The world's overcast with darkest gloom;
To North, to South, to East, to West
I look, I look in vain for peace:
I look, and find it not.
The Dove of Peace, with broken wing,
And deep pathetic look of woe,
Lies bleeding sore: strange wounds are these,
Bespeaking cunning, treachery.
Oh God! The pity of it all:
That friends of peace should cause these wounds
And bring that look of agony!
Where dwelleth peace?
'Tis eve; and high above the earth,
Resplendent in proud majesty,
Doth reign the moon. She is of herself
Not one bright ray imparts; yet she
With faultless lustre shines.
Unjealous of her feeble powers,
She smiles to grasp a meagre part
Of light's vast prodigality
That floods our mighty system. She,
Claiming her part, reflects the rays
From sun to earth; and this, e'en this,
Speaks soft to me of peace.

Where dwelleth peace?
I turn again to earth. I miss
The tumult, and the noisome strife;
I see the mountain and the dale,
I see the flowers with many hues:
I see that here is peace.
The tiny spring, the rivulet,
The river, with its mighty flow,
The trees, the fields of waving corn,
The hedgerows, and the song of birds,
The butterfly, with golden wings
All these with mighty voices speak
To me, that here is peace!

Mediation

(First published: July 23, 1915)

In this lyrical and sentimental poem of eight verses, George looks beyond the conflict to the day when the guns fall silent, and a new period of enlightenment and peace commences.

When softly fall the shades of eve,
I gather near
To where I ever would relieve
My every fear.
I rise above earth's noise and strife
And fateful war;
And here I find diviner life,
That nought can mar.

I ever have, when sore opprest
With anxious thought,
Repaired to that great home of rest
Its peace have sought.

And never have I been denied;
But this I find
My deepest needs are satisfied,
And calmed my mind.

On eagle wings upborne I fly,
Till sense of time
Is lost, with earth's despairing cry:
Its shame and crime.

I see the glow of fairer day
Than earth has known,
When nations walk the perfect way:
Their strivings flown.

When concord, peace and brotherhood
Reigns o'er the world;
When each will seek the other's good:
Hate's banner furled.

> I pray: I rise a better man
> For this blest sight
> And trust to do whate'er I can
> To aid the right.

Intercession
(First published: October 29, 1915)

This is the second of two rediscovered prayers by George, and it is rich in religious imagery. The prayer is arranged as a sestet, a format comprising six-line stanzas. This is more evidence of the fact that George saw the First World War as a righteous conflict that was ultimately the pitching of good versus evil.

Sunday, October 31, 1915, is set apart as a day of Solemn Prayer.

> O Father, if in Thy pure sight,
> Thou see'st our cause is just and right,
> If Thou, who judgest men their deeds,
> Bespeak to Britain guiltless needs;
> Then without fear we e'en may ask
> (For Thee) to help us in our task
>
> And we believe, O Father, God,
> We walk the path we should have trod
> Unquestionably Britain knew,
> That to her trust she must be true:
> And Thou who art the righteous Lord,
> Will own and bless her honoured word.
>
> Therefore we bring our cause to Thee
> And pray Thee in Thy wisdom, see
> Our struggles 'gainst Satanic might;
> Our bid for Liberty and Right –
> Now, by our side, Lord, make Thy stand
> And stay the proud oppressor's hand

And O our Father, be Thou near
The souls in sorrow and in fear;
Bid them remember, Thou art He
That guides the nation's destiny
That Thou art still upon the throne,
And Thou art God, and God alone.

The Air Raid of Jan 31st 1916
(First published: March 31, 1916)

This is a sestet of rhythmic variation in which alternate lines one and three, as well as lines two and four, are set to rhyme, as are the consecutive (and penultimate and final) lines, five and six. It tells of the events of the night of January 31/February 1, 1916, in which nine Zeppelin airships set out to bomb Liverpool, but instead ended up dropping a mixture of high explosive bombs and incendiaries over the Black Country and towns such as Loughborough, Burton and Derby, resulting in injuries to 113 people, and the loss of 70 lives.

'Twas eventide, and o'er fair Britain's land
Had come the calm that follows daily toil;
And weary men from workshops near at hand,
And husbandmen, the tillers of the soil,
Had homeward gone to rest by cheering fire,
And list to lips whose prattle ne'er would tire.

All nature slept; the birds scarce mated yet.
Were nestled close in reawakening love;
Perchance was one nonsuited, he would fret,
And restless be, oft like amorous dove:
The low of kine, the plaintive bleat of sheep,
Was hushed and stilled in Nature's kindly sleep.

It was the hour when mothers bending near
The sweetest form that consummates their bliss,
With gentle words, "May God protect thee, dear,"
Would steal away with loving goodnight kiss:
Ah, Father God, there breathed a gentle calm,

That spoke of peace, to weary souls a balm.
A whir! A sound! A sudden awful crash!
A rude alarm! Then sound of bursting shell,
And high o'erhead, the loud propellor's thrash
Of buoyant ship, a floating thing of hell;
And o'er the land, o'er Britain falls amain
The devil's hand that leaves a crimson stain.

All Nature wakes to view the wanton sight
That marked the path of ruin's poignant way,
As cowards slew, as cowards took their flight,
Ere yet had dawned the light of newborn day;
No honour gained, nor felt the glow of pride,
Be this their joy, some gentle women died!

Ope' wide the gates that leadeth unto death!
Blot out the sign of "three score years and ten!"
For there are some that scarce had drawn a breath,
Nor did they know what hatred was to men;
Yet ope' the gates, and pass them gently in,
These bairns must speak when judgement falls on sin.

Nurse Cavell
(First published: October 13, 1916)

The story of Edith Louisa Cavell was well-known to people across Britain during the First World War. She was born near Norwich on December 4, 1865, the daughter of an Anglican vicar. After training as a nurse in London, she eventually moved to Belgium, where she became the matron of a Brussels clinic. After the German occupation, she remained in post and was secretly engaged in the sheltering of British and allied soldiers, and the aiding of their escape to the Dutch border. She was eventually betrayed to the Germans by a collaborator and subsequently executed by firing squad for war treason, on October 12, 1915, despite being a British subject. On the night before her execution, she said: "Patriotism is not enough. I must have no hatred or bitterness towards anyone." After the war, her body was reburied within the grounds of Norwich Cathedral. Interestingly, George wrote the poem on the first anniversary of her death, October 12, 1916, a date also used by the Church of England as her day of commemoration in their Calendar of Saints. What George was probably not aware of at the time of writing his tribute is that it overlooks perhaps the defining aspect of Nurse Cavell's heroism, from today's perspective, which is that she tended to wounded servicemen from both sides of the conflict, without discrimination.

(Martyred October 12th 1915)

Sweet nurse, we still remember thee,
Nor shall we e'er forget;
Tho' dead, thou livest grand and free:
Unconscious of regret.

Could'st thou again thy life but live,
Could'st thou recall the past,
Still wouldst thou thy sweet succour give:
Thy comfort reckon last.

Dishonoured lies the evil hand
That struck the fatal blow,
And thrice dishonoured is the land
That breeds a race so low.

But acts of men are like the seed
When planted in the field:
It may be wheat, it may be weed;
Both must a harvest yield.

And bitter will the reaping be
To those who took thy life,
For Nemesis avengeth thee,
Nor fails she in the strife.

Shall we forget? Ah, yes we may,
When fades Britannia's might:
When chivalry is chased away
By demons of the night.

Till then we will remember thee,
Nor shall we e'er forget;
Tho' dead, thou livest grand and free:
Unconscious of regret.

My Sleeping Boy
(First published: October 20, 1916)

In the context of the other war poetry, some may be forgiven for thinking that this poem serves as an allegory for the grief of so many parents who witness their son's future being 'stolen' from them by war. Of course, George may have intended this, too. However, it's vital here to examine the date when this poem was written, October 1916 – when the Battle of the Somme had still not ended. George's second and (at that time) surviving son, Ivor Hedley Sidney Hobbs was less than six months old at this point and, in that context, the poem seems to have been written for and about him. The narrative is a father's natural desire to see his son grow up in a better world where nations live side by side in peace and harmony; nevertheless, it also holds out the prospect that such children may also be called to arms in the future to see this ambition fulfilled. And what parent would wish to know their child's fate in such circumstances? There is now a sad irony to this poem because Ivor died in May 1919, shortly before his third birthday.

What dreamest thou, my little one?
What visions dost thou see?
Just in thine own sweet language tell,
Those visions now to me.

Oft have I stood beside thy cot,
And watched thee in thy sleep,
Soon have I seen a fleeting smile
Thy little face o'ercreep.

Why dost thy smile? Oh yes, I see,
Thou roamest in thy dreams,
Thro' lands enriched by peace and love
Where light eternal streams.

Celestial beings take thy hand,
    And guide thy little feet
O'er sunlit hill, thro' starry dell,
    By rippling waters sweet.

And there on dreamland's happy shore,
    In innocence and bliss
Thou meetest other visioned babes,
    And with them play and kiss.

But tell me sonny, why the frown
    That oft thy brow perturbs?
Tell me its cause, for I would know
    What thus thy mind disturbs.

Do angels in thy visioned sleep
    Sometimes to thee reveal
That near the gates of Paradise
    Are thieves who rob and steal.

That in the path that thou must tread,
    When leaving babe's estate,
There standeth some to rob thy soul;
    And ever seal thy fate.

No, no, dear lad, thy lips are sealed,
    Thou canst not tell me this;
But oh, 'tis true thou e'en must fight,
    To win thy visioned bliss.

The Eventide
(Not previously published)

In this poem, George returns to more of his favourite themes, namely that of the heavens and the idealisation of nature. Full of clichéd imagery and classical allusion, it calls on society to be selfless and collegiate in pursuit of life's ambitions.

How still the eve: the twilight shade,
Falls on the world's work-wearied breast –
Man to his home, the beasts, to rest,
Couch to the earth within the grade.
Over vale and hill, o'er woodland fair,
Like Psyche's breath breathes soft the wind:
Each flower kiss'd and hush'd to find,
The balm of sleep that each may share.

The thrush that sang his goodnight lay,
And trill'd his joy that life was good,
Now cradles close in leafy wood,
In peace secure 'till dawn of day.

And nigh o'erhead the master hand,
Has touched the orbs as yet unseen,
And lo! the gems in richest sheen,
With joy reveal a magic land.

Anon, the Moon, in peerless white,
Rides to her court in silver'd car,
Oft as she rides, each glowing star,
Pays homage to the Queen of night.

O blissful calm of heaven's peace!
O wond'rous joy 'neath nature's care!
O tangled path that men must share,
'Till hate and wrong and SELF shall cease!

Lance-Corpl Gee
(First published: June 29, 1915)

This poem is an intensely personal account of the loss on the battlefield of a fellow Wesleyan lay preacher, Swindonian and personal friend. Through George we encounter the stark human cost of military conflict.

First World War historian Mark Sutton explained: "This is George Wilfred Gee. L/Cpl 13960 2nd Btn Wilts. He was killed on June 15, 1915, but has no known grave, and is remembered on the Le Touret memorial in France.

"George Gee had joined up in 1914, and was at the time working in the

GWR. He was drafted to France on April 1, 1915, to replace losses sustained in the Battle of Neuve Chappelle, in March. He saw action in Festubert in May, and on June 1 he was on parade with the whole battalion when it was inspected by Prime Minister Herbert Asquith and General Haig. Back in the line, they readied themselves for an assault on German lines near Givenchy on June 15. 'C' Company, of which George was a member, suffered a hundred casualties out of the 180 men that went on the attack. This included all the officers."

It's highly probable that George Hobbs also penned the obituary that appeared in the *Advertiser* on July 2, 1915, three days after the poem was published.

Swindon soldier killed in action
Memorial service to the late Lance-Corpl GW Gee

A memorial service to the late Lance-Corpl GW Gee who had been associated with the Cricklade Road (Swindon) Wesleyan Church as scholar and teacher, and latterly as local preacher, was held in that place of worship last Sunday evening. The young soldier was killed in action on June 15th, as was first reported in our columns last week in a letter we published from Lieut. H.H. Morris.

The service was conducted by the Rev. G. Oyston who, in the course of his sermon said that that was a most solemn occasion and one which, he was sure, touched all their hearts. The loss which had befallen one of their homes was a loss which was felt by them all, and was felt the deeper by that Church and Sunday School. Their dear young friend had many graces of character which attracted others to him, and that large gathering that night in which so many classes were represented, was a tribute to his memory. Their friends across the way at the Primitive Chapel had sent a message on behalf of their place of worship, signed by the Secretary, stating that he was "desirous of expressing the Church's sympathy with the members of your Church in the loss of so useful and prominent a member, who has fallen doing his duty for King and country."

Not only was his life full of promise but already his influence was felt, and it was a happy and helpful influence. Although only just past his 20th birthday, although taken from them so early in life, his works followed him. His years were few, but he was the means of bringing blessing to many hearts. He was converted at the early age of ten, and ever since he had loved the things of good report. He had been associated with them as scholar, teacher, Secretary of the Sunday School and leader of the Young People's Class, and on the last occasion when he was home on leave he visited that Class and had a heart-to-heart conversation with the members. He was one who carried his Christianity into his home life and business, but never let his light be hid under a bushel. Those who were over him in the Works had told him (the preacher) how they had admired him for his fidelity to Christian principles, and from the time he enlisted he was marked out for speedy promotion. He was always bent on improving himself intellectually as well as spiritually, and took advantage of the correspondence in connection with the local preachers. Probably he would have set up as a candidate for their ministry, the ranks of which would have been the richer for him. But events had turned out otherwise. He was the Secretary of the Band of Hope, and the arrangements of the anniversary of that body were made by him.

It was never thought that he had made up his mind to enlist – he saw no glory in fighting – but he faced his duty. As to why he enlisted they would let him speak for himself. Writing to a friend, he said: "I didn't join without a great deal of prayer and consideration, and before my way was made clear, but I have no regrets whatever, and humbly I say that God has made me a channel of blessing to more than one.

"My personal experience is that the man who lives his religion earns the respect of others, but the man who, while professing to possess something more than others, is no better than they, is held up to ridicule."

That he was admired by his comrades was proved by what they learned from other sources. When he enlisted he did not cease to do Christian work, but simply enlarged the sphere of his influence. He was plucky in a physical and in a moral sense. Those who ridiculed him came to admire him. A man who went down to Weymouth to see him came back with the remark, "If anyone has Christian principles, George Gee has."

It was the same in the trenches in France. A man who was not connected at all with their Church life remarked that George Gee was one of the best men in the world. After serving with the 8th Wilts he was drafted into the 3rd Wilts and landed in France upon Good Friday. He was killed in action on June 15th, saw rather more than ten weeks' active service and his body was found next day by a private in the 2nd Bedfordshire Regiment and was buried on Sunday.

They recalled his parting words: "If anything happens to me you are not to worry. I am all right."

Many a parent would give all that he possessed if he could say the same of his son.

Who was there who would come forward to help to fill George Gee's place? Never was the need greater for progress than it was today. That was a memorial service to George Gee. Might they give to him a memorial which would be his heart's desire by giving themselves to Christ's service.

The "Dead March" was played by the Organist (Mr A. Weston), and the anthem, "What Are These Arrayed in White?" was ably rendered by the Choir. A special hymn, "Lord God of Hosts, Whose Mighty Hand," was sung to the tune of "Eternal Father, Strong to Save."

Writing home on June 26, Lieut HH Morris said: "With reference to the late Lance Corporal Gee, I cannot say yet exactly where he is buried, but you can assure his mother that all men of the British Army who fall in action get a proper burial, and each grave is carefully marked, so that I have no doubt they can find his grave when this awful war is over and Germany crushed (as they will be for sure).

"I have no other details at present, but will make it my business to do the utmost for his parents, as I am also prepared to do for any other. If I get further details, I will communicate them at once.

"It was hard luck, for he was a good fellow, and had a splendid influence on the men."

In affectionate remembrance of Lance-Corporal George Gee,
whom I was privileged to know as a fellow Local Preacher.
Killed in action, June 15th 1915.

I mourn with those who mourn for you;
I mourn, yet oh I know 'tis true,
That in the realms of endless day
We'll meet when mists have fled away.

Tumult and strife will then be o'er,
Naught e'er disturbs, that peaceful shore;
Death then will be in fetters bound,
And sorrow's pangs can n'er be found.

I say farewell, and not good-bye;
Yet I can scarce repress a sigh:
Tho' conscious that we'll meet again,
The parting yields a poignant pain.

Scarce had you lived, when conflict came
And filled the land with grief and shame;
You heard the call – you saw the need,
And proved your worth in very deed.

Sincere in all you undertook,
You wavered not by word or look,
But undismayed 'gainst wrong and sin
You fought the fight the Crown to win.

Your duty you have nobly done:
The fight is o'er, the battle won;
The song is yours, of victory,
'Gainst folly, greed and tyranny.

Your barque has sailed the raging sea,
And near the port of Liberty,
You met your Pilot face to face,
And "crossed the bar," e'en by His grace.

No moaning now is in your ears,
No throbbing pain, no welling tears,
No thunder's roll, of lightning flash,
No cannon's verberating crash!

But in the calm and vernal air
There reigns supreme a rest so fair
That you have e'en forgot the strife
Which gave to you untrammelled life.

And so farewell, until that day
When joy has chased the gloom away
When you and I, in that fair land,
Shall clasp again each other's hand

*Lance-Corporal
George Gee*

Footnote 1: Poet's Corner

Correspondence in the pages of the *Advertiser*, in the wake of George's (and others') war-themed poetry appearing in the same paper, gives some insight into how it was received in some quarters. As early as April 1915, some readers found the continued reference to the (now eight-month-old) war wearing. One writer, signing himself 'Chiseldon', replied in kind, putting together a 16-line poem, which brought the following response from George, his letter being published alongside others to the editor:

Dear Sir, – In your evening issue of the 6th inst., some verses appeared entitled "The Poet's Corner," the signature at the end of the last verse being "Chiseldon." In the four verses written, the writer seems to have a complaint against those who send in the lines that are published in the "Advertiser" week by week.

With your kind permission, I would like to make a few observations, as one who contributes to "The Poet's Corner" week by week. Though I do not claim to be a poet, yet I take it I am included in the complaint that is raised by "Chiseldon."

In the first verse "Chiseldon" says:

"The Poet's Corner reeks with war,
The clamour and the noise of strife;
Death meets you there in every line,
Oh, let us have a note of life!"

Now, instead of using the word "Poet," I would substitute the phrase "Writer of verse" (Mr Alfred Williams excepted, for he is acknowledged, by anyone of judgement, to be a Poet), and as a writer of verse I would like to briefly explain why I write.

If any of my lines "reek of war", it is because I write as I feel. War is with us. Cruel, relentless, bloody war.

England is passing through an experience she has never passed through before, and I pray she may never be called upon to pass through such an experience again. Many, many precious lives have been lost, and many more may have to pass through the valley of death before peace comes.

I have tried, in a humble way, to point out that wars are caused through the selfishness of man, and this war in particular is a proof of that statement.

For 25 years the German Emperor has been planning for greater power, vaster dominions. In a word, he has planned for German Expansion. He planned,

I verily believe, not for war (no sane man would plan to kill and devastate), but he planned on the assumption that if he could only get his military system to the perfection he wished, then he would only have to say to the nations around him, "The time has come for Germany to expand, and woe betide the nation that seeks to stop her" – and it would be done.

The other nations, seeing her might, would tremblingly say, "We cannot fight her, even by co-operation; we had better let her expand peaceably, even if it means we are swallowed up by her expansion." This, I believe, was the Kaiser's intention, but it misfired.

The conflagration commenced before he was ready, and when he found he would have to fight, he decided to get his blow in first. In trying to get his blow in first, he threw honour to the winds, and worked on the principle, or lack of principle, that treaties to protect the weak were merely scraps of paper, to be torn up and thrown aside when it suited his purpose.

Up to the time of this base betrayal, England, subject to certain conditions, stood aside and when her honour was involved she stood inflexibly to defend her honour. She stood to defend the weak against an unscrupulous bully.

That England had no secret designs upon Germany is an acknowledged fact. To use the words of a prominent Statesman, "Britain was only armed for defence. Had we meditated a war of aggression against anybody, do you think we should have to improvise an army after the war began? We were not equipped for a war of aggression – even against a military power of the third rank."

This was, then, as far as England was concerned, a war of honour, and had England failed in her duty, she would forever cease to be an honourable nation. War is horrible, it is detestable, it is devilish, and the responsibility of this war rests, not upon the defender, but upon the aggressor. And there can be no two opinions as to who the aggressor was.

This being the case, when I write my verses upon some particular phase of the war, I do not extol war. Nor do I not rejoice at victory, because victory means death to someone. But, in that victory I see what our brave lads are fighting for.

They are fighting because the honour of England demanded it. They are laying down their lives in the defence of the weak. The cry of Belgium has entered like iron into their souls, and if I can pay a humble tribute to their courage, I want to do so, and shall continue to do so as long as the Editor consents to publish my verses.

I miss out the next two very fine verses and come to the last verse:
Amidst the crash of shot and shell,

We would the Poet dreamt, and cease
To write heroic verse of war,
And give us only thoughts of peace.

Yes, we want thoughts of peace. Oh, if we could only wake up tomorrow morning and know that the war was over.

I stood outside Bristol station a little while ago; a trainload of wounded had just arrived. There was a long line of ambulance cars waiting to convey them to hospital. As the poor fellows were being carried out, I went forward with the rest of the people that were assembled to see them.

When I saw the stretchers, and the poor bandaged heads, I felt a lump come into my throat, and the tears to my eyes. Yes, I thought of peace; I think of peace now.

When I hear the sobbing of the widow, and the childish prattle, asking for the Daddy that will never come back again; when I see the heavy eyelids of the mother, telling of sleepless nights, thinking of her boy in the trenches; when I see the father, bowed with woe, with the fateful telegram in his hand, I think of peace. I pray for peace. I write of peace.

Yet, with all this, I want to extol the brave acts of brave men, fighting not only for British honour, but for the British people, among whom there is one that is debarred from going out there to fight himself, or he would have gone, ere this.

Yours sincerely,
George E Hobbs

Footnote 2: Toy Soldiers

Long after the Armistice, and long after he had published his book of war poetry, George's thoughts about war came to the surface again in 1936, when he penned another letter, this time to the editor of the Derby Daily Telegraph, and it was published under the heading *Toy Soldiers*.

It shows that the George's thoughts on the war were still raw, but there is a great irony in that the very pose that he complains of in the toy soldiers is the same as a motif used on the cover of his volume of pro-First World War verse, called The British Solider, and Other Poems, 1914-15.

Sir, – I am a visitor on holiday at Chaddesden. The other day I went into Derby to look round the shops.

I stood for moment looking at the children's toy counter. Besides toys there were miniature soldiers, replicas of the various regiments, infantry and horse.

As I looked at soldiers, erect, kneeling and prone I was suddenly staggered at what met my view. Three or four of the figures were of soldiers in all the passion of killing, with rifles clubbed above their heads ready to dash out the brains of their opponents.

The sight filled me with horror, that this should be on view for sale to children.

Yours etc,
George E Hobbs (Swindon)

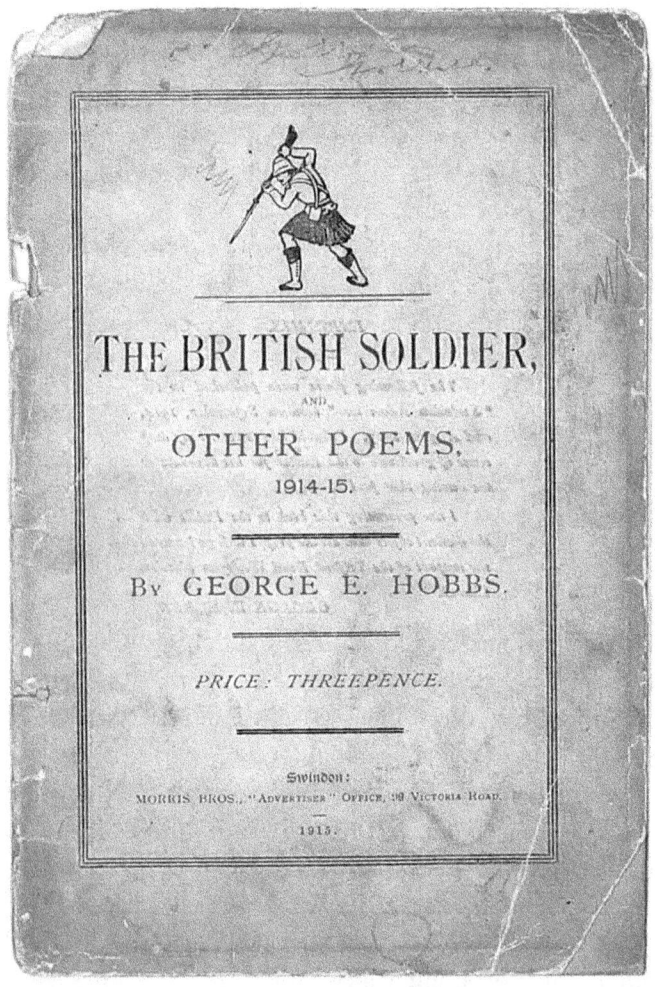

The cover of George's book of poetry. (Courtesy of Peter Field)

Chapter 5

Life in the Great Western Railway

Many have written about the history of the Great Western Railway and Swindon's glorious role in making it the greatest railway the world has ever seen, but there are relatively few who wrote from a point of personal experience. George Hobbs was one of those people.

It could be said, in fact, that he is the epitome of a Swindon railwayman, his comparatively humble origins being no bar to joining the ranks of the town's celebrated engineers, in a Works that earned a worldwide reputation and led a cutting-edge industry. What's more: he lived and worked through surely the golden age of railways and the GWR in particular, between the wars.

So it is fortunate, indeed, that George the storyteller, preacher and poet (and more besides) also put pen to paper to produce articles about his work in X Shop, where he oversaw the turning out of complex points and crossings for the company's permanent way, as well as other aspects of the GWR in Swindon.

A contributor to the prestigious GWR Magazine, George was also a member of a similarly notable engineering society in Swindon, and in 1929 was duly honoured by his peers following a talk about the manufacture of points and crossings, the business of X Shop, where he was foreman from 1923.

Formed in 1893 with 39 initial members, the GWR Mechanics' Institution Swindon Junior Engineering Society had as its object 'the mutual improvement of its members in Engineering Science, by the reading and discussion of papers, and by visiting places of engineering interest'.

Operating out of rooms at 2 Emlyn Square, in 1904 it changed its name to the GWR Mechanics' Institution Swindon Engineering Society, as it sought to embrace a wider selection of applicants for membership, from apprentices to older professional and time-served engineers.

George was elected as a full member on June 21, 1928, aged 45, five years after he had been promoted to the position of foreman.

Less than eight months later, he presented his one and only paper to the society, in the lecture hall of the Mechanics' Institute, the contents of which are reproduced in full, below.

Officially published on February 5, 1929, *Permanent Way Fittings and Their Manufacture (GWR Mechanics' Institution/Swindon Engineering Society Transactions 1928-1929, Pamphlet 169)* is a product of his role in X Shop, but also his constant thirst to acquire and pass on knowledge.

At the meeting of the Reading Sub-Committee on April 15, 1929, it was agreed to rank a number of recent papers in order of merit and, in so doing, decided that 'the Society's medal and award of £3' should be given to George as his paper was judged to be the best of the seven papers submitted for adjudication. This decision was duly endorsed at the meeting of the full committee on May 6, 1929.

Much like *A Brief History of Time* by Stephen Hawking, we don't really expect many people to read this particular article from beginning to end as it's a bit maths-heavy. However, merely having a copy, admiring the content and appreciating its arithmetic complexity should be enough to convey the fact that George's talents extended beyond the wielding of the pen.

Its quality as an engineering dissertation endures to this very day as it remains a primary source for information on the permanent way of the Great Western Railway.

Also included, below, is an article George wrote for the *Advertiser* in 1920, which also appeared in the GWR Magazine in 1921. His account of *The Heaviest Casting Ever Made at the Swindon Works* is nothing if not a demonstration of the versatility of George Hobbs as a writer. The man who is, on the one hand, able to put together a scholarly account of permanent way fittings, and, on the other, report the imagined antics of Mrs Crabthorn (see Chapter 13), is just as comfortable here, somewhere in the middle.

The piece successfully engages the engineer and the layman, and is reminiscent of Alfred Williams's seminal book, *Life in a Railway Factory* (published five years earlier), in its ability to bring to life an industrial scene that would have been familiar to many of George's associates and contemporaries, but alien to us today.

Where the two authors differ is in volume – George's account leaves us wanting to read more about his view of life 'inside' – and also in approach. George is delighted to report on this GWR triumph, whereas Williams produced a *warts and all* account of what was bad about life in the factory, as well as what was good. As if to underline this, George pays due deference to the Works Manager and other officials before embarking on his description of the casting.

It should be noted that even though the iron foundry (now a Marks & Spencer store, part of the Swindon Designer Outlet shopping complex) turned out many tons of material every day, the fact that this particular event was deemed of sufficient interest, at the time, seems to say much about local pride in the achievements of 'the factory'. Or, in George's words: 'The thoughtful mind knows that the local effect is but the reflection of combined genius, united enterprise and loyal energy.' It's a message further endorsed at the end of the article, where George ends his description with a suitably positive and philosophical footnote. Delivered without the aid of 'diagrammatic sketches', his description is so fine it deserves reproduction in full here.

But we begin with an article about a railway operation going on outside the Works, which was published in the GWR Magazine. In describing the work of a large team of track-layers, George is unnecessarily modest when he says: "Would that some inspired writer could have witnessed the rhythmic glory of that relaying job!" In reality, it is written with an efficiency and clarity with which Alfred Williams himself would have been satisfied.

A Relaying Gang at Work: An Observer's Impressions By GE Hobbs

(First published: December 1928)

Just after dawn on the day of occupation the gang is ready to commence. Each man knows his individual job, and when the signal is given the scene becomes one of perfect rhythmic animation. Ninety men working within a compass of 200 feet, yet so perfect is the organisation that no confusion is possible.

Keys are drawn, fishplates removed, fangs taken out, and the old worn components are ready for lifting. With the aid of the engine crane this is speedily accomplished. No sooner is one component removed than the men follow in systematic rotation, removing the sleepers one by one.

Other men immediately follow with picks, breaking up the compressed ballast. In process of time – much quicker than one could have imagined, and only possible because of perfect organisation – the old site is prepared for the new fittings.

Now follows a scene which must impress the most prosaic of individuals. For poetry of action and motion of exquisite rhythmic precision, there is nothing to surpass it. Skids have already been prepared. Standing behind the heavy block of fittings are eighty men, each with just sufficient room for the full play of his prising bar, waiting for the word of command.

In front of the block and at each end, the rest of the relaying gang grasp ropes in order to assist the prisers. No voice is heard but that of the ganger, who stands upon a sleeper near the centre of the fittings.

"Now boys!" and at the sound of his voice all bars strike the ground simultaneously. "Ready? Altogether!" Muscles stiffen and the strain is applied. "One, two, three!" until half the distance is covered.

But even with a block of inanimate rail fittings, caprice plays her unwelcome part. The angle of negotiation is difficult with the result that the block persists in travelling Londonwards. Halfway over, a halt is called. Then, "Bristol end held, London end prised!" and all in perfect order the arc movement is performed, and the combined prising forward continued.

Inches by inches the block is skidded until it rests over the site. Then come the lifting jacks and the skids are removed. Lower falls the block, and presently it is home. Although the block is home, the job is far from completion, for there immediately follow the multifarious details of connecting up to the existing fittings. Filling in rails are cut, drilled and "fished" and gauges and intervals checked.

There is a beautiful curve running through the fittings. Nothing is so calculated to jar the sense of the beautiful as to see a curve with the proverbial degree of rotundity of a donkey's head. But when the roads of a compound are perfectly curved, either with similar or contrary flexures (and with the added charm of perfectly curved slips) then it is indeed a thing of beauty.

In skidding the fittings over, "kinks" make their appearance, but with a straight prise here, and a cross prise there, under the relaying ganger's supervision, there is restored again the dignity of perfect curvature.

During this period the Signal Department staff, under the supervision of their local inspector, have made all preparation for their very important contribution to the success of the relaying, and at last, within the specified time of occupation, the job is complete.

Many mundane and prosaic things have inspired poets to "inscribe of them in a book." Even the wheel tapper has a ballad of his own. Would that some inspired writer could have witnessed the rhythmic glory of that relaying job!

Here was teamwork brought to a fine art, and all concerned from the heads of each department represented to the last man in the gang, deserve the highest credit for a job that was "well and truly laid."

The Heaviest Casting Ever Made at the Swindon Works: A Pen Picture of its Construction By George E Hobbs

(First published: October 22, 1920)

By the courtesy of Mr WA Stanier, the Works Manager, and with the kind assistance of Messrs Evans and Hyde, the foremen of the "J" Shop, I am enabled to write a pen picture of a notable achievement accomplished by the men of the Iron Foundry in the Great Western Works. The event is worthy of record in that it is unique in the annals of Swindon Works.

To the unthinking mind, a "finished article" may be admired for its ponderous bulk or its delicate, symmetrical beauty. But the thoughtful mind seeks to penetrate beyond the local qualities of size and beauty into the mysteries of its inception and the intricacies of its fruition. The thoughtful mind knows that the local effect is but the reflection of combined genius, united enterprise and loyal energy.

As it is to the lay mind I write, and as no diagrammatic sketches will be used, I want to describe in a simple word picture the details of the heaviest "cast" ever attempted at the Works. To have the interest stimulated and maintained, it will be best to begin at the beginning and follow the details of its progress, until we see it – even as it is now is – an accomplished fact.

An under block is to be cast, meeting the requirement of heavy steel being forged upon its face by means of a weighty helve, lifted under steam pressure and allowed to drop with its full weight. Attached to the helve is a "die stamp" and the combined weight gives it a gravitational fall of six tons.

The cost and labour of fixing the block is such that no split or breakage must occur at contact. Hence, size and weight must be worked out to secure safety from disaster. When this has been obtained, a pattern must be first made, resembling the shape and size of the finished article.

The Pattern

The pattern – for the details of which I am indebted to Mr Budding, the pattern shop foreman – is an important feature of the whole process. The utility of the finished article depends largely upon the accuracy of the pattern. Not only shape and size, but due allowance must be paid to the shrinkage of vital parts.

The pattern, in this case, is a hollow wooden structure, yet so large is the block to be cast that the pattern weighs approximately 25 cwts. Not only is there a main pattern, braced and supported to withstand depression during the process of sand ramming, but core boxes are made for the special features of the block. These, when finished, are conveyed to the Iron Foundry – there to await a suitable place being prepared for its reception in the sand.

Usually, patterns are placed within the confines of a metal box. But this pattern is so large that no box is found with sufficient capacity to contain it. It is therefore necessary to clear a space and excavate a hole in the ground not only large enough to contain the pattern, but also with sufficient space to allow the insertion of the special sand that will determine the shape and form the walls of resistance to the inrushing metal.

When the excavations are complete, a coke bed is formed over the entire surface of the base, having a vent pipe ascending to the top. This is for the draw and escape of the gases which will form when the molten metal is first introduced into the mould.

The pattern is then fixed with its narrowest dimensions downwards – and the first part of the moulder's work commences. Hour after hour the special sand is thrown in and rammed with patient skill until the top is reached. There must be no slip-shod work in the ramming, otherwise when the pattern is withdrawn the mould will be faulty.

After the removal of the pattern, the entire surface of the mould has to be dried and hardened – and is accomplished by means of a series of gas jets playing upon its face. Upon the completion of the hardening process, a coat of "blacking wash" is given to the surface to ensure a clean cast.

Ingenuity and genius

A special feature of the cast is now introduced, and it is here where ingenuity and genius must combine to prevent the whole process from becoming a costly failure.

If the required block merely had a plain base an "open" cast would be the easier and better way. That is to say, the molten metal would be poured in to the mould in a similar manner to that which the housewife would make a blancmange in a serrated or "fancy" mould.

But the base of this block has certain vital parts. A dovetail is to be formed which must correctly engage the corresponding block to which it is to be fitted. Hence, instead of the easier "open" cast, a "closed" cast must be employed. This, as I have already intimated, necessitates technical forethought and clear-sighted ingenuity in order to obviate certain dangers.

Merely to close the mould covering the top would not be sufficient. It must be securely fastened and weighted so that when the mass of metal is poured in, there will be no lift upon the part which contains the potential dovetail. The method of fastening the mould is by means of heavy longitudinal girders secured together by stout bolts.

Before details of the actual cast are given, some explanation is needed as to the outer structure of the mould, for this is an integral part of the cast.

The block is rectangular in shape and its mass may be judged by the fact that its approximate weight will be 63 tons.

The required amount of metal is much too large for a single draw from the furnace; also, it is of vital importance that the greater part of the molten metal should be in the near vicinity of the mould. To overcome the difficulty and to fulfil the conditions, two large dams are constructed, one on either side of the mould and each having a holding capacity of 20 tons.

The metal is prevented from premature intrusion by two geared sluice gates, easily manipulated at the right moment. Three inclined "runners" or conduits are constructed for the first introduction of metal to the mould, while upon the top cover six "risers" are constructed so that as the metal settles, the depressions are made good through them from a waiting ladle.

The First Draw

The furnaces, one in the "J" Shop and one in the Chain Foundry, have been cleaned and charged. The engines controlling the fans are running at full blast – and the first draw of metal commences.

First, by the aid of a 12-ton ladle suspended from an overhead electric travelling crane, the dams are filled, each with its capacity of 20 tons. Then, the five- and four-ton ladles are requisitioned, and it is from these that the first metal is introduced into the mould.

Immediately the first metal is run, a glowing iron rod is inserted down the vent pipe which ignites the escaping gases – and the first danger is over. Shaving piles are also lit around and on top of the mould to assist in obviating subsequent dangers.

When the bottom of the mould is estimated to have received its safe coating of metal, the sluice gates are opened from the dams and 40 tons of molten metal run simultaneously by means of specially constructed channel ways, into the mould.

The main cast is now practically over, but the work is by no means complete.

Condensation brings depressions in the cast, therefore it is necessary to "feed" the body of the block through the risers. Iron rods are obtained and in successive relays the feeding is continued throughout the stage of initial solidification.

The cast took place about noon, and during the whole of the afternoon the feeding process demanded the attention of a waiting ladle filling up the depressions through the risers as they occurred.

My work took me to the Foundry, and I was privileged to see some portion of the cast.

One deep impression I carried away with me: it was the united co-operation of all concerned for the success of the cast. A wonderful spirit of comradeship existed. Each was out to do his best, and there is not the slightest doubt the best was achieved.

The whole process reflects the greatest credit upon the organisation of the Foundry.

Above: Swindon Works' iron foundry, pictured in 1907. Opposite: two views of X Shop, where George became foreman. (Courtesy of The Swindon Society)

Above (with detail, left): the top brass of Swindon railwaymen gather for this team picture during the Second World War, including George (fourth row from the back, sixth from left). (Courtesy of STEAM Museum, Swindon)

Pamphlet No. 169.

Permanent Way Fittings and their Manufacture.

PAMPHLET NO. 169].

G.W.R. Mechanics' Institute.

Swindon Engineering Society.

"PERMANENT WAY FITTINGS AND THEIR MANUFACTURE"

BY

Mr. G. E. Hobbs (Member).

EXCERPT OF TRANSACTIONS, 1928-29

PUBLISHED BY THE SOCIETY:
G.W.R. LOCOMOTIVE, CARRIAGE & WAGON DEPT., SWINDON.
1929.

ALL RIGHTS OF PUBLICATION ARE RESERVED.

M. G. BURROWS, HON. SECRETARY.

The Society, as a body, is not responsible either for the statements made, or for the opinions expressed in the following pages

No. 169]

G.W.R. MECHANICS' INSTITUTE.

SWINDON ENGINEERING SOCIETY.

TRANSACTIONS, 1928-29.

ORDINARY MEETING.—FEBRUARY 5TH, 1929.

Chairman—MR. K. J. COOK.

"PERMANENT WAY FITTINGS AND THEIR MANUFACTURE"

BY

MR. G. E. HOBBS (MEMBER).

The term permanent way is a term used to distinguish the finished and permanent railroad from the temporary line laid down during construction. When completed the permanent track usually consists of two roads, each laid to gauge and each separated from the other by an interval not less than the Board of Trade requirements. The Board of Trade requires an interval between rails of 6' 0". The G.W.R. practice is to maintain an interval of 6' 6" between running faces. The rails are laid in chairs having a sleeper spacing of approximately 2' 6". If a 44' 6" rail be taken of the "OO" type, then there will be fifteen sleeper roads of 2' $6\frac{1}{2}$" spacing, and one shortened road at each end of 2' $1\frac{7}{8}$" (Fig. 1). This leaves 1' $0\frac{3}{8}$" at each end of the rail for fishing up to the next rail in line. The rails are held in the chairs by keys, either of teak or oak. These are placed on the reverse side to the running face, the drive being in the direction of the train travel. The reason for outside keying is fairly obvious: the wood keys forming a shock absorber or cushion.

The chair in which the rail is held will need a thought in passing. The chairs have other functions to perform beside that of housing the rail. On the chair base there are five serrations, each to a depth of $\frac{5}{32}$". Two are on the inside of the rail, three on the outside. On the sleeper there are similar serrations which engage with those upon the chair. The function of the serrations

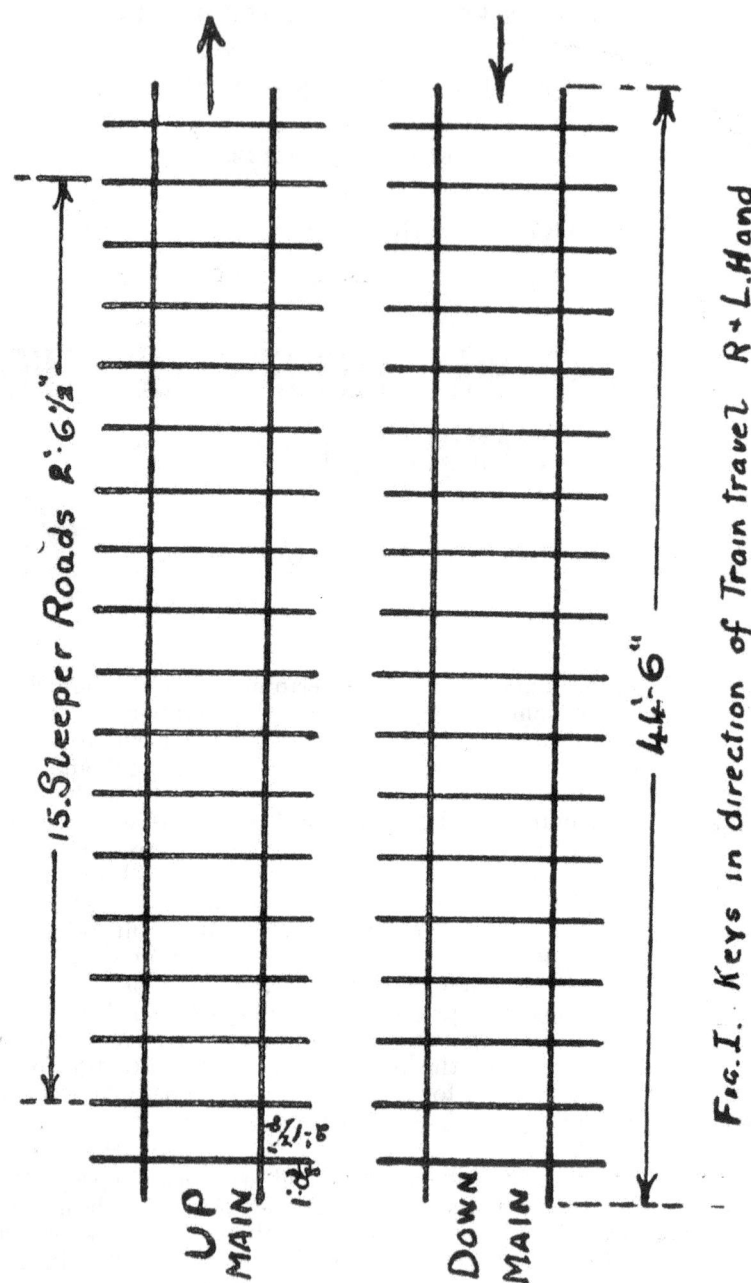

Fig. I. Keys in direction of Train travel R + L. Hand

is to assist against the widening of the gauge consequent upon the oscillation of heavy traffic. If the chair seat be inspected longitudinally with the rail it will be noticed that across the seat there is a slight curve. The rail actually, when free of a moving load, rests only upon the centre of the chair seat. From the centre to the outsides of the chair seat there is a curvature of $\frac{1}{32}''$. The Author is not versed in the subtleties of weight-loads upon wheels, so he cannot say if this law applies to the track in front of pony truck wheels: immediately preceding the driving wheel of an engine in motion there is a slight disturbance known as the "precessional wave." At every part of the wheel's journey there is a definite deflection of the rail. The slight curve of the chair seat admits the deflection being continuous. As the seat is $7\frac{3}{8}''$ across and, as already intimated, the chair spacings are approximately 2' 6", were it not for this slight curvature there would be a continual series of hard poundings. The probable result would be, at least, many broken chairs, if nothing worse.

This leads to the next point, that of the connection of rails. When rails are joined they are said to be "fished." The term is a nautical one, and is a relic of the days when wooden ships went into battle. It a mast were crippled it was rehoused as best is could be and supported by two pieces of timber, which were then bound with ropes. The seamen termed this a "fished" joint, and the term has been appropriated to railway use.

In the early days of railways the joint was supported by joint chairs. But in the year 1847 Mr. Bridges Adam introduced the method which is still in use—that of connecting by fish-plates. As the rail-joints lie between sleeper roads it means that the joints are suspended. The fish-plates, therefore, must be of design to support the joint. The support must be effective, yet not too rigid, seeing the precessional wave is very much in evidence at the joint. Many designs of fish-plates have been tried, a number of which have been rejected as unsuitable. One of the rejected class was known as the "Clip" fish-plate. This plate was designed not only to engage with the fishing-angle, but clipped round the foot of the rail in order, as was thought, to give increased vertical rigidity to the suspended joint. It was found to give too much vertical rigidity, actually amounting to a shearing stress. Fractures were constant in the rail-head fishing-angle, so much so that this type of fish-plate was speedily discarded.

The fish-plate now in use for bull-head rails answers all the requirements of a suspended joint. The slope of the rail fishing-angle is $1''$ in $2\frac{3}{4}''$, or in degrees, 20° 36'. The slope of the plate fishing-angle naturally agrees, and is such that while full support is given to the joint, the required elasticity is allowed for rail deflection under load. The plates in section are slightly arched in form, so that when the fishbolts are screwed up tightly the plates are always in tension. This is especially so when the joint is deflected and in consequence it is not necessary to apply locking devices for the nuts.

In passing it may be of interest to mention the "expansion gap." This is the gap allowed between rails when being laid, and is naturally determined by atmospheric temperatures. If rails are laid in winter they will demand a different expansion gap to those laid in the height of summer. For 44′ 6″ rails the expansion gap is $\frac{5}{32}''$ when temperature is at 80° F. In moderately cool weather, with the temperature at 60° F. the gap is $\frac{1}{4}''$. In cold weather, with the temperature at 30° F. the gap is then at its greatest $\frac{13}{32}''$. The fish-holes in the rails are elongated sufficiently to allow the maximum play between expansion and contraction.

Up to this point the Author has been speaking mostly of the plain roads, but the subject proper, "Permanent Way Fittings, and their Manufacture," is now reached. "Fittings," meaning units which are essential to main line cross-overs, single line working when one of a double track is under repair, refuge sidings, relief sidings and assembly yards. There are other fittings of a more complicated nature which will be dealt with in the course of the paper.

The simplest fitting of common usage is a "Turn-out." A "Turn-out" (Fig. 2) really comprises two fittings as understood by a manufacturing shop—a pair of switches and a crossing. The turn-out diverging to the right is termed a right hand turn-out, the one to the left a left hand turn-out.

Switches are manufactured in standard lengths and are identified by their individual lengths. The range of lengths is not strictly consecutive, certain lengths not being included. The range proper includes 10, 12, 14, 15, 16, 18, 20 and 30 feet switches; 6, 8 and 9 feet are sometimes manufactured, but these are used where the curves are very sharp and the leads, in consequence, are short.

A pair of switches consists of two outer, full section rails, and two inner rails, planed wedge shape to form the blades or tongues of the switches. The G.W.R. practice is to joggle the stock rail in order to give a stouter stability to the toe of the blades. The blades are planed to $\frac{3}{8}''$ thickness at the toe, so that when one of the two blades forms the running road, it rests with such precision in the joggle of the stock rail that no shock is experienced as the engine swings to the curve of the turn-out. When one blade forms the running road the opposite blade stands clear of its stock rail by a given distance. This distance for standard switches will be $3\frac{3}{4}''$; 18, 20 and 30 feet switches, irrespective of curvatures, have tongue openings of $4\frac{1}{2}''$.

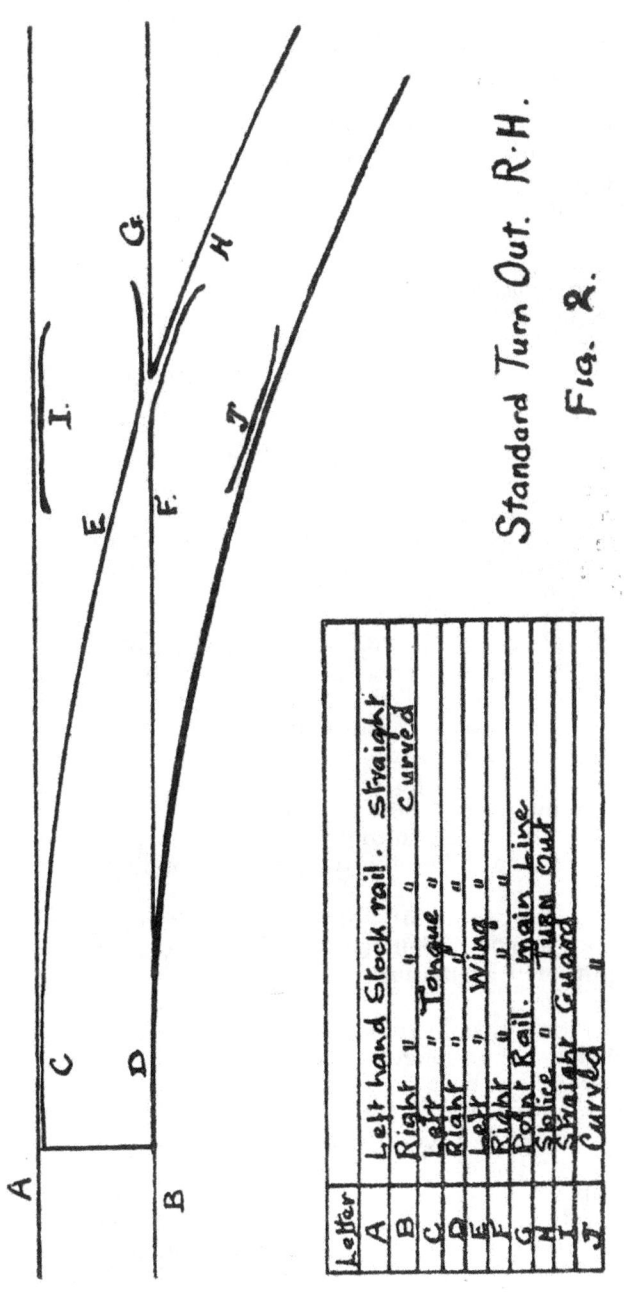

Standard Turn Out. R.H.
Fig. 2.

Letter		
A	Left hand Stock rail.	Straight
B	Right " " "	Curved
C	Left " Tongue "	"
D	Right " "	"
E	Left " Wing "	"
F	Right " "	"
G	Point Rail.	Main Line
H	Splice "	Turn Out
I	Straight Guard	"
J	Curved "	"

Switches demand a crossing. As will be seen later it is possible to have a crossing without a pair of switches. But for every pair of switches there must be a crossing—except in the case of a "throw-off," which is a different proposition.

Crossings are known by their inclination number. That is they are measured by the distance from their intersections at which the perpendicular offset from one running face to the other is unity. Thus an 8—0 crossing is one that measures 1' 0", from running face to running face of the vee-point, 8' 0" from its intersecting point. Crossings in Bull-head rails have been made as wide as one foot in one foot nine inches, and as narrow as one foot in twenty feet.

A crossing consists of four principle members, with accessories for connecting them into a complete unit. Two converging rails form the "Vee" point. One, the "point" rail, marks the main running road, and one, the "splice" rail, indicates the cross-over road or the turn-out from the main road. Two other rails converge from the opposite direction towards the nose of the vee-point. These are termed the "wing" rails. At a given distance from the nose the right hand wing rail bends to the right, and the left hand wing rail bends to the left. Up to, and including the shoulder of the bend, the wing rails are running rails: the running faces being on the inside and converging to the nose of the vee-point. At a little distance from the shoulder the wings cease to be running rails, and the rest of their length become wing guards to the vee-point. Consequently, when a crossing is complete with all its necessary blocks and chairs, the vee-point lies snugly housed within the protecting arms of the wing rails. A guard rail, chaired to each running rail opposite the vee-point, and separated from the running faces by an opening of $1\frac{3}{4}"$, completes the crossing for protective running conditions.

Turning to the manufacture of these fittings, for the purpose of this paper a pair of fourteen feet switches, with its crossing of one in eight, will be manufactured.

The first process in the shop is to prepare the tongues as this process will take the longest time. For convenience of this descriptive assembly the stock rails will first be prepared. As it is fourteen feet switches of the "OO" type, two rails of standard length as supplied direct from the makers are obtained. For these switches the stocks will be 28' 4" long. These are taken to a multiple drilling machine, having cross-traversing heads for adjustment to meet the needs of a range of holes. Four of the five heads supply the drilling, and one head has been adapted for a $1\frac{5}{16}"$ milling cutter. A jig-template is placed in the fishing angle of the stock rail and secured by two clamps. The holes are then drilled for chair centres and a double hole drilled, which afterwards is milled into an elongated hole for the convenience of the front push rod. After drilling, the rails are taken to a press for the joggling process. This is a very interesting process for it means that a $\frac{3}{8}''$ joggle is to be put in the rail within the narrow compass of $9''$. As the head and foot of the rail is $2\frac{3}{4}''$ across, the web $\frac{3}{4}''$ thick, the height $5\frac{3}{4}''$, and the steel with its carbon content in the region of .5%, it will be appreciated that great pressure is needed for the joggling.

The rails are joggled cold in a hydraulic press at a pressure of 800lbs. to the $\square''$. The ram is $1'\ 6''$ in diameter, so that the total pressure is approximately 90 tons. An average of 35 pairs of switches are turned out per week. This means 70 joggles per week, approximately 3,700 in a year. In a period of five years the Author has known perhaps a dozen rails break in joggling, but more than half that number have been "second-hand" rails. These rails have probably been in the road for twenty years and have become crystalised through the pounding received under wheel impact. These rails receive a local annealing at the joggle point and are joggled while still hot. Those that have fractured under stress have probably been allowed to cool too far before bending. The point the Author wishes to emphasise in regard to new rails is that while the stocks are given the severest stress a rail can experience, and in consequence certain disturbances are imparted to the rail, there is not one single record of a stock rail breaking in the vicinity of the joggle when in service.

The stock rail is joggled $5'\ 4''$ from the lead end of the switch and is so set that a string line, lined from the lead end along the running face, will again strike the running face of the stock rail exactly $14'\ 0''$ from the toe of the switch. This point is termed the "heel" of the switch, or in points and crossing parlance, the "$4\frac{1}{2}$." Here, when the tongue is home against its stock, the opening must register $1\frac{3}{4}''$. The full sectioned head of the tongue rail which is $2\frac{3}{4}''$ plus $1\frac{3}{4}''$ opening gives $4\frac{1}{2}''$.

As the pair of switches is a standard pair one stock rail will be left straight and one curved to a radius of 950 feet. The curve of the one in eight crossing will be 605 feet radius, but there is a reason for curving the switches to a flatter radius. A pair of 14 feet switches will lead into a series of four different angled crossings, namely—8, $8\frac{1}{4}$, $8\frac{1}{2}$ and $8\frac{3}{4}$. The radius of the switches is therefore flattened not only to meet the needs of the series, but also to give a more gradual entry into the sharper radius of the widest crossing of the series. As a matter of fact the lead curve from switch to crossing is a transition curve. From 950 ft. the curve sharpens to 750 ft. and then to 605 ft. as it passes through the one in eight crossing.

The rail is curved in a "Craven" rail bender which is motor driven. The push block of the bender is adjustable, the length of its stroke being controlled by the operator. The curve is given to the rail in versed sines on chord lengths. The formula for curves above 300 feet radius is a simple one, $\frac{C^2 \times 3}{2R}$. For curves under 300 feet radius the formula used is $V = R - \sqrt{R^2 - \left(\frac{C}{2}\right)^2}$. For all curves of high denomination five feet chords are used; but for turn-table race rails 2′ 6″, 5′ 0″ and full length chords are used. Every curve is checked before leaving the shop.

The stock rails are now placed upon the bench for the bolting on of the chairs. These chairs are termed "slide" chairs, and in shape are like a letter "L." The upper portion fits into the fishing angle of the stock and when secured throws the rail to an inward cant of 1 in 20. The horizontal portion has a flat surface, four inches wide, upon which the tongues slide laterally in their engagement or detachment with the stocks. The first chair is bolted on four inches behind the joggle. This is in order to give support to the toe of the blade when forming the running road. Six other chairs are bolted on to each stock rail at a nominal sleeper road spacing of 2ft. 1in. This narrow chair spacing gives adequate support to the switch blades through their weakest cross sections. A double jawed chair is placed 1ft. 2ins. from the heel end of the blade. One jaw is securely keyed to the stock rail, the other jaw being of easy width to allow the slight swing of the blade upon the adjacent fish-plates. It will be necessary to enlarge upon this point later.

The stocks are now ready to receive the tongues. In the meanwhile the tongue rails have been taken to a planing machine, first to be roughed planed. This machine is a "Hulse" planer having an adjustable tilting table. Four tongue rails are planed at a time, each rail lying on the flat. For 14 feet switches the tongue rails are planed on head and foot from full section, 8ft. 11ins. from the toe, to just under the web at the toe. Two of the rails are then taken to a "Stirk" planer for front planing and finishing. The finishing process to the tongue planing is of an interesting nature and will need a somewhat detailed explanation.

It will be assumed that the switches are a right hand pair. This means that the left hand stock will be straight and the right hand curved. Further it means that the two planed faces of each tongue will differ in contour, if the Author may be allowed to use such an expression where two straight lines are involved. The inside face of the left hand tongue must be straight, seeing it will engage with the running face of the straight stock. But its outside face must be curved to the radius of the opposite stock rail; for with this rail it forms the gauge road. The right hand tongue demands the opposite conditions. The inside face must be curved to meet the curved stock when in engagement and the outside face must be straight to form the straight gauge road. The method adopted to meet these varying conditions is as follows:—

The tongue rails are placed vertically in a series of four specially designed cast iron blocks and secured by side clamps. In the centre of the planing length there is a fifth block having a bolt tapped through its vertical wall. The duty of this block is to spring the tongue to its curve for the final planing.

The tongues are held in numbers one and four blocks and sprung in the centre block so that the two inner faces will show a verse sine of $\frac{1}{8}''$ in 8ft. 11ins., the length of the planing. The rails are then planed on their outer faces at a cant of 1 in 10. This is a reverse cant to the front of the joggle, as it also will be to the heel of the switch tongues. The reason for this reverse cant is to prevent the toe of the tongue being exposed at the joggle.

It will be seen that when the tongues are released from the blocks one will be true to its curve, the other will have a curve on the wrong side. The tongue that will be correct is the left hand tongue since upon release the straight face which has been sprung will resume its straightness. The curve is therefore where it is needed, that is, upon its running face. The second tongue has its curve upon the reverse side to that on which it is required. The curve is on the running face whereas it is wanted straight to gauge with the straight stock. The opposite face has sprung back to straight whereas it is required curved to engage with the curved stock. The problem of reversal is easy of solution. The tongue is placed in the rail bender and the curved face straightened. This at once pushes the curve through to the face that will engage with the curved stock. The heel chair is now fixed to the stock and tongue, and the switches are ready for despatch.

At one time the switches were gauged before leaving the shop, but this practice has now been discontinued. The front push rod is welded to a gauge length and the back rod is bent to a gauge length. As there is the correct curve in the stocks and tongues, and as it is known that the rods are correct to length, there is no need to gauge the switches.

The manufacture of the 1 in 8 crossing (Fig. 2). It has already been stated that a crossing consists of four principle members—point rail, splice rail, and right and left hand wing rails. Rails for point and splice rails are kept in three standard lengths—12ft. 3ins., 11ft. 10ins. and 10ft. 9ins. These three lengths will cover a series of graduating crossings from a one in two, up to and including a one in fourteen crossing. For this series an intersecting length of 12 feet is used:—That is the distance from the end of the point and splice rails to where their running faces will intersect is 12 feet. Above a one in fourteen it is the practice to cut from longer lengths, the intersecting length being advanced from 12 feet to 17 feet. The increased length for the series from and including a one in 14ft. 6ins. to a one in 20ft. is necessary for the advantages of fishing up to the next rail in line. At 12ft. intersection the spread of the vee legs would be too narrow to fix two pairs of fish-plates.

The first thing to do is to get the length of the point rail. In the shop there are tabulated lengths for standard vees, but for the present purpose they will be ignored. The "nose" width of every vee point is a constant $\frac{11}{16}''$ or .0573 of a foot. The length between the intersecting point and the nose of any angle may be obtained by multiplying .0573 by the angle. In the present case the point rail length will be $12' \ 0'' - (8 \times .0573)$ or $11' \ 6\frac{1}{2}''$. A projection of three inches is allowed in front of the nose for fanging down. The rail is cut to this length on a rotary saw, motor driven. In the old days with a steam driven saw this was a lengthy process, each rail-cut lasting fifteen to twenty minutes. With a Firth's "Speedicut" saw blade, 26'' diameter, $\frac{1}{4}''$ wide, and with a $\frac{7}{16}''$ tooth pitch, a rail can be cut through in two and a quarter minutes.

To an inquisitive person the splice rail length presents somewhat of a problem. The splice rail is to house into the point rail at a given distance from the nose of the point rail and will naturally vary for every angle. The wider the angle the nearer the splice rail will be to the nose of the point rail. The narrower the angle the farther away. When the combined point and splice rails form the completed vee, the housing depth of the splice must be $\frac{5}{16}''$. When therefore the housing point is determined the splice length is a simple matter.

The Author does not propose to worry over an intricate formula to obtain the housing point, he is simply going to state that the housing point will rise or fall in perfect ratio to the rise or fall of the angle. This means that the width of the point rail at the place where the splice is housed is also a constant. That constant he has found to be .1956ft. or $2\frac{11}{32}''$. The distance, therefore, from the nose of the point rail to the housing point of the splice is a matter of simple calculation:—Angle multiplied by .1956, or $2\frac{11}{32}''$, will give the right length to ensure a splice nose width of $\frac{5}{16}''$. As the two rails will be flush at their fishing ends the splice length for the one in eight vee will be $12' \ 0'' - (8 \times .1956)$ or $12' \ 0'' - 1' \ 6\frac{3}{4}'' = 10' \ 5\frac{1}{4}''$. The rails are then taken to the hydraulic press for setting and twisting. Each rail is set in a contrary direction for the necessary planing, and each twisted in a contrary direction for the necessary cant. It will be appreciated that no cant is possible at the nose of the vee, seeing that the nose forms a dual running road. The rails are set and twisted cold, the twist being obtained between reverse wedges. For a 1 in 8 point rail the set is $1\frac{1}{32}''$ in a length of $1' 7\frac{1}{2}''$, and for the splice rail $\frac{3}{8}''$ in a length of $1' 2''$.

The rails are now ready for machining. The point rail is placed upon a drill-shaper to shape out a planing clearance and to have a 3in. hole drilled through its nose end for subsequent slotting to form the 3in. fang projection. Both point and splice rails are then planed upon their housing faces on "Hulse" planers with tilting tables.

As the point rail will bear the fast running, the least possible planing is required. The major planing is given to the splice rail. The foot of the point rail is barely touched—just sufficient is removed to ensure a straight line bearing for the splice rail. This means that both point and splice rails are planed at two inclinations, necessitating double setting in each case.

The inside planing being complete the two rails are housed, secured by a clamp and drilled. They are then bolted together and machined upon their running faces to form the correct vee angle. The running faces are planed to a rake of 1 in 15, the rake being a reverse cant to the lead from the wing rail and also to the heel end of the vee. This is in order to give a safe negotiation from the wing to the vee point. The nose of the vee is given a top planing of $\frac{1}{8}$ins. to zero in a distance of $1' 4''$. The nose is then thinned at its apex so that it may be subsequently chipped and filed to a radius and the vee is ready for assembly.

In the meanwhile the wings are being prepared. This is an interesting process for it involves a principle which at first is not appreciated. To see the wings in a completed crossing it seems to suggest that the rails have merely received a straight push through, thus forming an obtuse angle. If this were the case the wing rails would be incorrect, as will be seen from an examination of the process of preparation.

As has already been intimated, the wing rails have a dual duty to perform. For one portion of their lengths they are running rails and for one portion they become wing guards to the vee. Both rails will converge towards the intersecting point of the vee. 1ft. 2ins. before meeting this point a shoulder is formed, the radius of which will be of the same denomination as the angle. From the shoulder each rail will diverge in opposite directions parallel to and $1\frac{3}{4}''$ from the running faces of the vee-point. They will remain parallel to the vee-point for a distance of 1ft. $4\frac{1}{2}$ins., when again they will diverge to form the lead in of a trailing crossing, or the emergence end of a facing crossing, and will be 3ft. 6ins. long. At the extreme end of the wing guard the opening must be $3\frac{1}{2}$ins.

Having in mind that the fishing end of the wing will be a running road the rail must be bent to throw an inward cant of one in twenty. But the wheels do not leave the wing at the shoulder of the bend; indeed, they will continue to find some bearing upon the wing until the bend has been passed by a distance of 2ft. 1in., or after the wheels have passed the nose of the vee by 5ins. This means an inward cant is wanted each side of the bend. To merely push the rail through—as it is termed in the shop—would not produce the desired effect. The rail would then be vertical on each side of the bend. The desired cant is effected by placing the rail upon its flat and curving it at the shoulder to a versed sine of $\frac{1}{8}''$ on a chord length of 5' 0".

The rail is then set vertically in the press and bent to a radius of 8ft., on an arc length of 8ins. upon its running face. Every wing rail is set to an offset chord length of angle divided by 4, which in this case is 2ft. The offset will be chord over angle—in this case, two over eight, which equals .25ft., or 3ins. When this offset is obtained each side of the bend, it will be found that the rail has in it an inward cant of 1 in 20. The guard bend is then effected by setting out the wing end to an offset of $1\frac{3}{4}''$ on a chord length of 3ft. 6ins. The wing rails are now ready for assembling. The necessary blocks and chairs are now obtained :— A pair of point, side and heel blocks, four double jawed chairs and the No. 4 chair, which will be a triple jawed chair.

The vee-point, which has now been straightened and riveted, is fixed in the centre jaw of the No. 4 chair and the wings fixed provisionally. The blocks are then fitted to flangeway clearance gauges and shoulder gauges; lined through with a straightedge for alignment and secured with clamps for drilling. The whole assembled crossing—irrespective of angle—is drilled at one setting. In some angles—say 1 in 2—the length of drill used is 3ft. 9ins. long.

At one time in the No. 3 chair position a nose chair was fixed. In renewals of crossing members in the line this chair constituted a big difficulty. It was cumbersome and required precise fitting to its position. This involved too much time when time was precious. The chair has now been substituted by two brackets, two blocks and a mild steel slab.

After drilling the crossing is brought back to the bench and bolted up. Brackets and slab are fixed at the No. 3 chair position and the crossing is ready for the final examination. Two 14' 0" guards have also been prepared to accompany the crossing. The guard rails have been set out at their ends to an offset of $1\frac{3}{4}''$ on a chord length of 3ft. 6ins. This gives a parallel flangeway clearance of $1\frac{3}{4}''$ for a distance of 7ft.

These two examples of manufacture may be termed the simplest of the work turned out in the shop. Coming to the compound benches, or the benches upon which the larger lay-outs are assembled, there are still jobs of easy grade. These are standard units comprising diamonds (Fig. 3), compounds, single (Fig. 4) and double (Fig. 5), with roads straight over straight. Standard diamonds are manufactured from angles of 1 in 2 to 1 in 8. Compounds, single and double from 1 in 6 to 1 in 8. Fig. 6 shows a layout having three diamonds and two double compounds. Fig. 7 shows a layout having a diamond with double outside slip or outside double compound.

But at least sixty per cent. of the work is out of standard. Before dealing with this aspect, examine the manufacture of a 1 in 8 double compound (Fig. 5). In essence a double compound is a diamond cross-over road with two slip roads having contrary flexures. Every component rail, except the guards, must have an inward cant of 1 in 20, while through the crossings and elbows there must be a flange way clearance opening of $1\frac{3}{4}''$.

The first thing to do is to prepare the elbows, which will gauge across the centre position of the compound. Each elbow consists of an elbow or back rail, two elbow points and an elbow guard. The elbow rail, forming as it does a double running road, will be set up similar to the wing rail of a crossing. The elbow points also will be treated along similar lines to the vee points already described. As the elbow guard will be vertical a straight push through with the ends bent out is all that is required. When assembled with the necessary blocks and chairs the elbows are laid out to gauge. If the roads gauge correctly each elbow is secured by clamps and each drilled as a unit. The drilling machine is of similar type as that used for the drilling of the crossings. Each machine is triple headed with a cross traverse and having independent motors upon each head. When the elbows are drilled they are again laid to gauge for the continuance of assembly from the crossing ends. The wing rails will differ from that of a standard crossing, in that they become stock rails for the two inside tongue rails and will fish up to the elbow points. The wing rails will therefore be joggled to receive the toe of the switch blades. The four outer stocks will be straight up to the joggling point, then curved to form the radius of the compound slip. Curved filling-in rails will connect to the outer stocks and curved filling rails will connect to the four inside tongue rails. The sleeper road spacings are standard, and when all the necessary chairs and brackets are fixed, the push rods secured and the whole compound laid out to gauge, the lay-out is ready for checking. Extreme intersections of crossings, elbow to crossing intersection, alignment of elbow rail to elbow point, flangeway clearances, tongue openings and verse sines of curves are checked before leaving the shop. These operations will be carried out by six men in about five days.

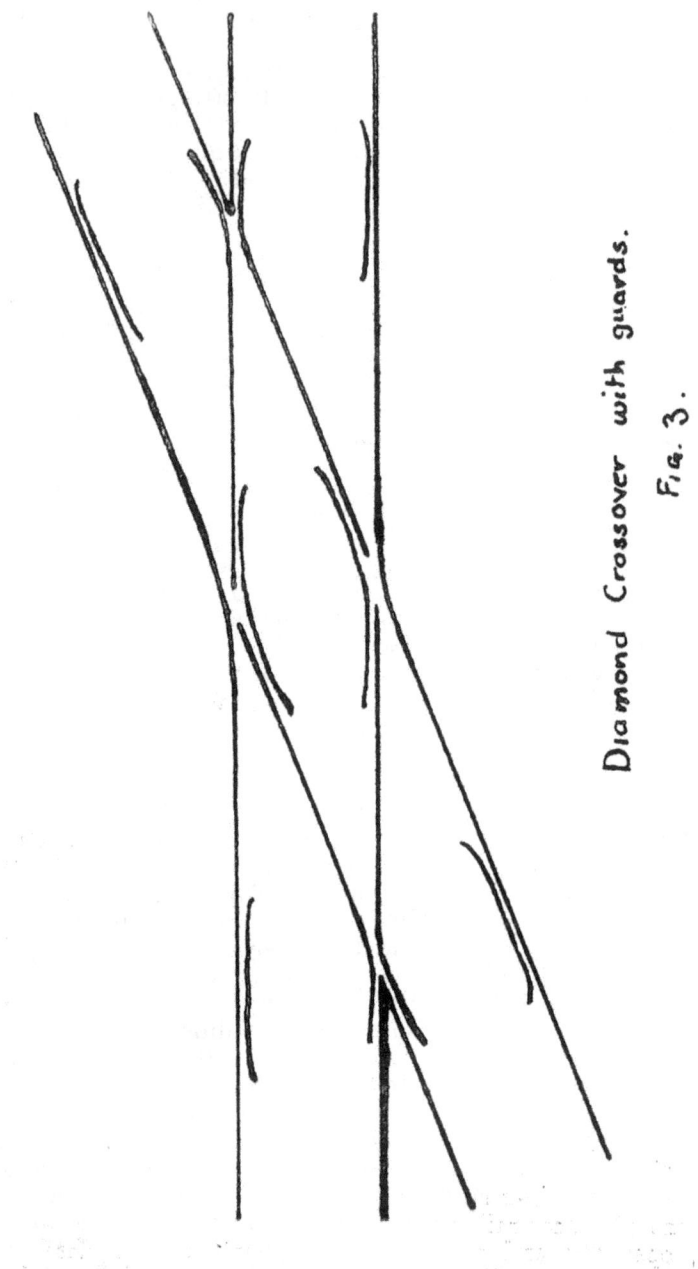

Diamond Crossover with guards.
Fig. 3.

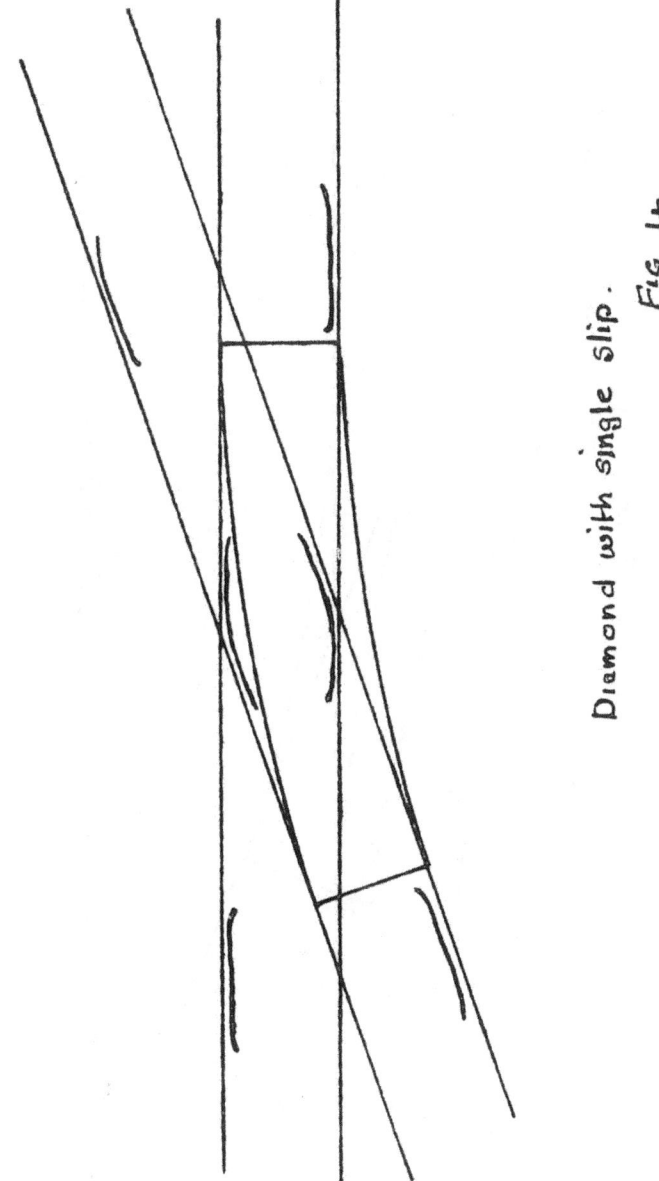

Diamond with single slip. Fig 4

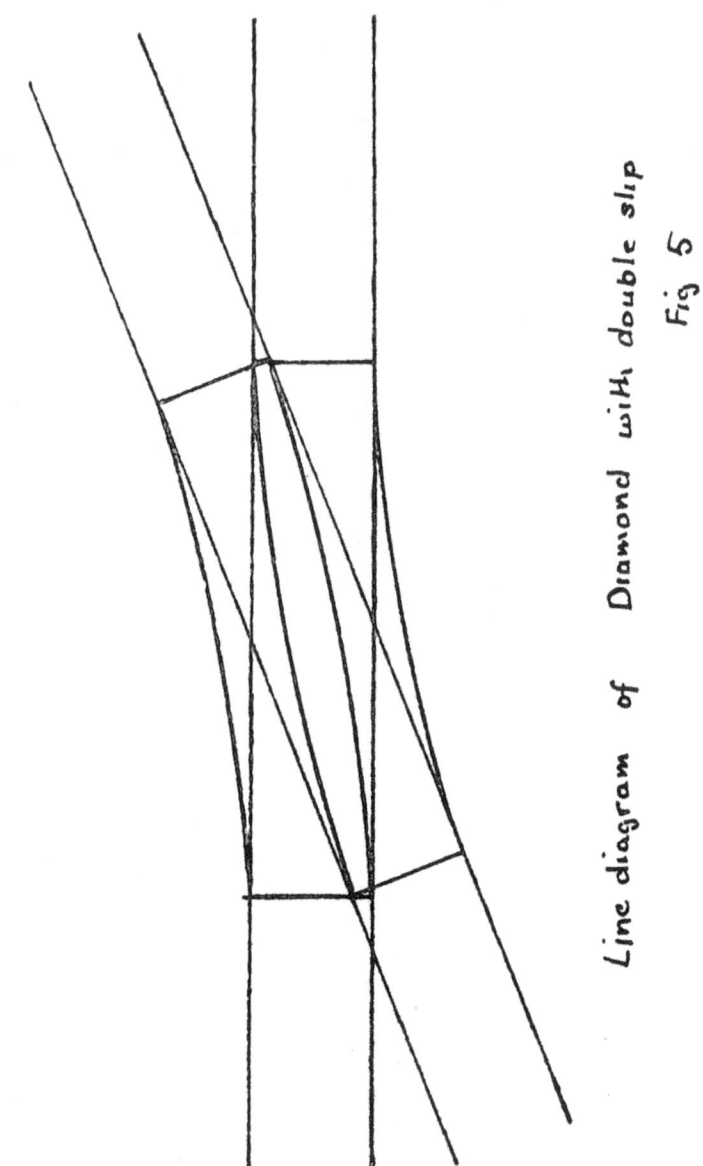

Line diagram of Diamond with double slip
Fig 5

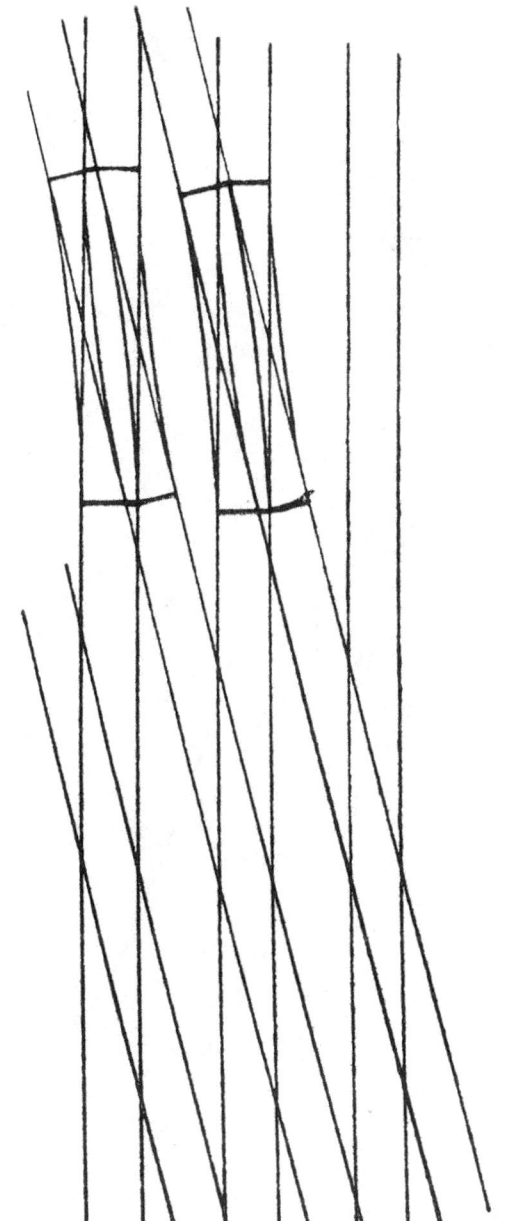

Line diagram of Layout. Showing 3 Diamonds and 2 Double Compounds.

Fig 6.

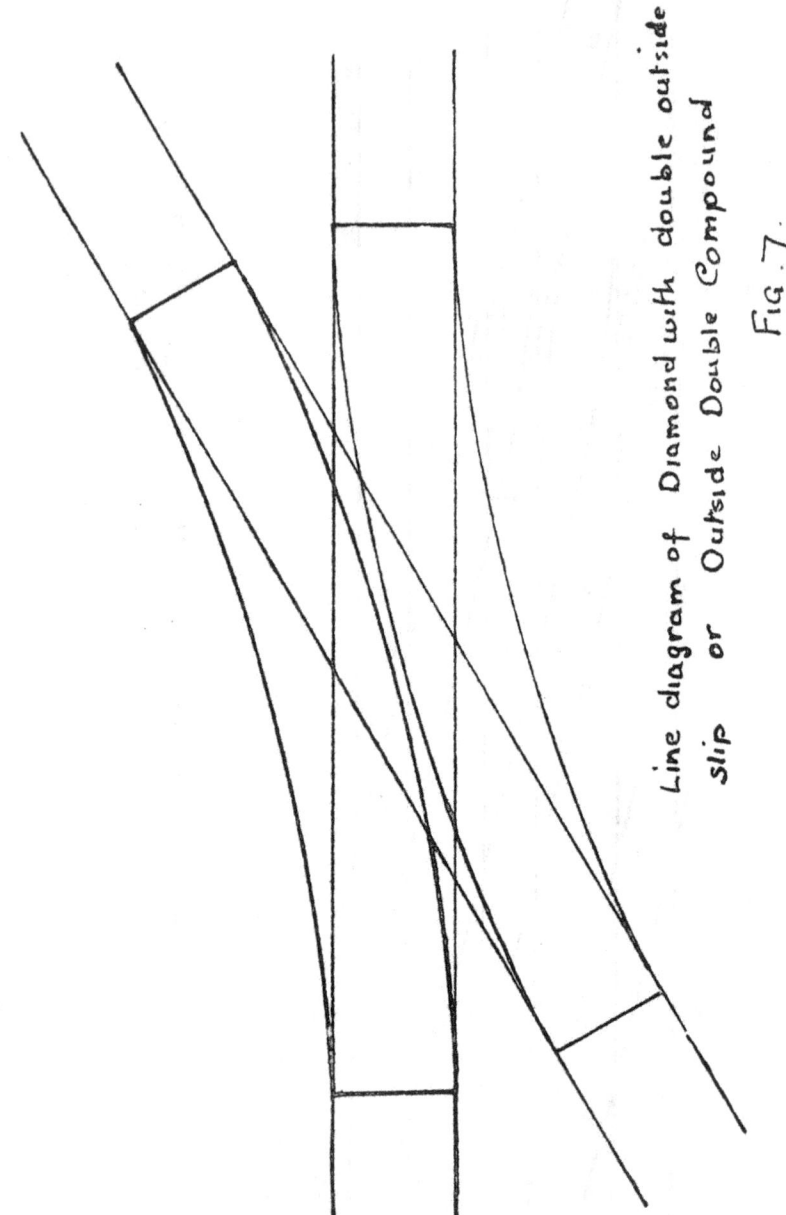

Line diagram of Diamond with double outside slip or Outside Double Compound

FIG. 7.

As has already been intimated, sixty per cent. of the work manufactured in the shop is out of standard. It is with these out of standard units that the more interesting work begins.

A tracing is sent down asking for a pair of switches with contrary flexure, attached to which is a check lump. (It may be said in passing that all slip roads having a radius below 600 feet must be guarded through by a check rail. Also all turn-outs where fast running obtains must be guarded by a check lump).

The pair of switches have already been described. For the present purpose the main road will be curved to a radius R, and the turn out in an opposite direction to a radius R^1. As it is a right hand turn out the check lump will fish up to the right hand switch blade.

The check lump (Fig. 8) will be a diverging pair of rails, the guard rail running parallel at $1\frac{3}{4}''$ flangeway opening to the right hand stock rail of the switches. The other rail will lead away to gauge with the left hand stock. The rails are so planed—the guard vertical and the running rail to an inward cant of 1 in 20— that at the end joining the switch blade the two rails will be the width of one rail only. This means that the two planed rails will gradually diverge until the planing ceases and they will each be of full section.

The information to hand is that a pair of switches and a check lump are to be manufactured, the radii only being given. The planing and an offset at the end of the lump have to be found. One knows that the planing will commence where the combined offset of the radii will be $4\frac{1}{2}$ ins.; that is, rail head plus flangeway opening. To save working each offset from the theoretical springing of the curve the mean radius is found which is the equivalent radius out of straight. This is obtained by the formula $\frac{R \times R^1}{R + R^1}$ —the + sign being used as the flexure is contrary. The formula to find the $4\frac{1}{2}''$ offset distance will be $\sqrt{2ER} \times .375$. The next distance to find is the point where the two diverging rails will be of exact full section. As the rail heads are $2\frac{3}{4}''$ wide the offset will be $5\frac{3}{4}''$, or including the flangeway opening of $1\frac{3}{4}''$, will be $7\frac{1}{4}''$. This distance is obtained in the same way $\sqrt{2ER} \times .604$. Subtract the $4\frac{1}{2}''$ offset distance from that of the $7\frac{1}{4}''$ and the planing is obtained.

It is also necessary to know the offset for the heel end of the lump. This is needed in order to check against the versed sine of the curves. Having obtained the $4\frac{1}{2}''$ offset distance add to this the length of the lump rail. This is now an extended chord

24

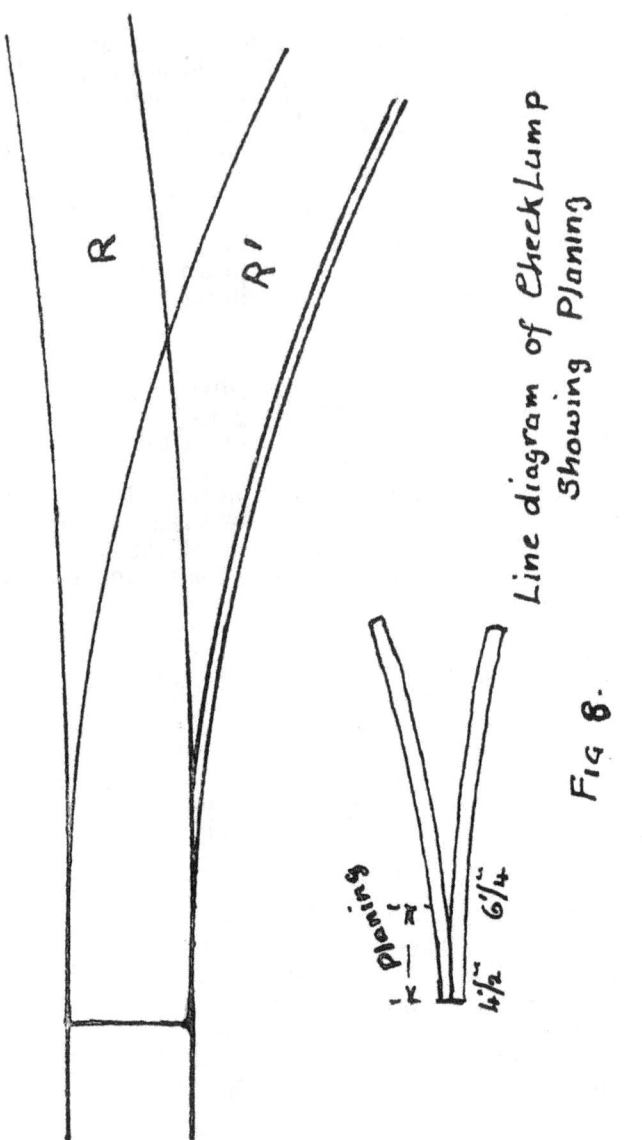

Fig 6.

Line diagram of Check Lump showing Planing

In this diagram $6\frac{1}{4}''$ should read $7\frac{1}{4}''$.

length and the offset will be obtained by the simple formula of $\dfrac{C^2}{2ER}$

Or take another example:—

It is required to manufacture a turn-out comprising a switch and crossing. This time the flexure will be similar. The only information is the radii, R and R¹. The angle of the crossing is not given. The formula for obtaining the angle of crossing is one that will give its inclination number, not the degrees of the angle. The formula is:—$N = \sqrt{\left(\dfrac{R \times R^1}{R - R^1} - \dfrac{G}{2}\right)2G}$.

Perhaps it will be of interest to tabulate a few of the formulæ in use in the shop:—

1.—To find radius when versed sine and chord are given:—
$$R = \dfrac{V^2 + \dfrac{C^2}{2}}{2V}$$

2.—To find versed sine when radius and chord are given:—
$$V = R - \sqrt{R^2 - \dfrac{C^2}{2}}$$

3.—To find chord when radius and offset are given:—
$C = \sqrt{2(RO) - O^2}$.

4.—To find offset of curve when radius and chord are given:—
$$O = R - \sqrt{R^2 \div \dfrac{C^2}{4}}$$

5.—To find radius when offset and chord are given:—
$\dfrac{C^2 + 4O^2}{8O} = 2R \therefore R = \dfrac{R}{2}$

6.—To find set of switches:—Let $D = 4\frac{1}{2}''$ offset. $R\ R^1 = $ radii.
Then set $= \dfrac{DR}{RR^1}$

Sometimes when measurements are given on arc lengths it is necessary to know the chord length. This is obtained by the following formula:—

Let $A = $ arc. $R = $ radius. $X = $ radians.
Then $\dfrac{A}{R} = X$. Chord $= $ Sine $\dfrac{X}{2}\ 2R$.

When crossings are at 6ft. 6ins. interval it is essential that their intersecting length be known. This length is needed so that it will be known where to break joint correctly. In the present case the interval will be 6ft. 6ins., and the two crossings will be of the inclination number 1 in 8.

It is known that the rail forming the angle from the down main will cut through the up main at a point where the vertical offset will be 6ft. 6ins., thus forming a right angle triangle. Let the angle be represented by capitals A.B.C., and the sides by small a.b.c.; "a" the vertical side, "b" the base, and "c" the hypotenuse.

As the angle is 1 in 8 first find sine A by $\frac{c}{a}$. Side "c" will be $\sqrt{8^2 + 1^2}$ or 8.0662. The sine will therefore be $\frac{1}{8.0662}$ or .1240. If side "a" of the large triangle be divided by sine A, that is $\frac{6.5}{.1240}$, this will give side "c" to be 52′ 5″. This measurement however is much too long. From side "c" construct another triangle the vertical length of which will cut through the intersecting point of the second crossing. This side, which will again be "a," will be true road gauge width—4′ 8½″. Side "c" of the smaller triangle will be $\frac{a}{\text{sine A}}$ or $\frac{4.708}{.1240} = 37′ 11½″$. The length required is 52′ 5″ ÷ 37′ 11½″ = 14′ 5½″.

The Board of Trade allows fixed elbow points up to and including angles of 1 in 8 for diamond crossovers. Above 1 in 8 diamonds must have movable points. In this fitting elbow guards and 1¾″ flangeway clearances are naturally dispensed with, seeing that when the elbow point engages with the elbow rail a continuous line is formed similar to an ordinary plain rail. The points are 31′ 0″ long and are made of a rail section stiffened at the foot. The points, when engaging or disengaging with the elbow rail, are sprung from the heel end. As they can receive no chair jaw support the slender points are assisted by fixed reinforcing rails, to which they cling when acting as the running road. One front push rod and three back rods tie each pair of points for their lateral movement.

In conclusion the Author would like to take an excerpt from a paper read by Mr. Raymond Carpmael before the Institute of Transport.

"During the past fifty years, until the unfortunate derailment at Sevenoaks, the permanent way can show a remarkably clean bill of health in regard to the prime causes of railway accidents.

27.

"For a quarter of a century past not a single railway accident involving loss of life has occurred in Great Britain as a result of defective equipment or maintenance of track."

The Points and Crossing Shop rejoice in this fact and take some little pride in that it has contributed to the safety of the travelling public.

Above: the medal (with reverse side also pictured, right) that was presented to George for his 1929 study, Permanent Way Fittings and Their Manufacture. (Courtesy of Peter Field)

Chapter 6

The Life of Charles Bradlaugh

A great deal has come to light in the course of researching the life and works of George Ewart Hobbs. It's clear he loved his family and his God. It is also the case that he loved his country, the Methodist church, liberalism, temperance and the theological pursuit of The Truth. Furthermore, it is also suggested that he was a fervent monarchist. But would it surprise you that one of his heroes was an ardent atheist?

This item (which is reproduced in full, below) is taken directly from surviving typewritten manuscripts that, in all likelihood, once formed an address given by George to a meeting of the Methodist Youth organisation, The Wesley Guild.

Undated and never knowingly previously published, the content does, however, provide a valuable insight into the life of Charles Bradlaugh (1833-1891) and the elements of his character and reasoning that George found absolutely compelling.

A renowned political activist, libertarian, radical, teetotaller and free thinker, Bradlaugh became the editor of the periodical the *National Reformer*, in 1860, and jointly founded the Reform League in 1865, in order to campaign for one man, one vote. He also founded the National Secular Society in 1866.

Although he was raised in an Anglican household and even once trained as a Sunday School teacher, Bradlaugh enthusiastically embraced atheism, believing that religion was an obstacle to progress. An avowed republican, he was also a strong advocate of women's rights, birth control and universal suffrage.

Such was his belief in liberal individualism that he opposed socialism and trade unionism. He was elected as the Liberal Member of Parliament for

Northampton in 1880, but soon ran into problems when he attempted to affirm rather than swear his Oath of Allegiance upon the Bible.

Insisting that it was his right to affirm in the Palace of Westminster (given that it was already permitted in the English courts of law) he decided to take on the might of the political establishment when this request was formally denied. Ultimately, this lead to him being stripped of his seat in Parliament on a number of occasions, but he always remained victorious at every consequent by-election.

Although he did eventually swear under sufferance in 1886, in order to break the impasse, he did, however, succeed in changing the law following the introduction of The Oaths Act of 1888.

In the following piece on Charles Bradlaugh, George declares that he is, in particular, an admirer of his theological reasoning, his principled stand against religious bigotry and his uncompromising honesty in thought and action.

To illustrate this, George highlights certain events from Bradlaugh's life that helped inform his social, political and secular thinking.

In George's own words '...this can be said of him without fear of contradiction: Never would he compromise with a principle. Never would he give way one inch in what he believed to be right, even though he knew it would mean suffering.'

The Christian imagery is not lost on me. And that really is putting Bradlaugh on a pedestal.

The Life of Charles Bradlaugh
(First published: unknown, date: unknown;
possibly published in the magazine of The Wesley Guild)

I make no apology for bringing to the Guild the story of an "Infidel". It is not a usual topic for a Christian Society, yet I venture to suggest we may make some enquiry into the life of Bradlaugh with profit to ourselves.

In writing the preface to the biography of Bradlaugh, his daughter, Hypatia Bradlaugh Bonner, writes thus:-

"This work comes before the public as a record of the life and work of a much misrepresented and much maligned man. A record which I have spared no effort to make absolutely accurate."

The record of the father's life and activities is written by a loving daughter. It may well be said then, that the record must be biased in favour of the father every time. Let us take that as granted. At the same time I want to take you into the opposite camp. You will find there, not bias to gloss over faults and failings, but bias which ignores the virtue of high endeavour. Bias so contradictory to logic and reason as to paint goodness with Satanic colours.

In the days of Bradlaugh – days not far removed from our day – Christians had yet to learn the virtue of tolerance. A lesson, I am afraid, not learned even yet.

From a purely Christian standpoint Bradlaugh's life was a gigantic tragedy. A tragedy which could have been avoided had sympathy and Christian guidance been extended at the crucial moment. Instead of these being given he was treated in the most insane manner by a Christian minister. And that action marked the commencement of the parting of the ways.

Charles Bradlaugh was born in 1833. His parents were respectable folk, suffering somewhat from penury, and from a religious standpoint, very nominal. His mother was of the old school, severe, exacting, and imperious. She judged by what appeared to be the obvious, and meted out punishment accordingly. One incident may be recorded.

One Christmas-time, when Bradlaugh was yet a small boy, visitors were expected. To mark the occasion some loaf sugar was purchased – an unusual luxury in poor households in those days. The visitors, with whom was a small boy, arrived in due course, but at tea-time it was discovered the loaf sugar had disappeared. Charles and his younger sister were charged with the theft, which they both strenuously denied. They were not believed by their mother and were sent to bed in disgrace. A little time after it was discovered that the little boy visitor had been the culprit. No redress or apology was given to the children, the mother probably thinking that an apology to children would be attended by loss of dignity, and a loss of disciplinary control. Bradlaugh never forgot the horror of that unjust punishment.

It may be worthy to note, in passing, the method adopted in teaching the young life of the middle of last century. And one wonders whether this glimpse into Bradlaugh's early training does not reveal one of the contributory causes of his later detestation of all things Christian.

At the ages of nine and ten he was given tasks in order to reveal his progress in writing, and to show if he possessed any artistic capabilities. At the age of nine he had to write upon and illustrate, "The Death of Ahab" (gruesome). At the age of ten he had to write upon and illustrate, "The Death of Absalom." The text selected to show this work was:- "Then said Joab, I may not thus tarry with thee. And he took three darts in his hand and thrust them through the heart of Absalom while he was yet alive in the midst of the Oak."

As a lesson in sheer wanton cruelty this can scarcely be surpassed.

As a boy, Bradlaugh was devoutly religious, and from being an exemplary scholar he became a promising Sunday school teacher. His church activities being confined to the Church of St. Peter's in Hackney Road, London.

At this time the Rev. John Graham Packer was incumbent at St. Peter's; and when it was announced that the Bishop of London intended to hold a confirmation at Bethnal Green, Mr. Packer naturally desired to make a good figure before his clerical superior. To this end he selected the best lads in his class for confirmation, and bade them prepare themselves for the important occasion.

Throughout Bradlaugh's life two virtues dominated his activities. An unequivocal love of and for truth, and a great passion for the highest freedom in thought, word and deed. Bold and courageous to a degree, he knew no fear where principle was at stake. In everything he was thorough.

Behold him then, at sixteen years of age, preparing himself for confirmation. The task allotted was the study of the 39 Articles of the C of E, and the four Gospels. Bradlaugh went farther than study them separately, he compared them and found to his dismay they did not agree. In his difficulty he wrote the Rev. Mr. Packer a very respectful letter asking for his aid and explanation. Instead of help there came a bolt from the blue. Mr. Packer had the consummate folly to write to Mr. Bradlaugh senior, denouncing his son's inquiries as Atheistical, and followed up his letter by suspending his promising pupil for three months from his Sunday-school duties.

A more colossal blunder could scarcely have been made by one who had the spiritual oversight of young lives, for this act marked the commencement of Bradlaugh's subsequent revolt against all things ecclesiastic. The lad, horrified at being called an Atheist, and forbidden his Sunday-school, naturally shrank from going to Church. It may well be imagined also, that under the ban of his parent's disapproval, home was by no means a happy place, with the result Bradlaugh wandered off to a place called "Sonner's Field".

"Sonner's Field", was in Bradlaugh's day, a great place for open air meetings. On week evenings the topics were usually political, but on Sundays theological or anti-theological topics were debated. It is therefore little wonder that Bradlaugh, wrestling under a sense of injustice, and filled with a vague doubt, turned to these meetings for light.

Now enters the Rev. J. G. Packer again. Realising he had made a most foolish mistake he attempted a remedy in which he commits a further blunder. Mr. Packer's right course would have been to see his one time scholar, admit his mistake, and do his utmost to right the lad's troubles. Instead of this, having heard that Bradlaugh had been seen consorting with Freethinkers, he obtained a foothold into the Bradlaugh household, and talked over the parents to such an extent that they consented to decorate the sitting-room with large texts of scripture. One glaring text, "The fool hath said in his heart there is no God", was hung up right in front of the place where young Bradlaugh sat to take his meals. You may imagine the effect this had upon him.

Finding that texts made little difference to Bradlaugh's attendance with the Freethinkers, Mr. Packer went farther. The lad was in employ with a firm of coal merchants, and this narrow-minded cleric threatened the firm he would withdraw his securities from them unless young Bradlaugh changed his attitude towards the church within three days. On the third day the lad left home and his employ, and from that day until almost the day of his death, his life was one long struggle against the bitterest animosity which religious bigotry could inspire.

Bradlaugh, at 16 years of age, was now left to his own devices, and having learned somewhat of the coal trade, he determined to set up for himself. Presently he managed to obtain a few customers sufficiently to keep him in bread and cheese. Not long was he to enjoy his determination to fend for himself. And for sheer pathos this story wants some beating.

Bradlaugh's principle customer was the good-natured wife of a Baker. As she required several tons of coal per week to bake her bread the commission on this transaction amounted to about ten shillings a week. This constituted the principle source of his income. Then came persecution. Some kind friend informed the dear lady of Bradlaugh's attendance at the Freethinkers' Hall. This was a severe blow to the good lady's feelings. She had prided herself upon being the means of helping this young man in his distress. When, therefore, he called again for orders, she said at once:-

"Charles, I hear you are an Infidel!"

At that time Bradlaugh was not sure whether he was an Infidel or not; but he instinctively foresaw that the question addressed him might interfere with the smooth running of his business. He therefore sought to avoid the issue by exaggerating the importance of the latest fluctuation in the coal market.

The stratagem was of no avail. The kind but painfully orthodox friend again returned to the charge. Bradlaugh then had to fall back upon the difficulty of defining the meaning of the word "Infidel". In this he evidently failed to impress his customer. Again and again he tried to revert to the more congenial subject of a reduction in the price of coal, and when, finally he pressed for the renewal of his usual order, the interview was brought to an end by the Baker's wife:-

"I cannot buy my coals from an Infidel," she said with a shudder. "I should be afraid my bread would smell of brimstone."

Thus ended the young coal merchant's early business career. I leave the story for your private digestion.

Bradlaugh was now reduced to poverty. In this stress he did what he never would have done under normal circumstances. Gaunt, hungry and with clothes threadbare, he joined the army, and became a trooper in the 7th. Dragoon Guards. The Guards were stationed at Dublin, and to that place, with the rest of the recruits, Bradlaugh journeyed.

On the way over to Ireland the rest of the recruits, seeing in Bradlaugh a quiet and unassuming individual, took recourse to horseplay with him. Finding he did not retaliate they ransacked his private box and when they found, much to their surprise, a Greek Lexicon and an Arabic Vocabulary, their scorn and derision knew no bounds. A wild game of football was at once organised with the Lexicon, and it came out of the struggle somewhat the worse for wear. The Arabic Vocabulary, being a smaller book, found better treatment. Bradlaugh recovered these battered relics and ever after kept them upon his study shelf as a memento of his early struggles and endeavours.

There are one or two rather interesting episodes of his army life which are worth recording.

While serving with his regiment Bradlaugh was a most active advocate of Temperance. Only a day or so after he arrived in Ireland he began his advocacy upon the quarter-master's daughters. It was a bold thing for him to do seeing that his action amounted almost to an insult. Bradlaugh was told off to do some whitewashing for the officer in question, and the girls passing by took pity upon him. Their pity was due to his appearance, for he still bore the marks of his privations. They brought to him a glass of Port Wine which he politely refused. Then came evidence of a strain in this young fellow which was brought out repeatedly throughout his whole life. He was never content merely to refuse the wrong but his very nature demanded he should do the right. It was a definite principle with him. With his refusal to take the wine he proceeded to give the young ladies a lecture upon the evils of intemperance. Luckily for him the young girls took the lecture in the spirit it was given and smilingly withdrew carrying back the wine with them.

I should like to emphasise this point. Whatever may be said of Bradlaugh in regard to whether he was a sinner or not, this can be said of him without fear of contradiction: Never would he compromise with a principle. Never would he give way one inch in what he believed to be right even though he knew it would mean suffering.

A curiously characteristic act made him the hero of the Inniscarra peasantry. A landowner had put up a gate across a right-of-way, closing it against soldiers and peasants, while letting the gentry pass through it. Bradlaugh looked the question up and found the right-of-way was real; so he took with him some soldiers and peasants, pulled down the gate, broke it up, and wrote on one of the bars:- "Pulled up by Charles Bradlaugh, 7th Dragoon Guards."

The landlord went to the Colonel of the regiment with a view of prosecuting Bradlaugh. To which the Colonel replied:- "You had better study the aspect of the law upon this matter, for Private Bradlaugh generally knew what he was doing." It is needless to record the landlord did not prosecute, hence the gentry had to share the way with the commoners.

One more episode of his army days, then we will take his later attitude towards Christianity.

On one occasion he was orderly-room clerk, and a newly arrived young officer came into the room where he was at work, and addressed to him some discourteous order. Private Bradlaugh took no notice. The order was repeated with an oath. Still no movement. Then it came again with some foul words added. Bradlaugh got up from his desk and walking over to the officer bade him go out of the room or he would throw him out. The officer went, but in a few minutes the grounding of muskets was heard. The Colonel entered accompanied by the officer. It was clear that the private soldier had committed an offence for which he could be court-martialled. The officer made his accusation and Bradlaugh was bidden to explain. The young soldier asked that the officer should state the exact words which had been addressed to him. The officer evidently had a stark of honour left in him and he gave to the Colonel the exact words used. Turning to the Colonel, Bradlaugh said he thought the officer's memory must surely be at fault in the whole matter, as he could not have used language so unbecoming an officer and a gentleman. The Colonel turned to the young officer and very pointedly said:- "I think Private Bradlaugh is right; there MUST be some mistake," and the Colonel walked out of the room.

Bradlaugh stayed three years in the army, and eventually was bought out by his mother, a reconciliation having taken place.

(Married on June 5th 1855. He 22. Wife 24. Not happy life. Wife died May, 1877).

To understand Bradlaugh's attitude towards the Christian religion one must first take into account the Rev. Packer's foolish conduct, and the effect it would have upon a mind like his. From his youth he was a thinker of a very intense type. Nothing would he take for granted. Essentially he was a reasoner, and in his reasoning he clashed with Victorian theological thought. The attitude taken by Bradlaugh was that the Old Testament was a book which recorded the genius, education, and manners of the earliest peoples. But when Theologians claimed for it absolute infallibility; that the Bible was written by men at the dictation of God, then Bradlaugh poured his scorn upon their reasoning, or lack of reasoning. The God of their logic was revengeful, inconstant, unmerciful and unjust. If God drowned the world then this act was of a particularly revolting character. There were barbarities and cruelties recorded in the Bible, which, according to the theologians, were attributed to the God of the Christians. If these were true then it stamped that God more Devil than God.

Bradlaugh was ever against theological exaggerations. On one occasion he was lecturing upon "The God of the Bible". In the discussion which followed a Christian gentleman informed the audience that "It was only by God's mercy they existed at all, as all men had been tried and condemned before they were born, and were now prisoners at large." Bradlaugh, in his reply, promptly took objection to this phrase, as implying that society was nothing more than a collection of "divine ticket-of-leave men". (Discussion. "All we like sheep have gone astray".)

Again, Bradlaugh was altogether against the theory of vicarious sacrifice or punishment, and that the Plan of Salvation through the Atonement was unworthy of the acceptance of the human race. So far as he personally was concerned he repudiated the virtue of Christ's work.

To put Bradlaugh's position in a nutshell I will quote his own words as given in a debate. Said he:- "I do not stand here to prove there is no God. If I should undertake to prove such a proposition I should deserve the ill words of the oft quoted Psalmist applied to those who say there is no God. I do not say there is no God, but I am an Atheist without God. To me the word "God" conveys no idea, and it is because the word "God" to me never expressed a clear and definite conception that I am an Atheist. The word does not, to my mind, express an eternal, infinite, omnipotent, intelligent, personal conscious being, but is a word without meaning and no effect other than it derives from the passions and prejudices of those who use it."

The question may be asked, as to the attitude of orthodox Christians in face of such sweeping statements. Bradlaugh conducted many debates upon public platforms and here is the amazing sequel. In nearly all the debates his logic was the more sound and his manner the more courteous. A prominent K.C. once said to a nervous junior:- "Do not be afraid. If you find you have no case then slate the other fellow." Whether Bradlaugh's opponents had a case or not, they followed out the famous K.C.'s advice. Instead of keeping to the subject matter in hand they contented themselves with trying to prove that Bradlaugh was a fool and a vagabond. Audiences were beforehand worked up to the highest pitch of indignation against Bradlaugh, and there were many times when he literally carried his life in his hand. It was characteristic of the man that, except to defend himself, he would never strike back at an adversary if that adversary attacked him from the front. But woe betide the luckless individual who attempted to attack him from behind. Bradlaugh was just over six feet in height, and if it did come to a struggle he feared no crowd, certainly he feared no individual.

In 1858, Bradlaugh became the Editor of the "Investigator". A journal, it was said, of the investigation of truth. The truth that Bradlaugh found was not the truth we know, yet just as we are sincere so he was sincere. We should have to go a long way to improve upon his creed. In his editorial he stated the journal's purpose.

"Our only wish," he wrote, "is to make men happy. We wish this because in so doing we increase our own happiness. The secret of true happiness and wisdom lies in the consciousness that you are working to the fullest of your ability to make your fellows happy and wise. Man can never be happy until he is free. Free in body and in mind. Free in thought and utterance. Free from crowns and creeds, from priest and king. Free from the cramping customs created by the influences surrounding him, and which have taught him to bow to a lord and frown upon a beggar. Liberty. Equality. Fraternity. That true liberty which infringes not the liberty of my brother. That equality, which recognises no nobleman but the man of noble thoughts and noble deeds. That fraternity which links the weak arm-in-arm with the strong, and, teaching humankind that union is strength, compels them to fraternise, and links them together in that true brotherhood from which we strive."

We who are ardent Monarchists may not go as far as Bradlaugh in his rule of conduct, nevertheless there is much we could copy in it.

Wherever there was distress, or tyranny there Bradlaugh was to be found. India and Italy, which in Bradlaugh's day was passing through troublous times, found in him a stalwart champion against oppression, and against all forms of religious intolerance. When asked why he did not confine his activities to

England alone, he replied almost in the words of John Wesley:- "The world is my country. To do good is my religion."

I think I have given now sufficient data respecting the life of Bradlaugh for us to form some opinion of this remarkable man. I have purposely left out all account of his parliamentary life, confining ourselves to his Atheistical convictions. The problem before us now is of a somewhat complicated character. Let the question be put this way:-

"Can there be any virtue in a morality without religion?" or, to put the question as we should better appreciate it:- "Is it possible for a person to be a real influence for good without Christ. Rather more, to actively repudiate Christ's Salvation?"

First, every rational human being must be answerable to his or her own conscience as to whether their attitude is right or wrong. "To his own master he standeth or falleth", and the master is the conscience. A Christian who says he believes when conscientiously he does not and cannot believe is guilty of falsehood. When I use the term "does not believe", I mean something that orthodoxy wishes him to believe but from which his inward conscience revolts. One cannot be honest by a mere profession, but when attitude has been stabilised after thought has passed from opinion to conviction and from conviction to belief, and from belief to action, then irrespective of the attitude taken, it is one of honesty. And honesty is a positive virtue. But it must be honest or there is no virtue.

There are folk who have taken up with Atheism, or have professed scepticism from various motives. Some because they refuse the rigid bonds of discipleship. Some from sheer perverseness, wishing to be different in order to fain notoriety. Some become sceptics through inaccurate thinking and reasoning. There are others, and they are very few, who are Atheists because it is utterly impossible for them to take any other course and be perfectly honest. Bradlaugh was one of the latter type.

As I have already said, he was a thinker and reasoner of a very intense type. There was no forming of judgement by superficialities. Right down to the dregs he went, sorting, sifting, arranging and rearranging, until he was satisfied he had the very milk of the nut. Then, fearlessly he told the world his findings.

Bradlaugh disbelieved in a God idea, or at least could not conceive the idea of a God. The doctrine of vicarious suffering or punishment was repugnant. The Bible had no virtue but the virtue of history. Yet to say he was an evil man or a man without morals would be untrue.

A writer has written:- "Nothing can be of practical value in religion but what is ethical". A theological creed is empty of help or meaning unless it has moral value. Bradlaugh laid all his emphasis upon moral ideals. Let me put his moral creed into my own words.

"I do not know God. Such a conception is too high for me. But I know man. I cannot look higher than man. In man I see possibilities of greatness, of nobility. I also see possibilities of depravity and lowness of aim. Seeing this I believe that the whole duty of man is to live for the service of man. Men are brothers and each should work for the good of his brother. Man should work to relieve the oppressed among them, and to give perfect freedom that man may develop into a perfect moral being."

Bradlaugh laboured for the freedom of the masses from industrial slavery, and he spared not the masses who wasted their substance in foolish living. In all things he was consistent to every principle of right and truth. Bradlaugh died as he lived.

Charles Bradlaugh

Chapter 7

Henry Day and Even Swindon School

George Ewart Hobbs entered Even Swindon Infants School on October 21, 1889, and left Even Swindon Mixed School on December 20, 1895, aged just 12.

Most of us will have a teacher that we remember with special fondness. There is no doubting whom George felt was particularly special to him.

Although he had left school while still so very young, George embraced the path of self-improvement like so many of his fellow Swindonians – whether by studying after-hours at the Mechanics' Institute in Emlyn Square (or at the reading rooms in Rodbourne Road), by borrowing books from the lending library there, or by attending the many lectures and meetings that were freely available around town to those willing to give of their time.

But we certainly get the impression that the love and respect that he had for his headmaster may – just may – have meant that George benefitted from his elementary schooling to a greater degree than many of his fellow pupils. After all, don't we all try that little bit harder for those we like?

Of course, we would also argue that Henry Day was an exceptional individual, too. The son of a letter sorter in the GPO, he was born in New Hall Street, Birmingham, on February 19, 1856. Having gained his Teacher's Certificate at the Birmingham Bishop Ryder's National School, he moved to Swindon in 1878, upon his appointment as one of the assistant masters at the old GWR Schools in Bristol Street.

Promotion was soon to follow when, in June 1880, he was appointed as the first headmaster of Even Swindon Schools.

Having set up home at 51 William Street, following his marriage to Sarah

Arabella Thomas in December 1880, the couple eventually moved to Brendon House, 57 Ashford Road, where they raised five sons and a daughter, namely Frank, Laurie, William, Arnold, Leslie and Dorothy.

The first known public tribute to Day from George appeared in the final part of his series of articles, *The Story of the Creation*, on June 19, 1917:

> As I look back upon the days that I spent at the Even Swindon School, I see many days when the lessons were irksome; lessons which, if I had only thoroughly mastered their initial stages, would be of incalculable value to me now. As I write, I seem to hear the headmaster, Mr H Day – whom I have to thank for a great deal – impressing upon us the necessity of being thorough in the initial stages of learning so that with the rudiments well assimilated, the building upon that foundation would be a pleasant task.

Day held the post until his retirement in September 1919, and a stone tablet was erected in his honour, at the school, bearing the inscription:

> Erected by Old Scholars
> on the Retirement of
> Mr. H. Day,
> The first Head Master of
> this School 1880 – 1919, as
> Evidence of Appreciation
> of his Meritorious Services.

(Although the original tablet disappeared from the original school building in Hughes Street just prior to demolition in late 2013, a splendid replica was prepared, courtesy of Cllr David Renard and Swindon Borough Council, and is now installed at the new school in Pasture Close).

Following the retirement presentation evening that took place at the school on September 22, 1919, the *Advertiser* published a fulsome report of the event in which Day heaped praise on his staff (many of whom were also former pupils) as well as other former scholars, and stated that:

> He was proud of them and the good work they had done and were doing in the world. Some had done good, unselfish work, like their friend Ald. Walters, and in a different way Mr George Hobbs, men who had done good work, of which any man might well feel proud.

Day went on to enjoy a long retirement, eventually passing away on November 24, 1941, at his house at 130 Croft Road, so chosen for his latter years because it was situated close to his son, Leslie.

Following his passing at the ripe old age of 85, a number of correspondents wrote in to the *Advertiser* with heartfelt accolades, extracts from which are recorded below:

Mr Day was one of nature's gentlemen, always kind and courteous to children, teachers and parents. He had wonderful sympathy and patience with little children and a perfect understanding of older lads and girls, winning their love and respect.

Mrs Frances J Gay

A master of detail, he worked faithfully in quietness to maintain a high standard and a fine spirit. He led the boys and girls to respect themselves and the school.

Mrs Frances J Gay

He was a strict but just and kindly master, beloved by scholars and parents.

Francis Lewis

As may be imagined, Mr Day had a somewhat rough passage to start with, as many of the boys were 12 years and upwards before commencing their schooling, and the loose life had turned some of them into petty hooligans.

TA Jarman

I met him about three years ago in Regent Street – the same smile, well-kept beard, and the ever-present leather bag. But, best of all, the same personality, which made him the most popular headmaster a school could possibly have.

FN Avern

I expect there are others who could give more glowing tributes than I have done, but I hope they will join with me in offering condolence to the bereaved relatives in the passing of one of the finest schoolmasters Swindon has ever known.

Francis Lewis

However, the most glowing tribute to Day was delivered during his lifetime, and made by none other than George Hobbs:

But to you, sir, I owe more than words can express.

So, as part of this chapter, we include one personal, handwritten letter from George to Day (reproduced on the following three pages), plus an open letter that appeared in the correspondence column of the *Advertiser*, as well as an account by George of the last prize-giving attended by Day as Headmaster of Even Swindon Mixed School, on July 31, 1919.

Last but not least, there is a short article by George about another Even Swindon School alumnus, namely the composer and arranger, Percy Lewis, who was originally from Guppy Street.

4. Jennings. Street
New Swindon
21. 2. 16.

Dear Mr. Day,

I am writing to ask if you would be kind enough to accept this little gift of mine, accompanying this letter. Though it is nearly twenty years since I was a scholar under you, yet I think you will remember me. It is also just possible you will remember that I was by no means quick at my lessons—; tho I do not remember failing at an annual examination, yet I think there were times when I only got through by the skin of my teeth. I will certainly say this; whatever success I have attained since my schooling days terminated, that success has been directly attributable to the tuition I recieved from yourself. I often look back to the last two years of my school days, when I was in the sixth and seventh standards, with great pleasure. One of the things, among others, that I like to remember, is the memory of morning prayers. I was certainly thoughtless in those days, that is, thoughtless to the nobler, and grander things of life, yet, as you conducted prayers morning by morning; there were times when I saw in you a something that I could not define then, but now I know it was the fact that you had indeed grasped the nobler and grander life,— and you revealed it to me (unconsciously, perhaps on your part) in the way you conducted morning prayers.

I have contributed to the "Swindon Advertiser" for some months now, verses of topical thought, and otherwise, and, believing I could help a little cause that is near my heart, I published some of those verses in booklet form. I am glad to say, in three months, I had sold 750; bringing in a profit of £3.17.6. for the Telford Road Wesleyan Mission Hall. A few I retained, to give to one or two friends, and I should count it an honour sir, if you would accept this one. Some of them, I have no doubt, you will find weak in expression, but I think you will find also some of them are more bold and robust. I may

(2)

say Mr. Alfred Williams has sent me a very kind letter on my contributions to the "Swindon Advertiser". I sincerely hope you will not mind my writing to you, and sending my little gift, and I may say I should have sent it before, but I was under the erroneous idea that you had retired from the Even Swindon school, and I have been trying to get your address.

Trusting that God's blessing will rest upon you
    I remain
     Yours Sincerely,
      George E. Hobbs.

An Open Letter to Mr H Day Headmaster of the Even Swindon Mixed School

(First published: August 1, 1919)

Dear Sir,

I have assigned to myself a task in the execution of which I find both pleasure and difficulty. In a little while you are retiring from the headmastership of the Even Swindon Mixed School, and I wish to embrace the opportunity of publicly paying my last tribute of esteem before you relinquish the post you have filled for the past forty years. I do this the more readily, because infinitely would I prefer you to see this tribute of your old scholar's love, than the evidence should be mistakenly withheld until – should the order of Providence be such – above your still form I planted flowers upon your grave.

I should be cold and meaningless were I merely to say you have done your duty. The bare phrase savours of mechanical routine and uninspiring monotony; of conformity to inflexible rules, wherein the lifeless influence of the letter retards the life-giving spirit of inspiration, expansion and self expression.

Many there are of whom one could say they have done their duty; and such is the law of cause and effect that the reaping corresponds to the measure of the sowing. For a bare legal duty they reap a bare legal joy. The phrase, 'naked and unadorned' would be a negation of your life's work.

We so often associate the good influences of our lives to the examples set before us by our parents and our Sunday School teachers; rarely do we acknowledge the good influences of our day school teachers.

Profoundly do I pay tribute to the memory of my home training, and to the memory of the various Sunday School teachers who undertook the guidance of a very refractory scholar.

But to you, sir, I owe more than words can express.

Not only do I refer to the years in which I was under your tuition, but also to the subsequent years in which you have given me your practical sympathy, inspiring me in the channels of effort you know my heart to be.

To return to my school days: I am glad I can write with the knowledge that I was never a favoured pupil. So far as you were concerned, favouritism was abhorrent and distasteful. In every dull scholar you saw potential culture; and in every refractory scholar you saw potential goodness, and you laboured faithfully to develop the potential qualities you believed you saw there.

It was ever your aim to develop the best your scholars were capable of producing.

I write too, with the memory that on more than one occasion you punished me. But the punishment meted out was ever corrective and never vindictive.

I never worried much about being punished, save once: And that was when you gave me six with the cane – three on each hand. In the whole of the time I came directly under you, I only saw this punishment administered three times. Once for gross insolence to a teacher, and twice for untruthfulness – and I was one of the two punished for presumed untruthfulness.

I admit with shame there were times when I could look a teacher in the face and not be quite lucid in my statements, but such was your influence upon me that I could not look you in the face and lie.

And the pain of that occasion was not due to the cane, but to the fact that you believed me untruthful. I did not fear the cane, but as keenly as a boy could feel, so I felt the shame, but this time, not the knowledge of guilt. No sir, you were not to blame – the circumstances are fresh in my memory as I write – it so happened that circumstantial evidence seemed to suggest to you the obvious.

And now you are laying aside the mantle of active work and are retiring to seek the rest I am sure you so much need. As you have lived such a strenuous life, the reaction may bring to you at times slight feelings of depression.

At such times, sir, may this thought bring you comfort. The sentiments that I have tried to express are not only my own personal sentiments, but they are shared by hundreds.

Evidence is to hand from various parts of the Homeland; from the Continent of Europe; from America, India, Africa, Australia, New Zealand, and from Fleet and Army, that your influence has had a positive bearing upon hundreds of lives; and you carry with you upon your retirement their love and undying esteem.

Though the sun may be far over the meridian, it has not yet begun to tinge the Western sky; and I trust the years that yet may be spared you will be years of gladness and joy; of peace and tranquillity of spirit.

And when in the fullness of time the bright hued colours of the sunset are yours, may this be your hope: Every sunset is but the anticipation of a glorious dawn – a dawn in which the victor is crowned and the "Well Done!" is heard.

That every comfort may attend you and yours is the wish of your old scholar.

George E Hobbs

Presentation to Mr H Day
By George E Hobbs
(First published: August 8, 1919)

Having received an invitation to attend the annual prize distribution at my old school, I decided to avail myself of the opportunity thus presented, and go. I came to this conclusion the more readily because of two reasons: the first being that I had not witnessed such an event for twenty-three years, and the second, that this would be the last prize day in which my old schoolmaster would take part as the head of the school. I therefore looked forward to my visit with no little degree of anticipation and pleasure.

Looking back upon that event – which took place on July 31st 1919 – I am sincere when I say I would not have missed it for a great deal. It was a time when the hallowed memories of bygone years stirred the soul; when a strange sensation came to the throat, and the eyes were luminous with unshed tears. To me, even as it must have been to others, it was a day of days.

Upon my arrival at the school, I found the hall packed with a bright-faced throng of boys and girls, a fair sprinkling of mothers and, I fancy, one or two of the fathers. On each side of the hall stood the teaching staff; while through the open classroom doors I caught a glimpse of the younger children who could not be accommodated in the hall itself. Upon a small raised platform stood my old schoolmaster; while upon his left were seated Councillors T Butler (Chairman of the Swindon Education Committee), AE Harding, R George and Mr W Seaton (Secretary to the Committee).

I had scarcely apprehended these details when my eyes ceased to wander, and I turned to listen to what my old schoolmaster had to say. He told us of the memories he retained when he was a scholar and took prizes. How, on one occasion, he knew the sensation of "treading on air" as he went forward to receive such a prize as would gladden the heart of any boy. He walked back to his place the proud possessor of a full-sized guinea cricket bat.

He told of the time when the school was first opened; when Even Swindon was very different to what it was today. In those days prize-giving was a problem of some magnitude; for as no money was granted for this purpose, the purchase money had to be raised by means of concerts. And as no books could then be bought in Swindon, he had to journey to Bristol in order to select and purchase them.

Very powerfully did Mr Day remind the children of the glorious heritage into which they have come – that of free education; telling them of the days (which I can remember) when on Monday mornings, 3d and 2d had to be taken to school by the respective members of families. Concluding his remarks, Mr Day called upon Mr T Butler to distribute the prizes.

In a very happy speech Mr Butler delighted the children with reminiscences of his own early days in which, in contradistinction to the reminiscences of Mr Day, he told them of an occasion when he received punishment for indulging in laughter during school hours.

The punishment was not administered in a vertical position and upon the hands, but the posture was horizontal and upon a more painful part of the anatomy. And the young folk, evidently visualising the somewhat painful episode, roared in sheer delight.

Sincerely did Mr Butler pay tribute to the sterling qualities possessed by Mr Day, and of the faithful service rendered by him during the 40 years of his headmastership. He reminded us too that the teaching staff must also receive their meed of praise; for the efficiency of the school could not be maintained but for their faithful and hearty co-operation with him.

Though the hands of the clock insisted on continuous movement, Mr Butler found time to congratulate each prize-winner upon the receipt of their prize. I am glad he did this, for as prizes are now given for work done and not so much for attendance, the child with a second or third prize has worked probably as assiduously as the child who was fortunate enough to take a first prize. While we bow to genius, we must not forget to take off our hats to the conscientious plodder. If any of the young folk should read this article, prize-winners or non prize-winners, let me say to them: Work, not so much for prizes – gratifying as the receipt of them may be – but work so that you may lay the foundation of such usefulness as will tend to add to the sum total of happiness in your day and generation.

No meeting, in which "prizes" and "children" are features, is complete without the presence of our old friend Mr Reuben George. And he gave us, what I may term, a jolly and ennobling ten minutes. Fun and serious advice were intermingled on Mr George's own inimitable way, and we each felt the better for listening to his address.

Then followed the thrill of the afternoon.

Evidently the children sensed what was about to take place; for, as soon as Mr Ballinger the assistant headmaster mounted the platform, the hall became tense with silent yet eager expectancy.

Mr Ballinger told us that for practically 40 years, Mr Day had been the headmaster of the Even Swindon School; and now the time had arrived when he was relinquishing that position and seeking rest in retirement. For practically the whole of that period he had been associated with Mr Day and, he believed, he was fitted in a unique sense of estimating the worth of his chief.

He had the opportunity of studying him from every standpoint appertaining to school life, and also in those general paths of life wherein man is judged as man.

He had a scholar's knowledge of a schoolmaster, a pupil teacher's knowledge of a chief, and an assistant's knowledge of a colleague. In each and every aspect, his estimate of Mr Day's worth was very much higher than mere words could express. His rule to the scholars had ever been upon the lines of moral suasion; never upon threats of punishment. To his staff, he had ever been a sympathetic friend; and one and all trusted that he would long enjoy the rest he was about to enter into.

It was a tense moment when Mr Ballinger, removing a large chair cover, revealed to our view a beautiful upholstered easy chair and asked Mr Day, in the name of the teaching staff and scholars, to accept this token of their esteem. In addition to the chair – on which was recorded a suitable inscription upon a brass plate – a beautifully executed illuminated address was presented. It is indeed a real work of art, and one must believe that the soul of the artist is reflected therein. Beneath Mr Day's name and the record of the occasion are the names of the present teaching staff, and a few, who could be reached of those who had served under Mr Day in the years that are gone.

In tones controlled only under strong force will, Mr Day replied, thanking the teachers and scholars for these evidences of their affection. In the years to come it would ever be his joy and comfort to know that their love and esteem would follow him to the end of time.

It was very fitting that the afternoon should close with a concert by the children. And with Miss Routledge at the piano and Mr Ballinger conducting, the children sang to us of their best. Every item was splendidly rendered, and great credit is due both to the children and to those who trained them.

With the singing of the National Anthem, one of the most enjoyable afternoons I have ever spent was brought to a close. And I can only conclude by joining with the teachers and scholars in wishing Mr Day and his wife life's best joy in the years that are coming.

Councillor AJ Gilbert who kindly supplied the frame of the illuminated address, sent a letter appreciative of the work accomplished by Mr Day and of the fact that he is a true type of an English gentleman.

A Swindon Product
Mr Percy Lewis of "Laughter (Un) Limited" Musical Director
By GEH

(First published: September 28, 1923)

Mr. Percy Lewis, the musical director of "Laughter (Un) Ltd" the revue that is being played by an excellent company at the Empire Theatre, Swindon this week, is a Swindon man – the fifth son of Mr & Mrs J Lewis of 13 Guppy Street, Rodbourne Road, who well may feel proud of their son's achievements in the musical world.

Mr Lewis received his scholastic education under Mr. H. Day, a former headmaster of the Even Swindon School, and completed his course at the Higher Elementary School in Clarence Street. Mr. J. Gale, the well-known pianist, was Mr Lewis's music teacher, and Mr. Lewis's first appointment in orchestral work was at the Swindon Empire Theatre.

Not finding sufficient scope here for his talents, Mr. Lewis journeyed to London where, after passing through various vicissitudes of fortune, he eventually became a conductor at the Surrey Theatre, the principal suburban music hall.

Mr. Lewis conducted the orchestra at the Lewisham Hippodrome for six years, and here met with a poignant experience. A new song had been composed for Miss Marie Lloyd, entitled "Good Old Iron", and Mr. Lewis was commissioned to arrange the band parts but whilst he was in the midst of the work, the news reached him that Miss Lloyd had died.

Mr. Lewis has also toured with the George Edwardes' No. 1 Company, conducting in "The Dollar Princess" and other well-known musical comedies.

That music is his natural element is revealed by his accomplishments. Not only does he conduct but several music scores have been written by him. The orchestral parts of a foxtrot entitled "Jolly Times" is from his pen, also a concert waltz entitled "Autumn Leaves".

Mr. Lewis wrote the music for two of Gulliver's pantomimes, and Dorothy Mullord is indebted to him for the music of her several plays. "Jolly Times" and "Autumn Leaves" have proved big favourites with devotees of the terpsichorean art.

Mr. Lewis is now at work upon a beautiful musical suite called "The Seasons," which it is thought will be the acme of musical perfection."

Top: Henry Day in c1885 and 1930. *(Author's collection)*

Middle: Even Swindon School, where George was a pupil, and later returned as a guest for headmaster Henry Day's retirement presentation. Pictured here in the 1960s, it is now the site of an Aldi supermarket. *(Courtesy of The Swindon Society)*

Bottom: Donald Day and Noel Ponting with the plaque installed in honour of Henry Day at the new Even Swindon Primary School, in Pasture Close. *(Author's collection)*

Chapter 8

A Red-Letter Day

On Monday, April 28, 1924, the *Advertiser* announced the first official visit of a reigning British monarch to Swindon – King George V, along with Queen Mary – with the banner headline 'Wholehearted Welcome to Royal Visitors'.

George Hobbs was given something of a ringside seat during this landmark day in the town's history, and his account, published in the GWR Magazine, is reproduced in full. But first some background. The *Advertiser* reported that:

> For the first time in its history, Swindon was today honoured by a visit from the King and Queen, and Their Majesties received a warm welcome from the inhabitants of one of the most loyal boroughs in England. All classes of the townspeople joined in – according to the Royal Visitors a reception worthy of the great occasion, and there can be no question that the King and Queen very highly appreciated this spontaneous expression of the loyalty of a town so representative of industrial England.

The piece went on to describe the way the route from the station to Victoria Hospital had been decorated in celebration, particularly Newspaper House, headquarters of the paper, which it described as being 'profusely embellished with flags and streamers, and the windows were relieved with red, white and blue bunting.' And:

> The Coate Amateur Rowing Club had quite a novel display. On the long wall facing the Advertiser offices, a boat was placed and embellished with oars, flags and balloons. The officials spent many hours on this scheme but their efforts did not meet with their full reward owing to the weather conditions.

'The Queen,' it was stated, 'was stylishly dressed in Navy marocain and cerise, and the King wore a bowler hat and lounge suit with a white flower in the buttonhole of his overcoat.'

The royal couple proceeded in convoy to the Town Hall and attended a wreath-laying ceremony at The Cenotaph, in memory of the men of Swindon who had fallen during the First World War. Amongst those introduced to the King was Mr W Gosling, known as 'The Wroughton VC.'

Upon arrival at Victoria Hospital, they proceeded to the women's ward in the new wing, and then to the children's ward. At one cot, the King enquired after how the little girl within was progressing, to which she replied, "I have had them all out." The King, clearly surprised by the response and appreciating her good humour 'patted her gently upon the head and laughed as he congratulated her upon her cheeriness'.

Following an inspection of the men's ward, the entourage then made their way by car to the GWR Works by way of the GWR Medical Fund Hospital, the Medical Fund surgery and baths, accident hospital and Mechanics' Institute.

As time goes on and as the Mechanics' Institute slips into further disrepair, it's worth recalling what was written about this venerable building at the time:

> From the commencement of the history of the railway, Swindon Works have been progressively and closely identified with admirably conceived plans for the instruction and welfare of the employees.
>
> An excellent example of this is the Great Western Railway Mechanics' Institution which was founded in 1844 'for the purpose of disseminating useful knowledge and encouraging rational amusement amongst all classes of people employed by the Great Western Railway Company'.
>
> In connection with the institution there is a fine library containing 50,000 volumes, Reading rooms, separate recreation rooms for billiards, chess and drafts, a large hall for musical and other entertainments and a lecture hall, form part of the institution. The management is in the hands of an elected committee of foremen and other employees.
>
> An interesting feature in connection with this institution is that under its auspices the Annual Trip or Works' Holiday is conducted. The directors provide, free of all cost, the requisite number of trains, and an idea of the extent of this function may be gained from the fact that each year some 26,500 employees, wives and dependents participate. The Trip was established in 1849, the number taking part on that occasion being 500.
>
> Early in the history of the Mechanics' Institution, special attention was paid to the establishment of evening classes for the study of subjects allied with science and art... The facilities for technical education at Swindon are considered to be amongst the foremost in the country...

In a summary of the Royal Visit, published the following day, the *Advertiser* also noted:

His Majesty spent a little time in observing how wheels are balanced and then proceeded to the weighbridge, adjacent to which there was a parade of 80 men still in the service of the company, who had each worked in the factory for over 50 years. His Majesty immediately spotted George Bayliss of 189 Rodbourne Road, Swindon who is credited with 58 years' service, being 69 years of age.

He is one of the old brigade and was conspicuous by the fact that he wore the old time white jacket and trousers. Though not worn nowadays, Mr Bayliss will not discard the old style and has a clean suit every week...

At the conclusion of their visit, the King and Queen boarded the Royal Train for their return journey and the King requested that the whole of the workmen should have an extra half holiday next Saturday morning and the request was readily granted.

George's account in the Great Western Railway's official magazine is reproduced below, to which we have added the timetable from the official programme.

A Pen Picture of the Royal Visit to Swindon By George E Hobbs
(First published: June 1924)

It may truly be said that Monday, April 28, 1924 will be a day memorable in the annals of the Great Western Railway Works at Swindon. For 82 years have the works been in existence, rising from infantile weakness, not merely to adult strength but to the proud position they hold among the railway works in the British Isles; yet up to the date just mentioned, their history does not record one visit by a personage of kingly or queenly rank. That defect has now been repaired.

Upon the arrival platform of Swindon station I was fortunate enough to be allotted a place facing the position which the Royal saloon would occupy upon its arrival.

There were still some minutes to wait before the train was due, and one had time to view and to appreciate the beautiful bower of variegated bunting displayed here. This, with the soft, scarlet carpet underfoot, transformed this part of the station into a veritable fairyland.

A distinguished company was assembled upon either side of the gangway to witness the arrival of Their Majesties, while in the centre were gathered the ladies and gentlemen who were to welcome the august visitors.

At that moment one's attention was removed from the incidental details to that for which we had come. An instinctive stiffening to attention, then softly, as though a sleigh traversed snow, the Royal train came to rest.

The hand-clasps of the King with the Mayor and Mayoress and with Mr CB Collett, the Company's Chief Mechanical Engineer, were the grips of virile manhood; and any idea that Her Majesty would be in any way remote was dispelled by the exquisite charm of her womanly smile.

It was the express wish of Their Majesties that the shops through which they were to pass should be under normal working conditions; and to the credit of every man and woman engaged in those shops, this wish was loyally respected.

The thrill of a unique experience was felt in the being of every man and woman in the shops, and there must have been constantly a subtle desire to cease work in order to view the Royal party at such close range. But one may say with truth that each individual job was executed exactly in the spirit wished for by Their Majesties and the management.

We must here pay tribute to the loyalty of those who remained in the shops not visited by the King and Queen. Many probably felt that the tour of inspection should have included their shop, but the route was wisely chosen, in that it took in the manufacture of those parts best known to the public mind. And, after all, visited or not visited, the fact remains that the day was essentially a "workers" day.

Many times have the King and Queen travelled in the Great Western Royal Train, with its wonderful smoothness of running; and it was the "worker" who demonstrated to Their Majesties how that excellence was obtained. What applies to the Royal special applies also to every train running upon the GWR system – the maximum of ease and comfort.

And now to come back to the impressions of the tour through the shops. That Their Majesties were keenly alive to the utilitarian as well as to the spectacular point of view of things inspected was evidenced time and again throughout the tour. The beauty of perfect symmetry, as displayed in the design of carriage and engine, was frankly admired by the King and Queen, but their interest and admiration were no less keen over the details of manufacture and the economy of integral parts.

The method of inspection differed somewhat in the Carriage Department from that in the Locomotive Department. In the Carriage Department the finished article – in the shape of a magnificent 70ft first and third class composite carriage and the latest design of dining car – was inspected first.

Then came the polishing, sewing and trimming shops; the skeleton carriages under construction; and lastly, the saw mills where a huge elm bole was being sawn longitudinally upon a multiple sawing machine.

One noticed repeatedly the great interest His Majesty took in the purely mechanical aspect of things; and while this is equally true of the Queen, Her Majesty revealed how intensely womanly she was by her absorbed interest in the work wrought by the girls in the sewing, trimming and polishing shops. The same interest was shown when Their Majesties inspected the dining car.

While both Their Majesties appreciated all the details of mechanical skill and ingenuity, the Queen revealed those domestic traits for which she is famous, by her thorough inspection of the dining car's economy in kitchen and pantry.

In the Locomotive Department the tour of inspection commenced at the Iron Foundry and terminated at the weighbridge of the AE Shop. And through that tour one felt that one thought must have been prominent in the mind of His Majesty the King – the thought of "power".

The King of such an empire as ours is familiar with the word "power"; the power of State, of Empire, of law, and so on. But now His Majesty saw power from a different viewpoint – power as mechanically applied.

Whether it was the 65ft turntable upon which has a gross weight of 110 tons, being turned by the efforts of one man, or the huge engine on the testing plant potentially eating up mileage, yet ever remaining stationary, or clinching home steel rivets between the 23ft deep jaws of the gap riveter, or the suspension of an 82 ton engine, carried up and down the shop by the 100 ton overhead crane – there His Majesty saw Power from the mechanical aspect.

And another thought must have occupied Their Majesties' minds: the power of a united industry, in which all departments working together for a common objective, and putting the best into every single effort, could produce the perfection, the symmetry, and the utility of the finished article.

One last impression, and one that will not be lightly forgotten. Upon the conclusion of the tour the hooter sounded, and like magic the whole north side of space adjacent to the main line was quickly packed by a dense throng. The line of employees reached nearly a mile in length.

Upon the footplate of the "Windsor Castle" stood Their Majesties, the King at the regulator.

Standing where I was, near to the engine, I saw that both the King and the Queen were thoroughly enjoying their novel experience.

In true workmanlike style, the King waited for the signal of the guard and when this was given His Majesty opened the regulator, and the Royal Train proceeded slowly towards the station.

Route and Time Table

2.10 p.m. Arrive at Swindon Station

2.15 p.m. Drive from Swindon Station by way of:

Fleet Street
Bridge Street
Regent Street
Regent Circus (Post Office side)
Cenotaph
Victoria Road
Wood Street
High Street
Newport Street
Devizes Road
Bath Road
to Victoria Hospital

2.30 p.m. Inspection of Victoria Hospital

2.45 p.m. Leave Victoria Hospital for Swindon Works by way of:

Bath Road
Victoria Road
Town Hall
Regent Street
Bridge Street
Farringdon Street

3.10 p.m. GWR Medical Fund Hospital
Medical Fund Surgery and Baths
Accident Hospital
Mechanics' Institution

3.15 p.m. Swindon Works
Enter works by:
Sheppard Street Entrance
Inspect Laundry
Polishing and Finishing Shops
Carriage Body-Making
Saw Mill
Iron Foundry
Engine being turned on balanced turntable by one man

Types of Engine in Yard
Engine Testing Plant
General Machine Shop
Engine Erecting Shop
Lifting Complete Engine by Overhead Crane
Wheel Shop
Wheel Balancing
Weighbridge and engine being weighed
4.25 p.m. Entrain Royal Saloon (outside Weighbridge House)
to be drawn by the "Windsor Castle"
4.30 p.m. Leave Swindon Station

The King looks on during the royal visit of 1924 as a railwayman demonstrates the ease with which locomotives could be marshalled on the Swindon Works turntable – a feat that George remarked on in his 'pen picture' for the GWR Magazine. The photos overleaf are from the same visit to Swindon Town Hall and the Works, and include a famous one of the King and Queen Mary observing a casting. George was among the gentlemen of the press making notes in the background, but we haven't been able to spot him! (Courtesy of The Swindon Society)

Chapter 9

George's Fables

George Hobbs was particularly well-read. And from his book-bedecked front parlour, where he sought privacy from the hustle and bustle of family life, he was often inspired to put across his thoughts in the form of fables. But these were not actually biblical *per se*.

Perhaps not wishing to alienate those who would baulk at the idea of going to church, he seemed happy to save his overt sermonising for the pulpit. Or at the very least, he was content to clearly label such writing so people were left in no doubt what to expect, such as in the case of the series entitled *Pen Pictures From the Pulpit*.

No, his fables were different. Doubtless inspired to share his moral, ethical and socio-political beliefs amongst a wider congregation (the readership of the *Advertiser*, in this case), he often used inanimate objects and animals as a vehicle for the conveyance of some awkward or uncomfortable subject matter. This was by no means uncommon. Many writers used this device.

But George sometimes went a step further. He gave the animals or objects featured in some of the tales an actual voice.

This prosopopoeia allowed him to speak more freely than perhaps he felt able to do in the first person. It may well be that this allowed him to reach a wider, secular audience without 'majoring' on the whole 'God' thing. Furthermore, it gave him an opportunity to vent some of his political views.

As a fully paid-up member of the trade union, the Amalgamated Society of Engineers, it will come as no surprise that he was a political animal – but no actual, official party affiliation is known. We can, however, be reasonably certain that George was broadly aligned with many of the skilled working class at the time who formed the backbone of the Liberal Party.

Such leanings were handed down to him by his father, Henry Hobbs, who gave him the middle name of Ewart as a tribute to Liberal politician William Ewart Gladstone. At the time of George's birth, Gladstone was into his second term as Prime Minister of Great Britain and Ireland.

By far the largest series of fables was known as *Conversations*, for that is exactly what they were. Comprising 25 individual articles, some seek to take tacit wisdom from Ancient Rome, Aretaic virtue ethics or from Greek Mythology. It is hard to imagine that those pieces, in particular, would have been accessible (or indeed a joy to read) by many in the wider *Advertiser* readership.

However, some of the most readable of the series involved a dog. Not just any dog. She was called Tiny, and was a Christmas present for George's daughter, Dorothy. And by a few strokes of a pen, Tiny acquired a personality – as did Nibby the cat, and a rather third-rate pencil. Even the moon received the gift of life!

Perhaps it came as no surprise that this style of writing did come in for some criticism within the correspondence pages of the newspaper.

However, George responded:

> ...it is by no means a rarity for an animal to be used as a medium for conversational writing. Even things inanimate have been made to speak that the writer may bring before his readers some matter of passing interest or of lasting vital moment. It is the subject matter that counts, and not the medium by which the matter is presented.

George rightly remains convinced that prosopopoeia is a useful device for his fables and allegories, and Tiny is his main ally, even when the message he is putting across is rather profound and serious. She makes her first appearance on October 25, 1917, in a piece entitled *Tiny and I*.

Her name, by the way, suggested not a little irony. As George himself said:

> As I watched her gradually develop, there came a time when I cried "Halt!" – but she halted not; and I became painfully aware that the name we had given her was a misnomer. In fact, it was grotesque. Tiny became elephantine in physical structure, hurricanical by nature and yes – still docile in disposition.

Through one of the fables we learn that George did his writing alone in the front room, which he variously termed his 'den' or the 'executive part of the home'. Tiny was certainly not allowed in there. Her normal place was either in the garden or on the kitchen rug.

> If, by chance, the wife has a suspicion that Tiny has been upon forbidden ground, she does not question me – knowing my laxity of government – but

questions Tiny; and when Tiny realises the seriousness of the indictment, she is so injured at the bare thought of disobedience that she immediately commences to bark at imaginary trespassers to show how alert she is in the protection of her mistress's home.

George is about to start reading a book in peace and quiet and in full knowledge of the fact that he had allowed Tiny into the parlour as a special treat, when he was immediately disturbed by a voice – which he immediately assumed came from the dog, who gets punished and exclaims: 'Why did you kick me like that?' When a somewhat upset Tiny argued that it wasn't her who had interrupted George's down time, it became clear that the villain of the piece was Nibby the cat, 'a nomadic feline, who often came into the house' and whom George often heard using bad language.

But what concerned George about this whole incident was that he had punished one animal for the apparent sins of another. But why should he worry? It was only an animal. Nevertheless, it still played on his mind. His internal debate was this: surely it was right that he admit his mistake and be contrite, but on the other hand, it was only visited upon an inferior being – in this case a lowly animal. Perhaps a palliative would be a far better way out of the situation rather than an apology?

Finally, George came to the conclusion that wrong is wrong, 'irrespective of position in the social order', and continued; 'There is no loss of dignity in acknowledging a mistake – rather dignity is enhanced.'

In the final analysis, his conscience accepted that a palliative was nothing more than a bribe. Bribery was immoral and could never right a wrong, and he concluded by saying: 'I felt convinced that what my higher nature advocated was the true course. Closing my book, I called Tiny to me, and said, "Tiny I admit my error. In arriving too hastily to conclusions, I punished you unjustly. I am sorry!"

'That is all I said, but as Tiny looked up into my face, and then licked my hand, I felt no loss of dignity, but rather peace came, and I was able to enjoy my hour of relaxation.'

The previously mentioned writing implement makes its appearance on October 30, 1917, in another piece laden with metaphor, entitled *Just A Common Stick Of Pencil*, in which he undoubtedly seeks to stand up for the handicapped and the marginalised of society.

George had settled down to do some more writing, and he wasn't getting on at all well. His pencil was either scratching the paper or the point kept breaking off, despite numerous attempts at sharpening it. In a fit of pique, he threw the pencil to the floor. A voice, which he assumed to be that of his wife, Agnes, told him off for doing so. When challenged over this, she rightly denied it was her, saying that 'if conversation writing is going to make you talk to yourself, or imagine that others are talking to you when they are not, the best thing you can do is to go into the yard and saw that wood up'.

When George feebly ventured that it must then be the pencil, she replied, "How is it possible for a pencil to speak? Don't be so absurd!"

He retired to the parlour to continue the conversation. During what followed, he admonished the pencil for not performing its duties particularly well... as a pencil. The pencil responded that it did the best it could and stated:

"If you do your best, you can do no more... You are very hasty with your condemnation... and I notice that a sneer lies not far from your lips; but before you indulge in recriminations and in sneers, you will prove your claim to being a wise man if you first of all inquire into the causes of why my best should be such a poor best."

The pencil then went into a lengthy diatribe about its history and, in its particular case, the manufacturing fault which caused it to be suboptimal. But rather than throw it away as part of a defective batch, the foreman decided it was just about good enough to be used as change for the equivalent of a farthing (a quarter of a penny).

In its defence, the pencil stated:

"There I was, rough and warped in my body, and a mixture of good and bad – more bad than good – in my essential part. From the commencement of my life I have had no kindly word said to me; nor have I ever had a hand grasp me with a sympathetic touch. Tossed here and there, I have been despised, ridiculed and laughed at, even by the infant humans whom I find usually like to have one of my family in their possession.

"From the factory, I was sent to the shop at which your wife purchased some material, and the money she tendered necessitating a farthing's change. I was given as the farthing's value. Today you took me from the vase, sharpened me – and the result you are familiar with. That is why my best is such a poor one.

"Before you attempted to see if I was useful you were biased against me; for, even as you sharpened me, I was conscious of your thoughts. I have been so used to lack of sympathy that I knew I had not misread you. I knew I should not be given a fair chance."

Upon hearing all this, George said that in the future he would try to approach things with 'a bias on the side of sympathy, rather than in the opposite direction'.

Just in case the reader has missed the moral, the piece ends with:

> As I concluded my conversation with the pencil, my thoughts went out to the multitude of human derelicts that may be found upon the ocean of life today. I wondered if there were many of them whose life story coincided with that of the pencil. Thrown out upon an unsympathetic world, warped in body, and seemingly without a chance of soul-expansion, they are foredoomed to failure and unhappiness.
>
> How many of them could have been saved if kindly sympathy had but been given them?
>
> If, instead of being contemptuous of their first feeble efforts, encouragement was extended to them, I feel sure that the history of tragic human defeat would not be so extensive as unfortunately we find it.

Who would have thought pencils could be so enlightening?

The next series of *Conversations with Tiny* appeared in four parts, commencing on November 22, 1917. Remember, of course, that the First World War was by then in its third year.

In Part One, called *Tiny Asks A Question*, the premise is that the dog senses that something out of the ordinary has taken place: certainly not in a supernatural way; it was just that Tiny thought that George was becoming mean.

The evidence for this was based on the fact that Tiny's food had undergone a change. And for that matter, her master's diet had changed for the worse too. George challenged Tiny to come up with reasons as to why there simply wasn't as much food on the table as there had been a few years before.

Was it the fact that George was earning less? Was he now spending considerable sums on pleasures and luxuries? Or was it the fact the price of food had by then risen so high as to be almost beyond the reach of the average household?

The first two were profoundly incorrect and the third reason was pretty close to reality. Indeed, by the fourth quarter of 1916, it is thought that household costs for the average working family had risen by 55 per cent since war began. Any by 1917 local bakers were selling 'War Bread', where anything up to 25 per cent of the ingredients were non-flour substitutes.

George explained:

> You are much nearer the truth now, Tiny. But even this answer is by no means a complete one; it is only a partial answer. The complete answer, in so far as your question is concerned is: there is a scarcity of foodstuffs, and in consequence of that scarcity food prices have advanced from, in some cases fifty per cent to, in others, as much as two hundred per cent. Then again, there are other things essential to life and legitimate comfort the prices of which have swollen to an abnormal degree.

Tiny responds:

> "If the prices of commodities say of three years ago were upon a certain basis, and since that time have advanced to the almost unbelievable extent you have intimated, then there must be a cause for this also; and therefore what you have given me as the cause of this alteration of my menu becomes really the secondary cause. The primary cause is still unknown to me."

George attempted to discourage Tiny from seeking any further information regarding the spiralling cost of food. But finally, he relented with enormous regret. And the reason for his reticence becomes abundantly clear:

> "There are humans today who are advocating the decease of such as you. I imagine them to be folk who have little or no love for dogs, and who certainly do not stop to consider what the result would be should a wholesale and ruthless destruction of dogs take place. But the time may come when even this drastic suggestion may be put into actuality and…"
>
> "What is the reason of such an absurd suggestion, master?" asked Tiny vigorously.
>
> "It is because – as I shall try to show you clearly if you force me to further discussion – there may come a time when even the scraps that you may eat may be precious to the maintenance of human life," I replied. "No," I hastened to add, "I am not pessimistic enough to believe that time will come, but it is within the bounds of possibility, and therefore, if I tell you all you wish to know, involving as it does, the reasons of food scarcity, high prices, profiteering, the need of loyalty in food economy, the cause of hoarding, with its attendant hardships upon the poorer of the community; the suggestion of equality of sacrifice and the possibility of your destruction, if I tell you of this you will come in time to dread my coming home."

In the next two articles, George seeks to explain to Tiny why Britain entered the war against Germany and how, as an island nation, we were dependent on imports of food and materials from overseas. However, given that British ships were falling prey to German submarines, it followed that food shortages would result. He continues to explain to Tiny that the prices of food and commodities were rising, given that two out of every three ships were being sunk and that the increased costs of production were being passed onto the consumer – although some unscrupulous manufacturers were certainly profiteering from this fact. Tiny replies:

> …it seems to me that if prices are raised to meet new conditions, then it is the consumer that pays every time; and if, as you say, the term embraces all grades of society, then those of the lower grades will be the first to suffer; and that to my mind is obviously unfair.

However, the idea that wages should be increased to meet these higher costs was proven to be bogus economics as prices in the shops would eventually increase as a consequence, putting everybody back to where they were in the first place.

But, George has a remedy...

This remedy is reproduced in full, below, followed by more George Hobbs fables, including one in which Tiny and Nibby feature again, promoting the virtue of honesty over fibs, half-truths and white lies; another in which new characters appear, namely Reynard Fox and Tab, the farm cat; and finally there is a somewhat dark New Year message as 1921 gives way to 1922, which perhaps demonstrates George's fabling at its best.

Conversations (14)
Higher Wages Not the Remedy: But "Equality of Sacrifice
By George E Hobbs
(First published: December 12, 1917)

"Now Tiny," I began, "as to-night will be our last conversation for a time we must make the most of our present opportunity. I propose, therefore, to give you my constructive policy – or what I conceive to be the remedy for the discontent due to the inflated prices of commodities. I believe that an article has been written under the title of 'Equality of Sacrifice'. I have not read its contents, and I only have, from hearsay, a hazy idea of its arguments. The suggestive force of the title, however, has gripped me; and I have come to the conclusion that herein lies the true solution.

"You will find that what I am about to advance is of a drastic and revolutionary character. Some will call it fanaticism; some will call it foolishness. Many will give to it ugly epithets, few will view it favourably. But whether it is received with acclamation or abuse, this fact remains, some plan will have to be thought out, and quickly, if England is not to follow in the footsteps of Russia.

"No scheme up to the present has been, or is, satisfactory. The panacea of higher wages, the scheme in which the workers placed such confidence, is, as I told you in our last conversation, a failure. Higher wages automatically increase the prices of commodities – even a rabbit is spoken of as 'a little dear' and I think somehow it is not said in an affectionate sense. Certainly those that use the term know in what sense they use it.

"As I say, Tiny, some scheme, other than those which have already been advanced, must be thought out – and I advance mine, conscious of its unattractiveness. It must be clearly understood that what was to Britain a war of honour has now developed into a war of existence. As a nation we live or die by the issue, and the scales held by fate are as yet but evenly balanced. There is one factor, and one only, that will weigh down the scales in favour of victory and life, and that is sacrifice."

"But sacrifice by whom, Master?" asked Tiny.

"By those who will live if Britain lives, or die in the nation's death," I replied.

"And who are these?" questioned Tiny again.

"Listen, Tiny," I answered, "In a book that is loved by many humans there is a story recorded of an angel visiting a young man whose country was in great distress. In the salutation of the angel he said, 'The Lord is with thee, thou mighty man of valour!' to which the young man replied, 'If the Lord be with us, why had this evil befallen us?' The singular was used in the salutation: the plural was used in the reply. In that reply is revealed the young patriot identifying himself with his country. If the Lord was with him, then the Lord was with the nation. If the nation was in distress, then he, being part of the nation, was in distress also. Whatever vicissitudes the nation passed through – suffering or joy – he also suffered, or was joyous. You ask who will live if England lives, and die if England dies, and I answer, myself and all those who go to make up our nation, and therefore, if equal advantages or disadvantages depend upon the issue of the war, then, to make victory a verity, all should participate in sacrifice – there should be 'Equality of Sacrifice'. Under no circumstances should it be possible for one section of the community to have an advantage over another section, seeing that the whole nation is involved in the issue of life or death. But what is the position? The nation is divided into two great and essential sections, viz. soldiers and civilians. Soldiers are essential to the nation's cause, and the service demanded of them is obedience and loyalty. Involved in this service are hardships, suffering, possible promotion – possible death. In return for this service they receive food – when they can get it; clothing – when it can be obtained; shelter – when it can be found, and one shilling and sixpence per day. Civilians are also essential to the nation's cause, and the service demanded of them is, again, obedience and loyalty. But whereas soldiers live, to a certain extent, under compulsion, civilians live under requests, pleadings, and partial self-choice. Under these conditions it is a lamentable fact that civilians take advantage of this partial freedom. It is of very little use pointing to one portion of the civilian section and saying that these are the culprits; the question is so intricate, and so interwoven with difficulties, that the truest thing to say is that all are involved. A large portion of the blame in this matter must lie with the Government, for they usually have taken the line of least resistance, and what they would not tolerate in the military section they have allowed in the civilian section. If obedience and loyalty is demanded and given in one section, then it should also be demanded and given in the other.

"The soldier section, of course, is recruited from the civilian section, but there are certain legitimate reasons why some civilians should be kept out of the army. There are reasons of age, physical reasons, essential trades in the production of munitions, land cultivation and the like. But again I say these reasons, however true and essential, ought not to carry with them an advantage over those who are daring with their lives to keep England clear of the fate of Belgium. If all are involved in Britain's fate, then all should be in the unit of effort, and in the unity of sacrifice.

"The only scheme, therefore, that seems to me to be fair, and that meets the requirements of victory, is for the Government to place at once all the civilians upon an equality with those who are fighting. That all civilians should be rationed with a sufficiency of food to meet the requirements of their individual household; that they should be clothed and housed on a similar scale to that of the army; and that rates of pay should also be placed upon a similar basis. That is not so impossible as it may appear at first glance. First let me take the matter of food – remembering that the Government supply to soldiers their need, and civilians, with their higher wages, are often turned disappointed away. For our argument we will take the butcher, baker, grocer, and milkman. These would first take an inventory of their present existing stock and supply to the Government, upon which the Government would credit them with its value. Then, instead of continuing to buy and sell, each would become ration depots, according to their own particular line, and the needs of their present number of customers. This would save the business man's fear of bankruptcy, the worry of the present demand and supply and, in addition, the dishonest and unscrupulous trader would have no advantage over that of the honest trader. Accessories necessary to each individual business would be repaired or renewed at the Government's expense, and upon the conclusion of the war, stock to the original value would be supplied to each, to be dealt with in the same manner as at present. In other words, they could again revert to buying and selling for profit.

"Not only should this be done in the matter of food, but all the supplying trades should be similarly dealt with. Coalowners should be credited with their stock, and then supply to coal ration depots, or where it is needed most.

"Then in regard to housing: Each civilian family would remain in the same house they at present occupy, but rents would be suspended. The landlord would be credited with the value of his property in its present condition. Accredited rates would be paid by the Government, and essential repairs executed by them. By this scheme the landlord would not lose, only in the same ratio as everyone else would lose, or gain as everyone else would gain.

"In regard to the worker, I would place him upon a similar basis as is at present existing in the army. Being rationed in all the essentials necessary to his sustenance, clothed according to his legitimate needs, and having no rent to pay, his extra needs would then be no more than those who are fighting. Certainly, I would respect Trade Union bonds and similar organisations involving principles of labour but, as all would be rationed, clothed, housed, and having medical and similar facilities given, payments could be suspended for the duration of the war."

"Master," said Tiny in a very solemn tone, "before you proceed farther I would like to make an observation, and it is this: If I am correct in my estimation for human opinions, they will declare your scheme to be absurd and unworkable. The workers especially will be against you, seeing that you are interfering with their Trade Unions. You must remember that on more than one occasion you have told me the cost of their inception. You have informed me that the steep hill of human progress has not only been deluged in tears, but that there are even graves to be found upon its route. Is it logical, then, to believe that the workers will forego the result of years of misunderstanding and patient suffering? And again, Master, if I may continue my observations, the business man will be against the scheme. Is it reasonable to suppose that after working hard to establish a sound business they would be willing to renounce, even for a time, the result of hard plodding?"

"Yes, Tiny," I replied, desperately, "you may continue to multiply instances of disapproval, I expect it. But as Englishmen to-day we must weigh against our selfishness the desire for a better and brighter future. If we say 'Damn the consequences I am going to live selfishly!' then God help England – No! that is a wrong expression, for God would not help England. Believing as we do that our very existence is in the balance; believing as we do that the world's future hangs upon the issue; believing as we do that we have nothing to regret in so far as commencing hostilities is concerned, it is wrong in the extreme to put self before right. You say Trade Unionists will be against the scheme? I am a Trade Unionist, and I say that Trade Union bonds should be respected – but often in my quiet moments of reflection I try to visualise the sodden fields of Flanders; the scorching, fly-infested deserts of Egypt and Africa; the grave-strewn routes of Palestine and Mesopotamia – and I ask myself the question, what am I sacrificing? Grumble? Complain? Yes, I know I do, but not when I am visualising those fields. Uncomplaining in the most trying circumstances, unflinching before an unscrupulous foe, these men are steadily going forward to victory. They are sacrificing their all, and in that sacrifice are emptily appealing to us for our unselfish support and co-operation.

"Let the Government take over all means of supply, not hesitatingly, but fearlessly and give to us, honest and dishonest, profiteer, hoarder, and the starving poor, the nearest possible scheme to "Equality of Sacrifice".

Conversations (10) Truthfulness By George E Hobbs
(First published: November 14, 1917)

My dog Tiny is a good dog – at least that is my opinion. I am quite aware that this claim may be refuted by others; my wife, for instance though she would not go so far as to say that Tiny was a vile dog yet would hesitate to endorse my opinion for her. It is strange how one's opinions alter. When Tiny was a puppy she was "a dear", according to the wife, now she is a "clumsy great thing", with many etceteras added thereto. I know that there are times when Tiny may reasonably be likened to a whirlwind – that much I have already admitted – and this is especially the case when she usurps the cat's duties and sets off a-mousing.

A little while ago I arrived home at 6 o'clock in the morning. Having let myself in and lit the gas, a whine indicated to me that Tiny was ready to give me a welcome. I let her in, and after her usual greeting she suddenly became very exerted. Looking to see the cause of her agitation, I espied a mouse hanging upon the curtains almost at the top of the window. Upon shaking the curtains the mouse, with acrobatic agility, landed lightly upon the floor, but not liking the look upon Tiny's face immediately ran under the nearest chair.

Now followed what I may justly call "Pandemonium", and justified, to some extent, the wife's opinion that Tiny was a clumsy great thing. The back of the mouse was clear of the rung of the chair by about seven inches: Tiny's back was about six inches above the rung. Seeing with what beautiful freedom the mouse could traverse the floor Tiny thought she could do the same, with the result that, as Tiny went to obtain a closer acquaintanceship with the mouse, the first chair taking a horrible list to port crashed with a mighty crash to the floor. Chairs number two, three, and four followed in quick succession, and as the fourth chair settled down in an inverted position I heard a squeak.

I was thankful indeed to hear that squeak, for it meant that the mouse had received its quietus. I scarcely cared to contemplate what would have happened had the mouse taken into its head to have visited each room in succession. The "lust to kill" was so strongly upon Tiny that she was in all truth an irresistible force, and being such, no article of household adornment or of utility would have been sacred to her. "Immoveable objects" would be a phrase unknown in her dictionary, for kill she must, even though the house came down about her ears.

In the midst of the upheaval there came a voice from above: "What is the matter down there? Have you taken leave of your senses?"

"It's all right," I exclaimed exultantly. "Tiny's caught a mouse! Good dog, Tiny!"

"A mouse!" mocked my wife, in tones of exasperation. "That's just like you. I suppose half the furniture is broken. I'd give her 'mouse' if I came down there – clumsy great thing."

There it was again, "clumsy great thing", and yet with all her peculiar canine characteristics, I repeat she is a good dog. I say it because I think it; and because I think it I am going to think her a conversationalist, and contrast her morals and mannerisms with another individual of the animal tribe whom I have unfortunately come into contact with.

It is rare that I find myself without an appetite for something. At all times I strive to profitably "buy up the moments as they pass". A day or two ago, however, I found myself without occupation. I was feeling ill, physically, and even pursuit seemed to have a nauseating effect. I could not read with profit; neither could I settle to write; so, making myself as comfortable as possible before the fire, I tried to direct my thoughts into those channels that are always a source of delight to me when I am "fed up". The vastness of space. Was there a centre of attractions? If so, where was that mysterious globe situated? A globe so mighty as to baffle all powers of mathematical calculation – or even of human conception. A globe around which all known and unknown suns and systems revolved.

Yes; an hour of riotous mental speculation, with all its significant spiritual stimulation, has often helped me when passing through a "fed up" period. (One of these days I would like to record my impressions of an hour of such riotous thinking.)

As I sat there, the quietude was broken by a rasping voice exclaiming "You are a fool-dog, and a ranting old hypocrite into the bargain. If you had half-an-ounce of pluck in you you'd do as I say." The voice was that of our occasional visitor, the scoundrelly cat, and evidently he was inciting Tiny into a course of action which, as yet, was not clear to me.

"Does it require pluck to tell an untruth, then?" asked Tiny quietly. Ah, that was the cat's game, was it? Well, I would listen to see what the outcome of this argument would result in.

"Untruth? you silly old duffer," laughed the cat, "where does the untruth come in? All that you have to do is to say you don't know."

"Look here." replied Tiny, "let me present the case as it appears to me. I was lying here upon the rug half asleep when a mouse ran across the room, and before I could prevent it, it climbed up the table-leg and got upon the table. There was, I know, a tiny hole in the table cloth, and in my eagerness to catch the mouse – knowing the master's aversion to mice upon the table – I accidentally tore the cloth. It –"

"That is just what I said," interposed the cat. "There was a hole in the cloth in the first place, and seeing that you made it larger in a praiseworthy effort to assist your master, as you term him, and seeing also that it was a pure accident, you would be perfectly in order to refuse all knowledge of the greater rent. In other words, if you are questioned upon the matter say you don't know anything about it. If you do acknowledge your guilt," he added, significantly, "don't forget it will mean a hiding for you."

"Yes," said Tiny, miserably, "I know what my confession will invoke. But!" and her voice took a clearer note, "I have heard master say that truth was like a straight line, having no curves or angles, and that if one wishes to be in possession of a good character, one must not side-step even by a hair's breadth from the line."

"Master," said the cat with a sneer, "who is he to set himself as an authority upon what truth is, and what it is not? Humans tell untruths, and I dare say when it suits his purpose he does the same; only, in his lordly way, he would call it diplomacy – an inexactitude justified by the circumstances – but he would be a liar all the same."

"Yes," replied Tiny, "there is no doubt humans are fallible and often do things which in their better moments they would scorn to do. But master says that –"

"I don't want to hear what master says," interposed the cat rudely. "All I ever hear from him is 'Out you go, you prowling thief' or 'Don't let that pirate in here' – but I'll be even with him yet. I'll –"

At that moment I heard an ominous growl, with sufficient menace in it to make the cat pause and change his manner of speech. "All right!" he exclaimed, "Keep your bristles down, I won't hurt your precious master. If I've got to hear what he said let's have it quick."

"Yes," replied Tiny, "I will tell you; but first of all let me advise you to cultivate a more civil manner, and to be less frequent with your threats. As I was saying, master says that two sets of principles are ever surrounding human life. One set he calls 'Positive' or right principles, the other he calls 'Negative' or wrong principles. He further says that these two can never be merged together because the one is the direct opposite to the other. Right principles must for ever remain right; wrong principles must for ever remain wrong."

"That's all right so far as it goes," said the cat, "but I've heard that humans, as good, if not better than your governor, say that circumstances alter cases, and that applies in the present case."

"In reply to that," observed Tiny, "Master says that irrespective of any circumstance that would suggest the contrary, wrong principles can never be converted into right principles. An act is either a right act or a wrong act. A thought, word, or desire can only be a right or a wrong thought, word, or desire. Especially did I hear him say that an untruth needed no adjective to indicate its status, but that white, black, little, and big lies all stood upon the same level. I feel, therefore, that the course of action I must follow must be to acknowledge, without equivocation, that I tore the cloth."

"And you know what to expect?" queried the cat. "Yes," replied Tiny; "but whatever is involved I must tell the truth."

At that moment I thought it was time to test the sincerity of Tiny's resolve. Casually walking into the kitchen I glanced across the table, and there I saw that there was indeed a rent in the table cloth. It was not a large one, but certainly large enough to be noticeable. "Who's torn the table cloth?" I asked with a show of temper, at the same time taking down the dog-whip from the nail upon which it was hung.

"Was it you?" turning to the cat, and raising the whip above my head – but the cat had fled. I turned to Tiny, still in a menacing attitude. "Was it you?" I asked roughly. Poor Tiny: how she trembled. "Yes, master," replied Tiny bravely, "I tore the cloth in an endeavour to catch a mouse that had got upon the table. It was quite an accident, and I am sorry." I lowered the whip, and patting her upon the back said, "Ah, Tiny, if we humans only followed your example and, irrespective of the consequences to ourselves, lived, and spoke the truth, our characters would be more robust than what we find them at present."

The fire had burnt low; the gas had ceased to radiate the room with its light, but I awoke conscious that my sleep had done me good.

Conversations (25)
The Fox and the Cat
By George E Hobbs
(First published: March 14, 1919)

Young Reynard Fox was on the prowl. He had left his home in true fox-craft fashion; carefully selecting his way, he glided rather than walked, until there was no longer any danger of the precincts of the home he had just left being discovered. Once out of the copse he felt free, and off he started at a swinging gait across the fields to where he knew he could obtain food.

It was night, or rather early morning, and as he had been carefully instructed by his mother, he knew there would be no humans about to interfere with his objective. Over one field, down another, across the locks of the canal, and there lay the farm. But he did not stay there as one would have judged he would – in fact, he passed on without a turn of his cunning head. It seemed inexplicable; for it was known to the fox family that the farmer had a brood of nice young chicks. The explanation must be that young Reynard had been warned not to raid too near home. Away he went until he came to a farm several miles from the home-copse. And then he paused.

Though there was no need for any such action, yet one instruction of his mother's had entered deeply into his mind. "My son," said she to him one day, "the best time to hunt for food is just before the dawn, for at that hour humans are in their deepest sleep. "But," she added impressively, "I am sorry to notice that you exhibit traces of boastfulness and over-confidence in your own abilities. If you are not careful it will lead you into serious difficulty. When hunting for food at night never be too confident that danger is absent; always try the air!"

Thus it was he paused, and lifting his pointed nostrils into the air he carefully sniffed for the presence of humans. Feeling satisfied that all was clear, he moved towards the place where he knew the hens to be.

Not far away, another form moved, but so silently that Reynard had no knowledge of her presence. It was Tab, the farmhouse cat, and she was also prowling around. Tab's favourite relish was the sleek mice who daily fed upon the farmer's rich store of wheat. Often had she gone forth of a night and satisfied her hunger upon these well-fed creatures. Tonight however, her hunger being already appeased, she was venturing farther afield, and being in a sporting mood she was on the prowl for barnyard rats.

Something moved; and just at that moment the moon, which had gleamed brightly, now became obscured by a passing cloud. Reynard was crouching low upon the ground, and Tabby, a little bewildered by the sudden gloom yet knowing that something had stirred, sprang with true feline agility, and landed right upon young Reynard's back.

Now no self-respecting fox, old or young, could tolerate such an indignity, and Reynard (much to the distress of Tabby), demanded an instant and complete explanation for such conduct.

Poor Tab; how her heart fluttered as she felt herself shaken from Reynard's back, and the loose skin at the nape of her neck seized in his mouth.

"Oh! Oh! Reynard!" gasped Tab, "I must have made a mistake. The sudden darkness confused me – and I'm truly sorry!"

"Are you indeed?!" replied Reynard heatedly, releasing her from his mouth. "And I've a good mind to shake the life out of you!" This he said with more fear than temper in his voice; for Reynard had received a greater shock than he cared to own. In truth, as subsequent events will prove, Reynard was nothing but a boastful coward. "At any rate," continued he, trying to steady his voice so that his fright should not be known to Tab, "I'll look over it this time, because now we are here, I wish to ask you a question and I want you to answer it."

"All right, Reynard," said Tabby, grateful to think the incident had closed so easily for herself. "What is the question?"

"Suppose," began Reynard deliberately, "that on one clear, crisp morning you heard close at hand the huntsman's horn, and turning in the direction of the sound you saw a large pack of dogs making their way at full speed towards you. You knew without a vestige of doubt it was you they were hunting, and if caught it would mean death. Tell me, Tab... what would you do?"

"That needs very little consideration," replied Tabby promptly. "I should jump towards the trunk of that tree," (indicating a poplar tree with her right paw). "And as quickly as possible climb to the top. The dogs could not touch me there, and I do not think the humans would take the trouble to climb up and bring me down. That is what I should do, Reynard."

At this, Reynard laughed so uproariously that Tab wondered wherein the joke lay. Shaking the tears of laughter from his eyes, and proudly expanding his chest – as young Reynard could – he said (with emphasis upon the pronoun), "I should not do anything so undignified as to run up that tree." ([Of course,] he would [never] admit to Tab that he could not.)

"First of all, I should face them boldly to show that I defied them. Then, with perfect composure and ease, I should perform the tricks in which I am adept. I should run straight, double on my tracks, cross my tracks; in fact I should lead the dogs such a dance they would be glad to give up the chase in very disappointment and weariness. I..."

"Yes! yes!" interrupted Tab sarcastically, "you would, no doubt. But I notice that the tense of every verb you use is future. Is there no sentence in which you could use have instead of should?"

"Yes," sharply replied the nettled fox. "If you do not take care the sentence will be, 'I have killed Tab, the cat, for insolence.'"

"Oh, no offence!" said Tab hastily. "I only wondered if you had done these things, seeing you speak with such confidence. Then again," continued Tab with a sly look, "how is it so many of your tribe are caught? Do they not know these tricks?"

"Oh, yes," replied Reynard loftily, "but..."

At that very moment there came a sound which caused Tabby to bolt up the poplar tree in a very energetic manner. They had both been so engrossed in their conversation that the dawn and the ever strengthening day had escaped their notice; and the very circumstances suggested in Reynard's question had suddenly burst upon them.

As soon as Tabby felt herself to be safe, she settled down to watch how Reynard would conduct himself. Peering down she saw that the fox was indeed facing the direction in which the dogs and the huntsmen were approaching; but the look upon his face did not suggest bold defiance, but rather that of abject fear.

"Buck up, Reynard!" Tabby could not refrain from shouting at him. "That look of defiance ought to frighten them. Still, I wouldn't count too much upon that, if I were you. Get on with the tricks; they will soon give up in disappointment and weariness!"

The derision in Tab's voice pierced Reynard like a lance, and turning with a snarl of frightened rage, he attempted to run away as fast as he could. But what a sorry figure he was. His terror was so acute that his trembling legs refused to carry him. Again and again he fell to the ground, and at last with a piteous moan he turned, sank upon the green sward and awaited the coming of the dogs.

On they came in full cry, and surrounding Reynard they literally tore him to shreds. Not one tooth did he show in temper. Not one effort did he expend in defence of his life; it was thus that Reynard died.

Tabby sat very still for a while in an attitude of profound meditation. At last she roused herself and philosophised thus: "Ah, yes; I can see that words and deeds each have their respective values; and deeds must ever have the higher value. I see too that words and deeds have a relative value; for words must rise or fall in worth according to the worth of the deeds.

"Though I had a fair knowledge of Reynard's character, yet I can imagine there are beings who could make others feel small and insignificant as they recite what they would do under given circumstances. The poor, puny listener stands enthralled at the magnificent courage of the reciter, wishing in their deluded minds they also had equal propensities.

"Then comes the test – and deeds proclaim the value of words. The boasted feet of brass are found to be but feet of crumbling clay; and the apparent potential fighter is proved to be nothing but a resistless coward.

"I think," Tabby mentally concluded, "I will try and reverse the order a little. I will be a 'doer' first and a 'speaker' after – if I can. At least, I'll try."

[It's unclear which political figure of the day this is aimed at, but it may have been British Prime Minister David Lloyd George, who promised to wrestle war reparations from Germany "'til the pips squeak", but in private sought a settlement which was more akin to peace and reconciliation.]

A Good Riddance
The Message of 1921
By George E Hobbs
(First published: January 6, 1922)

In a large, brilliantly lighted room a company of people were seated around a table in an attitude of deep concentration. At the end of the table facing the West, an old man stood, whose flowing white beard revealed that his race was nearly run.

Deep furrows across his forehead revealed too that the race had been a hard and bitter one. He knew his time was short, and if he was capable of any feeling at all it was one of thankfulness that soon he would turn his back upon that assembled host and pass from their midst forever.

Over the west door was written: "Exit to the unknown," and even now the bolts were being slowly drawn for his passage through. Yes, he was ready to go.

He cast his gaze over the assembled folk, and a cynical smile flitted across his face as he saw them turn towards the East door. Mentally he followed their thoughts and read with them the mystic sign over its portals: "Entrance from the unknown."

He knew what they were waiting for; and he also knew their hopes could not materialise while he remained with them. A few brief moments yet remained for him, and though he dared not speak until spoken to, he trusted that speech would be forthcoming so that he may reply thereto.

The opportunity came simultaneously with his thoughts. Reluctantly the assembled folk withdrew their gaze from the East door and frowningly fastened their eyes upon the old man.

"Old man!" said the chairman, "in a few moments you will have left us and there is not one of us here present who will regret your departure. When you came through the East door from the shadowy unknown we welcomed you with open arms. We saw you as a sweet lovable babe. Innocence was stamped upon your brow and the virtue of many graces was delineated in your countenance.

"You grew rapidly and we were proud of your youth. But ere you had reached maturity we realised a gross deceit had been perpetrated upon us. Your innocence we found to be simulated. It was a cloak that hid your subtle intrigues. What we thought to be the virtue of many graces developed into vice of the most devastating form.

"You had the charm of an angel and with it, the sting of a devil. During your reign (for to a certain extent, we must acknowledge your sovereignty), men and women have been broken and children have wondered at the meaning of existence. We are glad you are going, old man and we trust never to see the like of you again!"

It was speedily evident that the assembled company fully endorsed the chairman's tirade against the bent old man, for loud and sustained applause followed his remarks.

Then there came a pause, and again an eager glance went towards the door. But the time was not yet fully come. When they looked again at the old man, they were astonished to see his form standing erect, while from his eyes there flashed the fires of a controlled passion.

The Old 'Uns Message

"Gentlemen!" said he, sweeping his eyes over the company. "I am glad you have given me an opportunity of speech. My time, as you say, grows short.

What I have to say must be said quickly. I am glad to see assembled here all classes of society: businessmen, politicians and ministers of the Gospel. I see employers of labour and the workers. In your company I see men of utility and human parasites. A goodly company, gentlemen! A goodly company indeed!

"Fearlessly I have been indicted by your chairman, and the applause which followed is clear proof you are in agreement with his indictment. I do not even pretend to be upon my defence. Fearless as your chairman was, I turn the tables upon you, gentlemen, and tell you that the crime is not mine – but yours.

"Even as you indict me so you have indicted yourselves. I am what you have made me and I could be no other. My crime pales before yours, gentlemen. You are lords of your own actions. I, and my order, must ever be the creature of circumstances.

"How much of my failure is due to you who are politicians, I leave to your own conscience. If you have played fast and loose with the sacred cause entrusted to you, if you have allowed "party" to take the place of integrity, the mills of Divine retribution will render to you your dues.

"And you businessmen; you who dare not show to the world the difference between your buying and selling, how dare you applaud when you know your hands are filthy with the grime of fraud and deceit.

"And what of you who are ministers of religion. How you applauded with the rest! And yet there are some of you who are flagrantly responsible for my failure. There are some of you who think more of adherence to a ritual than the salvation of men. Some of you from the soft ease of your pulpits have dealt out platitudes and indulged in insipid generalities to those who were hungering for man's food.

"Some of you have hurled challenges to the devil from the pulpit but you dared not come down and challenge him in the world of everyday commerce and industry. And yet you applaud your chairman's indictment of me!

"And you workers that toil in the busy marts. Are you guiltless in this matter?

"You who profess fidelity to equality and practice inequality. You who say all men should be brothers and daily contradict your word. You who ask for honesty to yourself yet will not be honest to others!

"Gentlemen, the East door is opening. My little successor will be with you in a moment. I, Anno Domini nineteen twenty-one, bids you farewell. All that I ask is that you will be kinder to my little successor, Anno Domini nineteen twenty-two than you have been to me.

"It is actions that count, gentlemen, not words. Farewell!"

Chapter 10

George Hobbs and the Spirit World

Arguably the most curious of the curiosities in George Hobbs's body of work is his seven-part excursion into 'the spirit world'. It is a lengthy exploration of spiritualism, but what kind of spiritualism?

Written towards the end of the second decade of the 20th century, when the fad of spiritualism as a religious movement was coming to an end, it appears to dabble in that more formal theology, which is based on mortals making contact with spirits, either through mediums or directly. But it seems just as much concerned with the more philosophical definition of spiritualism as we might define it today, which explores ideas about the spirit that might be within all of us, and how looking within ourselves might lead to enlightenment.

Although his report is delivered through an imagined conversation with his dog, Tiny, it seems George actually experienced what he considered to be a genuine meeting and 'conversation' with a spirit. We know this because of an exchange of letters in the pages of the *Advertiser*, which we have attached to this chapter as a footnote.

To discover that George is not only open to the idea of deep meditation, but has practised it, puts him decades ahead of the time when it might have been freely accepted (in Britain, at least) as being of potential benefit to the human spirit, and confirms what all his writings tell us: a deep-seated desire for knowledge.

In Part One, Tiny is the first to observe the apparition whom George is seeking to contact, but he finally succeeds (albeit briefly) in achieving the concentration necessary to establish his own higher spiritual intercommunication. Then, in

Part Two, he recounts his second visit to the spirit world and details his conversation with a spirit messenger, lamenting that man's pursuit of knowledge and reason has adversely impacted on his capacity for faith and, thereby, on his ability to reconcile 'the seen and the unseen, the discovered and the undiscovered, the material and the spiritual'.

By the fourth instalment, George draws parallels between the Old Testament story of Naaman, and his own situation, whereby his attempt at seeking spiritual revelations from the messenger in Part Three had been rebutted – all because he was more intent on pursuing his own transcendent fulfilment at the expense of his duties to those around him.

The series then segues into The Revelation of Love. This time, he goes on to recount the details of his latest spiritual jaunt in which an old man commands him to research the meaning of love, followed by his mysterious meeting with a young girl and her broken doll – and then a tragic encounter with a mother and son.

Finally, he witnesses the betrothal of two star-crossed lovers. But with an end-game that is highly suggestive of a thinly-veiled plea for sexual equality in relationships, the girl declares that women must be wary of men's motives – as lust and possession may be masquerading as love. And yet, according to George, the only pure love is the love of God.

Remember that while all this sounds like The Beatles and others experimenting with 'new' ideas in the 1960s and coming to the conclusion that *all you need is love*, what we are actually witnessing is an ordinary industrial worker and Methodist Churchman doing something not dissimilar, almost exactly half a century earlier.

Curiouser and curiouser!

Conversations (18)
Can Mortals Hold Communion With the Spirit World? Yes!
By George E Hobbs

(First published: April 19, 1918)

"For goodness sake, don't be so restless, Tiny! Here have I been trying to concentrate my thoughts sufficiently to write, and you have done nothing else but wander about the room and whine. Whatever is the matter with you?" I said with a feeling of intense irritation. Tiny paused in her relentless wandering, and coming close to me said in a shaky whisper, "Didn't you see it, Master? It was quite close to you."

"See what?" I asked sharply, putting down my pen and turning round to her. As I looked at her, I found that she was in a state of keen agitation, and in her faithful eyes there lurked unmistakably the look of fear. "What is it, Tiny?" I asked more gently. "What did you mean when you said, 'Didn't you see it, master?' What is there to see?"

"Master," replied Tiny, looking round apprehensively, "this is the third time it has come."

"What has come?" I asked. "Do try and compose yourself, and at the same time, be more lucid in your explanations."

"Master," replied Tiny quickly, "you know that you have moods of abstraction; when, though you breathe, you seem to lie inert and unconscious. You have told me that during those periods you try to force your spirit away from its physical encasement; that it may journey into realms unknown to ordinary mortals, and that there you may converse with the higher spiritual intelligences."

"Yes, Tiny," I answered, "that is so; but so far I have not met with positive success. It was very difficult at first to command the requisite power of concentration, but gradually it has come. Just recently, on three different occasions, it seemed as though I were about to realise my desire, but at the crucial moment something has intervened and broken the spell."

"Ah! That must have been the same three occasions of which I speak," said Tiny, reflectively. "The first time I saw this being," she added, "I tried to rouse you, for I could see at a glance it was no ordinary mortal. It was certainly of human aspect, but shadowy and ethereal in substance, and as I tried in vain to rouse you, the being vanished.

"As it vanished I heard a voice, which said, 'I have some of your bidding, but you are not yet ready to receive me.' On the second occasion the same thing happened, except that the voice intimated that, though you were not yet ready, you were nearing the goal. Tonight master, you were not in a state of absolute concentration, and the being vanished without a word."

"Thank you for what you have told me, Tiny," I replied. "It convinces me that I am nearer success than I thought. Success will come," I cried exultantly; "It will! It must! And now leave me, Tiny," I continued, when I had become calmer. "But before you go, let me tell you that should you see this being again, do not fear, for no harm will come to you."

When Tiny had left me I continued to sit for a time in deep thought. Was the time ripe for another, and perhaps this time a more successful attempt in my effort to commune with the spirit world? Were not the words of the celestial visitor as repeated to me by Tiny, pregnant with hope?

"I have come at your bidding, but you are not yet ready to receive me," the messenger had declared. Yes, I mentally resolved, so soon as earth sounds are hushed, and night has wooed restless nature to sleep, I will make one more attempt; this time I believe success will attend my effort.

As the shades of night settled down upon the earth, the conviction came to me that, writing as I had been in the earlier part of the evening upon a subject totally different to the one upon which my thoughts were now turning, my mind was not in a fit state to apprehend the discovery of communion with the spirit world. I must cleanse my mind of all materialism; and for that purpose I went into the open air for a while.

How beautiful was the night! It was full of the fragrance of Divine whisperings. The sky was devoid of clouds, and over to the West, the moon, a thin golden crescent, was gradually lessening her altitude. Around the pole star, in countless numbers, revolved the stars, in obedience to the laws of the Great Architect.

There shone the neighbourly Sirius with bold lustre, challenging through millions of miles of intervening space the supremacy of our own sun. There, the Great Bear, ever keeping its nightly watch upon our island home, still retained its beautiful symmetry of order and distance. There the mysterious Pleiades, holding in its grasp the secret of universal control. Here again was the fiery Mars in all the glory of reflectivity; and as I watched I felt my soul stir within me.

The day certainly "uttereth speech", but it is the night that "showeth knowledge".

My first act upon returning to my room was to stop the ticking of the clock. It was intensive concentration that was necessary, and I wanted nothing to irritate or retard the progress of that concentration. Making myself as comfortable as possible, I made one more attempt to penetrate the veil. This time the struggle for spiritual ascendancy proved to be the most severe I had as yet passed through.

The physical retained a tenacious grip upon the spirit, refusing to release it even temporarily from its prison. After a time the physical grew weaker, and gradually to my intense joy, I begin to lose the sense of natural surroundings. One more struggle of awful intensity, and with blissful ecstasy I realised I had at last reached the goal of my desire.

"I have come at your bidding, and this time you are ready for me," said a voice at my side, and looking up I beheld a being of supernal splendour, whose regal bearing filled me with awe.

"Spirit!" I answered, "the desire of my heart has at last been realised. I had long believed it possible for the spirit of mortals to hold communion with the 'higher' intelligences of spiritual existence; but my difficulty, in the first place, was the means by which this was attainable. While brooding over this possibility I felt that concentration of the mind was the medium."

But the difficulty again manifested itself by my apparent inability to concentrate with sufficient intensity. The consciousness that spiritual intercommunication was attainable was the hope to which my soul has ever been anchored, and helped me against my constant failures. Slowly but surely I was enabled to detect, and to eliminate the hindrance that barred my progress.

"Now, I have attained?"

"Yes," replied the spirit, "you have attained to that which few mortals have done; but which is the possibility of every human. We in our sphere are often saddened at the inability of mortals to hold communion with us; but, as the means of communication must ever lie in the hands of man, we are powerless to establish communications until man has discovered the means. As you now know, pure, uninterrupted concentration of the mind is the means by which intercourse is secured. And now, what are your wishes?"

"My wishes are many and various, O spirit!" I replied. "But chief among them is the desire for knowledge."

"But you have your philosophers and teachers, your scientists and logicians," objected the spirit. "It is to these you must look for knowledge. Mortals have been endowed with reason and..."

"Spirit, that is true," I interposed. "But, though it may seem a paradox, it is also true that with the increase of human wisdom there comes an increase of confusion. Mortals are ever discovering 'solid rocks', and even as they stand in bold and haughty defiance upon them, they find to their dismay that the solid rocks are, after all, only sinking sand."

"And what can be the cause for such a deplorable state as this?" queried the spirit, interestedly, yet aghast at such a statement.

"Spirit!" I answered, "I do not profess to a knowledge of philosophy; neither am I teacher, scientist, or logician; but, thinking long upon this matter, I have reached an opinion, which humbly, I will unfold to you."

At this point my physical part, having recovered from its recent struggle, reasserted its power, and brought back again my spirit to its prison.

But, I do not fear. I have the secret!

I shall journey again to the spirit world.

Conversations (19)
A Record of My Second Visit to the Spirit World (2)
By George E Hobbs
(First published: April 26, 1918)

Before I set on record the happenings that be-fell me on my second journey to the Spirit realm, I wish to say that as spirits are sexless I ought to address such as "It" or "Its" according to the case of the pronoun. But as spirits are also personalities, I think it will be better – at least I shall be better understood – if we assume the masculine gender, and address such spirit as "He", "Him", and "His" according to its cases. And now to resume:

Upon my return to the spirit world – which event I found easier than at the first – I made two important discoveries. They were discoveries which verified certain conclusions that I had already formed in my own mind. First, I found the celestial spirit in the same attitude of attention as when I had left him two nights previously. This for the moment puzzled me, for, as I say, one whole night and two whole days had intervened since I had last conversed with him. Suddenly, my own convictions came back to me, and I remembered that I had already formed the opinion that time was a thing unknown to the dwellers of infinity. To me a space of time had elapsed – to the spirit it was merely the continuation of our conversation without a break or pause.

The second discovery that I made was one upon which I had not been quite so pronounced; hence, not having definiteness, I have spoken in orthodox language by saying that my spirit "journeyed" to the spirit world. We speak of "rising", "ascending", and "journeying" when the spirit leaves the body, but I discovered that these terms are merely figures of speech. I found that the spirit "land" was simplified into a state of being, rather than complicated by localisation.

The severity of the struggle in my first spiritual cleavage was so intense that a detailed account of its separation was impossible. But as the second effort was less severe, I was able to pay more attention to the process. Even now the physical struggled to retain the spirit; and I realised that it was due to this very resistance that gives rise to the idea of "ascending" and "rising". The spirit, whose very nature is to be free and untrammelled, ascends to escape the restraining clutches of the physical. From my experience, I suppose that when physical death takes place, the ascension of the spirit would not be so noticeable owing to the fact that there would be no physical resistance.

To recapitulate a moment: As a full revelation can only come by passing through the gateway of physical death, I do not hereby claim that I received a full revelation. But I assert most emphatically that my discovery was such as to lead me to understand that the spirit "land" was essentially one of individual conscious perception. I want to remember this great discovery; for not only do I now know that spirit life is ever around me, I also know that when the final change is at hand, I have no "journey" to face, but merely a change of perception.

Another discovery I made, and one which I wish to deal with later, was that when once the clogging elements of the flesh had been laid aside the feeling was one of exhilaration and contentment. So much then for my first discoveries. As I have already stated, the spirit was in an attitude of attention waiting for me to continue our conversation. So, adapting myself to the situation, I said: "My humble opinion why confusion grows simultaneous with human wisdom is that mortals have allowed the servant to become the master. Nay, even further, they have allowed the creature to assume the rank, and claim the prerogatives of the "Deity".

"As I am not a disembodied spirit, and therefore not of mortal extraction, you must pardon me if I say that I do not quite follow you," replied the spirit.

"Let me explain in detail," I answered, "for I realise that you will wish to understand the position fully before you grant my request for higher and more advanced knowledge. He whom you serve in serenity and in faithfulness, endowed man with a capacity for knowledge, and the faculty by which that capacity is served we call reason. This divine faculty, however, was not poured upon man in its completeness and full fruition, but, for reasons which appear to me to be obvious, was hedged about with flexible limitations. For the moment we will say that to limit this divine gift was an act of short-sighted stupidity. Reason fettered by boundaries leads to suppositions of grotesque proportions, and diametrically opposes the end that I opine the Deity had in view."

"Enough, mortal!" cried the spirit vehemently. "Dare you an attempt to pierce the veil that hides the will of Omniscience? Your presumption outruns your discretion!"

"Spirit!" I replied, "were I within the confines of the physical I should indeed hesitate; but here in the spirit, even as I have been conversing with you, spontaneous insight has come, and the gaps that I so much feared in my recital are now filled and connected before me. On these grounds, and having mortal experience behind me, I dare to propound an opinion as to the end the Deity had in view concerning man."

"You are presumptuous, mortal!" said the spirit decidedly. "But pray proceed."

"The Supreme Intelligence," I continued, "wished mortals of human mould to be creatures of thought and of responsibility, hence the endowment of the capacity for knowledge and the faculty of Reason. By the limitation of Reason, O Spirit, it means that the capacity for knowledge would be served but slowly; that, as generations of men succeeded each other, the mind of the race would gradually develop and expand; with the result that the limitation of each succeeding age, being flexible, would be thrown farther and farther back. This aspect, however, held the possibility of bitter disappointment and despair. The men of an age would tremble upon the brink of discovery. Failure after failure would be recorded in the attempt to unravel the mystery, and just as the great discovery was about to be made, that age would pass away. But would they die disappointed? No! for Divine Wisdom has given to man another faculty which links up the seen and the unseen, the discovered and the undiscovered, the material and the spiritual, and to which we give the name Faith. Reason, then, was given to man to guide him to a knowledge of his resources, and to lead him right up to the barrier of temporary impossibility. And Faith was given that he may look forward into the darkness and see – how, he would not know – the impossible becoming the possible. Such, O Spirit, is the opinion that I hold regarding this matter. Am I intelligible to you?"

"Fairly so," replied the spirit in a non-committal tone, "but how works this combination of gifts?"

"Ah, spirit!" I answered sadly, "we are now coming to the tragedy of which I spoke in the opening sentences of my remarks to you. As the mind of the race developed, and the items of temporary impossibility became the items of accomplishment, man gradually allowed his faculty of Faith to fall into disuse. This, as you may well suppose, has proved fatal to the advancement of real knowledge and wisdom. Reason of itself leads but to confusion. Every conceivable subject has its schools of conflicting thought. But had the faculty of Faith been allowed equal development with Reason, Faith would have lessened the distance between these conflicting thoughts and converged them to a common centre. Then that which is most desirable would have been brought about and man would have experienced, not unison of thought, but harmony of thought. As it is, O Spirit, the higher reaches of knowledge are now denied to man, for knowledge or power by Faith is a lost possession. There are exceptions, but they are the exceptions that prove this rule. Modern opinion says in effect: "Faith! Poof! Reason is the arbiter of knowledge! And in the enthronement of Reason to the sacrifice of Faith lies the cause, in my opinion, of the lack of true wisdom, and of the confusion of thought. It is for this cause that I ask for higher and more complete knowledge."

"If it be as you state, do you think it possible for man's position to be retrieved?" asked the spirit.

"Yes," I replied, "it is possible. But it can only be brought about by developing the faculty that serves man's capacity for spiritual knowledge – Faith."

"Well," said the spirit, "you have now given me the position as far as you can interpret it, and now what is your request?"

"I would know, O Spirit," I replied, "Death in its power and process! Life and its graduations! Love in its essence!"

"You ask hard things," answered the Spirit, "but such as is needful you shall know."

Upon my return to the physical I felt there were great revelations awaiting me, and I laid myself down to sleep, content.

Conversations (20)
A Record of My Third Visit to the Spirit World (3)
By George E Hobbs
(First published: May 3, 1918)

In setting out the record of my third visit to the spirit world, I am painfully conscious it is not the record I should like to have written. It is true I made some valuable discoveries and was taught some useful lessons; but in so far as the great revelations are concerned my visit was a failure.

And the cause of that failure lies with myself. I know that by a stroke of the pen I could easily make the record read more attractive, and by doing so, place myself in less odious light. In fact, perfect candour demands the truth – that such temptation did assail me; but if I had succumbed to such mental suggestions the records would not then have been a faithful one. As it is my wish, however, to record experiences and not to weave a phantasy, I must be true to those experiences, and I therefore record the following:-

There are times when impetuosity may be classed as a virtue; there are other times, alas, when to be too precipitate ends in disaster. I use the interjection "alas" because I have found to my sorrow that such is true.

Through man's enthronement of reason to the sacrifice of faith, much of the knowledge that should have accrued to him has been denied him; and I, falling into the same universal error, have had to pay toll in lack of understanding.

When, therefore, the spirit with whom I had conversed promised to reveal the knowledge that I sought, I not only looked forward to those revelations with keen delight, but I also made a mental resolution that the following evening should see me once more in the spirit world.

Having my mind thus made up, I turned contentedly into bed and enjoyed a repose that was wholesome and dreamless. My first thoughts upon awaking were such as brought humility, and filled me with awe. Soon, within a few short hours I should be experiencing what but few mortals have experienced, and in possession of knowledge that even still less have known.

How often had I dwelt upon that great elusive mystery – life! And as once more I thought of it, there came to me the first stanza of some lines I had written only a little while before:

What is Life?

To human minds a mystery:
A puzzle, maze, an unsolved quest!
Deep e'en as man may probe, yet still,
Are deeper depths beneath his feet:
The sages of the years agone,
The mystics of medieval age,
The schoolmen with their hoary locks,
And modern philosophic mind,
Have sought to solve the mysteries
That lie beneath the cloaking veil:
Have sought, and still are searching yet;
Have sought, and searching, find it not.

And then, love! How many and varied were the interpretations given to this attribute. I remembered how on one occasion I was pondering deeply upon the essence of love, and finding no satisfying answer, fell asleep. The experience resulted in the writing of some verses, one of which was:

> What is love then in its essence: What its scope and energy?
> Did it give but for reclaiming, was it circumscribed, or free?
> This is what I pondered deeply, while the stars their vigil kept,
> 'Till old Somnus came and claimed me, and I laid me down and slept.

And then, Death! That mysterious change that once I feared, but now no longer feared. This was the knowledge I sought; it would soon be mine – and I went about my daily duties with pleasurable energy, anticipating the forthcoming joy of the evening. Suddenly, in the midst of my joy, there came a reactionary shock. My memory had proved faulty, for on this very evening I now remembered there were certain duties that had to be performed. Here, then, was a problem of some difficulty. The duties were essential – that I knew, and at any other time the fulfilment of the obligations involved would have been pleasurable to me.

But now a greater pleasure was anticipated. What should I do? I knew, too, that if I failed in these mundane responsibilities it would create disorder of some magnitude, as well as bring pain to faithful hearts. But what of that compared to the great revelations that were about to be unfolded to me? Debating thus with myself, I set my face steadfastly against all that it would mean, and chose the revelations in preference to those duties that should have been performed.

Having settled this difficulty to my own satisfaction, I now made preparations for my visit to the spirit world, and in so doing I came face to face with another difficulty. I found upon this occasion it required much more force of will to realise spirit perception than at either of the previous times. The reason of this was that my mind had a dual function of some complexity to perform: that of expelling the thought of my neglected duties, and of impelling thoughts consistent with my intended change from the physical to the spirit.

Even this experience had an educational value, for it taught me that uncongenial thoughts can only be expelled from the mind by impelling other thoughts that are congenial. Intensive concentration upon the object that is wished for will so absorb the mind as to leave no room for thoughts antagonistic to that desired object. Thus, by impelling thoughts harmoniously attuned to spirit perception, I was finally able to leave the physical and visit again the spirit world. My attainment of spirit perception was rewarded by seeing the spirit ready to receive me; yet, for the moment, I scarcely knew whether it was fancy or fact, but my reception seemed less cordial than at other times.

"All hail, Spirit!" I exclaimed in salutation.

"Hail Mortal!" replied the spirit. "What would you?"

"What would you?" I answered, at a loss to understand his apparent forgetfulness. "I am come that you may reveal to me the knowledge that I seek. Did you not say that such was as needful should be revealed to me? Why then this question?"

"Mortal," replied the spirit, with keen emphasis, "none can apprehend the higher reaches of knowledge who fail in the lower – and you have failed! Spirits live ever in the present. They know nothing of time except as they meet certain needs of mortals. The present is therefore always at your disposal for higher knowledge. One short evening of time was asked of you to bring happiness to others, but you thought of your own happiness in preference; and, in consequence, no revelation can be given you until this wrong has been remedied."

"But it is now too late, O spirit," I objected, crestfallen to think that my selfish impetuosity had caused me to fail. "And, indeed, I am sorry," I added, hoping that an expression of contrition would have the effect of reversing the edict.

"There are two things I wish to say to you," replied the spirit, "and then this interview must end. It is this: Your experience should have taught you that opportunities once lost can never be recovered. You had to-night an opportunity of doing good, of bringing solace to some soul burdened by the cross of adversity. When you return to the physical, you will do your best to remedy the wrong you have done; but even then it will only be a partial recompense.

"Exactly the same circumstance will never present itself to you again, and consequently a lost opportunity can never be fully atoned for. Remember this if you wish for higher knowledge. Then, too, you expressed sorrow. What for? Do I need to ask, or you to answer? Your sorrow is the sorrow of ungratified desire, and not the sorrow of contrition. You are sorry for yourself, at being found out, you have not the sorrow of shame for neglecting your duty. Return to the physical, mortal, and remember that he who would attain to the greater must first of all be faithful in the lesser."

Such is the record of my third "visit" to the spirit world. The lesson that I am trying to assimilate is that one cannot ride roughshod over duty, without bringing in its train due castigation.

Conversations (21)
My Fourth Visit to the Spirit Land Leads Me to a Strange Experience (4) /The Revelation of Love (1)
By George E Hobbs
(First published: June 7, 1918)

I suppose it is the natural sequence of human nature mentally to decide the mode by which anticipated blessings will come to us. We see the end from the beginning – and are often thereby deceived. The example of Naaman, the Syrian Captain General, is a case in point. My own experience is another case in point – the details of which, in a moment, I will explain.

To take the case of Naaman, the Syrian. The circumstances are so well known – or, at least, I assume that they are such – that to rehearse them in detail would be but a waste of time. Suffering from the loathsome disease of leprosy, he was cut off from all social intercourse, and in consequence lived the life of a recluse, isolated and lonely. It is therefore no wonder that when he saw a straw floating by him, he clutched at it, and seizing it, held on tenaciously. A little Hebrew captive maid in the household of Naaman's wife had spoken and said, "If my master would journey to Samaria, the prophet there would recover him of his leprosy." And Naaman, with costly presents and a large retinue of servants, went down to Samaria.

On his way to the city, Naaman followed the usual order of human beings, and [orna]mentally dressed the stage and arranged the various actors to their respective positions. He would stand here as one of the chief actors, the guards and attendants as minor actors would stand there, and then silence waiting for the dramatic entrance of him by whom the cure was to be performed. But it did not work according to the envisioned rehearsal. The prophet merely sent out a message by one of his servants: "Go and wash in Jordan seven times," the message ran, "and thou shalt be healed!"

Naaman, mortified because the actual performance did not coincide with his prearranged plan, turned angrily away, saying as he did so, "Behold I thought – !" There lies human nature, and but for this advice given by one of his servants, and accepted by Naaman, he would have lost the great blessing that eventually came to him.

This brings me to my own case. Behold I thought – and my mental conjecture of ways and means proved to be different to the actual happening. I cannot be blamed, I think, for the mental arrangements I made. I believed that after faithfully fulfilling the conditions laid down by the celestial being – conditions of duty that unfortunately I had hitherto neglected – I should, by intensive concentration, again "visit" the spirit world, when the knowledge that I sought would be imparted to me. Certainly, the revelations came, but the circumstances surrounding them were totally different to what I had conceived they would be. For the moment I can offer no explanation, but merely record the dramatic happenings as they came to me.

* * *

It was strange, very strange. But who I was, or where I was, I had not the slightest knowledge. Subconsciously, I believed I had existed before, but where or under what conditions I did not know. Nothing stirred. Everything around me was cold, colourless and still. Suddenly, I experienced a tingling sensation pass through my whole body, and I became sensitive to warmth and light. Scarcely had this happened when I experienced another sensation, and I became sensitive to movement and sound. Then followed an exquisite sensation, and I became sensitive to emotions.

Looking back upon my experience, the cry of my heart is – O, for the power of description! O, that I had command, not only of a perfect vocabulary, but also that I knew the supreme relative value of words. But this embellishment is not mine, and my descriptions must become the poorer for this lack. When nature assumed her resplendent garb, the barren wilderness around me became covered with a beautiful carpet of green. The trees became suffused with variegated hues, and through their branches the soft wind made beautiful music. In the air, the birds, rising upon their wings, trilled in joyous ecstasy; and all around was peace and gladness.

As yet I had not seen any of like being to myself, and I fell to wondering if I was the only one of my kind existing. Even as I communed with myself, I was at first startled, and then interestedly gratified to see, approaching me, one of like being to myself. And yet scarcely like myself; for whereas I was young, strong and rigorous, he that approached me came with halting and feeble steps. Snow white were his locks, and his face was scarred and wrinkled. As he came near he evinced no surprise at seeing me, either by manner, look or speech: though I must confess to a feeling of curiosity in myself as I waited for him to speak.

"Peace be with thee!" exclaimed the old man, and I, not quite understanding his salutation, merely repeated his words, "Peace be with thee!" My reply, or the tone in which I uttered it, caused him to look at me for a moment in a strange way. It was only momentary, however, for his brief but searching glance had told him the truth, that I was ignorant and untaught.

"What troubles you, son?" he asked, gently. "What is it you have upon your mind?"

"Sir!" I replied, "a while ago, how long ago I cannot tell you, I was inanimate and unconscious of the beauty around me. By a series of processes that I can only describe as sensations I gradually became sensible to this grandeur and its beauty has caused me to be greatly exercised in my mind as to how it came into existence. Can you tell me?"

"Ah!" exclaimed the old man with a smile, "that is the trouble, is it? Well, I will tell you the secret. Love brought it into being. Love is the creating and sustaining factor of all existence. The carpet of green, the blooming flowers, the sweet-scented hedgerows, the leafy trees, the mountains, hills and valleys, the boundless ocean, all this was brought into being by love."

"Love?" I exclaimed wonderingly, and there came to me, like the distant surging of the sea, an echo of memory. It was the solution of this very problem that I sought yet so vague were my reasoning powers, and so faint was the echo of memory that I could not interpret its message.

"Love," I said again, "what is love?"

"Son," replied the old man, "the world in which you and I find ourselves is occupied with sentient beings. Go, I pray you, among them, ask their interpretation of love, and bring the answers back to me. This much I will tell you: Supreme Love is a Being; therefore if you can discover what Love is, you will discover at the same time something of the personality whose name and nature is Love."

With this the old man left me, and there was nothing left for me to do but to commence my pilgrimage. But where should I go to find the people of whom he spoke? There was no one in sight, and no road to direct me to the dwelling place of these people. But staying winding along the valley and climbing the mountain side was a path which hitherto had escaped my notice. I decided, therefore, to follow this path wherever it may lead; and with the point of direction settled, I started on my journey to find from those I came into contact with their interpretation of Love.

Upon reaching the foot of the mountain, I climbed laboriously up its steep hill side till I reached a point where I could see the houses of those I was about to visit. Here I paused for a while to rest, and to try and form some method of procedure when I should reach these people. Though I thought long upon the matter, I found I could form no definite plan of action; so at last I proceeded on my way, resolving to be guided by the circumstances attending each individual case.

It was not long before I reached a town of fair size, and, entering the streets, the first thing to attract my attention was a being, similar to myself, but smaller and very fair to look upon. Bright blue eyes had this little one, and tresses of a rich golden brown; and she was seated upon a raised step in front of a house not far from me. Fearing to make my presence known, I stopped at the corner of the house and enchantedly watched her actions. Carefully folding some piece of material, she placed it round something that lay below her knees, and straining it to her little breast, commenced to sing in a low, sweet voice:

> Baby, dear baby, there's nothing to fear;
> Angels, bright angels watch over you, dear;
> Sleep then contented, O sleep on my breast;
> Folded in love, dear, secure you may rest.

Folded in Love! – Love! then this little one knows something of Love, I thought, joyously. She will be able to help me and thinking thus I approached the little maiden. When I had reached her side, I saw that what she had been singing over was a small lifeless image of herself. She called it a dolly, and smilingly held it up for me to see it. One of the legs and both of the arms were missing, and its face was cracked and broken.

"Yes, yes," I exclaimed somewhat impatiently, "but little one, I heard you sing of Love, can you tell me what Love is, for I am so anxious to know?"– and eagerly I awaited her answer.

(To be continued)

Conversations (22)
The Revelation of Love – continued (Part 2)
By George E Hobbs
(First published: June 14, 1918)

"Can you tell me the meaning of Love?"

That was the question I asked of the little maiden who had been singing over the lifeless image of herself. She called it a dolly, and when she held it up for my inspection I found it had one leg and both arms missing and its face was cracked and broken. "Love!" replied the little one – and her face became suffused with a wonderful light – "Yes, I know what Love is, it's what I gives my dolly. P'raps you'd like to hear about dolly and then you will know what Love is. Come and sit down here and I will tell you."

Being anxious to hear the little one's explanation of Love, I complied with her request and sat down beside her on the step.

"You know," she began, "we are very poor, and this is the first and only dolly I have ever had. Before I had her she belonged to a rich little girl; but when the arms and the legs came off, and the face was broked, I s'pose she got tired of her – and dolly was gived to me. I used to dream I had a dolly of my own, and when I waked in the morning and found it was only a dream it made me cry, for I was so lonely. But I am not lonely now I have got dolly, for I love her and she loves me. That's all."

"Yes, yes, little one!" I exclaimed, somewhat impatiently, "you say you love your dolly – as you call this lifeless imitation of yourself – but even then you have but explained to me what love is; that is what I am anxious to have told me."

The little girl gazed into my face with a look that clearly indicated she did not quite understand me. Evidently she thought that the declaration of love should explain itself. After a short pause she said, "Sometimes my dolly cries cos she's in pain or is lonely. When she does I just folds her in my arms and kiss her and she is happy again."

Then her childish voice sank to the lowest of whispers, and she looked about her apprehensively to see that no one was eavesdropping. "My dolly has never been hurted since I have had her," she whispered, "but one night she would have been hurted if I hadn't been there to protect her. When my daddy came home that night he frightened me. I don't know what it was, but he fell against the chairs and then the table. On the table was dolly, and when he saw her he tried to throw her to the floor. I don't quite know what he meant, but I heard him say in such a funny voice, 'My girl's as good as any other girl – not likely she's going to have others' left-off toys.'

Quick as I could I rescued my darling, but it made daddy angry; and taking a big stick, he shouted, 'Give the thing to me an' I'll break it into bits!' Course I wouldn't let him have her – and that made him worse. He said he would smash her in my hands if I did not let him have her. But I folded dolly in my arms, and turned my back to daddy – and – and, the marks are on my back – but he didn't hurt dolly."

And then she laughed with a gay sweet laugh. "But it isn't always like that," she said, "Dolly and I have lots of fun together, and we are happy 'cause we have each other. There!" she concluded with a smile, "I think you know what love is now, don't you?"

When the little maid had concluded her explanation, I sat for a time in deep meditation. I must confess that her simple recital had strangely moved me. Love, according to the tenets of this little girl, expressed itself in yielding protection when danger threatened; in bringing comfort to the heart bowed down with sorrow; in giving sympathy, and bringing ease to the pain-wracked, and in being the constant companion of the loved. The burdens were cheerfully borne by the lover, and the beloved became the happy possessor of joy unspeakable. Was this love? Oh thought sublime! Its rich fragrance caused my heart to race madly within me. But I suddenly placed a check upon my feelings, for my analysis was not yet complete.

As yet I had had no previous experience to guide me, consequently I identified the ideals of this little girl only with the broken and crippled doll. I could, in a crude way, appreciate the beauty of circumstances. The doll was a cast-off – despised and forsaken by its previous owner – and the starved soul of this lowly maiden had responded to its helplessness and hopelessness and she, in her own way, had discovered love.

Then my mind seemed to become more clarified, and with startling rapidity thoughts came to me that proved very disconcerting, and caused me finally to test the practicability of her ideals. How did the rich girl, who owned the doll before it was broken, interpret love? I conceived that when the doll was new it was a beautiful work of art. Eyes, ears, nose, hair would be the acme of perfection, and the clothes of the softest and richest texture. Would she have interpreted love to be protection, comfort, sympathy and companionship? If so, there was something that I could not fathom. Protection had not saved it from being broken, and the idea of companionship had not prevented it from being discarded and given away. If the poor girl's interpretation of love was the correct one, why did it contradict the acts of the rich girl?

And then I thought again. What would happen if a better doll was offered to the little one who still sat silently by my side? Would she forget in the dazzling beauty of a new and well-dressed doll, the helpless condition of her first doll? Would she scorn its missing limbs, and ragged clothes and its scarred and broken face? I remembered the touching pathos in her voice as she said, "It is the first and only dolly I have ever had" – would her interpretation of love stand the test of a trial? I felt afraid to try and experiment. Suppose she failed. It would mean not only that I should lose faith in my little friend, but also that the temple I was beginning to erect – wherein I was at last to find the divine – would be razed to the ground. I could not, however, bear the suspense, and I decided to put her to the test.

With this end in view I thanked her for what she had told me, and bade her good-bye. As she turned her sweet little face to me, and I looked into the limpid depths of those eyes of blue, I felt she would not – she could not – fail me.

Proceeding through the streets of the town, I was attracted to a house which stood apart from the rest, and to the front of which was a large window. When I reached the window I gasped in surprise, for here was a perfect galaxy of dolls, of every conceivable size and colour. Right in the centre of that bright army was one which surpassed all the rest in beauty of features and sumptuousness of dress. In peerless grandeur and regal bearing she stood, queen of that throng of inanimate beings. As I took a closer survey of that beautiful image, I realised with a quaking heart that the test was to be one of the utmost severity. Silken eyelashes adorned eyes that opened and shut at will. In the lobes of the delicately moulded ears were rings of pure gold, and around the shapely throat was a string of miniature pearls. When I looked at the waxed hands it seemed as though hands of flesh and blood were before me, so perfect were they in shape and upon one of the carefully detached fingers was a ring of great worth.

The clothes were of the richest texture, and were like the softened harmonious rays of a reflected rainbow.

It was with this radiant vision of inanimate loveliness that I was to test the validity of my little friend's statement. I must confess it was with faltering steps that I proceeded towards her with my burden.

As I approached the house I stepped softly, and her sweet voice reached me as she sang again, "Folded in love, dear, secure you may rest."

Abruptly I stood in front of her and held out my present. For a moment she scarcely understood the situation, and then I saw her face go deathly pale. She looked down at her ragged, limbless, broken doll, and then slowly returned her gaze to the lovely vision I held in my arms. Suddenly, with a cry that pierced my heart, she threw her poor broken dolly far out into the road, where it fell with a sickening crash and folded in her arms, the new doll.

"Little one! Little one!" I cried in an agony, "remember your words!" – but she heeded not my despairing cry; and at that moment a heavy cart came by and the forsaken dolly was crushed to a powder.

Blindly I turned away. I could not bear the sight of the little one in an ecstasy of delight; and I dared not look at that mangled mess in the road. Bitter thoughts surged through my brain, and my throat hurt at the intensity of my emotion. Those lofty ideals that I thought so real were after all only a mirage. My temple was demolished even before I had commenced to build. Love, instead of something to be desired, was vacillating and capricious; nay, it was even more deadly, more intolerable. It succumbed to ravishing beauty of form and dress! And pitilessly banished the old, the broken and the poor.

And then I thought of the old man's words. "Love is a being," he had said, "and when you have discovered love, you will then know the being whose name and nature is love." Know him? I hate him, if that is his character.

Conversations (23)
The Revelation of Love – Part 3
By George E Hobbs
(First published: June 25, 1918)

Note:- Having achieved, by intensive concentration, intercourse with the spirit world, I wished to have revealed to me "Love in its essence, Life in its graduations, and Death in its power and process." I am taken to a world occupied by sentient beings, and from there I am to learn what I wish to know. The following is the third part of the Revelation of Love. – GEH

When I had left the town wherein my hopes had been so cruelly shattered, I journeyed along the highway until I came to an isolated and deserted spot, and there I cast myself down on a sandy mound in a spirit of utter dejection. In sheer delight I had followed my little friend as she constructed her beautiful edifice of love. Protection, comfort, sympathy, companionship – joy! The masonry was of too substantial a character to sustain a fracture even and the building and the builder seemed to me to be conjointly one. How true had seemed her eyes; incapable of playing false. Yet, not only had the masonry sustained a fracture, but had been demolished; and even now was lying in a ghastly ruin. Those seemingly true eyes had glowed with a false light, and had lured me on to disaster.

And then came to me other thoughts. Perhaps her explanation was, after all, a correct one, but the failure had been in herself. That the trial had been severe I well know, and – yes; that must be the solution. The dazzling beauty of the new doll had temporarily deranged her judgement, and had caused her to falsify her own heart. Perhaps ere now she had repented of her weakness, and was yearning again for the one she would never more see.

Whether this was the explanation or not, I would not go back, but conquering my despair, would search in other directions that the real meaning of love may be revealed to me. Thus heartened, I resumed my journey, determining in my mind to hold myself in hand for the future, and not allow my emotions to lead me again through my former experience.

Soon I saw in the distance two persons walking towards me; and as they drew near I saw that one was attired after the manner of my little friend, and the other similar to myself. The one was tall and beautifully proportioned; the other was of diminutive stature, and about the age of the little girl whom I had recently left. In the conversation that ensued I found that they were mother and son. To the mother I addressed myself, and pleadingly asked if an explanation of love could be given to me.

"Love!" she replied. "Yes, I think I ought to be able to give you an explanation of love, seeing that I just deluge my boy with that quality."

"Then perhaps you can give me the details of its constitution and operations?" I asked with quickened interest – for whereas the little girl had only an inanimate doll as the object of her declared love, here was a living object on which love was said to be expended.

As I put my question to the mother, the little fellow detached himself from her detaining hand, and began to wander aimlessly about. She called to him in a gentle, coaxing voice to come again to her side, but he took not the slightest notice of her, and conducted himself as though she had not spoken.

"With anxious care I watch over my boy," said the mother, turning to me again. "And I shield him from every threatening danger. If he is in pain I comfort him, and, as I am his constant companion, the burdens that come upon his little shoulders I carry."

Then the explanation of my little friend was true after all, I mused thoughtfully. Here, again, it was given me almost in the words she had uttered. Protection, comfort, sympathy, companionship.

At that moment I was startled to notice that some distance from the road on which we were standing was a precipitous drop of great depth, and to which the little boy was getting perilously near. I called the mother's attention to this fact, and, with a cry of warning, she ran towards him: "Come back with mother, dear!" she exclaimed, pantingly, catching hold of his little hand.

"Won't!" he replied with asperity, and shook her restraining hand from him. "Boy's going to stay where he likes!"

"But look!" cried his mother, fearfully, "you are almost upon the edge of a steep cliff, and if you were to fall over you would be dashed to pieces. Come back with me to where it is safe and play there."

"Won't!" he replied again, and shook his little body in temper. "Don't want mother – boy's going to stay here!" After a while, however, his petulancy left him, and he allowed his anxious mother to lead him back again to safety.

During this little episode, my thoughts had been progressively at work. I felt that love must be somewhere along the track that the little girl, and this boy's mother had marked out.

I realised, however, that there was a mark of distinction between the two declarations; for the mother's statement of love had something about it which was lacking in the declaration of my little friend.

True, the little girl has been anxious about her dolly – taking the stripes upon her own poor little back rather than that her dolly should be hurt. But in the gestures and the general bearing of the mother, in the expression of her face, and the light of her eyes, all seemed to suggest to me that the anxiety was intensified. I could form no opinion as to its cause, hence I decided to question the mother further.

In reply to the questions I put to her, she replied, "He is my very own boy – my only child. He is a part of myself, and my whole life is bound up in him. No hurt can come to him but what the pain of that hurt is also felt by myself." And then she paused, and I saw the blood mount to her cheeks.

"The people that live near to us say that my sonny is naughty and wilful," she said slowly. And then her mood changed, and she exclaimed fiercely, "But it is an untruth! He is not wilful and naughty! And if he was," she added more calmly, "I love him too well to chide or correct him. Whatever he may wish for I give him. There is nothing but what I would do for his sake! – that is real love. What sinks beneath that is worthless!"

As I was about to reply, I noticed that the boy was making his way dangerously near to the edge of the cliff again. His mother and I had been so engrossed, she speaking and I listening, that we had for a moment forgotten the child. But now she too noticed his proximity to the dangerous edge, and quickly made her way to his side.

"Come away, dear," she said. "If you fall down there you will be killed! Come and play over here where it is safe."

"Won't!" he exclaimed decisively, "going to stay here! Don't want mother! Go away!" As he threw off her restraining hand he edged nearer to the cliff. Seeing the danger, I went over to the mother's help and took hold of the boy to carry him back to safety. In a moment he began to kick and scream, and his mother, with fury upon her face, exclaimed, "Put my boy down! How dare you lay rough hands upon him like that! Put him down at once!"

"But I am only doing it for his good," I replied, surprised at the mother's anger. "If I leave him here I am afraid he will fall over the cliff."

"Put my boy down!" she said again; and complying with her wish I placed him down upon his feet. The moment I had done so, he began to walk backwards from us, and his mother, with fear stamped upon her face, went towards him.

"Come back, dear," she cried. "Come – Oh!" – it was too late. The boy fell; and in trying to save her child, the mother, with an awful shriek, fell too.

Some distance away I saw a path which tortuously wound itself down into the ravine beneath. To this path I hastened and descended. The sight that met my view was terrible. The boy was injured so frightfully that to describe it would be nauseating. There he lay, injured and dead. I turned to the mother and found that though she had also received terrible injuries, she still lived. I did what I could for her, and presently, with a shuddering sigh, she opened her eyes.

"Sonny – my sonny," she panted.

"He is dead! I said sorrowfully.

"Dead?" she breathed rather than spoke, as though she tried to grasp what was meant. She tried to rise, but I gently laid her down again. "Ah, I know now, but it is too late," she cried, brokenly. "I have killed my sonny, and have caused my own injuries. Give me something to drink! Keep me alive till I have told you the fault. My idea of love was wrong. It caused my boy to be sullen and discontented, he was not happy in my love, and I can see now that I had spoilt him. Love is not what I said – that was mistaken love. Oh, sonny: if I had but remembered that love, real love, at times must find expression in correct – "

It was too much for her. Her heart had broken, and after a terrible convulsion she lay still. I called to her, but she answered me not, for she was dead.

How long I remained there I could not say; but presently I tore myself away from the hateful spot. The thought that hammered itself into my brain was, were there many young lives ruined through a mistaken idea of love? I hoped not. At any rate I was glad for this fact: The tragedy had been caused by a false idea of love, and that still left me with faith to believe I should yet discover the real love.

Conversations (24)
The Revelation of Love – Part 4
By George E Hobbs

(First published: August 30, 1918)

Note: Having achieved, by intensive concentration, intercourse with the Spirit World, I wished to have revealed to me Love in its essence, Life in its gradations, and Death in its power and process. I am taken to a world occupied by sentient beings, and from them I am to learn what I wish to know. The following is the fourth part of the "Revelation of Love." – GEH

It was a long time before I could throw off the feeling of depression that had come upon me as a result of the scenes I had lately witnessed. Poor little lad. Poor mother – according to her own statement – literally sacrificed upon the altar of a false ideal.

Viewing dispassionately the circumstances that had led up to the tragedy, I realised there was much that was beautiful in the declared love of the mother for her boy. She lived for him and him only. His joy was her joy, and his sorrow was her sorrow. "No hurt can come to him," she had said, "but what the pain of that hurt is also felt by myself. And the burdens that come upon his little shoulders I carry." Easing the burdens that seemed so great to him that he may be happy.

Happy! Ah! There was the difficulty, for she told me he was not happy, but sullen and discontented; and the sullenness and discontent was due to her misinterpretation of Love. Then it seemed to me that instead of easing his burdens, she had, by her own action, increased it; and how could she ease from him that which she pressed upon him?

Then again: What was it she was about to say to me when death supervened? "Love," she was saying, "sometimes finds expression in correct –"

And then death came.

Truly, I was in a maze, and in my present state I felt I could not solve the difficulty, or rightly to distinguish between the real and the ideal. I hoped, however, that as my knowledge increased I should be able to revert to the experiences I had passed, and should pass through and be able to give to each its true value. As it was, I must continue my investigation until at last I should discover real Love.

My next experience was prefaced by a series of events which, if not remarkable in themselves, led me to see how little things may become stepping-stones to the larger and more important things.

I had been walking for a long time in a reverie, scarcely knowing, or heading, in which direction I travelled, when I became conscious of a rich and beautiful melody. At first it seemed quite close to me, but though I gazed around me with eager intent, I could see nothing from which such music could emanate. Now it was growing fainter, and at last, with a trilling cadence, it ceased.

Puzzled at not being able to find the cause, and feeling somewhat tired, I sought some place in which I could rest a while. Some distance away I saw a green sward that looked refreshingly inviting, and to this spot I hastened. I had scarcely reached it and was about to throw myself down amidst its luxuriant growth, when a small feathered object rose hastily before me and swiftly ascended into the air. In a moment the beautiful song burst out afresh, and I saw that this little bird was the mysterious songster.

In an ecstasy of delight I followed its course. Up, up, up it went into the blue vault of space, ever singing its glorious song. Now it seemed to stay in its flight, resting on fluttering wings; then up again, with no cessation of its notes of joy. Now it was descending, slowly at first, then faster and faster, until, with lightning velocity, it seemed to hurl itself to the ground – and with its return to the ground the song abruptly ceased. I felt a new being for that song, it cheered and inspired me, and gave to me a degree of pleasure and happiness I had not as yet experienced. Could I not possess that little feathered friend that he may ever charm me with its silvery notes? I would try, and with this thought in my mind I threaded my way carefully and silently to where I had seen the little bird descend. Close by was a hedge full of the bursting blossom of rose and honeysuckle, and to this hedge I kept close, obscuring my movements as much as I possibly could.

Suddenly I paused with every nerve a-tingle and with hope rising high in my breast. Strong as my desire was to possess my little feathered friend, it vanished before the flood tide of a stronger purpose. Voices had reached me, and the theme of the conversation was love.

I had no consciousness that eavesdropping was wrong, consequently I listened with careful attention to all that was said. But first, who were these beings conversing upon the great problem, the solution of which I would give much to know? – conversing, too, in such a manner and tone as to suggest a familiarity with their topic. Peering between leaf and branch I obtained a view of them, and the sight thrilled me to my heart's core. I had seen the old man, the little girl, the mother and her boy, but here facing each other were two beings of the noblest mould and bearing.

The man was good to look upon; tall, strong, and broad of shoulders; yet, even with his height and breadth, he did not appear to me to be at all slow or awkward. Every attitude of his suggested to me alertness, energy, determination and intelligence. Yes, he was indeed good to look upon. And the maid with whom he conversed. Scarcely so tall as him, but I had the idea if she had been with herself, without the comparison of the man's height she would have appeared much taller than she now seemed. I could not imagine features more perfect, or limbs more graceful, and as she moved to and fro her very action was the rhyme and rhythm of poetry.

Passionately the man looked at her as though he would like to have taken her to his heart, yet he hesitated. Turning at last to her, and with arms outstretched, he said with thrilling intensity, "Dearest, I dare not live longer without a knowledge of my fate. I love you with the whole strength of my manhood. I want you – want you dearly. My speech is poor; I cannot frame the sentences as I would, but the longings of my heart are great! My love for you is wide as life, deeper than death, and strong as eternity. Will you come to me?"

Slowly the maiden raised her wondrous eyes to him, and evidently he read his answer there, for with one stride he had taken her in his arms and her fair head rested upon his shoulder. "You do love me then?" he whispered.

"Yes!" she replied simply. "Your speech is nothing to me, but the magnetism of your presence is everything. I am yours dear. I give myself to you wholly and freely. I will marry you when you wish."

"Marry?" he said, holding her close. "We need no Church or Priest to sanctify, and no law of state to ratify our union."

"But that is only your fun," the maiden replied, smiling happily. "Of course we must bow before the altar of God, and His Priest must bless our bond."

"Yes, yes, dear," he said hastily, "I did but jest with you. You mean so much to me I cannot, I dare not lose you. My life shall be given to shielding you from danger. In sorrow I will be your comfort. In darkness I will be your light. I will be your joy, and you shall be my great happiness."

There they stood smiling, happy, radiant – and then they were gone. I would follow them. I wanted to know more. There were things still unexplained – No! I would stay here and meditate upon what I had heard.

So this was love: The surrender of two hearts, each to the other, and the merging of two lives into one. A yielding of two wills to mutual interests, so that in the yielding a true and harmonious blend is formed. The man to give, the woman to take. The woman to give, the man to take. Yet paradoxically I reasoned that in each case so beautiful would be the blend that all receiving would resolve itself into giving. Love then was giving; ever giving, and taking but to give again.

Reasoning thus, I gradually felt a drowsiness steal over me, and finally I lost consciousness. How long I remained in this state I could not say, but at last consciousness again came back to me, and feeling refreshed, I passed on my journey. How I wished I could meet again those handsome young creatures. How easily would they complete the revelation for me, proving to my satisfaction that the beautiful ideal they had placed before me was real.

At that moment I was startled to see a wild looking figure coming towards me. By the dress I saw it was a woman, though her attire hung strangely upon her, and from her eyes there gleamed a wild, mad light. Feeling that she was in distress, I essayed to stop her in her mad flight.

"Let me go!" she panted. "Let me go to the river. I can stand it no longer! Oh! let me go."

"What is the matter?" I asked gently, and as I turned her face to me I was staggered to see it was the very girl who I thought I had but recently left with her lover. But what a change. Her once beautiful eyes were now sunk far back in their sockets. Her cheeks that I had admired so much were now ghastly and hollow, and her poor form was fearfully emaciated. "What is the matter?" I asked again. "And where is he who loves you?"

"Loves me?!" she cried scornfully. "His words at our betrothal should have warned me. He wished me to yield myself to him unconditionally, but I thought he did but jest. I know now he meant it all the same. Again and again he suggested it, and when he found he could have me on no other terms he knelt with me at the altar. But his passion was possession, not protection; and his interests were selfish and not mutual."

"There is true love," she cried passionately. "Pure love. Holy love. God-like love – and there is a hellish, cruel travesty; and the quality he had for me is known by a very ugly name."

"But can such a man, and such words, be so false?" I protested.

"Yes," she said wearily, "I now know that there are many beside myself who have been deceived by a fair countenance and pleasing words – where the woman has merely become the sport and plaything of the man. But let me go! I can stand no more"– and she was gone.

Footnote: Communion with the Spirit World

George's revelations about his apparently successful attempts to commune with spirits through meditation apparently ruffled the feathers of some of his readers, and set the authors of this book wondering whether the story is an allegory, or whether it was an actual 'experience'.

In both cases the method of relating it through a 'conversation' with his dog, Tiny, clouded the issue. A conversation with a spirit is one thing, but one with a dog is another thing entirely!

An exchange in the letters column of the *Advertiser* in June 1918 provides us with the answer, so here follows the letter, which accuses George of hallucinating, and his response.

To the Editor of the "Swindon Advertiser"

Sir, – It is a great question which has been placed before us by Mr Hobbs in his article on "Conversations", which appeared in your issue of April 19th 1918, "Can mortals hold communion with the spirit world? Yes." These conversations have been in part a dialogue between Mr Hobbs and his dog Tiny (a most uncommon procedure).

The sense of sight is by common consent placed first among the senses as regards intellectual importance. From it we gain accurate knowledge of external objects. It gives us the power of discriminating and appreciating colour and form. The object of all science, whether it refers to matter or to mind, is simply to ascertain facts, and to trace their relations to each other.

The powers which regulate these relations are entirely hidden from us in our present imperfect state of being; and by grasping at principles which are beyond our reach, we leave that path of enquiry which alone is adapted to our limited faculties, and involve ourselves in error, perplexity and darkness. When we endeavour to pry into the causes of this order, we perceive the operation of powers which lie far beyond the reach of our limited faculties.

For now we see through a glass, darkly. Thus psychology deals with the growth and nature and faculties and methods of the mind in its widest sense – how we feel, and think, and will; and can never legitimately treat the further question, as to what we think, and why we think "all things end in mystery".

In Bacon's work, Novum Organum, it says: "The human understanding is like a false mirror which, receiving rays irregularly, distorts and discolours the nature of things by mingling its own nature with it."

[The writer then proceeds to quote Berkeley, Dean Stanley, and Prof Ward in the same connection, but we are unable to give space for these quotations].

Now I have been surprised to hear Mr Hobbs, being carried away by his own imagination to believe with the spirit:

You have attained to that which few mortals have done. An inspired writer says: "He that exalted himself shall be abased."
I do not profess to a knowledge of philosophy.

Why complain? An inspired writer says: "If thou incline thine ear unto wisdom, and apply thine heart (the reasoning faculty) to understanding then shalt thou understand the fear of the Lord, and find the knowledge of God."
Now Plato defines philosophy as "the passion for divine wisdom". Therefore you must observe how futile your attempt, knowing your lack of knowledge in philosophy. Your argument resolves itself into an hallucination of the mind, a spectral illusion. That which is seen is temporal, that which is unseen is spiritual.

Yours truly,
CH Hollick
26 William Street, Swindon

To the Editor of the "Swindon Advertiser"

Sir, – Will you be kind enough to permit me space in your columns that I may attempt a reply to Mr CH Hollick's letter of the 28th ultimo? First, I should like to thank Mr Hollick for his letter. Adverse criticism is infinitely better than than non-interest.

But while I thank him for his letter, I must confess there are portions I do not understand.

The Conversations, as he says, are in part a dialogue between myself and my dog "Tiny". But why the parenthetical phrase? Surely Mr Hollick, whom I believe to be a student of literature, will know that it is by no means a rarity for an animal to be used as a medium for conversational writing. Even things inanimate have been made to speak that the writer may bring before his readers some matter of passing interest or of lasting vital moment. It is the subject matter that counts, and not the medium by which the matter is presented.

The information following the parenthetical phrase is of real value, and for this I thank Mr Hollick again. Following the informative quotations, Mr Hollick takes me somewhat to task and in a subtle manner cautions me against pride. The subtlety lies in the Biblical quotation, "He that exalteth himself shall be abased."

But surely, Mr Hollick will not confuse things that differ. The softened pride of achievement is legitimate; the noisy swank (if I may use a modern term) of presumption is illegitimate. If mine is of the latter type then I deserve the implied rebuke.

May I ask Mr Hollick, considering the number of folk who are living, whether the proportion is great or small of those who are in touch with the spiritual? Without labouring the point, I am proud that the pride of humility belongs to the minority.

Mr Hollick tells me that, being my stated lack of knowledge in philosophy, "my argument resolves itself into an hallucination of the mind, a spectral illusion".

Well now, suppose I said I do not profess to a knowledge of mathematics, but I know that three multiplied by three equals nine. Technically, I should be telling an untruth, but generally I should be understood to mean that I knew one of the simple stages of mathematics, but as yet I had not ventured into its higher or more intricate reaches.

It is just possible that I know a little of philosophy, but I do not presume to the extent of knowledge that my friend has in this direction.

In conclusion, let me remind Mr Hollick of the young man who was born blind. He will remember the story and how the people used their arguments to prove that he was a fraud and that what he claimed for himself was impossible, and therefore untrue.

But the young man said, "One thing I know, that whereas I was blind, now I see."

Argument is futile against reasoning like that.

And if I know that by intensive concentration I have attained actual communication with the spirit world; if I know that I have seen and spoken to a spirit, "hallucination of the mind" and "a spectral illusion" will not, by any means be the right solution.

Yours sincerely,
George E Hobbs

Chapter 11

Heaven(s) Above

'I cannot imagine,' wrote George Hobbs, in November 1919, 'any normal human being contemplating the unclouded night sky, without having an intense desire to know more of those beautiful gems of light in the "vaulted dome of heaven".'

Indeed, George was alternately fascinated by, and in awe of, both the idea of Heaven (the paradise some believe they will rise to, after death) and the reality of 'the heavens' (the universe) for the whole of his life. They are themes that crop up, again and again. Or maybe *theme*, singular.

Notice the choice of word in that sentence, above. While it might have been reasonable to expect George to call the sky 'the heavens' (plural) – a euphemism we still use today – instead he calls it 'heaven' (singular). In George's world, his faith and his fascination with all things astronomical were sometimes (and perhaps ultimately) the same thing; his mission, it seems, was to find out what divided and what united them.

While this book was being written, the world celebrated the 50th anniversary of the first moon landings, and while we remind ourselves that half a century has now passed since that auspicious day in July 1969, George Hobbs demonstrates that our fascination with what lies beyond our own planet is, in fact, rather older.

We will see, in Chapter 12, how George's consideration of Heaven/the heavens inspired him to write science *fiction*, but first we should look at his attempts to understand science *fact* whenever his curiosity led him to wonder at the night sky.

His studies didn't always bring him to the conclusions that we (with the benefit of much greater knowledge) would come to, and we should not blame him for that. It must have been a strange twilight era to live in, where writers and their readers began speculating about space travel – and yet powered flight was in its infancy, and had not been achieved when the first works of science fiction were published.

Rather than sneer at answers that we can now be sure are way off the mark, we should applaud George – not just for wondering, but also for encouraging his readers to do the same. It shows us how people like him were trying to make sense of what little information they had access to.

In his obituary in the *Advertiser*, under a paragraph entitled 'Keen Astronomer' we are told that 'being a keen astronomer he went up to Stockport [sic] in order to gain the best point of vantage for studying a total eclipse of the sun' [in 1927].

But as early as 1915 he was speculating, in a poem, *Ode to the Moon*, that 'upon thy surface vast/Roamed sentient life amid the verdant green'. He probably had his own telescope because another line in the poem tells us that 'I seem to see thy lunar Apennines/Thy lofty Alps', even though the poem also talks of 'tall and stately pines' and 'commerce ships' sailing on the moon's mares (which no-one ever saw through a telescope!).

Here he is clearly fantasising about the possibility of life there, rather than believing it existed, but he seems to suggests that he believed 'sentient life' had once lived there, and he speculated that they may have built civilisations.

He used another poem from the same year to explore the idea of *The Central Sun*, informing us that 'There is a theory, long held by astronomers, that the stars (our own solar system included) are in orbital as well as rotational motion.' Unfortunately, George makes the unfortunate assumption that these spiralling galaxies mean 'that there must be a central sun, around which the stars revolve'.

He wrote a number of poems dedicated to the sun and the moon, and in his 32-part series, *Conversations*, four articles are actually devoted to (and, dare we say, are in devotion of) the moon – in which our nearest celestial neighbour is actually afforded a personality.

And it doesn't stop there. The moon, stars and planets not only feature in the 18-part *The Story of the Creation*, but the planets and their satellites take centre stage as George takes us on his epic, 12-part, largely science-based analysis of the solar system in the series entitled *Other Worlds Than Ours*.

Here, George offers 'some personal views upon the plurality of worlds', giving us perhaps the best insight into public interest in astronomy, space and life on other planets in the early part of the 20th century. It is dated April 1920.

It starts with caution, George warning: 'Astronomy as a science does not teach other than what can be verified. It will subscribe its authority to planetary law;

but it cannot subscribe its authority to the inhabitants of Mars. The one is indisputably established; the other is merely an hypothesis.'

In other words: *let's not get carried away*. Here the conflict is not the one that is evident elsewhere in his writings, namely between science and faith, but rather science and fantasy.

However, even as a man of science, apologising for speculating about life on other planets, George offers up something of an excuse, suggesting his hypothesis 'may be logical' and that the existence of life on other planets 'may indeed be the only possible answer'.

Even when he seemingly puts a brake on his speculations by concluding that 'until certitude be established it must remain under the heading of speculation', it is telling. What he is clearly saying here is that, while it was as yet unproved whether there was life on Mars or not, he was fully expecting science to, one day, prove it to be true.

Throughout his writings on this subject – as well as elsewhere in his works – there is an overwhelming sense of a man glad to have been born into an age of relative enlightenment, but frustrated not to have been born into a future one, so that some of the mysteries of space could be revealed. It is, in fact, impossible, not to feel sympathy that he was not born into the Space Age that was just around the corner.

Can we draw the conclusion from George's writings that most other people, in the first quarter of the 20th century, had come to see the existence of alien life in the solar system as more likely than not? It's hard to be sure, but George is one layman who has considered this deeply.

Other Worlds Than Ours contains theories based on knowledge available at the time, and demonstrates, if nothing else, that the author is extremely well-read. Unfortunately, science and then space travel would prove these early 20th century theories to be completely unreliable.

He believes, for example, that 'the far off Neptune and our near neighbour the Moon are formed from the same elemental family', even though we now know that the former is one of the 'gas giants' of the solar system, probably with oceans of liquid ammonia and carbon, which could hardly be more different from the moon.

However, this idea of the solar system being like a family is key to George's thinking as he uses the analogy of a family with eight children to describe the eight planets that were known at the time (Pluto, the ninth (and subsequently demoted) 'planet' not being discovered until ten years later).

His theory is that everything in the solar system was once part of the sun, and centrifugal force was responsible for its current form, claiming: 'portion after portion was hurled into space', and curiously using 'the words of the Hebrew story of the Cosmos' to confirm this.

He also makes a fatal error about the earth's atmosphere and the effects of this as a 'greenhouse'. While we now know the atmosphere to be a crucial and delicate barrier that protects life from the radiation of the sun, George comes to virtually the opposite conclusion.

He believes the heat of the sun 'is modified by the atmosphere, the atmosphere being to the inhabitants of a planet what the glass of a conservatory is to that which is cultivated within its confines', but goes on to conclude: 'If it was possible to dispense with the atmosphere, ice belt, surrounding our globe, it would be impossible for us to feel at all the mighty heat which emanates from the sun.'

Eventually, George comes to his grand theory about life in the solar system, which is nothing if not novel to 21st century eyes:

> I believe life is moving out from the Sun. That is to say, I believe that life – so far as the Solar System is concerned – first dawned upon the planet Mercury. And life which flourished upon Mercury was small, similar to that which is found upon the earth. It highest creation was sentient beings – men and women, as we know men and women upon this planet. I reason so because it seems to me out of harmony with logic to believe that earth is the only planet upon which sentient life can exist.
>
> I imagine the Great Architect had a more utilitarian purpose in creating the host of heaven than merely as a spectacular display for the special delight of earth dwellers. To believe otherwise is to reduce the Great Intellect to that of a common or garden type of showman...
>
> Mercury, then, in all probability, had had its prehistoric man, crude and underdeveloped in intelligence. Then civilisation grew and developed with science, philosophy and art. And then Mercury grew old, his glories were departing. But life was not being annihilated from the system: for as life was ceasing upon Mercury, it was commencing upon Venus, and, ceasing upon Venus, commencing upon Earth. As each planet radiates its heat away and becomes a solid globe, so I believe it becomes a world with sentient beings as its highest tenants.
>
> Lastly, I believe that this progression will continue until Neptune, the outermost planet of the system, will be the only world upon which life is found. Then possibly, upon the decay of Neptune will come the great cataclysm – and when the system will be born anew.

What this ultimately tell us is that, despite being a man of curiosity and science, who is prepared to confront centuries-old ideas about the existence of life and its meaning, George is always inclined to find a theory that sits comfortably with what his faith is telling him: that the hand of 'the Great Architect' is ultimately still involved, even to the extent that the planets exists to enable His long-term plan for life in the solar system.

'Yes, these speculations are unorthodox,' concludes George, 'but sometimes accepted orthodoxy is in error. Whether this be error or truth, one thing I know: it has provided me with hours and hours of keen enjoyment.'

Although we don't know how much his interest in astronomy was shared by his fellow Swindonians, George's reference to one or two astronomical 'sensations' of the era suggest the rest of the population were sometimes wont to join in the fun.

In 1920, for instance, he enjoyed speculating about life on other planets by latching on to a distraction that intrigued people worldwide, and Swindon was apparently no exception as George offered his readers his interpretation in an article he called *The Marconi Sensation*.

'The world and his wife,' he states, 'are standing with bated breath before the curtain that veils the mysterious and the unknown.'

The Marconi Sensation referred to was not Guglielmo Marconi's work on radio transmission; that had taken place more than 20 years earlier. What gripped the public imagination, now, was the scientist's discovery of 'mysterious interruptions' at wireless stations which Marconi made the mistake of calling 'signals'. To many, this presented the real possibility that we were receiving intelligent messages from space, and George began speculating about their origin, the strapline of his article in February 1920 being 'Signals from whence? The Sun? The Moon? Or Mars?' It also inspired him to write science fiction, based on the 'sensation' (see Chapter 12).

It is worth noting that, at this point, science had not ruled out the possibility of life on the moon, although George had other ideas about the origin of these potentially intelligent messages, and was looking further into the night sky. 'A much more feasible suggestion,' he wrote, 'is that the signals come from the planet Mars,' before admitting that 'even here there are difficulties of gigantic proportions in the way'.

For a start, he argued, although radio waves were able to 'traverse the entire circuit of the Earth', it was doubtful they could have come all the way from Mars ('what is 25,000 miles compared to 49,000,000 miles?').

But the odds against there being life on the planet was less of a hurdle, George thought, claiming:

> I believe it to be a reasonable supposition that Mars is inhabited. The pole caps have been seen to be covered by a white substance, which increases and diminishes according to the Martian seasons. It is reasonable to believe the

white substance to be snow and ice... It is suggested that the "canals" found upon the surface of Mars are artificial, and in consequence, is a proof of intelligence.

The supposed 'canals' were discovered in 1877, six years before George was born, but by the end of the second decade of the 20th century – when George is writing – the idea had largely fallen out of favour, and was thought to be an optical illusion, caused by comparatively rudimentary telescopes. To be fair to him and other believers in a habited Mars, however, it wasn't until 1965, and the arrival of the Mariner V spacecraft, in orbit around the planet, that both the canals theory and hopes of higher forms of life being present were finally extinguished.

His fascination with the sky at night continued until at least January 1938, when he wrote an article called *Reinmuth, 1937*.

This was an object that had been reported as a 'baby planet', and which appeared in the sky, the previous October. Passing just 400,000 miles from the earth, it was, indeed, the closest recorded encounter with any object, save for the moon and meteorites, and there were concerns that it was on a collision course, before it apparently (in George's words) 'veered off into space'.

The popular interest this caused may have been linked to the fact that a photograph of the fast-moving object was published, and it was visible to the naked eye, although it is uncertain whether George or anyone in Swindon actually observed it.

His interest, of course, was somewhat deeper, so he wrote to Greenwich Observatory, and he forwarded the reply to the editor of the *Advertiser* for publication in the letters column. Readers need not worry, he said, because the collision had been cancelled rather than Swindon Town's home match against Bristol Rovers, that same week!

So we learn that astronomy can be fun, although, as George proved in 1927, it could also provide never-to-be-forgotten moments...

Pen Picture of the Solar Eclipse
An Enthralling Drama of Nature
By George E Hobbs
(First published June 30, 1927)

All roads on Tuesday and the small hours of Wednesday morning led to North Wales and to the North of England. Hundreds of thousands of people hurrying with one fixed purpose – to witness the unique and awe-inspiring spectacle of a total solar eclipse. A similar phenomenon has not occurred in England within living memory, and will not occur again until August 11th, 1999. The total eclipse of that year will cross the Duchy of Cornwall.

For many years I have looked forward to the 1927 eclipse, ever hoping that the opportunity would be mine to witness this rare event. It was therefore with great joy I set out on Tuesday for Southport, 18 miles north of Liverpool. I very much wished to get within the narrow belt of totality, and as Southport was delicately near the centre of the belt, I felt that would be a good place.

I had read much upon this phase of celestial phenomenon, written by those who had been fortunate enough to witness it, of the physical glory revealed during the short period of totality, and of the psychical effects produced. Writing of the total eclipse which occurred in Norway in 1851, one astronomer, after depicting the physical wonders he saw, wrote of the effect it produced upon the purely scientific mind.

"Life and animation," he wrote, "seemed indeed to have now departed from everything around; and we could hardly but fear against our reason that if such a state of things were to last much longer, some dreadful calamity must happen to us also." The writer went on to say that the "Norse peasants about us fled with precipitation and hid for their lives."

If therefore a feeling such as this existed within the breast of a purely academician, what sympathy must one extend to the Norse peasants to whom the sight must have been truly awesome. How easy it is now for us to see the early races performing their incantations in order to scare away the Dragon which was attempting to devour the sun.

What then should I see? What would be the psychological effects produced? These were questions I asked myself as the train raced to the north.

Teeming with People

Southport was literally teeming with folk. The town did not sleep one wink. From boys and girls of tender years to hoary old age, all turned the night into day. A vast fair upon the sea front – very similar to Wembley, and a veritable fairy land continued its fun all the night, and a thousand cars and motor cycles were parked adjacent thereto.

At 3.30am I took my stand upon a huge sand dune at "Hill Side", some four miles from Southport, and waited patiently for the sun to rise. A chill north-easter was blowing and it needed enthusiasm to remain. Presently the dunes for miles were covered with folk, each with their dark glasses ready for the event.

Anxiously one scanned the heavens. Would the low clouds obtrude? No! – for at 5.13am the limb of the sun was seen. Gradually he rose higher, parting with the clouds as Psyche would shed her filmy draperies. At 5.31am (Swindon set time) I noticed first contact, and the sun was gloriously free of obscuration.

When the moon had blotted out just over half the sun's disc, a thick vaporous cloud enveloped both. Optimist as I tried to be, my heart almost failed me. But no! Ten minutes before totality they again emerged from the pall, like lovers who would not [be] parted.

Full-Visioned Totality

Then came the wonderful period of full-visioned totality, with clear visibility throughout.

How shall I describe that half minute of breathless glory? I think the thrill, the wonder, the awe – aye, and the divinity of that half-minute, will remain with me as long as consciousness lasts. It cannot be described. It must be witnessed. Yet I will try to describe the indescribable.

Just before totality, the heavens became a dark blue. Every person around me assumed the same weird hue.

And then I saw the shadow band. It was easily traceable, for totality occurred with the rapidity of drawing down the blind, and the sun was blotted out. No, not blotted entirely out for there immediately appeared the wonderful Corona. I watched for that peculiar phenomenon known as Bailey's Beads, but failed to detect them. Nevertheless I saw another feature which thrilled me even as I saw it. The Corona on the left hand limb was a pearly white, but my binoculars revealed the upper right hand quarter of the limb to be fiery red. Almost in the centre of the red quarter I had the great good fortune of witnessing an eruptive prominence. I have no means of judging its height, but this probably will be given later in scientific journals when the astronomers tabulate their data.

A Weird Sight

I spared a second from this wonderful vision in order to glance around. And I can honestly say it was the most weird sight I have ever been privileged to witness. The forms were phantoms, not human beings of flesh and blood. They moved as intangible beings would move, airily and silently. In fact it was a sensation of being in a world of spirit.

And just as I likened totality to the drawing of the blind, so light came with the rapidity of releasing the blind, and the light shone out once more. The shadow line could be seen receding even as it had been seen approaching.

The whole phenomenon was wonderful in the extreme, and one I shall never forget. Swindon readers will understand when I say that the commencement of totality, totality and the termination may be likened in effect to the two minutes' silence of Armistice Day – the signal to cease, the silence, the signal to commence. I do not think I can describe the sensation better.

I am glad for the memory. I would not have missed it for a great deal.

The 1927 solar eclipse.

Chapter 12

Science Fiction and the Paranormal

Science friction burns my fingers.
Electricity still lingers
Hey, put away that ray.
How do you Martians say 'I love you'?
(Andy Partridge)

Speculating about the mysteries of the universe and the possibilities of alien life is one thing, but George Hobbs also liked a story. His obituary referred to him as being 'a story writer of no mean ability' and it should come as no surprise that some of his works of fiction took on an element of make-believe, and sometimes even *scientific* make-believe.

It is impossible to know what first stimulated his interest in the science of astronomy, the mysteries of space and fantasies about life on other planets, but it is perhaps no coincidence that when HG Wells published his seminal masterpiece of science fiction, *The War of the Worlds*, in 1897, George Hobbs was a (perhaps impressionable) young man of 14.

George would certainly have been aware of Wells's book, but it's unclear whether he actually read it. In the pre-amble to one of his own stories, he tells readers that "I have never read any of the fiction writers upon this subject." However, this may refer, specifically, to the subject of travel to the moon.

It is safe to assume, at least, that *The War of the Worlds* inspired him to the conclusion that if HG Wells could write science fiction, then why not George Ewart Hobbs? Meanwhile, we have already discovered that it was only natural for George to raise his eyes up to the sky and wonder, so it was perhaps inevitable that the storyteller in him would find astronomy and other sciences to be fertile ground for fiction.

Just in case we forget the context in which George was writing his science fiction, we should remember that although the genre had been *launched* by the first part of the 20th century, it had barely registered on the literary scale, compared with the *galactic* appeal it has today. So, while we have the benefit of *Star Trek* and *Star Wars* and any number of other subsequent giants of the genre on which to base our interpretation and expectation of science fiction, George Hobbs had little. He wasn't exactly going *where no-one had gone before*, but he was one of the first to explore *the final frontier*.

Just as he showed himself to be something of a pioneer in his attempts to write situation comedy (as we will discover in Chapter 13), so we should recognise that George was ahead of the game in science fiction, too.

As far as science fiction was concerned, his honest (albeit sometimes flawed) ideas about the possibility of life on the moon or Mars no doubt fanned the creative flames. Meanwhile, great advances in technology and the continuing sense of wonder at the rapid pace of scientific innovation, which he made sure to stay informed about, must also have been an inspiration.

The following transcriptions are a sample of three of his voyages into science fiction that were serialised in the *Advertiser*.

Evidently inspired by the real-life phenomenon of *The Marconi Sensation* (see Chapter 11), *The Mysterious Message* is set in the year 2136, with the earth threatened by an approaching apocalypse from deep space. But did the coded alien warnings decoded by Professor Fellows turn out to be right all along? Or was it just a momentous false alarm?

In the mammoth, eleven-part *A Visit To The Moon*, George 'publishes' the edited journals of his late friend, Christopher Jackson, who (we are told) had previously documented his secret journey to the moon and back. We learn of a close encounter of the third kind, involving the mysterious Lunarians, along with interstellar semi-detached homes and, in all probability, a story to which George hoped to return to at a later date.

Thirdly, another professor features as one of the main characters in *Doctor Nickols*, along with other members of the Psychical Research Association. This story, in four parts, is about mind control and the nefarious motives of one particular doctor of psychiatry: someone whose strange behaviour was arousing suspicion once it was realised that young women were falling under his spell.

The Mysterious Message
Chapter 1
By George E Hobbs
(First published: March 24, 1922)

Like a piece of wet rag, Prof Fellows, Chief Astronomer of Federal Europe, fell back into his chair. It was the purest chance he found such a resting place, for he scarcely had knowledge of his surroundings. Had he fallen to the floor it is questionable if the sudden and violent impact would have conveyed to his dazed senses that he had fallen. Twenty years of patient study and at last the riddle was solved. That was the thought hammering upon his brain: "At last! At long last – solved!"

It was little wonder that his discovery had unmoved him, for it was nothing less than this: He had discovered that a mighty cataclysmic change was about to visit the earth. Two short years more, to be precise, in the March or June of AD 2136, half of the earth's surface would be plunged into eternal night, while the other half would experience perennial day.

Feverishly he pulled his scattered senses together and brought them to some semblance of coherency.

"This is terrible," he muttered, "and much too big to keep to myself. I must call Maxwell and let him check my data."

And in a few moments, a handsome young fellow of about twenty-eight years of age appeared.

"What's the matter, Professor?" asked Maxwell, seeing the extreme pallor of his face. "Are you unwell? Let me get you..."

"No, no, Jim! Close the door, lad and come here quickly. I have solved it at last – and it's terrible. Some of us will not be here in two years' time. Millions will die, but if I could only determine upon which part of the globe the disaster will fall, steps could be taken to save some – perhaps all. But that is impossible to determine. It seems that fate will work her own capricious will. For myself, I do not mind. My work is nearly done. But for you and my little Ada (the child of my old age), it is different.

"But come, lad, I must give you my whole confidence. I want you to check my data. Perhaps even now I may not have understood."

Jim Maxwell's face betrayed no surprise as he listened to his Chief's startling pronouncement. None knew better than the remarkable genius of Professor Fellows. He knew him to be a veritable superman. The "grey matter" was in no way strained, even as he fought out the problems of astronomy, mathematics, wireless, telegraphy or etymology – in all of which he was a master hand. And although Jim Maxwell had assisted his chief during the past two years in the incidental and more mechanical routine of the Observatory, he knew the Professor had been ploughing a lonely and definite furrow.

A Secret for Three

"But mind, lad," continued the Professor, after a short pause. "For a time we must keep this to ourselves. We…"

"You are too late for that, Daddy," came a girlish voice, and to the dismay of both men there stood behind them the Professor's pretty daughter Ada.

At sight of her standing there in all her girlish grace, the father groaned aloud, while Maxwell's face betrayed the deep emotion surging through his whole being.

"You must not stay here, dear!" implored the elder man, desperately. "Maxwell, add your entreaty to mine. God, man! She must not stay and listen. It will unnerve her. It…"

"Father," said Ada softly, "I do not often disobey you. It was quite an accident I overheard what you said. You were agitated when you called up Mr Maxwell and you did not notice that you used the Duaphone instead of the Monophone and consequently you called me as well. If it is universal disaster, or semi-universal disaster, I am going to stay with you now, Daddy, just the three of us."

It was the last sentence that decided Jim Maxwell. "Ada will stay with us, sir," said he quietly. It was the first time he had spoken her name aloud, though he had often addressed her so to himself. "This is no time for confessions of love; but if your findings prove true and destruction is about to visit our planet, destruction in which we personally may or may not be involved, then I do not hesitate to confess I have always loved Ada. And whatever fate has in store for us, nothing can alter that fact. I love her, sir!"

Very gently Professor Fellows looked at his young daughter. Swiftly his thoughts raced back to the day he wooed and won her mother. And in his child's eyes he saw the shining light of love that she was too honest to hide; the light that he remembered meant consent – and he was content.

For one brief moment the rumblings of approaching cosmic convulsions were forgotten as he assigned his daughter a seat by Jim Maxwell's side. One close hand grip, and then…

"We are ready now for what you have to tell us," said Jim contentedly. "Let us have your discoveries, sir. And if Fate decrees our death, we three will meet it together."

"Some of the information I am about to impart, lad, will be familiar to you," began Professor Fellows, "especially that part which deals with the economy of the solar system. And you, my dear, as a student of History, will also be able to follow some portions of my narrative.

"You will know that two centuries ago, in the beginning of the Twentieth Century, a war known in our history books as the 'Great War,' raged throughout Europe. At that time the world was divided into nations; some having kings at their head, while others were more or less constituted as Federal Europe is constituted today. Our history books, as you are both aware have so fully dealt with that black page in human wretchedness that further mention need have no place here.

"During the progress of that war, a scientist by the name of Marconi startled the men of his day by stating that mysterious sounds had been heard by his wireless operators at Marconi House (Marconi House, by the way, was situated in London, the chief city of Western Europe. In the great earthquake of 1970 it was destroyed, and for many years its site was a matter of conjecture.)

"These myst..."

"But, Daddy," interrupted his daughter, "you speak as though the site has now been discovered. I have only lately read Dr Salvage's book on the 1970 earthquake, and he says among other things that the site of Marconi House is utterly impossible to locate."

"I located it twenty years ago, dear," replied her father. "And it was by a discovery I made there that caused me to devote my life to a special branch of research. I found a message there, written in a code peculiar to those days, and written by one whose insight into the reality of things was most remarkable. But I will tell you of this as I come to it. Also I will tell you the reason why I have never disclosed my secret.

"These mysterious sounds were a matter of much controversy by the leading scientists of the day. Some attributed their origin to solar magnetic disturbance. Others would go further, yet with true scientific reserve, declared they would not rule out the possibility of the sounds being signals by intelligent beings from some neighbouring planet.

"Through the intervening years successive wireless stations have constantly recorded similar sounds. And though improvement has followed improvement in wireless installation, no further progress has been recorded in the interpretation of those sounds.

"But I have discovered both the origin and the interpretation of those sounds."

(To be continued)

The Mysterious Message (2)
Chapter 2
By George E Hobbs
(First published: March 31, 1922)

Synopsis:- In the year 2134, Professor Fellows, Chief Astronomer of Federal Europe, discovers that partial destruction will visit this planet in the year A.D. 2136. He places his facts before his only daughter Ada and her lover, Jim Maxwell, who is the Professor's assistant at the Observatory.

The claim of Professor Fellows, that he had discovered the site of Marconi House – the wireless station that first recorded the mysterious sounds in the early years of the Twentieth Century – was after all but of small moment. Certainly it was interesting to Ada in particular and not a little gratifying to think that her father had achieved where so may had failed; especially after reading the history of the terrible earthquake that had demolished the wonder city of the Twentieth Century – London. But such a claim faded into insignificance in the face of the larger claim: that he had now proved those sounds to be messages and had deciphered their meaning. It was startling in the extreme. Breathlessly the young lovers awaited his further revelation.

"Perhaps it will be well for me to remind you," continued the Professor, "that these mysterious sounds were subsequently believed to have originated from intelligent beings upon the planet Mars. And from the physical investigation of that planet the suggestion seemed to have some weight.

"As you have long been familiar, lad, Mars is about 4,200 miles in diameter – just a little more than half the diameter of the earth. Believing as we do that primarily the planets were very hot and then cooled by radiation, it is logical to believe the Mars would have cooled long before Earth parted with her surface heat. It is therefore permissible to conclude that having cooled before Earth, sentient life would be flourishing there thousands of years before even the seas were formed upon this planet. Observer after observer constantly recorded facts which strengthened such a belief.

"The findings of earlier astronomers have been verified and amplified by our own observers of to-day. The Martian day is about equal to that of Earth, and the year about twice that of our planet. But I want to suggest to you that though these things are accepted as facts, life upon Mars is of much more recent date than upon Earth, and consequently there must be a lower grade of intelligence."

"But further evidence refutes such a suggestion," objected Maxwell firmly. "The unmistakable presence of canals, which, owing to the rapidity of construction, and the colossal magnitude of the enterprise surely must point to superior methods in scientific irrigation."

"Yes, lad, so it has been during the last 150 years," replied the Professor. "In fact so far back as 1877 these canals have been noted, and the periods in which double canals take the place of single canals has been duly tabulated. But where astronomers have been wrong is in attributing the canals to intelligent beings at all.

"I myself have observed two parallel canals, each thirty miles wide and at least 1500 miles long, formed in just over two months. Such an undertaking would be impossible by human agency – I use the term "human" for convenience of speech – unless Mars was tenanted by millions more human beings than is found upon this planet. And that, Jim, you know to be utterly at variance with possibility."

"That is so," asserted Maxwell thoughtfully. "And you infer?"

"That the canals are formed by the periodic melting of polar ice and snow," replied Professor Fellows.

"But let me lead you farther, for time grows short," he continued earnestly. "We have to conserve our mental and physical strength for that which I fear is inevitable.

"When I began my scientific career I must admit that the romantic intrigue surrounding those mysterious sounds touched a sympathetic chord within me. The normal scientist, dealing as he does with circumscribed law and hard material facts, is of necessity prosaic and intensely practical. But I am afraid I am not normal in this sense. I find a joy in stepping out of the rut of orthodoxy and striking out a lone path, either to find a negative result, or, as in this case, a positive discovery.

"My first step from orthodoxy, then, was to formulate the creed that sentient life was a consequential necessity of planetary economy; and that as life flourishes upon Earth in all its diversified forms, so it has adapted itself to the conditions of the two inner planets, and will adapt itself in the process of years to the five outer planets. In other words, as Neptune, the outermost planet, was first formed and subsequent formation worked inward to the sun, so, like a wave that had recoiled from the beach, sentient life has worked and will continue to work outward from the sun. Upon the surface of Mercury, therefore, nestled close to the genial warmth and light of our luminary, I premised life to have first dawned in our system. I ruled out the probability of Mars maintaining life superior to Earth as being opposed to my theory, and formed the opinion that superior intelligence could only be found upon –"

"Venus!" exclaimed Maxwell involuntarily. "Sorry, sir, but I was so interested in following your line of thought that I spoke unconsciously."

"And you only said what I was going to say, dear," said Ada with a smile, which transformed itself into a blush of embarrassment as she realised she had uttered aloud her first term of endearment to her lover.

Though neither of the men presumed to notice her embarrassment, yet, to one of them, coming disaster faded for a moment in the bliss of that sweet utterance. And then serious attention held sway once more.

"Yes, Jim, and you, dear," said the Professor, "you stated my thoughts correctly. I formed the opinion that life had ceased upon Mercury, and that superior intelligence could only be found upon Venus. Having formed that opinion, the next step was to associate the mysterious sounds with that planet.

"But," objected Maxwell, determined to raise all the logical opposition he could muster, "discovered facts would preclude such a supposition. Life would be far less likely upon Venus than upon Mars. You must admit the facts, sir, and the fact that Venus only turns once on its axis in the same period as it takes to go round the sun; in other words – as you are quite aware – that Venus always presents the same hemisphere to the sun, rules out superior life, or life at all upon that planet."

"Yet my opinion has been crystallised into fact!" replied Professor Fellows quietly. "I told you at the beginning, Jim, I had trodden a lonely path; a path unchartered in scientific research. And I tell you my apparent eccentricities have led me to the truth. It is true that Venus ever presents the same hemisphere to the sun. But if, for the moment, I must argue from the discovered facts by astronomers, let me remind you of what was discovered during the transits of Venus in the years 2004 and 2012. You know by the records we have that a dense atmospheric belt, 300 miles deep, was discovered completely surrounding Venus. And the presence of an atmosphere does not preclude the existence of life.

"But I have greater proof than mere prosaic details. I have been in communication with intellectual beings upon Venus, and they have told me that the same fate which has attended their planet is about to overtake ours. Their ancient records state that millions of their ancestors perished; and that it is utterly impossible to foretell upon which hemisphere the disaster will fall."

"But how on earth, sir, was it possible of you to understand their language signs?" asked Jim incredulously.

"A very natural question, lad," replied the Professor. "And I will tell you."

(To be continued)

The Mysterious Message (3)
Chapter 3
Arresting Story by George E Hobbs
(First published: April 13, 1922)

Synopsis:- Professor Fellows, Chief Astronomer of Federal Europe, discovers that in two years' time – A.D. 2136 – partial destruction will overtake the Earth. He claims that his discovery is the based upon information given him by scientists upon the planet Venus. He proceeds to give this information to his only child Ada and her lover, his assistant at the observatory.

Jim Maxwell had followed closely the narration of his chief's arguments. But when, with abrupt boldness, he informed his two listeners he had been in communication with scientists upon the planet Venus, Jim looked at the Professor with a questioning glance. And his chief caught that glance and interpreted its meaning correctly.

"I think my sanity is above reproach, Jim," said Professor Fellows with a quiet smile. "I knew I should startle you, but I can prove my claim, never fear. It's quite all right, lad, you need not apologise. I am quite aware it is a strange claim. But let me tell you how I obtained my information.

"Thirty years ago I suffered a severe nervous breakdown, and I went to Budia in Southern Europe to recuperate. While there I discovered in a second-hand bookshop an old MSS [manuscript] book in which was contained a partially faded pen sketch plan of Marconi House and district. I believe this book provides the only reliable information extant of that historic wireless station.

"When I arrived at the presumed site I found workmen excavating a foundation for a new electric Power Plant. They had discovered old foundation walls as they thought, but I came to a different conclusion.

"I worked at night, going secretly, and was rewarded by the discovery that one of the walls was really a portion of a vault. In that vault I found notes which eventually proved to be written by one who, like myself, was investigating along unorthodox lines. Either from the fear of ridicule, or that he wished to keep his investigation secret, he had written his notes in code. And it took me many weary months finding out the key. Just have a look at this."

Code and Key

Maxwell took the proffered papers upon which was written: "Ivxliwvw hlfmwh ziv hrtmzoh. Mlg uiln Nzih yfg Evmfh. Mveg uzelfyzov. Ikkvigfmrgo

– Mab 1980 – Hsaoo gib gov." On the second was written: "1980. Zn xlilvxg. Szev szw wvuurmrgv ivhklmhv yig wi mlg fmwvihgymw ozmtfytx. Nth yv z xlmmlm yahrh. Droo gib zytrm."

"What on earth does it convey, sir?" asked Jim, utterly perplexed.

"Just the question I asked myself a thousand times, lad," replied the Professor. "And yet the key was simplicity itself. It is written in the English language of the Twentieth Century. And by a reversal of the alphabet of those days the meaning is clear. This, then, is the meaning: 'Recorded sounds are signals. Not from Mars but Venus. Next favourable opportunity – May, 1980 – shall try again.'

"And the second is:- '1980. Am correct. Have had definite response, but do not understand language. Must be a common basis. Will try again.'"

Understanding a little of the Old English tongue, Maxwell and Ada, assisted by the Professor, compared the code with the interpretation and found it to be correct.

"And his problem was my problem," said the Professor. "After I had perfected my intensifying apparatus I too had a definite response. And though now and again I fancied I had a fleeting knowledge of some of the words, I could make no intelligible sentences. I believed with my unknown and long-since dead friend, that with intelligent beings, wherever found, there must be some common basis of language. But I went farther than he did. I assumed that the beings upon Venus who were striving to communicate with this planet were intellectually in advance of us. Consequently I determined to tune out my own messages and leave them to decipher and interpret.

"When Venus was in a favourable position compared to the Earth, night after night I turned out my request – 'Third planet from Sun. Anxious to know meaning of Signals!'

Their Difficulties

"As Venus is not always conveniently placed, my request was turned out over a long period. But after a weary period of waiting I was rewarded with a definite answer. It appeared subsequently their difficulty had been twofold. First, my mode of expression was ancient to them, in consequence of which they had to wade through volumes of their old literature in order to obtain the basis of my mode. When they had obtained this I further confused them by the first part of my request, viz., 'Third Planet from Sun.' As a matter of fact, Jim, what we have long thought to be true is proved beyond all doubt. There is another planet between Mercury and the Sun. We know it as the 'Planet of Romance', or

'Vulcan', but the astronomers of Venus know it as 'Alphanus' – the first planet. We are therefore in the fourth position from the Sun, or 'Deltos', as we are known by those upon Venus. Their planet, being the third in order of distance, is known by the name of 'Gammath'."

"Then that explains the vagaries of Mercury's orbital motion!" exclaimed Maxwell.

"Exactly, lad," replied Professor Fellows. "As you are aware, astronomers have long believed theoretically such a planet to exist. That is why the definite name 'Vulcan' was given to it. Yet neither transit nor reflected light has ever revealed it to practical observation.

"But to return to my first difficulty, that of language.

"It is interesting to note the successive races upon Venus have passed through the evolution of languages even as we have. The very names they know the planets by suggests a period when their language had a close affinity to Greek. Alphanus, Betau, Gammath, Deltos – all have an affinity to ancient Greek.

"Soon coherent messages were flashing to and fro between us, and then they revealed to me why they had been so anxious to communicate with this planet."

The Peril in Store

"They told me that our deductions of their planet were specifically correct. One hemisphere lies in perpetual night, frozen and silent; while the hemisphere on which they reside basks in perpetual day. By natural selection the race that now lives upon Venus have adapted themselves to the conditions prevailing there.

"Their records state that the present condition of the planet was due to the disturbing influence of a periodic comet. Their ancestors had been warned of the danger by the fast disappearing race of beings upon Mercury or Betau. But as no one could tell upon which part of their globe the disaster would fall millions perished. And I have discovered, lad, the same fate is imminently ours. The cause of the disruption you will probably guess?"

"The comet known as Halley's," replied Jim. "Your predecessor, I remember, recorded a disturbing influence in its last return to the Sun in the year 2061. But it was thought the deflection was merely nominal and due to the proximity of Jupiter."

"Yes, that is so," said Professor Fellows, thoughtfully. "But it appears that the derangement in the orbit of Halley's Comet is cyclic, and is believed to occur every 6,000 years. Its next return, in two years' time," added the Professor significantly, "will decide the fate of millions upon our planet – perhaps ours – we do not know.

"And now I will leave you young people. I am tired and weary and must have rest. Don't let it weigh too heavy upon your heart, dear," concluded the Professor, wistfully. "We are all in the hands of God. And – and we cannot prevent it – but we have – yes, we have immortality. And there's life beyond, dear. Goodnight!"

(To be concluded)

The Mysterious Message (4)
Chapter 4
Arresting Story by George E Hobbs
(First published: April 21, 1922)

Synopsis:- Professor Fellows, chief astronomer of Federal Europe, in the year 2134, discovers that in A.D. 2136 partial destruction will visit the Earth. He claims that his discovery is the result of information given him by scientists upon the planet Venus. That information he has imparted to his only child Ada and her lover, his assistant at the Observatory.

Fifteen months sped swiftly by. In the interim Jim Maxwell, with the full approval of Professor Fellows, had married Ada. For twelve months now they had been husband and wife.

Though the shadow of impending disaster was ever present, yet each had found one degree of happiness and solace in the near presence of the other.

As Jim said one evening, folding his young wife in his arms, "I cannot say, dear heart, that every moment of the year has been a dreamless joy. But what joy has been mine, you have been its creator. Whatever fate has in store I say here and now, thank God for this one year."

All three had their moments of tortured depression, but Professor Fellows in particular suffered. His was a pain race-old in its cause and effect. That "knowledge was power" was discovered by the first man and woman in Eden. But what they did not discover until too late was that the quality of the power was determined by the quality of the knowledge. The fragrant tree of knowledge flourishes in the garden of every intelligent being; but a merciful Providence has placed danger signs beyond which it is imprudent for man to venture.

Professor Fellows had ventured, and his venturing had driven him and his daughter from their Eden of peace. He had discovered that which was to prove inevitable. He could not avert its progress, neither could he control or direct its activities. Knowledge was his, yet he was powerless to save even one life from destruction.

"We Must be Silent"

Jim and Ada often talked it over: whether it would not be better to publish to the world the news of the impending disaster. But Professor Fellows had learned his lesson. "No! no!" said he emphatically, when the idea was mooted to him. "It is better the world should not know. In fact, Jim, I sometimes think it would have been better if I had not pursued my investigations. If, with my knowledge of the event, I could also know where the disaster will fall, then would my investigation be of help to the world. But I am helpless, and the knowledge which I thought would place my name upon the honoured roll of fame now nauseates me. No, no, we must be silent. If the world knew, and knew also its utter helplessness, it would go mad. Better a swift and unanticipated destruction than months of agonised suspense."

And so it was allowed to remain the unenviable property of three.

A Final Conference

In the November of the year 2135, Professor Fellows called Jim and Ada into his study for what he called 'a final conference'. Both saw that his face was grave in the extreme, and they waited to hear what he had to say.

"In a month's time," said he without preamble, "I should judge about 21 December, the comet that is to work its fell purpose upon our planet will be visible in our Central Refracting Telescope. As soon as we detect it, lad, I propose to take a certain course which I trust both of you will believe is for the best. I do not want the three of us to be caught in the catastrophe, so I propose that as soon as we detect Halley's Comet, you two will remain together, and I shall go either to South America or New Zealand."

"No, no, Daddy!" cried Ada in agony, sensing with filial intuition a deeper reason for his course of actions. "Let us all three remain here, whatever happens! Jim, dear, persuade Daddy against it!"

But no reasoning upon the part of Jim, nor the tears of his loved child, could turn Professor Fellows from his determination. Nor would he satisfy their persistent demand for further explanation.

It was because he dare not tell them of his continued agonised investigations.

Feverishly in solitude he had worked out his calculations and eventually it seemed to him that the disaster would fall on 21 or 22 April when the western hemisphere was turned away from the sun. But he dare utter no word for there was still a large degree of uncertainty both as to time and place.

He had reached that stage when his tremendous secret made him feel almost a murderer. He knew there would be no more peace in his life. And while he would give all his possessions could he but save the unsuspecting ones who would be involved in the disaster, he prayed that he himself might be a victim.

On the night of the 20 December Professor Fellows stationed Jim at the giant refractor. Long and anxiously Jim gazed into that part of the heavens where he knew the comet would make its appearance. Careful measurements were taken and star charts assiduously scrutinised, for that part of the heavens where he was looking was thickly populated with stars, and a mistake could so easily be made.

The 20th, 21st and 22nd of December passed with a negative result. At 11:30p.m. on the 23rd Jim went to snatch a few moments' rest, while his chief took his place at the eye-piece.

The Coming of Doom

Presently the eagle glance of Professor Fellows detected a point of light that arrested his attention. At once he consulted his star-chart and found there was no star charted in the place where he had found this one. With limbs that trembled he again sought that object through the refractor. Yes, there it was, and he knew without farther questioning it was Halley's Comet returning to the sun.

"I have found it, lad," said Professor Fellows quietly, as Jim returned to the room. "Just check my measurements and you will find that I am correct." And Jim, with fast beating heart, by observation and measurements, found that it was indeed true. The destroying medium was almost at the door.

Very affecting was the parting between the old chief and the two whom he so much loved. But at last it was over, and he had gone.

On 17 April, earth tremors of slight power were recorded upon the recording chart at the observatory, and Jim knew that the crisis was at hand.

On 19 and 20 April, 2136, the tremors increased in power. It was as though a huge brake had been applied to the earth's surface, which, shudderingly, persisted in its revolution.

It was on 21 April that it happened. All through that weird day vague apprehension was expressed upon the faces of the people. Even the animals, particularly those of wild breed, shared that vague apprehension, coming from the woods as though to seek comfort from the presence of those who formerly had hunted them.

And then apparently the sun stood still over Europe, and the days which followed were terrible in the extreme. By wireless it was learned that the western world had been trapped upon a receding tide, and the tides having now ceased, vessels could neither get in nor out of port. Only those upon the edge of the darkness could be saved, and these hastened towards the light and warmth and safety.

The fate of the Western world, plunged into the abyss of night and freezing solid by the intense cold, can never really be known. No news came through after two days. The rivers became frozen so that the electric power station could not work, and power and light failed for ever.

One message only came through to the broken-hearted Ada and the sorrowing Jim. It was wirelessed in code six hours after the catastrophe occurred. It was brief and poignant: "I was right after all. Don't grieve, dearest, and good-bye! Good-bye Jim! Be good to my little girl!"

And the old world settled down to its new conditions, carrying its ghastly burden of death upon its hemisphere of perpetual night.

The end.

A Visit to the Moon (1) Recorded by George E Hobbs

(First published: August 17, 1923)

Synopsis – My friend Christopher Jackson had long been obsessed with a desire to visit our satellite, the Moon. He disappeared for three years. Suddenly he came to me again, dying in my arms after declaring he had positively visited the Moon. He requested me to edit his journal for publication. My friend's request is here obeyed. – GEH

Part 1 of Journal

I have returned from a voyage unique in the annals of adventure and discovery. What many have ridiculed as the flight of an imaginative mind; what a few have dreamed of as a probable achievement, I have accomplished. I have visited our Satellite, the Moon!

Let me say at the commencement of this strange narrative that though

I understand writers of fiction have romanced about this subject, I have never read one word of their writings. I am honest when I say I have no knowledge of their suggested method by which they would reach the Moon, neither of what their imagination would lead them to see when they arrived there. Plagiarism for the sake of sensationalism, or for ephemeral notoriety is abhorrent to me. (In justice to everyone concerned I also may state that I have never read any of the fiction writers upon this subject. – GEH).

I am perfectly aware this narrative will be met by scientific incredulousness, if not with scornful abuse. I shall be called a charlatan, a fool, a romancer without knowledge. I expect this because my discoveries are somewhat different to that of accepted popular astronomical declarations. In this direction one request only is mine. I have a conviction I shall not live to see the publication of my notes. If this should prove my fate then I must leave my MSS in the hands of my lifelong friend G. E. Hobbs. He will believe in my integrity and will see that justice is done to my memory.

In judging the value of my discoveries I would ask the reader to remember this fact. The topography of the Lunar disc is obtained by means of the terrestrial camera situated 240,000 miles from its objective. The most powerful telescope in the world cannot show to the human eye the wonderful details brought out by the camera. Hence, the declared knowledge of the Moon's economy is obtained at best from the photographic plate. My knowledge is obtained not by means of the camera, but by personal visitation!

The possibility of visiting our satellite had fascinated me for a number of years. But there were so many difficulties to surmount that there were times when, in utter despair, I saw only the foolishness of the attempt. Presently out of chaos came order. Difficulty after difficulty melted into thin air, and at last I accomplished that which was declared to be foolish and impossible.

My means of transit will be the first thing I shall touch upon. The reader must pardon me, however, if at times I am somewhat vague. The means of transit is my own particular invention; consequently, not wishing at present to give the world my secret, I shall give only a general outline.

I eliminated at the very start the idea of any and all types of existing aeroplanes. Planes and propellers are of use only where a resisting medium is encountered, consequently such means of transit would be of use only within the narrow limits of the earth's atmospheric belt. I knew I should have to traverse a region in which the etheric density would be so low as to be a negligible quantity. So low indeed that meteors may traverse that region with prodigious velocity without igniting or disrupting.

Sufficient for me to say, then, that with the assistance of three deaf mutes, brothers, and all skilled to the highest degree in aeroplane construction, and in the science of electro-magnetism, I constructed a machine, the outer shell of which was made entirely of aluminium.

This, when completed, was tested to resist an internal and external pressure of 2,060lbs. to the square inch.

The central portion of the machine was made a perfect sphere, with pear-shaped appendages upon the vertical plane. Inside the spherical body I constructed a second shell, detached from the outer casing, and perfectly poised upon the gyroscopic principle. The reason for this will be obvious to the intelligent reader. From the earth I had to take an ascending flight; while upon reaching the moon the order would be exactly reversed. Not only so but somewhere between the two worlds – the exact region I have no means of judging – the vertical appendages would slowly fall to the horizontal plane. It was, therefore, very essential that the inner shell – my living and observation room – should be entirely free from the outer structure. Communicating passage-ways with collapsible sides were made so as to engage with the outer shell in any of four positions.

Four windows of specially tested glass were fixed in both the outer casing and inner shell, so that in whatever position I may find myself, two windows in each would be in alignment for vision. My food and drink were made in concentrated form, and though I took what I considered to be a twelve months supply, the whole occupied a space of but six cubic feet.

Between my observation room and the pear-shaped appendages, two storage tanks were constructed, into which oxygen was pumped under high pressure. Atmospheric gauges were placed on the outer casing, connecting through the oxygen tanks to the space surrounding my perfectly poised room. Here were fixed automatic release valves, designed by the elder of the deaf-mute brothers, and so gearing that as the mercury in the gauges fell so the automatic valves would release the precious life restoring oxygen. I tried several experiments with the valves and found they gave every satisfaction. As the mercury fell to zero in the tubes the amount of oxygen released was sufficient for my needs. An indicator in my observation room controlled by the velocity of the escaping oxygen, by inverse action indicated atmospheric density. When the valves were closed my indicator recorded 14.7lbs. atmospheric pressure. But when the velocity of the escaping oxygen was at its highest, the indicator recorded zero. By this means I felt sure I should be able to tell not only when I had left the earth's atmosphere and had penetrated the awful void of space, but also be able to tell the amount of atmospheric density upon the moon's surface. But the strangest part of my machine's economy was the "motive" power of transit.

(To be continued)

A Visit to the Moon (2)
Recorded by George E Hobbs
(First published: August 24, 1923)

Synopsis – My friend, Christopher Jackson had long been obsessed with a desire to visit our satellite, the Moon. He disappeared for three years. Suddenly he came to me again, dying in my arms after declaring he had accomplished his objective. He requested me to edit his journal. A description of his machine has been given. – GEH

Part 2 of Journal

Up to this point I have dealt rather fully with the details of the mechanism of my machine. Now I intend to be less open. The "motive" power of my machine is my own particular invention, and for the time being will be my secret. I have no fear that either of my deaf-mute friends will betray my secret. They were and are true friends, and all the wealth in the world would not be inducement enough for them to be disloyal. I shall therefore give but a general outline of my secret.

My "motive" power was situated in the extreme end of the pear-shaped appendages; and was designed to throw out, from either end, powerful magnetic antennae. It was so arranged that from a deflection indicator in the observation room, I could, at will, reverse the poles of attraction and detraction. When commencing the upward flight, the apex of my discovery, 'local velocified magnetism'. By the aid of multiple intensifiers, so compact as to occupy but a cubic foot of space, I was able to throw out magnetic antennae forty million times the length of my machine. And – here lay my secret – I could localise, or isolate this force within any required diameter. That is to say, I could throw out this wonderful force on a 240,000 mile line, having a radius of influence not greater than four feet. It was as though my machine could slip into a tube and be conveyed to the moon within its solid walls. So localised was the magnetic field that a compass placed six feet away on either side of my machine remained unaffected.

At the same time in the appendage at the base I was able to set up detraction;

which gave me, after several experiments, more power than I needed to resist terrestrial gravitation. When therefore the moon was in a favourable position I had a 'pull' from our satellite, and a 'push' from the earth.

I calculated that my speed would be about 200 miles per hour making the voyage about seven weeks' duration. Subsequent events, however, proved I could easily maintain a speed of 300 miles per hour, which reduced the voyage to just over 33 days.

After everything was ready I spent a further fortnight going over again every part of my equipment, to see that nothing was wanting. Several times my three friends besought me, by signs I understood, to let at least one of them accompany me. But not through any motive of selfishness I refused their request. I believed I should succeed. On the other hand some unforeseen circumstance may cause me to fail. And if I had to fail and die, then I would fail and die alone.

Never shall I forget the sensations which coursed through my body as the time arrived for my departure. Three hearty grips of the hand – then I passed through the communicating door into my observation room. Having detached the collapsible passage ways and closed the outer and inner doors I was ready to start. As I was particularly anxious to test my atmospheric gauges and automatic release valves under proper conditions, I set my forward control at 25 degrees above low power and my rear control at quarter retardation point. This would ensure a low rate of speed through the earth's atmospheric belt, and, at the same time, give me a more detailed account of the belt's depth.

I am not emotional by nature, yet I must confess to a momentary dimming of the eyes and clutching at the throat as my machine began to rise into the air. I suppose it was a perfectly natural emotion; for was I not upon an enterprise never before attempted? But I fought down my weakness with stern repression, and commenced to log my voyage.

I was greatly startled to find that at an altitude of only 3 miles the escape of oxygen from the release valves indicated drop in the mercury gauges of seventeen inches. That is to say atmospheric density upon the earth balanced a column of mercury 30 inches high. Here, only five miles above the surface of the earth, atmospheric density had decreased just over a half. I did not expect to meet with such a loss until I had reached an altitude of at least 100 miles.

In the next five miles I indicated a further decrease of five inches. This meant that at an altitude of ten miles above earth, atmospheric pressure stood at about 3lbs. to the square inch.

From now onward the decrease became less and less rapid until at 150 miles the indicator recorded two inches in the mercury columns. At 250 miles the mercury fell to zero and I knew I had at last passed out of the earth's atmosphere.

And then I had a surprise which startled me into an amazed wonder. I had just written in my log-book, "Earth's atmospheric belt 250 miles deep. Mercury at zero. Automatic release of oxygen full and satisfactory" – when I happened to look up at the indicator. To my surprise it now registered half an inch in the mercury gauge. I was certain it recorded zero when I began to log, but now it indicated a rise. I threw my controls, both fore and aft, into full capacity; my speed increasing to 300 miles per hour.

Hour after hour I continued to watch that indicator, but the half an inch remained constant. For the moment I could give no explanation for such a strange phenomenon, and at last, dazed and weary, I partook of some refreshments and turned into bed.

How long I slept I do not remember but when I awoke my eyes fastened themselves upon the indicator. That half an inch had remained constant during my sleep and still remained steady.

And then the explanation came to me! It was undreamt of, but true. It was that an aether of measurable density pervaded the whole universe. There was no aetherless space, as some had supposed, no useless vacuum: But a connecting medium of life to every planet and to every sun. It was the first discovery of real importance I had made.

(To be continued)

A Visit to the Moon (3)
Recorded by George E Hobbs
(First published: August 31, 1923)

Synopsis – My friend, Christopher Jackson, had long been obsessed with a desire to visit the moon. He disappeared for three years. Suddenly he came to me again, dying in my arms after declaring he had accomplished his objective. He requested me to edit his journal. A description of his machine has been given, with the log of his journey through the Earth's atmospheric belt. – GEH

Part 3 of Journal

Having determined the depth of the Earth's atmospheric belt, and discovered that the surrounding aether had a measurable density, I now turned from my anxious watching of the atmospheric indicator to view the rapidly receding Earth.

From the spectacular point of view the sight was exhilarating in the extreme. No living person had ever witnessed the sight that now met my view. When I left the Earth's surface the weather had been fine. Not a cloud had been visible in the sky. But now I had been upon my journey for 56 hours and had travelled nearly 17,000 miles.

As I looked through my observation windows I saw that the weather had changed upon Earth. At one time I could see vast areas of the Earth's surface, at another time it would be obscured by the fitful clouds. Presently, after I had been refreshed with food and sleep, I looked again, and this time I was rewarded with as wonderful a sight as human eye had ever gazed upon. Gone were the clouds, and the Sun's refulgent beams poured down upon the world that a short while ago had been my home. My ravished gaze passed slowly from one wonder to another. I could still distinguish the continental areas by their colouring of darkish brown. And not only could I trace portions of the oceanic areas by their green-greyish hue, but I actually caught a glimpse of the Sun's reflection reflected like a point of light from its waters.

And then my attention was fixed upon a most wonderful phenomenon! I ought to have anticipated this sight, for, after all, it was an elementary feature of the Earth-Moon system. Hundreds of times had I watched the Moon wax and wane. First from crescent to full and then from full to crescent again. But now I saw the phenomenon in a reversed aspect. It was the Earth that was passing through phases instead of the Moon, though in an inverted direction. Three-fourths of the Earth's hemisphere turned towards me in brilliant sunshine, the other fourth was in the shade of night.

Needless to say this discovery afforded me the liveliest satisfaction. It revealed to me I had now left Earth-influence behind me, and I was journeying with the Moon. Our satellite tenaciously held the magnetic antennae projected from the apex of my machine. It was immaterial now how long my journey would take. I knew that my machine was bound to alight upon some portion of the Moon's surface.

It was simply glorious to watch the gradually changing aspect of the Earth; to see the darkened portion extending and the light portion assuming the ever beautiful crescent. That the old Earth revolved upon an axis I now proved from actual observation. The topography of its surface changed every hour. Out of the shaded gloom would steal a dark brown or greeny-grey area, and moving across the field of light, would disappear round the limb of the Earth's disc.

But there was one contingency I had not reckoned upon: and when it came upon me it filled me with a vague and indefinable dread. I had been so fascinated with the changing aspect of the Earth that I had taken little notice of the globe to which I was rapidly approaching.

Even when I did look through my forward observation window at the moon no thought of impending disaster crossed my mind. It was the wonderfully enhanced dimensions of her disc that first held my attention; for at this moment the moon was full-orbed. She now appeared to me to be at least six times as large as when I was upon the earth. From the growth of her bulk I passed to a detailed examination of her outstanding features. I had long been familiar with these features, but only as I saw them through my 8-inch aperture equatorial telescope. But now I saw them with the unaided vision as no telescope on earth could show them.

I easily picked out the wonderful walled plain of 'Ptolemaus', centrally placed upon the moon's surface and a little to the south of the equatorial line. Immediately beneath and practically adjoining was another ringed plain I knew to be 'Alphonsus'.

'Ptolemaus' had long fascinated me in my research work because of the number of unexplained details that lay scattered upon its floor. I saw now that they appeared to be small craters, of which I should judge the number to be about 150. How joyfully I anticipated my descent upon the moon's surface, for then I should have the secret of their construction within my grasp.

From a study of 'Ptolemaus' I turned my attention to the 'Mare Imbrium' situated almost on the western edge of the moon. I saw now many details situated on the Mare that were impossible of detection from earth.

And then I saw the thing that filled me with alarm and dread. The western edge of the Mare was tinged in a dark, foreboding shadow. I saw in a moment I had miscalculated the timing of my journey. I had been at pains to work out the time of my arrival upon the moon so that it should coincide with our satellite's full-orbed phase. I should then have time to find my position and be able to move my machine as to be continually in full daylight. By some terrible mischance I had miscalculated. The moon was already beginning to wane upon its western edge. Even though I could speed up my machine another 100 miles per hour I knew I should be too late. I did not fear the cold of the Lunar night. That could not touch me housed as I was in the machine. It was the fact I should have to make my landing upon an unknown and practically unchartered surface. In the terrible darkness I should not be able to see when to retard my power in order to make a safe landing. I had not anticipated the presence of such a danger and when I realised what it meant I turned sick with a haunting fear.

(To be continued)

A Visit to the Moon (4)
Recorded by George E Hobbs

(First published: September 7, 1923)

Synopsis – My friend, Christopher Jackson, had long been obsessed with a desire to visit the Moon. He disappeared for three years. Suddenly he came to me again, dying in my arms after declaring he had accomplished his objective. He requested me to edit his journal. A description of his machine and the log of his journey through the Earth's atmospheric belt has been given. He fears he will alight upon the night side of the Moon. – GEH

Part 4 of Journal

If I was engaged upon writing a novel instead of recording the happenings which befell me on my journey to the Moon, I could alter my position with a mere stroke of the pen from that soul-stirring danger to one of absolute security. But as it is my desire to record the incidents just as they happened I cannot be false to my experience.

Again I looked through my observation window, hoping against hope my eyes had deceived me. But no! There upon the Mare was the fateful shadow. The change which had taken place was almost imperceptible. Yet I knew that awesome gloom was rapidly extending. I knew that long before I reached the Moon the hemisphere turned towards me would be covered with an impenetrable mantle of darkness.

But the reader of this journal may well ask why I made no provision for external lights to my machine. The answer is a simple one. I had been overconfident. As I explained in my previous journal, I had calculated upon reaching our satellite when her hemisphere turned towards me was full-orbed. The only lights I had thought necessary to take were six fully-charged electric flash lamps. And these were taken so that I could inspect at any time the internal parts of my mechanism.

I shall remember to my dying day the hour of my despair. Even now, safe as I am, and joyous at the knowledge of my success, there are times when the horror of that hour overwhelms me. For a time I completely lost my nerve, and gave myself up for lost.

Presently, however, calmer thoughts prevailed. My wild, senseless ravings ceased, and I rose weak and shaken to obtain the refreshments I so much needed.

There was but one chance in a thousand of a safe landing. And I prayed fervently for that one chance to be mine.

I come now to the thirtieth day of my journey. I calculated I had traversed 216,000 miles, and had yet somewhere about 25,000 miles yet to traverse. Another three days would see me at my journey's end: Either to be smashed to a pulp, or with a safe landing, there to await the welcome return of the Lunar day. As no danger could possibly accrue for at least two days, I determined to obtain as much sleep as I could, so that my nerves would be well braced for the coming ordeal.

Two days passed. I had entered the momentous stage of my journey. Everything around me was darker than the darkest night I had ever experienced upon the Earth. I set my forward power to half retardation point and then, to distract my mind from any thought of impending disaster, busied myself with inspecting, by the aid of my flash lamp, the indicator and essential equipment.

For eight hours I maintained my perambulating vigil. The half-an-inch was still constant in the atmospheric gauge. I avoided the observation windows as one would avoid a plague spot. I dare not look. I would not look! But just as the scene of a murder fascinates the murderer and compels his return to the place, so was I partially hypnotised by those windows, and compelled at last to look through them.

And what a sight met my gaze! For a moment I thought the strain of the past hours had crazed my brain; or that I saw a mirage, even as travellers in the great sandy deserts see them. But self-analysis proved I was perfectly normal. And it could not be a mirage, for that which I saw remained fadeless and constant. Like a phosphorescent glow I saw the rugged surface of the Moon. It was no phantasy, but real. Oh, how my heart beat with unrepressed gladness. The danger I had anticipated melted into thin air. And the explanation of this phenomenon was so simple. Let me explain.

I wrote in my previous journal that after I had left Earth's influence, instead of the Moon I saw the Earth passing through phases. The fuller experience which I had just encountered proved that I was partly wrong in making that statement. My timing miscalculation had caused me to see a double phenomenon. Both the Moon and the Earth were passing through phases. As, therefore, I should alight upon the night side of our satellite – that is, its "new" phase from the Earth – it followed as a necessary, natural sequence that the Earth would be full-orbed.

And even as Moonlight – at full moon – is reflected upon the Earth, so Earthlight, when the Earth is full-orbed, would be reflected upon the Moon.

This, then, was the simple explanation, the cause of my joy. The delicate phosphorescent glow which revealed to me the rugged surface of the Moon was light reflected from the Earth. I now retarded my forward power another 25 degrees but, finding no reduction in speed, I brought the pointer to zero, which shut off my power completely. To my surprise even this brought no retardation, but rather was there an acceleration. In a moment I divined the cause. I was now within Lunar gravitational influence and was, indeed, rapidly descending towards the Moon's surface.

It was the work of a moment to throw my forward into negative action, thus setting up detraction. At the same time I threw the aft control into positive action, and immediately the magnetic antennae became attracted by the Earth. It was just as though a powerful brake had been applied, and gradually the machine steadied down to 25 miles per hour.

Having now made all safe for a controlled descent, I worked out the distance I was from the Moon. I was particularly anxious to be accurate regarding my position for this reason: I knew that popular theory discountenanced a Lunar atmosphere. In my own mind I believed one to exist. I intended, therefore, to be extra vigilant in watching the atmospheric indicator, so that not only could I tell if an atmosphere existed, but also its density and depth.

My calculations proved I was 400 miles form the Moon's surface. Hour after hour I watched the indicator, but at 200 miles there was no difference in the mercury tube. As I could watch no longer I held the machine stationary by the controls and slept.

At 150 miles from the Moon, there being no change in the tube, I steadied the machine down to 10 miles per hour. In five hours, or exactly 100 miles from the Moon's surface, there came a sensible alteration upon the indicator. In the next 50 miles descent the mercury rose to the extent of two and a half inches. Higher and higher it rose, until it stood at exactly 10 inches.

At that moment I was thrown violently to the floor of my observation room. In watching the atmospheric indicator I had not been careful to observe my near approach to the Moon's surface. I fell forward upon my face, and for a time everything became blank.

When eventually I regained consciousness and could look around me I found that my machine was firmly held between two giant boulders. I had not the slightest idea of my position. But one consolation was mine. I had at last reached my objective.

(To be continued)

A Visit to the Moon (5)
Recorded by George E Hobbs
(First published: September 14, 1923)

Synopsis – My friend, Christopher Jackson, had long been obsessed with a desire to visit the Moon. He disappeared for three years. Suddenly he came to me again, dying in my arms, after declaring he had accomplished his objective. He requested me to edit his journal. A description of his machine and the log of the initial stage of his journey has been given. He has arrived upon the Moon, but, through miscalculation, has arrived upon its dark or night side. – GEH

Part 5 of Journal

It is, I suppose, a psychological fact of human experience that mental joy may supersede physical agony and discomfort. At least this seems to be true so long as the mental ecstasy endures. When my machine crashed I had been thrown so heavily as to lose consciousness for a considerable period. But when consciousness returned, the knowledge of success completely banished from my mind all thought of physical hurt, or of what damage my machine had sustained. It was enough for the moment to know I had achieved that which was declared to be impossible.

Presently, however, the evanescence of my feelings spent itself, and with its waning powers there crept over my body the agony of my hurt. To my intense relief I found upon examination that no bones were broken. What I should have done had a collar bone, arm or leg been fractured I really do not know. Even so, thankful as I was, the pain of my hurt was almost unendurable. From head to toe I was one mass of bruises.

When the agony became less intense, I ventured out from my observation room in order to take a survey of any damage done to the machine. In doing so I strapped around my shoulders a portable oxygen apparatus. The damage, if extensive, would naturally cause internal and external atmospheric conditions to equalise. And as I was venturing into circumstances that were purely experimental, I determined to take every reasonable care.

In making an exhaustive examination I found to my intense satisfaction that no damage had been encountered. It puzzled me greatly at the time why no damage had been sustained. But when presently the Lunar daylight came, I found the problem very simple of solution.

The reader of this journal will remember that, finding myself within Lunar gravitational influence, I threw my forward control into negative, and my rear control into positive action. This sudden transference of power caused the outer casing of my machine to tilt towards the north pole of the Moon. The result was, instead of making a perpendicular descent, the machine was deflected to an angle of 60 degrees. My descent, therefore, instead of a sheer drop, became a glide, and the machine, passing over a huge chasm, had become wedged in a "V" shaped crevice of a volcano crater summit.

This, of course, I was not to learn until eight terrestrial days, or 192 hours, had passed, and the Lunar daylight had revealed to me this cause.

The stars all around me were visible, but as I was unfavourably placed for strict observation, they afforded me little satisfaction during my period of waiting. But there were other points of interest. Points which helped me to possess my soul with patience in awaiting the welcome return of the Sun. From my observation windows I could still see – though somewhat indistinctly – the tracery of wonderful formations. Needless to say these intrigued me greatly. Upon every feature that came under observation a soft mantle of white seemed to rest. But whether this was due to reflected earth-light, or hoar-frost I could not at the moment tell.

Never shall I forget the dawn of the Lunar day. My limitations as a descriptive writer will prevent me from portraying even a semblance of its wonder, its magnificence, or its glory. Had I the pen of a Sir Sidney Low I should still feel the futility of words in attempting the description of that wonderful pageant of glory. It baffles description. It must be seen to be appreciated.

I had been to sleep, and upon rising I remember calculating that in 48 hours' time the Sun would be making his appearance. Feeling elated that the period of darkness would soon be over, I placed my log book in the locker and stood and glanced through the west observation window. To my surprise I saw that the features facing me were somewhat brighter than when I had last observed them.

Turning to the eastern aspect for comparison, I saw what was the commencement of the most wonderful sight I had ever witnessed. Stretching away to the East, the lunar features were bathed in a soft radiant light. As my eye traced the higher levels the light became of an increasing splendour, until, far away, the peaks of a magnificent mountain range were flooded with a silvery whiteness.

In rapturous awe I gazed upon the scene. It was the Lunar dawn, but so slowly did it advance that one was almost led to imagine it was a permanent feature of the Moon's economy. Hour after hour I watched with no thought of food and no thought of rest. My whole being was galvanised into vision. I only felt as I saw; and as the soft rays of light tired not my eyes, so was I free from weariness in my body. Presently I saw what I knew must be logical and natural. The dawn was advancing. Mountain peaks at lower altitudes were flashing out the message of advancing light.

Then the limb of the Sun made its appearance over the peaks of the distant range of mountains. And what a Sun it was! The same luminary I had served upon the Earth each succeeding day – and yet a different Sun! The orb I was familiar with upon the Earth was a huge ball of incandescent gas. One that could not be observed without the aid of tinted glass, and by that aid one saw merely a perfect round disc of utter passivity. But now the Sun transformed into the liveliest activity. I could gaze upon the Sun's disc with infinitely less hurt to my eyes than when upon earth, while from his limb there shot forth those wonderful red prominences which can only be seen by terrestrial astronomers during a total solar eclipse. Spurts of flaming gas shot forth in all directions, making one of the weirdest, yet the most beautiful pictures I had ever been privileged to see.

As the Sun rose higher in the heavens, wonder succeeded wonder until I scarce knew whether I was an ordinary Earth-dweller, or had died and passed into an enchanted land.

Upon Earth I had been familiar with the blue sky during the day time, with the entire absence of stars. But as the Sun rose upon the Lunar landscape the sky was not blue, but blue-black. And the crowning feature of celestial phenomena was the fact that stars of the first magnitude were visible all the time.

But now it was perfect daylight, and when at last I could take myself from the wonders around me, I began to make preparations to leave the machine. It was here that the most perilous part of my adventure would commence. Was it possible for me to roam the Lunar landscape? That was the possibility I must now attempt.

(To be continued)

A Visit to the Moon (6)
Recorded by George E Hobbs
(First published: September 21, 1923)

Synopsis – My friend, Christopher Jackson, had long been obsessed by a desire to visit the Moon. He disappeared for three years. Suddenly he came to me again, dying in my arms, after declaring he had accomplished his objective. He requested me to edit his journal. A description of his machine, and the log of the initial stages of his journey have been given. He has witnessed the sunrise upon the Lunar landscape, and is now about to leave his machine in order to explore the Moon's surface. – GEH

Part 6 of Journal

I have ever found it good policy, when venturing into paths hitherto unexplored, to think twice before acting once. Even when a decision has been arrived at I invariably weigh again the pro and con of the venture, in order to see that the chances of failure are reduced to a minimum. It was well I obeyed the rule upon the occasion of leaving the machine. Had I made my exit upon the first impulse the chances are this journal would never have been written.

The Sun was now a beautiful object in the heavens, fringed around his limb with a wonderful corona. Every formation upon the Moon's surface was bathed in sunlight, even to the lowest valley. And the mantle of white I had observed previous to the sunrise had now entirely disappeared. I had no hesitation in believing it was a fairly deep covering of snow.

I had made up my mind the time was now opportune to leave the machine in order to explore the Lunar landscape, but before putting this into execution, thought over again my plan of procedure. I slid back the door of the observation room and stepped out on to the small platform which was between this room and the outer shell. Through the outer window I saw a ledge about five feet square which engaged splendidly with the outer door, and upon which I could step with perfect safety. But glancing to the right and then to the left of this ledge I saw there was a precipitous drop of some two or three thousand feet. Had I attempted an exit upon the first impulse, not knowing what effect the attenuated atmosphere of the mountain peak would have upon me, the attempt would probably have ended in disaster. It was altogether impossible for me to gain the valley safely by way of those cliffs. There was only one thing to be done, and done it was at once. I threw my rear control into strong positive action, which had the effect of not only dislodging the machine from the crater cleft, but also of placing my machine upon an even keel. When once clear of the cleft I reversed the power, and the machine, with a graceful curve, slowly descended to the valley below.

When the machine came to rest I noticed with a start of surprise that the atmospheric indicator recorded a rise of two inches in the mercury tube. This meant that the surface pressure of the Lunar atmosphere was about six pounds to the square inch. This was rather low compared to the Earth's atmosphere. Still, I thought there was probably some other elemental factor which would operate in favour of my breathing without using my portable oxygen apparatus. For the time being, however, I strapped the apparatus around my shoulders, adjusted the valve and mouthpiece, threw back the outer door, and by the aid of a short rope ladder, descended to the ground.

I felt such sensations as Peary and Amundsen must have experienced, when, after arduous and anxious labours, the North or South pole was reached. I was the first Earth-dweller in the whole history of the universe to stand upon Lunar soil. The world "soil" is not a misnomer, for the ground upon which I stood was soft to my feet, blue-gray in colour and of a composition which I verily believed was capable of sustaining vegetation.

It was even as I thought. Casting my eyes towards the base of a range of hills which formed the west side of the valley, I saw a long patch of what appeared to be dwarf vegetation.

As I did not wish to move far from the machine until more certain of my bearings, I raised my binoculars to my eyes in order to verify my assumption that the patch was indeed vegetation. I had scarcely adjusted the sight and focused the patch when a startled exclamation escaped my lips. I judged I should be three miles at least from the range of hills, but clearly through my binoculars I saw a score of objects emerge from a cave-like passage and move out amongst the vegetation. The crawl of some of these objects convinced me they were animals, and the upright posture of four convinced me they were of an intelligent order.

Here was a discovery indeed! Hastily I regained the machine; shut and locked the outer door, and sat down in my observation room in a maze of wonder and thought. Why I retired so hastily to the machine I scarcely knew. Probably it was instinctive self-preservation. At any rate I was conscious of the fact I possessed no weapons, either offensive or defensive; and, therefore, until I knew the character and disposition of the Lunarians, I made up my mind to stay within the security of the machine.

After I had recovered somewhat from the mental excitement which had assailed me, I went to the outer window again and took a survey through my binoculars. The Lunarians had evidently caught sight of my machine, for a large group were now standing outside the cave entrance, and one, who seemed a sort of leader, was gesticulating wildly among his fellows.

The vision of those beings must have been wonderfully keen, for though I searched carefully with my glasses, no optic apparatus was visible among them.

Another thing that impressed itself upon me was the height of these beings. Although I was not less than three miles from them I could see that the shortest of them was taller than the tallest man upon the Earth. For an hour I continued to watch them, and then the band, forming a semi-circle around the animals, drove them back into the cave.

I can honestly vouch that if fear had been the cause of my hasty flight into the machine, all vestige of that emotion had now vanished. I continued to remain where I was, not because I feared these beings would kill me upon their return, but because I wished to study them at close quarters unimpaired by having to fight for my life. Anxiously I awaited their return; and presently from out of the cave, there emerged a troop of about thirty. Eagerly I trained my binoculars upon them. However much I had speculated upon their appearance, speculation would soon give place to verification, for I saw that the band had decided upon a concerted advance towards my machine.

As the band approached nearer I was amazed both at their physique and their manner of advance. The shortest of them was fully seven feet in height, while the tallest would be at least seven feet nine inches.

The band was still some distance away, but to my eyes, the nearer they approached the more grotesque did they appear. Not a sign of fear was visible in their gait. They approached boldly and with confidence. But – I know of no better figure of speech – they were just like walking posts. Upright as an arrow, lithe and pliant in their step, but the most corpulent would scarcely measure more than twenty inches around his girth.

At fifty yards from the machine this band of unique beings stopped, and I eagerly awaited their next move.

(To be continued)

A Visit to the Moon (7)
Recorded by George E Hobbs
(First published: September 28, 1923)

Synopsis – My friend, Christopher Jackson, had long been obsessed by a desire to visit the Moon. He disappeared for three years. Suddenly he came to me again, dying in my arms, after declaring he had accomplished his objective. He requested me to edit his journal. He has arrived upon the Moon, and from the observation window of his machine he sees a band of Moon dwellers approaching. At a distance of fifty yards from the machine the Lunarians ceased to advance. – GEH

Part 7 of Journal

Many things absorbed my mind as I continued to watch that band of unique beings standing some fifty yards from my machine. Although their attenuated appearance and lofty stature presented a somewhat grotesque picture to my eyes, I could well conceive that the natural economy of the Moon was solely responsible for their physical condition. I had long ago reasoned that the two principal modifying factors of physical evolution were atmospheric pressure and density. I conceived that aeons before, when the Moon was at the zenith of her planetary existence, she possessed an atmosphere comparable to that of the Earth's present atmosphere.

At that time the sentient beings upon her surface would also be comparable in physical structure to present day Earth dwellers. But in the subsequent process of decay – which process must attend all things material – the Lunar gravitative power would decrease in proportion to the decay. Consequently the lighter gases which primarily surrounded the Moon would escape into the surrounding space.

But – and this is an important factor – the escape would not be sudden but gradual. No single generation, nor, indeed, several generations could possibly have detected the escape. Had the escape been the work of a month, a year, or even a hundred years, then, long before that century had passed, the whole sentient life of the Moon would have been ruthlessly exterminated. No, I conceived the change to have been of true evolutionary grandeur – slow, majestic and sure. And in the slow elemental change came of necessity, corresponding physical changes to the sentient life of the Moon.

I had no cause to doubt my reasoning. Here before my eyes was concrete proof. The very forms of the Lunarians had been modified by the gradually diminishing pressure and density of the Lunar atmosphere.

But my cogitations were at that moment interrupted. The Lunarians had evidently decided to take a closer inspection of my machine. Boldly they advanced, until they were right beneath the window at which I was stationed. Not one of them attempted to touch one single portion of the machine, though I saw they were greatly interested in my atmospheric gauges which were attached to the outside casing. With perfect composure the whole band circled the machine, then halted once more beneath the window.

I thought it was now an opportune moment to reveal my presence. Passing from the side I advanced to the centre of the window in such a position as to be visible to the whole band of the Lunarians. The effect upon them was truly electrical. They had viewed the machine with stoical calm. But now a strange vocabulary assailed my ears. Excitedly they spoke and gesticulated, and then, spontaneously and unanimously, their long arms shot above their heads, with palms open and extended towards the machine. Thus they remained for a moment of time; then, with perfect grace of movement, bent forward until the fingers touched the ground.

However much I may have misunderstood the worship like posture of these strange beings, of one thing I was certain. Their actions denoted amity and peace. One thing, however, made me hesitate for a moment to join them upon the ground. Through the window they had seen me without the paraphernalia of my portable oxygen apparatus strapped around me. What would they do when they saw my nose and mouth covered by the respirator? Yet I dare not descend without it. It was but for a moment I hesitated, then, adjusting the apparatus around my shoulders I threw back the doors and descended to the ground.

In perfect silence the band received my approach. But the instant I had reached the foremost of them the whole company raised aloft the right hand, which, in its descent, touched first their right then their left shoulder. This, I concluded, was their method of salutation, and, believing this, I returned their sign of friendship by the same mode. The look of awesome wonder upon their faces quickly gave place to that of respectful pleasure and delight upon my returning the salute; and at the time it puzzled me greatly why this should be so. In my subsequent stay among them, however, this became quite clear to me. I found that in greeting one another the Lunarians merely doubled the right arm and touched the right shoulder with their finger tips. But when, in the attitude of worship, they approached the altar of their Deity, the right hand was raised above the head and, in its descent, touched first the right and then the left shoulder. The symbolic meaning of this ritual was very beautiful – though to me, upon learning its significance, it was embarrassing. In simple language the personal salutation between the Lunarians, in touching the one shoulder only, meant – "I am at your service in virtue of our common brotherhood."

But when in standing before the Deity both shoulders were touched, the implication was that of complete surrender of body and spirit – the whole being – to the service of their invisible Lord. It said: "Wholly am I thine. Therefore do I serve thee with my whole powers, by virtue of thy Lordship and Kingship!"

When I discovered the meaning of this ritual I saw at once why the look of pleasure and delight had shown itself upon their faces: It was that I, a supernatural being, had "condescended" to greet them in their own peculiar way instead of showing superior aloofness. Upon its discovery, too, I hastened by every means at my command to show them I was one like unto themselves. That in knowledge and in power I was hedged about by limitations.

But I digress. Let me return to my first meeting with these wonderful and unique creatures. As there seemed to be no common basis of language between us (this I shall discuss later) I tried to make them understand me by signs. Naturally the first thing I wished them to know was the place from which I had come. And in this I found little difficulty. I first pointed to myself, then to the machine, and then, with a wide sweep of the arm upwards, I pointed to where I could see a thin illuminated crescent. I knew that to be the Earth emerging from its "new" phase.

I looked towards the band to see if they understood what I wished to convey. They understood perfectly. Yet I noticed a shade of disappointment pass across the countenance of the Lunarians. I was at a loss to understand this until one bolder than the rest pointed to the Sun and then to me. At the same time he uttered words which sounded like "Aura Boreal". I certainly did not understand the meaning of his words, but I instinctively divined the meaning of his action. He, with the rest of the band, thought I had descended from the most important orb in the Lunar sky – the Sun. I shook my head and pointed again to the crescent-shaped Earth.

The look of disappointment passed, and having satisfied them from whence I had come, I made signs to them that they should inspect the interior of my machine. But under no circumstances would they comply with my request. Rather did they urgently wish me to leave the machine standing where it was and accompany them to their homes.

(To be continued)

A Visit to the Moon (8)
Recorded by George E Hobbs
(First published: October 5, 1923)

Synopsis – My friend, Christopher Jackson, had long been obsessed with a desire to visit the Moon. He disappeared for three years. Suddenly he came to me again, dying in my arms after declaring he had accomplished his objective. He requested me to edit his journal. A description of his machine, his voyage through space and his arrival upon the Moon has been given. He is now with a group of Moon-dwellers. – GEH

Part 8 of Journal

I now come to the part of my adventures which proved to be the most astonishing, yet, the most fascinating of all I passed through. And yet I ought not to use the word "astonishing," for I had already encountered such unique experiences that nothing further should have occasioned me surprise. The fact that I had stood upon Lunar soil and was even now in the midst of a group of Lunar men, should have so inured me against further surprise, so to make me believe that all subsequent happenings were just ordinary and perfectly natural. But it was not so, as the sequel will show.

A strong and unanimous request was urged by the Lunarians to abandon the machine and accompany them to their homes. But I felt this was an impossible suggestion. Even now the supply of oxygen in my portable apparatus was beginning to fail. I began to find my breathing restricted and this was sign enough to me that it was time to replenish the supply. I therefore made signs to the Lunarians that I must adjourn to the machine, at the same time making them understand the adjournment was but temporary.

Upon reaching the machine I recharged the apparatus, and then sat thinking how best I could overcome the difficulty of having to wear constantly the respirator. I hoped not only to be able to understand the language of this strange people, but also to converse with them. But conversation would be impossible, if, during my stay, I always had to have the respirator over my mouth. Then there was the difficulty of food. Out on the plain it would be fatal for me to remove the respirator even for a moment.

But invention has ever been the child of necessity, and after an hour's toil I designed an arrangement which I trusted would meet my requirements. From the light rectangular reservoir strapped upon my back, I connected a flexible metallic tube to a perforated aluminium receptacle, which fitted around my forehead immediately beneath my cap. An automatic restrictor allowed just the amount of oxygen to pass through the perforations to meet my needs. I found upon testing the arrangement in the open that it performed its duty admirably.

Even the small amount of oxygen released through the perforations, being heavier than Lunar atmosphere, was able easily to displace the attenuated Lunar elements and give to me perfect freedom in breathing. As I dare not go far from my machine I conveyed to the Lunarians by signs they easily understood, that I would rise into the air and take the machine near to their cave-like home. The company immediately started for home, and I landed the machine about 20 yards from the cave.

Previous to rejoining my new friends I made sure of at least a 96 hour supply of oxygen in my portable tanks and, not knowing the quality of food partaken of by the Lunarians, I also took with me a 96 hour supply of concentrated rations.

When I descended from the machine only four of the Lunarians were waiting for me. I was informed by signs that the others had gone to bring out their cattle to browse again upon the vegetation in the immediate vicinity of the cave. The vegetation was really a coarse plant of exceeding rapid growth. I was informed that within an hour of the melting of the snows, consequent upon the Lunar night, the plant had already shot through the ground. And within eight hours it had grown to such an extent that the cattle could feed upon it. The roots of this plant were untouched by the snows and nature had decreed the roots to be practically everlasting.

The cattle I found to be as grotesque as the Lunarians had appeared to me. No animals existing upon the earth could be compared to them. The head and neck resembled that of a giraffe, the forequarters that of a kangaroo, and the hindquarters that of an elephant. There was this difference, however, that while the hindquarters resembled in bulk that of an elephant, the hind legs and feet resembled those of a gigantic hare. In other words, these creatures had a strange resemblance to the prehistoric Iguanodon.

Here, it seemed, that nature had produced one of her paradoxes. The animals both in its forequarters and its elongated neck seemed to me to be adapted for obtaining its food from the leaves of trees – as did the prehistoric Iguanodon. But they were more or less in a prone, and seemingly an awkward posture, browsing upon the plant life of the plain. As far as my sight guided me there was not the slightest indication of a tree anywhere. But I found shortly afterwards that I had been altogether too precipitate in my conclusions.

I had barely noted these facts when my guides intimated they wished me to accompany them into the cave. And I scarcely need say that I obeyed their request at once.

At the mouth of the cave I paused in sheer amazement. The ground sloped downwards at an angle of about 15 degrees and the perfectly natural tunnel was roomy and very lofty. But what caused me amazement was that instead of the tunnel being dark it was as light as though we were still upon the plain. I saw at a glance that the light was not artificial but natural sunlight. And presently, after we had traversed about half a mile, the cause was made plain to me.

High up in the vaulted roof double layers of a transparent substance – similar to glass, but of a different texture – and of a toughness that necessity had demanded of the former Lunarians, were fixed. I found there were thousands of these "skylights," and they were fixed from the Lunar surface in the great "ringplains" of the moon, where the feet of the Lunarians rarely trod and which was unsuitable for plant cultivation. In other words the "skylights" were fixed in the huge craters of extinct volcanoes.

We had traversed about a mile and a quarter, with the ground still on the downward grade when the tunnel opened out on either side, and I came upon a scene so wonderful as to make me think I was dreaming. But no. There it was, as real and as substantial as the moon herself. Broad cultivated patches of land, hedgerows, trees, streets, houses, and even a wide lake of clear water met my view.

Could one but forget the roof and the massive basaltic pillars which supported it, the scene may have been compared to that of a typical township scene upon the Earth. I noticed that the houses were of the semi-detached type, roofed and windowed as houses were upon the Earth. Although the town was built underground I found that there was a substantial reason for roofing the houses in the "pitch" roof style.

During the Lunar night, which lasted fourteen days of terrestrial time, each cave entrance was barred by massive doors. Grids of a given area were fixed in the doors to allow a circulation of air. But as the Lunar night air was of a treacherous character the grids were so made as to allow a restricted air entry. The result was that towards the end of the Lunar night the underground temperature began to rise and the atmosphere became more or less humid. The high vaulted roof of the cave was, of course, cold, owing to the snows above it: and as the rising temperature came in contact with the cold roof, condensation was caused and water particles dropped like a shower of rain upon the houses and the ground beneath.

This water was not suitable for drinking purposes, but was collected in huge cisterns and distributed to the houses by means of conduits, for ablution purposes only. The water for drinking purposes was obtained from the melting of the snow, running through channels into underground reservoirs, but at a higher level than that of the houses.

No mechanical means therefore was needed to control the water supply, as it fell by gravitation to the house taps.

(To be continued)

A Visit to the Moon (9)
Recorded by George E Hobbs
(First published: October 12, 1923)

Synopsis – My friend, Christopher Jackson, had long been obsessed by a desire to visit the Moon. He disappeared for three years. Suddenly he came to me again, dying in my arms after declaring he had accomplished his objective. He requested me to edit his journal. A description of his machine, his voyage through space, and his arrival upon the Moon has been given. He is now with a company of Moon-dwellers, learning many startling things of the life upon the Moon. – GEH

Part 9 of Journal

I have already explained that the Lunarians in their excusable ignorance, had mistakenly given me the status of a supernatural being. And though I had repeatedly striven to convey to them the fact that I was just an ordinary individual, my mode of conveyance had been singularly ineffective. In a multitude of ways they still affirmed their belief in my supernatural constitution. Although, at times, this belief had its compensations, there were times when it was exceedingly embarrassing. It was so when the following experience befell me.

I had been upon my feet now some twenty hours. What with the walking and the continual strain upon my nerves, excited as they were by each new discovery, I was beginning to feel physically and mentally fagged. Had I been upon the earth, six hours of exercise would have physically exhausted me. But under the very low pressure of the Moon's atmospheric belt, I found each movement of my limbs so light and buoyant that I could endure a much longer period of physical exercise without distress.

But twenty hours of continuous sight seeing had fagged me, and I longed for a period of rest. To my surprise, however my guides were as fresh as when I first came in contact with them. Not a sign of fatigue did they show. A vague suspicion took possession of my mind, which not only grew stronger as the moments passed, but eventually proved itself to be a question of fact. It was this. With the changing conditions of the Moon's economy there came not only corresponding physical changes to the Moon-dwellers, but also changes in the manner of living. As the day and night lengthened so the Lunarian's powers of endurance extended, refreshed by the longer sleep and rest attained during the Lunar night. Now the lunar day corresponded to 14 Earth-days, and the Lunar night to a similar period. So that the Lunarians were awake and active for 672 Earth hours, and rested and slept for 672 Earth hours.

It was a mental and physical impossibility to attempt an emulation of the Lunarians' endurance. At the same time, as they insisted upon accepting me as a supernatural being, it would not do to show signs of weariness so early. It was a dilemma of the greatest delicacy, yet I smile even now at the simple and childish way I extricated myself from the position without loss of dignity.

Through one of the 'skylights' I caught a glimpse of the crescent-shaped Earth. Clasping my hands together I laid my cheek upon them in an attitude of reflective repose. Then, raising my right hand, I slowly described a semi-circle from the Lunarians towards the earth. Here my hand remained poised for a moment, then, slowly I moved it forward to where I knew the Earth's position would be in 8 hours' time. I then described another semi-circle in the opposite direction, from the Earth's assumed position back to the group watching me; thus completing the circle. Pointing to the nearest house I laid my cheek again upon my clasped hands, then looked to see if they comprehended my meaning. I found that they understood perfectly what I wished to convey; that for a period of eight hours I wished to be left in reflective seclusion. And when I found myself reclining upon a soft, seductive couch, and my friend had differentially withdrawn, I promptly went to sleep.

I am quite aware that my method was childishly simple. But then I had to deal with beings not only whose language I did not understand, but also, who, though intelligent enough to cope with every-day exigencies, were but creatures of their age. They formed for me an exceedingly interesting study; for I saw that they typified the last stages of planetary sentient life. I conceived it was logical to suppose that evolution had played its part upon the Moon even as it had upon the earth. And that even as life had developed from a lowly origin, and had passed by successive stages – by adaptation to environment – to the zenith of its intellectual capacity, so in the decay of the Moon's constitution its sentient life would also be adversely affected. In fancy, I could see the earth in the dying condition of the Moon: And I conceived that the time would come when, even as there had been the first man and woman, so there would be the last man and woman.

That even as the first human pair were the joyful possessors of a garden world, with powers of reproduction to people the world with a widening intelligence, so there would be a last human pair; the sorrowful possessors of a desert world; with powers of reproduction abortive and sterile. The last man would lay the last woman to rest, that he himself may lay down to die.

But let me return to my narrative. It will take much too long for me to detail every incident in their consecutive order. Not only so, but since my return to earth I have found cardiac troubles which have caused me disquietude. I have a conviction my time is at hand; though I pray for strength that I may complete my journal. I must therefore record only the outstanding features of my two years' stay with the Lunarians. It was during the first long Lunar night that I began to understand the language of the Moon-dwellers. And though eventually I was able easily to converse with them, it is a language impossible to translate into any of the known languages of earth. Some of the phonetic sounds I may be able to indicate by written letters, but even these are very few. Their words seemed to be richly interspersed with sounds corresponding to L.R.S.Y. But probably owing to structural changes of some of the head and throat organs there was a curious absence of the "Dentals," D. and T., the "Gutturals" G. and K., and the "Nasals," Ng., N. and M.

I went with my friends just before the Lunar night set in, in order to close the great doors which barricaded the cave-entrance, first obtaining a plentiful supply of oxygen of my fourteen day's need. After the doors were closed there followed a period of twelve hours in which final preparations were made for the long night's sleep. It was during this twelve-hour period that I gleaned a great deal of interesting information regarding that side of the Moon which is never seen by dwellers upon earth.

(To be continued)

A Visit to the Moon (10)
Recorded by George E Hobbs
(First published: October 26, 1923)

Synopsis – My friend Christopher Jackson, had long been obsessed by a desire to visit the Moon. He disappeared for three years. Suddenly he came to me again, dying in my arms after declaring he had accomplished his objective. He requested me to edit his journal. A description of his machine, his voyage through space and his arrival upon the moon has been given. He is now with a company of Moon-dwellers, learning many startling things of the life upon the Moon. – GEH

Part 10 of Journal

It is an elementary feature of the Earth-Moon system that the Moon always presents the same hemisphere towards the Earth. Solar and terrestrial influences have so operated upon the Lunar tides as to steady down the Moon's axial rotation to that of her journey around the Earth. The Moon therefore turns upon her axis once in about 27 days.

The off-side of the Moon has ever intrigued astronomers to conjecture upon its appearance: And it is generally assumed that the hemisphere not seen by terrestrial observers is the physical replica of the hemisphere that is seen. But this assumption I found to be scarcely correct. There are no huge mountain ranges on the offside of the Moon. Nearly the whole of the hemisphere is a vast flat plain, strewn with a medley of gigantic boulders. And the cause of this was made plain to me when I began to understand the language of the Lunarians.

They informed me that upon the 'Serl' side (the off-side) of their world there were no living creatures. It was only possible to exist upon the 'Lour' side (the Earth side). From their ancient records they understood that the cause of the devastation, and the uninhabitable condition of the 'Serl' side was due to the tremendous difference between the night temperature and that of the day. The vigorous cold of the Lunar night was so intense that in its effects it almost resembled a pressure. Everything upon the 'Serl' side during the Lunar night was frozen to the solidity of granite. But during the Lunar day the temperature ascended so rapidly as to disintegrate the mountain range and crumble them to the plain. For centuries this had continued until the whole hemisphere was one vast plain. Why the 'Lour' side had not shared the same fate was due to the fact that it constantly faced the Earth: And foolish and insouciant as it may seem, it was nevertheless true, the 'Lour' side was saved this fate from the higher temperature caused by the transmission of the sun's rays from the Earth.

I was really glad when the long Lunar night was over. It was very trying to have no companionship, for, of course, after the Lunarians had prepared for their night's sleep, I had no one to talk to for nearly 13 Earth days. But when the glorious sun shot his rays athwart the 'sky-lights' it was not long before I had my guides with me again.

I was very interested and not a little amused at their method of ploughing the soil of their underground lands. Two of the unwieldy, Iguanodon-like animals were yoked together. In between them and extending some eight feet behind them was a stout pole of hard wood. At the rear end of the pole was a cross-piece of wood to which was attached, curving downwards and inwards, six other pieces of wood, each about three feet long, and spaced about 9 inches apart.

The cross-section of the curved pieces was pear-shaped, the stoutest portion projecting outwards. In appearance it was like a curved comb, and as it was light in structure, pressure had to be applied in order to penetrate the soil. Six furrows were therefore made simultaneously after which the seed, somewhat resembling barely, was sown. It took four Lunar days and nights for the "corn" to reach fruition; which time was just equal to sixteen Earth-weeks. Moisture was supplied to the soil each Lunar night by the "rain," that I have already written of, and which fell from the caved roof caused by the rising temperature.

Another feature that afforded me much interest was the entire absence of localism in the dialect of the Lunarians. And this fact seemed strange to me when I remembered that the edges of Lunar civilisation were separated by a distance of 2,000 miles. It was one of the guides – "Ralsee" by name – who first brought this fact to my notice, as well as other interesting facts arising therefrom.

I was down by the broad stream with Ralsee and four other of the Lunarians intending to do a little fishing. I had scarcely baited the hook when I saw a company of about forty approaching. Ralsee at once requested me to forego the fishing in order to be introduced to this company. Ralsee informed me they were passing through their township to another town situated some 20 miles away in order to participate in a religious festival. From all over the habitable area, irrespective of distance, delegates were sent to attend the festival which was held periodically to a time corresponding to three Earth-years.

I asked Ralsee to interpret for me, but one of the company who heard my request told me there was no need. In surprise I turned to my guide. 'No, lord!' he said to my look of surprise. 'There is no need to interpret, for we all speak the same tongue.'

This remarkable fact led me to question Ralsee closely, and he informed me there was nothing strange in this seeing that they were all one community. They knew nothing of barter, for everything was the property of the community at large.

I have no desire, here in my journal, to enter into comparisons. But my opinion of the general life upon the Moon was that progress was as dead as the off-side of the Lunar world. Development was merely that of senility. And it could not be otherwise by the very system under which they lived. The occupation of the father was the occupation of the son. The father ploughed the soil until the plough was worn out. The son ploughed the soil with a new plough, built exactly to the pattern of the old one. There was no choice in the matter at all. As father did, so did the son. And Ralsee informed me that this order of things had prevailed for countless years.

In vain I tired to interest my guide by detailing him some phases of Earth life. But he raised his hands in horror. Their system, he said, was the best that could possibly be found. So reasons all schools opposed to progress. Earth life has heard many such opinions stated. But when a system is declared "Best" and not "Better" progress ceases.

(To be concluded)

A Visit to the Moon (11)
Recorded by George E Hobbs
(First published: November 2, 1923)

Synopsis – My friend, Christopher Jackson had long been obsessed by a desire to visit the moon. He disappeared for three years. Suddenly he returned to me again, dying in my arms, after declaring he had accomplished his objective. He requested me to edit his journal. A description of his machine, his voyage through space, and his arrival upon the moon has been given. Also many startling things of the life upon our satellite. He is now contemplating his return to the Earth. – GEH

Part 11 of Journal

I have just recovered from another severe heart attack, so severe that the doctor who was summoned predicted that one more such attack would be fatal. I must therefore condense what I have to write in as few words as possible.

The means of locomotion among the Lunarians was of the most primitive order. In fact, the oldest known to the human race. The longest distance had to be negotiated afoot. Even with this disadvantage I was able to accomplish quite long journeys without fatigue.

Yet was I ever careful to see that my supply of oxygen was sufficient for my needs.

The time came however, when I saw that the supply in my machine was getting low and that I should be wise to commence my return journey to the earth without delay. But here I met with a formidable difficulty.

When I mentioned the fact of my return to the Earth, the Lunarians were vehement in their demands that I should remain with them. And though I knew them to be a peace-loving people, I saw they were determined to detain me even to the point of force.

Sorry as I was to do it, I clearly saw my only way was subterfuge. And while pretending to comply with their wishes, I secretly made preparations to leave them.

Never shall I forget the commencement of my return journey. The uncompromising attitude of the Moon-dwellers made it impossible for me to leave by day. I had to await the coming of the Lunar night. It took four Lunarians to close and bar the cave doors, but I believed that in the lighter atmosphere I could equal the strength of the four. The difficulty did not lie here, but in the intense cold and darkness of the night.

To show that I was well-intentioned (and to make it easier to locate the machine in the darkness), I brought the machine closer to the mouth of the cave. I then stored a good supply of oxygen in my portable apparatus and returned with my guides.

Presently, preparations were made for the Lunar night. The doors were shut and bolted, the grids opened; and then followed the usual custom of 12 hours' wait for nightfall. No 12 hours ever passed so slowly. Each moment seemed weighted with lead. But gradually the light of the Sun failed through the 'skylights'. 'Goodnights' were said, with right hand uplifted and shoulders touched – and I was alone.

I found it a more difficult matter than I had anticipated to remove the bars and open the doors. I accomplished it at last, however; but it was with much loss of energy. As I emerged from the cave, the intense and bitter cold chilled me to such an extent that I could scarcely command my limbs. A new fear assailed me. It was that before I could reach the machine, the intoxication of a benumbed body would cause me to collapse into the dreaded sleep, so feared by terrestrial polar explorers. Such sleep I knew would mean death.

With every ounce of faculty and energy I could command, I struggled in the direction where I knew the machine to be. To my intense joy I found the rope ladder and with a prayer in my heart for strength, I painfully climbed the ladder, crawled through the doorway of the outer casing and closed the door.

With the singing of many waters in my ears, and thunders roaring through my brain, I crawled to the oxygen valves and released them. It was as much as I could do. I just remembered their release when I collapsed to the floor of my observation room. Luckily, however, what with the higher temperature of the machine, and the life-giving properties of the oxygen my swoon was but momentary. And when I came round a great cry of gratitude escaped my lips that I was safe and free.

Although I knew I had 13 days of Earth-time before the sun would return and the Lunarians reawaken, I proceeded at once to make all snug for the return journey to Earth.

There was no difficulty in taking my bearings for the Earth; and having set my forward control at positive and my rear control at negative, I found the machine beginning to rise into the Lunar skies. Having nothing else now to worry over, I took as hearty a meal as concentrated food and drink would allow, and then sought my couch to sleep. Twelve hours I slept without waking. For the first time in many many months I had been able to dispense with my portable apparatus, consequently I was restful and easy.

There is little need to detail my return journey. It was simply a repetition of the journey out. The same depression and excitation occurred in the mercury gauges, and as I had already tabulated these changes, I merely checked them to see if my observation had been correct. I found that my tabulated list was correct in every detail.

There is little more to add. I have been back upon the Earth now a little over three months. I found my three deaf-mute friends had calculated an approximate date for my return. But it was one month after the date they had calculated upon when I descended into their camp. They are there now with my machine, snugly hidden. I shall not name the place in my journal, but shall give the geographical position only by word of mouth to my friend Hobbs.

If I live, I shall return again to the Moon when I hope my dear old friend will accompany me.

Christopher Jackson

Note: I have faithfully given to the world the details of my friend's journal. I cannot vouch for the accuracy of his claim. I can only do as I have done – record his journal. One thing could have established his claim, but unfortunately that proof is impossible of production.

My friend died before he could tell me the location of his machine. The deaf mutes may know of my existence, but even then they would not betray my friend's secret – even to me, without his permission. That permission cannot now be given.

What those three friends will do I have no idea. Probably they will journey to the Moon themselves. If they do, the probability is we shall hear later of their exploit.

Until then, I can say no more.

Doctor Nickols (1)
A Tale of Weird Happenings
By George E Hobbs
(First published: November 16, 1923)

The dull, cold November day was fast drawing to a close, and as Professor Newcombe took one last look through his study window before drawing the curtains for the night, he felt glad he had a cosy nook in which he could shelter.

He had been rather unwell of late, and the damp foggy air of November had compelled him, much against his will, to remain within the shelter of home.

Some of his friends, however, knowing the state of his health, and the necessity of his remaining within doors, had, on several occasions, shown their practical friendship by dropping in of an evening for a chat. And these evenings were to him very pleasant indeed.

There were three of them who usually came to visit him, Craik, a Scotsman, sub-editor of the City Times, Doctor Negross, of the Sandwell Asylum, a specialist upon mental diseases, and Captain Johnson, now home for rest after two years of exciting experiences in the South Polar regions.

Though their callings were so diverse they were a very pleasant company indeed. A strong common bond bound them together. They were all lovers of the mysterious and active members of the Psychical Research Association.

His three friends had promised to call again, and to-night he was expecting them.

It was not long before they came, and by the bustle in the hall he concluded there were more than three of them this time.

His conjecture proved correct, for when his man ushered in his three friends, there entered with them a stranger.

As he gave them welcome and bade them be seated, Doctor Negross, turning to him, said: "I must apologise, Professor, for saddling you with an extra one to-night – a fellow medico – but when you understand the reason you will forgive the liberty."

"What nonsense!" exclaimed Professor Newcombe indignantly. "There is no need of an apology. Your friend is most welcome," – and he held out his hand to the young stranger with a smile of warm greeting.

"Thank you, Professor," replied the young fellow, quietly. "Negross told me you would not object to my joining you, and so upon his invitation I came."

"Rest your mind content," said the Professor heartily, "and Negross," turning to the Doctor, "place the decanter upon the table, there's a good fellow; the cigars you will find in the cabinet, and draw up all of you around the fire."

After each had lit his cigar and made himself comfortable, there fell a silence for a moment or two between them.

"Now Jim," said Negross, turning to his young friend, "we are ready to hear your story. Tell the Professor exactly what you told me yesterday, and let us see if we can elucidate this terrible mystery of yours."

"First of all, Professor," began the young fellow, with a smile which had a strange shadow of sadness in it, "let me commence by introducing myself – which Negross in his own inimitable fashion failed to do. You will all know my father, I believe; he is President of the Association of which we all are members."

"What!" ejaculated Johnson, interrupting. "Are you the son of Lord Ferrydale, the President of the Psychical Research Association?"

"The same," he replied modestly, "James Tregus, second son of Lord Ferrydale," – with a bow to the little company.

"From my early days," he continued, "my father paid tribute to my common-sense by confiding in me his many adventures in psychical research. In fact, before I took up my life's work he took me with him on several occasions to scenes of reputed mysterious phenomena.

"It was this very confidence that led me to a study of, and a consecration to, this branch of scientific research, and, believing that I should be the better equipped for the work, I studied and took my degree as a physician and surgeon. I specialised – as Negross did – in mental diseases; and as I knew there would be no need for me to practise privately, I determined to be free to go anywhere and everywhere there was an opportunity to investigate and study the mysterious operations of the human mind.

"In my college days I met a fellow student, a little older than myself, for whom I conceived a great liking. His name was Harry Nickols, and he, like myself, was studying along psychical lines, in which branch of study he seemed a perfect genius.

"There were times when I felt he was using his powers and knowledge to improper ends. But as he was always a jolly, care-free chap, his sunny disposition disarmed any permanent suspicions upon my part, and I felt a veritable Judas in even thinking wrong of him.

"I will be true to my experience, however, and tell you why these suspicions came into my mind.

"One day while I was with him in his room, he took from a locked cabinet a photograph album, and turning his back to me, began to turn the pages over one by one. Facing him was a large mirror, and chancing to glance into the mirror, I was shocked at the expressions upon his usually benevolent features. It was perfectly satanic in its gleaming malignity. Before I could turn away I saw him take a photo from an inner pocket and place it in the album. 'Ah!' he exclaimed, with a laugh that made me shudder, 'another of 'em towards my supreme happiness – the beautiful darlings.'

"At that moment he must have remembered me, for he closed the album with a snap, and placing it in the cabinet, locked the door. When he turned to me the expression upon his face was one of child-like simplicity. 'Ah, Jimmy,' said he with a smile, 'some of my dear ones which your sacrilegious eyes must not look upon.'

"Being a man of the world and knowing a little of harmless flirtation, I thought I understood his meaning, and smiled indulgently.

"A little while after this incident, Nickols took his degree, and wishing me good-bye, apparently passed out of my life. And the effects of that satanic laugh gradually wore off.

"And now I come to an incident, to the details of which I want your closest attention.

"Some little time after taking my degree – which occurred twelve months after Nickols had taken his – I received an invitation to stay with some friends in the country. They live in a delightful part of Wiltshire, and when I tell you there is excellent accommodation for boating and fishing, two of my most ardent relaxations, you will not be surprised that I accepted the invitation with alacrity. It was just what my jaded nerves needed. The quietude of the country, sport that needed no arduous exertions, and the charming restfulness of my host and hostess and their daughter. Oh, no, I was not in love. I had been too busy for that kind of thing, and she, Norah, was eighteen years of age.

"On the second day of my visit, Norah and I went for an afternoon's enjoyment upon the river. It was a glorious day, and after we had gone some distance, Norah said suddenly: 'Doctor Tregus, did you ever meet with Doctor Nickols?'

"'Yes,' I replied, 'we were fellow students. We chummed together, and I found him a most delightful companion.'

"'I, too, found him so,' she answered with slight hesitation, while a faint carmine tinged her cheeks. 'He was a friend of Daddy's and before he left England he stayed with us for a while. Yet there were times when I thought him a little strange – when I even felt a little afraid of him.'

"'Yes?' I interrogated smilingly, 'and what made you afraid of Nickols?'

"'I can scarcely explain my feelings,' said Norah naively. 'We were, as I said, friends, and one day Doctor Nickols asked if I had a photograph of myself I could give him. I replied I had not. I had in fact one only and that I wished to retain.' 'May I see it?' he asked. 'Yes,' I replied, and going to my room I returned with it for him to see. I am not vain, Doctor Tregus, but his evident admiration for my poor photograph caused me to turn away embarrassed.'

"'Suddenly I heard a laugh that sent the blood cold in my veins. You will not laugh at me, Doctor Tregus, but you will remember where Mephistopheles, in Faust, determining to blast the soul of Marguerite, sings, or rather says, in leering satanic tones: "Marguerita!" – and laughs. Oh the awfulness of that laugh! And the laugh of Doctor Nickols was like that.'

"'I was veritably shaken by its malignity, but as quietly as my beating heart would allow I requested the return of the photo, and proceeded to my room.

"'Next day the photo was missing, and though we searched almost everywhere it could not be found. Strangely enough, two days after, it was again on my dressing table, and though I interrogated my maid, she denied all knowledge of its disappearance and its subsequent reappearance. So evident was the truth of her disclaimer that I was forced to believe her. The solution of the problem was altogether beyond me, but as I had received it again I was quite content to forget the incident.'

"'This morning,' she continued in a low voice, 'I received a letter informing me of the death of Doctor Nickols, and with the letter a photograph of himself. I do not know the manner of his death but upon the back of the photograph is a request which lends me to believe he knew the end was approaching. It says:

Dear Miss Norah,
Farewell! Place this upon your dressing table, and for old time's sake
think of me occasionally before retiring to rest. Good-bye.
                                                                        H Nickols.

"'What do you think of it, Doctor Tregus?'

"I was indeed shocked to hear of old Nick's death, but as I realised there was not much chance of finding out particulars I said to Norah: 'By all means do as he wished you to do. There can be no harm in that now he is dead. Poor old Nick! I am truly sorry to hear of his untimely end.'

"By the look on Norah's face my answer did not seem to please her overmuch, but instantly her manner changed and she smilingly requested we should return to the house.

"Perhaps you have already anticipated my story," continued Doctor Tregus in a low tone. "It was not long before I had proposed to Norah, and she had made me happy by giving her dear self to me. Her father and mother were quite pleased to give their full approval to our engagement, and after a week of exquisite bliss I returned again to town.

"The very next day I received a telegram urging my return at once. Norah had been taken ill. And I need scarcely tell you I returned to her with all speed.

"Her father met me at the station, and during our walk to the house told me a most distressing account of my sweetheart's indisposition.

"Norah, he said, retired to rest in quite a happy frame of mind. But when her maid went to awake her in the morning she found her young mistress unconscious with a death-like pallor upon her face. Neither her maid nor Norah's mother could awake her, and becoming alarmed they were about to phone the local doctor when she came out of her mysterious swoon. 'She is in a deplorable state of fear over something or other,' he said huskily. 'She has no knowledge we have sent for you, my boy; in fact she forbade us doing so. But seeing that you are her accepted lover, and a medical man, we thought it best to send for you. I know you will do your best for her, for you love her as we do.'

"I accompanied her mother to where Norah was lying, and when she realised it was I she turned her face away with a pitiful moan of anguish.

"'Mother!' she cried in tones of heartbreaking despair. 'Why is Jim here? He must not come! He is lost to me for ever. Oh, why has he come?'

"I felt the blood stagnate in my veins, and I staggered with the intensity of my feelings. I was a lover, gentleman, as well as a doctor.

"'Norah,' I said as gently as my shaking voice would permit me. 'What is the trouble?' – and despite her agonised resistance I gathered her in my arms.

"I raised my eyes to her mother, and she, dear soul, understanding my mute request, left us together. Norah did not struggle now, but just lay passive in my arms.

"'Oh, Jim!' she said after a pause, 'is it true? Can he claim me? I was never anything to him. I feared him – and he is dead. Yet he told me he would compel me to go to him. He told me last night. I went to him. It is too late! Too late!' – and she cried out in the convulsed grip of an awful terror.

"To say that I was in a hopeless maze would simply be to juggle with words. There was something so inexplicable, so incomprehensible, that I felt I was living in a world of unrealities. By a supreme effort of will I pulled my scattered senses to some semblance of order, and gently but firmly asked Norah to tell me as coherently as possible the trouble from the beginning.

"'Of whom are you afraid?' I asked.

"'Jim!' she gasped, 'keep me close to you and I will tell you all.

"'You will remember our conversation about Doctor Nickols? Well, I did not follow your advice, but locked his photograph away in a drawer. Last night I remembered it. And feeling happy in your love I ventured to pity his memory. So much so, that I took his photograph from the drawer and placed it upon my dressing table. In my new-found joy I could afford to feel sorry for one who had been cut off in the vigour of his early manhood. I had no sooner settled myself to sleep, when a strange sensation overcame me. I felt myself lifted apparently into space, and carried with lightning velocity through the air. Presently I found myself upon a beautiful sunlit island, and walking towards a house cosily nestled at the roof of a flower-decked hill. Although the environment was so enchanting, I experienced a strange thrill of fear, only to be intensified as a door opened and I saw the leering face of Doctor Nickols. Oh, Jim! I can't tell you more. His suggestions were dreadful, and though I refused his overtures, he told me I belonged to him, and when he willed it so he would have me for his pleasure. Even though I married I should still be his when he willed – "

"Norah could say no more, gentlemen," said Jim huskily, "for she had fainted."

"Tenderly I brought my darling round. I saw in a flash what had happened. And I saw clearly, too, the devilish result of Nickols' perverted powers. He had gone deep into the laws of psychical phenomena, and had discovered, even as I had, that personal contact was not necessary for psychic control. Given reciprocal photographs of operator and subject for the initial contact, uninterrupted concentration by the operator will do the rest.

"Nickols was evidently ahead of me, for it is only recently that I have discovered distance does not prove a hindrance.

"But to resume: When my sweetheart came out of her swoon, I was able to assure her the evil spell cast upon her by Nickols was broken. The first thing I did was to destroy Nickols' photograph, and gradually but surely Norah is recovering.

"But, gentlemen!" cried Jim with fierce intensity, "I fear there are other victims – fool that I was not to have foreseen this, and destroyed his cursed album – and for Norah's sake, for the sake of those whose minds will be blasted by his satanic proclivities, something must be done, Gentlemen! Nickols is not dead! He lives – and he must be crushed."

(To be continued)

Doctor Nickols (2)
A Tale of Weird Happenings
By George E Hobbs
(First published: November 23, 1923)

Chapter 2

It is impossible to describe the horror with which the little company received this terrible recital. Though they had understood a little of psychical phenomena, neither had thought it possible for such as this to occur. But of this they were agreed: something must be done – and at once.

Captain Johnson was the first to break the silence: "Do you think your sweetheart could give us a description of the island with sufficient detail to locate it?" he asked of Jim.

"No, I am afraid not," replied Jim with evident reluctance.

"If we only knew the geographical position," resumed Johnson, "we could charter a small steam yacht, and hunt the devil out of his lair. The Association would foot the bill, and I would undertake to navigate the yacht to his place of concealment."

"Do you think," interposed Professor Newcombe quietly, "that Norah –"

"No, no; for God's sake don't suggest that Professor!" cried Jim in an agony of apprehension. "I know what is in your mind, but – oh God! I couldn't."

"Jim," said Negross, laying his hand caressingly upon his young friend's shoulder. "You know I would not suggest anything to hurt you, or her. But what Professor Newcombe half suggested you can do – though not in the way you were thinking. Listen to me! You can place your sweetheart in a trance-sleep, carefully instructing her what she has to do. You know how to control her in such a manner that she will not meet Nickols, impressing upon her subconscious mind it is the position of the island we want. We can find the house after we get there – and that devil in human form. It will not harm Miss Norah and think of those poor victims who cannot help themselves. Miss

Norah was fortunate in having a student of Psychology as her lover! But, Jim, others are not so fortunate, and they are being sacrificed to Nickols' passion. What do you say?"

"Yes," replied Jim slowly, "I think that could be arranged, providing that Norah is willing. You must forgive me, but you will quite understand how this has knocked me over, and prevented me from thinking clearly. I –"

"Don't worry about that, lad," interrupted Professor Newcombe kindly. "Pull yourself together and let the knowledge you have acquired in psychical research suggest to you the best means for circumventing the scoundrel's power. We will arrange the expeditionary part of the business."

"Good!" exclaimed Craik, who up to this moment had made no effort to join in the conversation. He was a typical Scot, deliberate and taciturn. And though possessed of a heart that could melt into tenderness at the sight of helpless woe, he had the nerves of a granite rock.

He had listened to every word of that terrible recital. Ordinary minds would reject the whole story as grotesque – an impossible phantasy. But he knew it was true; and being true, the means to crush Nickols must be substantial and real.

"Good!" he exclaimed again. "Let our young friend do his part in obtaining from his sweetheart the geographical position of the island. But, gentlemen, neither the Psychical Research Association nor the public must know of this for the present. Get the position of the island, and we five will go for a pleasure cruise. I am part proprietor of the paper of which I am sub-editor, and my paper will supply part of the funds for the expedition providing we can claim the sole right to publication after the event."

So it was decided. And Tregus accompanied by Doctor Negross, journeyed down to Wiltshire to interview his sweetheart.

It was quite a relief to Norah to see Jim again. Poor girl, she had not entirely shaken off her feeling of dread. But now Jim was with her again she felt strong and safe.

When he put his proposal before her, she looked at him apprehensively, and with reproach in her eyes. "But girlie," said Jim, "no harm will come to you. If you will but be passive I will control you in such a way that you shall not be brought into contact with Nickols. It is the position of the island we want, and you are the only one that can supply it for us.

"And, Norah," continued Jim, gathering her tenderly to him. "Think of those – and there must be many – who are helpless in his power. We do not know them; but if there is only one more, then for her sake, dear, consent."

That evening Jim placed Norah under psychic control in the presence of Doctor Negross. It was an anxious moment for each knew how important it was that Norah should definitely locate the island from which Nickols scattered broadcast his evil influence.

As soon as Jim saw that Norah was under control, he said in tones of gentle authority: "Norah, by the will of Nickols you went upon a journey to an island upon which he lives. Now, by my will, I wish you to find that island again and tell me its position."

It was a weird situation and the two watching the face of the beautiful girl before them, suddenly drew their breath sharply as she began to speak.

"It is midnight," said she in a far away voice. "Yet I have no difficulty in seeing the way I go. I am journeying South by East. Paris? Yes, I have long since passed Paris – and sunny Italy: yes, I know Rome. It is even now behind me. I have passed the Pyramids – and it grows warmer. Sand – sand – all sand! Ah! but now the beautiful blue waters! I have passed the Equator – still South by East. What did Doctor Nickols mean – five South, fifty-five East. I do not know! Ah! Here it is – so beautiful, and yet so lonely – so inaccessible. No landing place – cliffs perpendicular. And the interior like a cup. Yes, interior – beautiful, verdant, luscious – and there is the house. I see the house – and by the door is –" It was enough! and Tregus, with perspiration standing like beads upon his forehead, recalled the wandering spirit of his sweetheart back again.

Signing for Negross to leave him, Jim was alone with Norah when she came out of her trance sleep; and tenderly he ministered her needs.

"You have done us great service, my darling," said Jim with a world of love in his eyes. "And now to bed dear, and rest. Have no fear, Nickols will never hurt you again. And please God he will hurt you again. And please God he will hurt no one else when once we lay our goodnight!"

The next morning Jim, accompanied by Negross, journeyed back to Town. They had all arranged to meet at the Professor's house at eleven o'clock that morning, to hear the result of Jim's effort.

"The direction Norah gave me," said Jim when they were all assembled, "seems fairly simple. But I am afraid we shall need greater detail before we can definitely locate the place. South by East, Norah said. And then [again], what did Doctor Nickols mean by five South, fifty-five East? I do not know! – and I am bound to admit that I too, see no direct solution. I –"

"What did you say?" asked Johnson springing to his feet. "South by East. Five South, fifty-five East – Professor that sounds familiar! Ah, I remember! Five degrees South latitude, fifty-five East longitude – it is the Seychelle group," he continued with emphasis. "The islands lie about two hundred miles South of the Equator, and nearly one thousand miles off Malinda on the coast of British East Africa."

"Yes, I remember," replied Professor Newcombe. "You commanded our expedition there, Johnson, when we went to photograph the Solar corona during the total eclipse of 03. But the group consists of thirty scattered islands. How are we to know upon which one we shall find Nickols?"

"I have a fancy I know the very place," said Captain Johnson thoughtfully. "The description given by Tregus re-calls to my memory a fantastical yarn told me by a native when we were at Mahe – the chief island of the group.

"On the east side of Mahe there is a large cave, which at high tide is partially covered by water. About eight miles to the North-East is an island, apparently quite barren of verdure, and surrounded by high precipitous cliffs. The native told me there is a subterranean passage running from Mahe to this island, and from which, those who dared to adventure its dark interior never returned. It is impossible to gain a footing upon the island except through this passage. And that would be impossible, he said, because of the evil spirits lurking therein.

"If it is true that Nickols is somewhere in the Seychellean group, then that is the island upon which we are most likely to find him. Evil spirits would have no terrors for him, seeing he is such a fiend himself.

"We seem to be making excellent progress," said Craik as Johnson paused, allowing himself to show more feeling than his wont. "And now, gentlemen, there is only the details of the expedition to arrange. I have taken my chief and senior partner into my confidence, and my place is to be provisionally filled for six months. We are placing three thousand pounds towards the expenses of the expedition, providing we have the sole right of its journalistic bearing. Secrecy, gentlemen, is our one great asset. What do you say?"

"It is most generous of your paper to do this, Craik," said Jim simply. "I think there is no difficulty in the way of acceding to you request. Secrecy, as you say, is our one great asset. But I do not think we shall need so large a sum as you suggest. I shall, of course, speak to my father about this, and if he will allow me I shall use his electric yacht. As it happens, her captain is now lying at his home very ill, so there will be no difficulty in placing Johnson to her command. The crew will answer admirably for our purpose, for they are all picked men, secretive and loyal, and are all humble members of our association."

So it was arranged. Without a moments hesitation, Lord Ferndale placed his electric yacht, *Iris*, at his son's disposal. And though he would have given much to have accompanied them, he felt that if he did, some enterprising journalist would suggest a sensational reason, and thus hazard the chance of success. He decided, therefore, to remain quietly at home and await the return of the expedition.

(To be continued)

Doctor Nickols (3)
A Tale of Weird Happenings
By George E Hobbs
(First published: November 30, 1923)

Chapter 3

It wanted just an hour to sunrise when the *Iris* slipped from her moorings, and crept silently out upon her mission of deliverance – and retribution. Her crew consisted of twelve able-bodied seamen, all strong active fellows, bo'sun, second officer, first officer, three electrical engineers, and Captain Johnson. Beside these were Professor Newcombe – for him a health cruise – Jim Tregus, Doctor Negross, and the taciturn Craik; making a total of twenty-three.

To ensure the greater secrecy Johnson had joined the *Iris* at Tilbury, and had thereupon taken her round to Weymouth, where Jim and his party joined her.

Before sailing, Captain Johnson had called the entire crew together and had given them a brief outline of the circumstances that had necessitated the cruise. And each had given a solemn pledge to relax no effort until Nickols was crushed beyond the power to work further evil.

Silently, but swiftly, the *Iris* swept down the Channel away into the gradually dawning day.

They had previously decided to make no call, but proceed straight to Mahe – the chief island of the group – with all speed. So rapid was their progress, that at the end of the seventh day out they emerged from the Suez into the Red Sea.

It was now decided to call a further council: and the five friends assembled in the Captain's cabin to settle their plan of action upon reaching Mahe.

That they were opposed by a mind of wonderful capacity and exceptional cunning was a fact they were already acquainted with. But what they did not know was whether Nickols was assisted in his nefarious work, or working alone.

Reviewing the situation, they believed he must, from sheer necessity, have others with him. But whether they were accomplices, and shared his guilty secret, or were merely attending the capricious fancies of an eccentric recluse, they could not tell. In any case they would prepare, not merely for servants attending the reclusive habits of a master, but for the resistance of an armed and unscrupulous band.

Instead of running direct into Port Victoria – as they had first intended – they remained about twenty miles off Mahe until after nightfall. And then, the night proving beautifully clear, they proceeded at reduced speed towards that part of the coast where the cave was situated.

Creeping noiselessly forward, and with the leadsman constantly taking soundings, they approached the vicinity of the cave. Here fortune favoured them in the shape of a small bay, having sufficient depth of water in which the *Iris* could be taken and anchored.

The morning's light proved that a better spot could not have been selected; for as they looked anxiously out to sea, they found that no other island was in sight from the bay. If Nickols, therefore, was where they believed him to be, whatever watch was set from his place of concealment they knew the *Iris* could not be discovered.

Captain Johnson now proposed to lower the small pinnace, wait until nightfall, and then institute a careful search for the cave. This was done, and to their unspeakable relief they found no difficulty in locating it.

It was now that the most trying part of the adventure began. Did Nickols have accomplices, and if so how many? What devilish devices were concealed in that subterranean passage as a check to inquisitive explorers? They did not know, and so extreme caution must be exercised.

Provisioned and armed, five of the crew directly under Captain Johnson kept a constant vigil: and towards late afternoon of the second day their patience was rewarded by seeing a boat steal cautiously out from the darkness of the cave, in which was contained a man dressed in the picturesque costume of a Spanish peasant. Having satisfied himself there were no watchers, he proceeded out a little way, threw out a grappling iron, and settled himself to fish.

"Whitlock," whispered Captain Johnson to the engineer. "Take the pinnace at half speed round the point and into the cave. Keep well inshore, and don't make a sound. Use the magnetic control. We don't want the sound of engine exhaust now."

Luckily the fisherman was absorbed in his work and stood with his back to the pinnace. It was the work of a few moments, therefore, and they were covered by the darkness of the cave. They found ample room within and water deep enough to turn the little craft round, ready to meet the boat as it re-entered the cave.

"Simpson!" whispered Johnson to the most powerful of his little company, "When the boat returns, wait until it is opposite us, then spring on board and seize its occupant at once. Whatever you do, don't let him make a sound. We don't want the rest of the devils brought about our ears."

"Right Sir," replied Simpson. "I'll see he makes no sound; you don't want him settled I suppose sir?"

"No, no," said the Captain. "Play on his wind pipe; but don't kill him. We want information from – silence! Stand by. Here he comes!"

Slowly the boat came through the mouth of the cave and, just as the two crafts were in line, Simpson sprang.

For a moment it seemed as though the small boat must go under; but it righted itself, and in Simpson's practised hands the prisoner was noiselessly secured and gagged.

"Bring him alongside smartly, Simpson!" urged Captain Johnson in a hurried whisper. "That's it. Now tie it up to the stern of the pinnace. Keep in the boat with him, we'll tow you to the *Iris*. Now lads, quietly. Use the control, Whitlock. Half-speed ahead! Splendid! Now full speed. Keep her at that," – and in a quarter of an hour they had rounded the point, and were alongside the *Iris*.

The Captain's cabin had already been prepared, with curtains drawn and lights switched on. Here they conveyed the prisoner and kept him under strict surveillance until Captain Johnson could summon his four friends.

When they had assembled, they found before them a young Spaniard, about twenty-five years of age. He was well set up, keen eyed and with an air of good breeding about him.

Without preamble, Captain Johnson, drawing a bow at a venture and speaking in Spanish, said: "Now look here my lad: An Englishman by the name of Nickols is living in seclusion somewhere about here. We want to know where, and the best means of reaching him. We want the truth; and the quicker you are in giving this information the better it will be for you. I need scarcely tell you we have means of extracting what we want, if you refuse to give it of your own free will."

"You can do with me as you please, Señor," replied the young Spaniard decisively. "But I shall tell you nothing."

"Very well," said Captain Johnson quietly, "then we must adopt other means.

Simpson, tell Whitlock to bring the battery. Sharply now! we can't afford to waste time. Gentlemen," turning to his friends and speaking in English, "it is evident we are on the track of Nickols. Our friend refuses to divulge anything, but he will speak in a moment, never fear."

At that moment Whitlock entered the cabin and placed upon the table a small compact battery.

"Now," said Captain Johnson to the young Spaniard. "You have information which we must have at all cost. You refuse to impart that information. We shall see. Let me explain what this little contrivance is capable of doing.

"In case of mental trouble due to shock, this battery will restore sanity completely. But if used upon persons who are in full possession of their faculties, it will render them hopelessly insane. You are intelligent; and to the intelligent person there is nothing so full of horror as insanity. Yet I tell you plainly, unless you give me the information I seek, this devilish contrivance shall work its full power upon you. It –"

"Oh, Señor!" exclaimed the young fellow, horrified. "Anything but that. Yes, I will tell you. He will kill me; but I would rather die than become a maniac. But, Señor," he added, piteously, "What will it mean to my beautiful Rosa – my little sister? I cannot tell you what, but he has a hold upon me which I dare not break. And to keep me loyal to him, he holds the spirit of my dear little Rosa in his power –" and strong and courageous as he was, the tears fell fast down his cheeks.

"Take the battery away, Whitlock," said Captain Johnson quietly. "And Simpson, you may go too. But tell the bo'sun to have an armed party of eight men ready to accompany me at a moment's notice.

"Now, my lad," he continued, kindly, turning to the young Spaniard, "take a sip of this brandy; you need have no fear for yourself or your sister. When once we can lay hands on Nickols his power will be broken for ever. I have a friend here who has specialised in psychical research, and he, understanding Nickols' power, will see no harm befalls your sister."

"Señor," he replied tremulously, "if you and your friends can save Rosa, you may do with me as you wish. Oh Jesu Mary! I would do anything to save her.

"The Señor Nickols lives upon an island, inaccessible from the sea, but which can be reached through a subterranean passage commencing in the cave in which you captured me. Exactly what he does I have no knowledge; for we are rigidly excluded from the house – except the kitchen where we prepare his food.

"Yes there are others, in fact four of us. All with unfortunate incidents in our past. And in each case," he continued bitterly, "the circumstances are bound up with Señor Nickols.

"Our work is to guard the passage and maintain a complete commissariat for his needs. To do the latter we have a house upon the high ground immediately above the cave, and which is reached from the passage by a spiral stairway. We are, therefore, safe from intrusion.

"Señor I need say no more. I will take you through the passage to Señor Nickols' house. You need not fear," he added, as he saw suspicion upon Captain Johnson's face, "I will not play you false. If Rosa can be saved and my life made less burdensome I shall be your debtor."

"But if there are four of you, how is it you have not been able to devise some means of giving Nickols his quietus?" queried Captain Johnson.

"Ah, Señor!" he replied shudderingly, "We have tried; but Señor Nickols has some mysterious power around him through which we cannot break. We are helpless. In each case he holds the spirit of a dear one in his grip. We do not know how, but the fact remains that he does."

When Johnson had given a verbatim account of the conversation to his friends, simultaneously they turned to Doctor Tregus. To them the situation was one of grotesque impossibility. It could not happen in the twentieth century. And to their unspoken request, Jim replied: "What seems so inexplicable to the uninitiated is abundantly clear to me, gentlemen. You will remember what I told you in regard to my own experiments. Between Nickols and his victims there has been an interchange of photographs; and the contact cannot be broken until one or the other has been destroyed.

"Nickols selects the photograph of the victim he wishes to bring to his side; then by concentrated telepathy he compels them to come to him. He has previously requested in a pathetic appeal – as he did with Norah – that his photograph should be placed in such a position, so that when they retire for the night – the mind being then in a state of restful receptivity – his photograph will be the last thing they see. And seeing it, they will think of him.

"If by any chance they neither see it nor think of him, then it is impossible for him to work his fell purpose upon them.

"No more need be said, gentlemen," concluded Jim, rising from his seat with a look of grim determination. "The next thing is to act – and at once!"

Captain Johnson found his party all armed and ready; and with them went Jim, Doctor Negross, the Spaniard, and the silent Craik.

"Now, Señor," said their guide, when they had all landed in the cave, "I want you to trust me and do my bidding. Under no circumstances must a word be spoken until I give permission.

"The island is situated eight miles away, and in the old days was used as a rendezvous by pirates. In a rough fashion they had constructed a kind of track, upon which was conveyed their booty to the island upon trolleys. The Señor Nickols has had this track brought up to date – for strangely enough the four of us who serve him are engineers – and we shall travel by car.

"There are lights along the passage which automatically switch on and off as we pass. Every 100 yards of track controls one light. As the car leaves one section, the light controlled by that section is immediately extinguished; while the next light is as immediately ignited by the car entering the next section. There is, therefore, a light throughout the entire journey. This is done, may I say, so that if the car breaks down we can use the hand trolley, and still have light in the passage, seeing that the lights are controlled from the track and not from the car.

"There are also automatic sound transmitters connected in the same way; and the Señor not only can hear the car, but if he so wishes, can see upon an indicated chart, the progress of the car through the tunnel. Once more, Señor, there must be no talking. Now, quietly forward to the car."

(To be concluded)

Doctor Nickols (4)
A Tale of Weird Happenings
By George E Hobbs
(First published: December 7, 1923)

Chapter 4

They found the car large enough to accommodate all of them. It was used for the conveyance of food and other necessities to Nickols' house. Silently they crowded in and the journey commenced.

It was just after midnight when the car emerged from the passage, and their guide, bringing it to a halt, motioned for them to leave the car and conceal themselves behind a low-lying hedge of brush wood. The car was then taken forward to a shed close by and the Spaniard was lost in the surrounding gloom.

Scarcely more than five minutes elapsed when Johnson saw four human silhouettes creeping towards them, and becoming suspicious, passed the word for the men to have their revolvers ready for instant use.

"Señor," whispered the young Spaniard, for it was he and his three companions, "I have told the rest of the situation, and they are each ready to give you assistance, but, Señor, you are certain our dear ones will be safe?"

"I have given you my word that no harm shall befall them," replied Captain Johnson. "Now lead the way to the house."

"One moment, Señor," said their guide in a low tone. "The Señor Nickols believes himself to be safe from intrusion here, so you need have no fear of secret devices for your hurt. When he is awake he is quite aware that we cannot harm him. It is only at night, when he is asleep, that he allows himself protection. It is impossible to gain admission to his bedroom; were we to step even upon the landing we should be all dead men.

"The Señor will not be retiring for another hour yet, so you will find him in the north room upon the ground floor.

"Ten yards away from the house is a privet hedge. It is for that part we must make. When I have conducted you there I will leave the rest to you. That is all, Señor."

"Now, my lads, forward!" commanded Captain Johnson, just above his breath, "and no talking."

Like a company of phantoms they went forward, the guide leading the way, until they came to the gap and passed through towards the house.

All was in darkness, and Johnson, still fearing treachery, took hold of their guide and placed him and his three companions in the midst of his little company.

"I want to trust you," he whispered in explanation, speaking in Spanish, "but I am taking no chances. Remain here all of you," he continued in English, "and you too, Craik, if you do not mind. I am going forward with Tregus and Negross Bo'sun. You follow behind us, and if there is treachery let the lives of these four pay forfeit – then help us the best way you can. How is it there are no lights in the house if Nickols has not yet retired?" turning to the guide for explanation.

"There are no windows in the room where you will find Señor Nickols," he answered. "That is why we do not know what happens there. When you arrive at the north door you will find upon the right hand side of the door, four feet from the ground and one foot from the door frame, what appears to be an electric bell push. Do not press it in but down, and the door will open immediately and noiselessly. The room in which you will find the Señor Nickols is upon your left hand, and will open in exactly the same way."

Quietly and with revolvers ready, the three crept forward. After a little search Captain Johnson found the unpretentious "knob", and pressing it downwards the door opened at once.

Without a sound, Jim Tregus switched on a pocket flash lamp and speedily found the second point of contact.

Ranging themselves side by side, Jim pressed the switch, and as the door opened the three sprang into a brilliantly lighted room.

For the moment they had eyes only for the white-faced hound before them. That he was startled goes without saying – believing as he did that he was safe from intruders. But so great a command had he of himself that the look of fear upon his face was but fleeting, and quickly passed to one of malignant hatred and devilish cunning. Keeping his eyes fixed upon Johnson, his right hand began to move slowly from his side.

"Keep your hand where it is, Nickols!" said Jim Tregus in a voice of intense hardness. "Keep it still I tell you, or I shall fire."

In a moment his manner changed, and, sinking back into his comfortable chair, his face assumed an expression of smiling benevolence.

"Well, Jimmy, my friend," said he, mockingly, "is it really you? Rather an unceremonious way of visiting an old acquaintance, is it not? Especially at this hour. And you have evidently forgotten your manners. Could you not say how d'ye do to my lady friend behind you?"

"I know his game," broke in Johnson quickly. "Keep the devil covered, Jim, while I look to see who is – oh, my God! – Stella! What in heaven's name are you? – ah, I see! You damnable cur! What is my daughter doing here?" And with an agonised passion he sprang upon Nickols.

With the grip of a bulldog he would have choked out the life of the gasping Nickols, but Jim sprang forward and took hold of the rage-blinded Johnson.

"Stop Johnson!" he cried. "Don't kill him. You'll do more harm than you think! Release the devil and leave him to me," and with a Herculean effort he separated the struggling pair.

"Now you dog," said Jim in a voice of terrible calmness, pushing Nickols back into his chair, "sit there, and as you value your miserable carcass, don't move!"

"I shall do just as I please," answered Nickols, with an evil smile. "I hold the trump card, as you very well know. If you kill me – and I may say you can do so if you wish – the girl dies with me. Her spirit, her very life, is in my keeping, and I can save her or damn her as I please – or as you please I should have said. What you do to me will happen to her; so you may do your best, or your worst – and to hell with the three of you."

"Is this true, Tregus?" panted the agonised father. "Can nothing be done to save my Stella? I would kill him here and now, but will his death hurt her?"

"Leave him to Jim, Johnson," said Doctor Negross earnestly before Jim could reply. He knew that Nickols' claim admitted of no contradiction. There was one way by which Nickols could be crushed, and that was by bringing to bear upon him a will stronger than his own. He knew by intuition what was passing through the mind of Tregus. Could he do this? It was the only way – and he must try. "Leave him to Jim, Johnson," he said again. "And Jim!" – he glanced at Tregus. "Jim?" It was enough; Jim Tregus understood.

It was to be a duel then. And the most terrible duel of all. If it had been a struggle decided by physical force, the excitement of attack and defence would so occupy the brain and muscle, that the horror attending mortal combat would be largely eliminated.

But here the full horror of the struggle would be manifest. Especially to Negross and Johnson, who would be helpless. They could only watch the progress of the struggle of wills, as each tried to dominate the other. Nickols, too, realised what was about to transpire, and for a moment he paled with anxious solicitude for his own success.

Both knew what the result would mean to the loser. The will power of the dominated would receive such a blow that even if he lived he would never be the same man again. The mind of the defeated would be injured forever.

But neither dare refuse to accept the challenge that circumstances had thrown upon them. Nickols knew that if he won neither the father nor Doctor Negross would injure him for the sake of the helpless girl who was even now in his toils. And Doctor Tregus knew that if he himself lost, not only would his own fate be sealed, but the fate of Johnson's daughter, and perhaps the fate of many more would also be sealed. It was then that he waited no longer – and the struggle began.

Jim Tregus had seen that momentary sign of fear, and speedily sought its advantage. With the full power of his personality Jim concentrated telepathic influence upon Nickols, immediately securing initial advantage by forcing his opponent upon the defensive.

For a full quarter of an hour eyes glared into eyes. Tregus, stern, resolute, fighting for the deliverance of the enslaved, and Nickols with diabolical intensity, fighting to retain his satanic power.

To Johnson and Negross it was the most terrible quarter of an hour they had ever passed through, when, to their unspeakable horror, they saw Tregus begin to slowly lower his eyelids.

With hearts beating well nigh to suffocation, knowing they dare not speak, they watched what they believed to be the final crushing of their hopes. Tregus was losing – and was even now relaxing the rigidity of his body.

It was then that Nickols moved; he could afford to relax his efforts. To him the struggle had been of the utmost severity. But he was winning; had, in fact, won – and he closed his eyes for a moment to ease him from the strain of concentrated watching.

Then came the end! But not in the way Johnson and Negross had thought. Jim realised how formidable was the opposing will of Nickols, and decided to stake all upon a fluke.

It was so simple an experiment that he believed Nickols would fall by its very simplicity. He lead Nickols to believe he was failing, and he, falling into the trap, relaxed his efforts, and closed his eyes for a moment's rest.

Then followed the inevitable reflex action. A moment's thought would have shown Nickols the utter foolishness of relaxing any effort until Tregus was psychologically down and out. But he was certain of success; and the closing of his eyes brought to him a slight sense of relief – and drowsiness.

In an instant Tregus took a step forward, and Nickols, sleepily opening his eyes, found himself confronted by the fierce, unrelenting gaze of his erstwhile victim.

"Nickols!" said John, scarce above a whisper, yet with terrible intensity. "You are beaten! Do you hear me? You are beaten! I, Jim Tregus, am your master! Now tell me you dog; where is the photograph album? Your master demands it!"

"The album!" said Nickols in maudlin voice. "Oh yes, I know – the pretty dears. In the cabinet – doors open, yes, bring it to me – the darlings!"

It was the work of a moment for Negross to find the cabinet and draw out the album. Jim still keeping ward over Nickols.

"I have it, Jim!" said Negross triumphantly. "What had we better do now?"

Without replying Jim bent over Nickols and said to him authoritatively: "Sleep, Nickols! Sleep until I tell you to wake. Gently! That's better" – and Nickols fell back in his chair in a profound slumber.

In the meanwhile Johnson had taken the album, and eagerly looked for what he believed he must find there. He found it. It was the photograph of his daughter Stella. Taking the photograph he tore it to shreds and scattered the pieces upon the floor.

"Stella, my darling!" he cried in the bliss of the moment. "You are free dear. You – Oh God! Where is she?"

"She is free in very truth Johnson," replied Tregus, laying his hand upon Johnson's shoulder compassionately. "It was her spirit that Nickols held in his control. The destruction of her photograph has given her relief, thank God. Now let us see what we have in the album."

Thirty-five photographs were found in the album, and among them, Norah's! "Ah!" said Jim reflectingly, "I see it all now quite plainly. It was Nickols who stole Norah's photograph; evidently he had one taken from it and then returned the original to her dressing table."

"Yes," he continued decisively, "we will destroy them all. Send the bo'sun back for the young Spaniard, Johnson. Perhaps he can tell us where there is an empty fire grate. I shan't be happy 'till this thing is destroyed."

When the young Spaniard arrived, he led them by means of Jim's flash lamp to the kitchen, where they had the satisfaction of seeing the album and its contents reduced to ashes.

"Now, Johnson," said Jim with a smile, "tell our young friend his Rosa is safe. No further harm can come to her from Nickols, or to the dear ones of his friends."

When this was translated to him, the young Spaniard's joy was unbounded, and in the delightful vocabulary of his race, with the tears streaming down his boyish face, he thanked them for what they had done.

Telling him to go back and join the others, Jim and his two companions made their way again to Nickols' room.

"What are we to do with him?" asked Negross, looking to Jim for answer.

"I scarcely know," replied Tregus, hesitatingly. "The cur deserves no pity: but we can't murder him in cold blood."

"Better bring him round," suggested Negross, "and let circumstances decide."

With this Jim made his way to the side of Nickols, when something about him caused him to pause.

"Nickols will trouble us no more," he said quietly, "for he is dead."

Such proved to be the case. All his medical knowledge had not been sufficient to prevent him from weakening his constitution by his excesses. He must have known what the outcome would be, yet he was held an uncompromising slave to his passionate desires. If it had not been for the severe mental contest he had but lately passed through, he might have lived for years, ruining and blasting hundreds of innocent victims. But the contest had proved too much for him – especially taken off his guard as he was – and when Tregus had sent him into a compulsory sleep, his brain, already overtaxed – snapped – and he died.

It was a few moments before the three friends could realise that the devilish mind of Nickols had ceased its activity; and when they were fully conscious that this was indeed so, they could scarcely repress a shudder.

"What had we better do now?" asked Johnson, looking askance at the dead Nickols. "We cannot very well leave him here as he is. Had we not better call the others up? Craik may have some suggestions to make."

"Yes, by all means," replied Jim, "call them up at once."

"Craik," said Jim when the party had arrived outside the north door, "we will give you all the details presently. Sufficient for now, Nickols is dead – in fact, died about ten minutes ago. What do you suggest we had better do?"

"Do?" replied the Scot, whose thought was quicker than his speech. "Send back to the yacht for some dynamite and bring down this house for his grave. And bring sufficient," he added after a pause, "to blow in the seaward end of the tunnel and let's have done with it for good."

So it was arranged. The house was left in ruins, and in the tunnel the debris was such that no human being could ever pass that way again. The soul of the erring Nickols was left with his Maker.

Very little is left to be said. The hold that Nickols had upon his four serving men proved to be of a very shadowy character. They had committed no crime. In each case Nickols had put them into a trance sleep, procured, by some means, a dead body, and waking up its victim, swore he had seen them commit murder. Promising to be their friend if they would only do as he wished, they consented to do so – each believing they had been guilty of this crime.

Each was sent away happy from Mahe, and returned to their homes to find their dear ones safe.

When eventually the City Times published the complete records, not only did it stir England, but the whole of the civilised world.

From the standpoint of finance – to come down to a prosaic ending – the City Times found what they had put into the enterprise proved to be the best investment in the history of its career.

One last scene. The five friends are standing upon the steps of a fine old country mansion, bidding God speed to one of their number. Standing beside the lucky one is a fair specimen of English girlhood radiant in the graceful folds of her "going away" dress. It is Jim and Norah who had just plighted their troth, and Professor Newcombe – who had now completely recovered his health – Negross, Craik and Johnson had met to bid them God speed.

Going up to Professor Newcombe she raised her face to him invitingly with a little blush – and her eyes sparkled with the tears she could not repress. "Thank you for what you have done!" she said simply.

"God bless you, my dear!" he said huskily as he pressed his lips to her brow.

"And you, Doctor Negross. And you, Mr. Craik. And you, Captain Johnson." And Jim was not one whit jealous as he saw his little sweetheart kissed by each in turn. He knew what the past had been to her, and how thankful she was of her deliverance.

"Come, dear," he said, "we must be going." And as the car whirled them away upon their honeymoon, Jim gathered his sweetheart to him.

"Are you happy, sweetheart?" he asked tenderly.

"Oh, Jim – !" was all she could answer as she nestled to him in the blissful rapture of pure contentment.

(The end)

Chapter 13

The World of Mrs Crabthorn

Mrs Crabthorn appears in many of George's articles and short stories. She is a larger-than-life comical character, and apparently fictional. But was she based on somebody George knew?

Just in case, we did check the 1911 census, but she didn't appear anywhere in Swindon, let alone Rodbourne, which was a bit of a relief, to be honest. And in any case, we would not have expected George to have actually named her, even if she had existed (although Alfred Williams, writing at the same time, did name real people in his books).

We expected she was an amalgam of numerous, working-class matriarchs that George had encountered on his travels in and around the town. Perhaps someone extraordinarily like her had once been one of his neighbours.

But, having said all that, in one sense we may have found her – not in the pages of a census, but in the pages of a book: *Tales in Verse*, written by Mary Botham Howitt, and published as far back as 1836. In particular we find her featuring in a poem entitled *Madam Fortescue and Her Cat*. Originally intended as a verse for children, the story is about an odious woman who is employed as a maid to her elderly mistress, and who promises to look after her cat when she dies. In return for this promise, Mrs Crabthorn is bequeathed a generous annual sum, which would allow her to not only provide for the cat but have enough left over to keep her in comfortable retirement – so long as the cat lived. These two stanzas provide some background:

> She makes believe to her lady,
> To be very fond of the cat;
> But she hates her,
> And pinches when she pretends to pat.

> But the lady never knows it,
> For the cat can but mew;
> She can tell no tales, however ill-used,
> And that Mrs Crabthorn knew.

You can also get a flavour of the woman from the line: 'Cross Mrs Crabthorn rules the house,' and it's a story that doesn't end well for the cat; nor, for that matter, Mrs Crabthorn, who reneges on her promise and ends up penniless, having been betrayed to the solicitor by her accomplice after having had the cat killed.

It's not hard to think that this may have been one of George's favourite poems and a character he loved to hate, and perhaps some elements of this original Mrs Crabthorn have found their way into the character that George employs for his series of fictional, tragi-comic domestic situations, all lovingly played out in a Wiltshire dialect, with walk-on parts played by, among others, her long-suffering husband, John, and their ten children.

John and Sal enjoy a sometimes troubled relationship. You would even go as far as to declare John a battered husband. Think of them both as a kind of proto Andy Capp and Flo (if you are old enough to remember the strip in the *Daily Mirror*). Or perhaps (if you are younger and read *Viz*) then think of a woman a bit like Mutha Bacon, but following a largely unsuccessful anger-management course.

Interestingly, George writes about his character: 'It appears she once had a mistress whom she loved; and from whom, upon the mistress's decease, she received certain relics to keep her memory green.' This is surely more than just another coincidence.

In the course of the pieces selected, below, we find out that Mrs Crabthorn has ten children – or has it since increased to twelve? That her first name is Maria. But it's really Sally, isn't it? And then her surname gains a letter E. So she is nothing if not a moveable feast, but no less endearing – all with an added hint of menace! And then there are the many local references which truly identify this lady as one of our own.

When originally putting this chapter together, we set out to select no more than half of the pieces that feature her. Having re-read them all, however, we confess she's grown on us, so we're going to include them all – all twelve.

It could be argued that she grew on George, too. As time goes on he started to refer to his fictional construct as his 'lady-friend', and you get the feeling that she was popular with *Advertiser* readers, too.

On one level, the stories about Mrs Crabthorn amount to profound social commentary. On another (and in context), it's biting satire. Others might think that this seemingly hapless female character is being cruelly lampooned, particularly in relation to her size.

However, she's super-assertive, motivated and clearly aspirational. Perhaps this was George's way of acknowledging that the place of women in society in post-conflict Britain was changing for the better? We hope so.

Before we introduce her, it is important to put the Mrs Crabthorn sketches into context, because this reveals George's attempts at situation comedy to be every bit as ambitious as the science fiction featured in Chapter 12.

As well as being related to the comic characters already mentioned, Mrs Crabthorn could be described as a Frankenstein's monster of a woman, made up of all the best and worst qualities of the red-faced large ladies we recognise in saucy seaside postcards; buxom battle-axes in Ealing comedies and cartoons; the unseen mother-in-law who was the butt of jokes by Les Dawson, or Les Dawson himself, in drag; the ample, rich widows with an explicable mutual attraction for Groucho in Marx Brothers films; the unforgiving wives of Laurel and Hardy; Sybil Fawlty on a bad day; possibly even the headless figure that chased the cat with a rolling pin, sometimes, in *Tom and Jerry*, along with countless other similar caricatures in popular 20th century culture. What we should recognise, however, is that Mrs Crabthorn predates all of these.

So if she appears quite crude, especially compared with some of the more sublime examples of the craft that we have experienced since George's era, and compared with more refined examples of his writing craft, remember that almost everything we know about comic characters and modern comedy came after he put pen to paper to create Mrs Crabthorn. His was a comedy, indeed, that pre-dated not only the best of sitcom traditions, but also the model of radio comedies.

Mrs Crabthorn is so far ahead of the game, in fact, that it is difficult to see where the inspiration for her came from, apart from the music hall – although, somehow, George doesn't seem to be the kind of person who would spend much time watching such entertainment.

The only clue comes in something that slips out of the mouth of Mrs Crabthorn ('E would 'ave served longer, only armistice came, an' 'e got demoralised'), which is a hint that George had either seen or was aware of *The Rivals*, featuring Mrs Malaprop, which saw the invention of malapropisms in 1775; not that Mrs Crabthorn and Mrs Malaprop had much else in common.

So, while Mrs Crabthorn and her sketches may not be the finished product, they are, at least, at the head of a great tradition. So – notwithstanding all of the above – we dare you not to smile…

Trip Eve and Trip Day:
A Comedy of the Train and of the Washtub
By George E Hobbs
(First published: July 1, 1920)

"Now then children, off with them boots. No, Peter 'Enery, don't get too busy, I'll tell you when to take off your clothes. Sit round and I'll take you one at a time, then I shan't make a mistake.

"Where's your father I'd like to know! Round at the Blue Nose, I'll be bound. It's a blue nose he'll be getting, and a thick ear in the bargain; leaving me to clean boots as well as bath you lot. Trip to-morrow and all.

"Fred'rick James! Drat the kid: 'tis'nt your turn yet. – Fell in! Then fall out quick, unless you want to feel the weight.

"What's that Billy Johnson? Yer mother wants to borrow the bath? Well tell her she can't have it then. She's a'ready got my frying pan, tell her to bath you in that. An' tell her to teach you yer manners, bustin' in 'ere when young ladies are bein' bathed. Get yourself off, quick!

"Will you stop pullin' the cat's tail, Florrie Janet, and get those clothes off.

"There, that's one. No, no supper tonight. All the grub's packed up for on the sands to-morrow.

"What's that, John William. I'm bathin' you again? Bless the kid, so I am. 'Op out quick and don't jaw. You changed places with Ebenezer on purpose, you young rascal. Don't answer back, or (whack) – shut yer noise and don't snivel.

"What's that? Mrs Johnson bin and bashed the frying pan up the yard? I'll bash her over the head with it next time I see her – the ungrateful hussy. There, thank goodness that's the lot. 'Op off to bed the 'ole bunch and no noise, or look out for a visitor. 'Ere Jonathan, what you grinning at? Let me look at you – snakes alive! You ain't washed. Missed you did I. Next time I'll bang the lot in together and swish you round like spuds. I won't miss any then, I'll lay.

"That you, John? Nice time I've got to look forward to to-morrow, an' you started on the fuddle a'ready – only went to have a drink? You was born wrong, John. You ought to have been a whale – except a whale's got a small quilt an' yours is like pouring soap-suds down the drain. An' then if you was a whale the new earth would be 'ere 'fore time, for there'd be no more sea. You'd guzzle it all up. Yer name ought to be "blotting pad" for you soak up everything wet.

"Didn't talk like this 'fore we were married? No, an' I didn't have ten kids and a porous husband 'fore I married either. You'll clean the boots, and won't touch the beer to-morrow? Oh, well, John, p'raps I was a bit hasty. P'raps my bite is worse than my bark, or vice versa. I'm goin' on John. Good night, I'm tired.

"Now children, go steady and keep together. What's that jack-a-napes? Is this a Sunday School party? You mind your own bisness.

"'Ere's the train. Help the nippers John. Don't stand there looking as tho' you've a'ready got there and waitin' to come back. 'Ere Peter 'Enery, hold the grub. Come on, one, two, three – what, no room? You 'old yer hush. We wants to go to Weymouth as well as you.

"Weston train? 'Ere, 'op out quick! What d'ye mean, John, by saying this was the Weymouth train? You didn't say? Don't start the say by telling me no lies! Yer brain's fuddled from the "Blue Nose". Don't stand there gassing, find the train. 'Ere who you pushin'? That ain't the train, John, engine's London way.

"'Ere we are at last, and last is right, for 'tis the last train. That's like you, John, spoilin' a good hour of the nippers' day before they start. Pull yer 'ands out of yer pocket and give the kids a leg up. They ain't got no wings to fly up with. Letting everybody 'ear what I be saying of? Taint me, 'tis you and yer addled wits they be noticing. 'Tis hardly a word I ever speak. Too quiet I am, an' I gets put on for it.

"Courtin' couple in there; don't like to intrude? 'Ere you get 'em in, I can do some good this morning at any rate. Wot do I mean? Why let the turtle doves see this little lot, an' let them 'ear you a-jawing me, then they might reconsider about gettin' spliced.

"No need to shift honey, I can stow this little lot away easy. You ain't close enough to yer young man – or boy they calls 'em to-day, don't they! Move a little nearer. That's it. John William, keep yer hand out of the gentleman's pocket. See's the door's shut, John. Don't want the kids a-fallin' out on the line.

"Let's have the baby's bottle, John. That's not the one, an' you told me you'd keep off the bottle. Law sakes, blotting pad's yer name as I told yer yesterday.

"Not jaw in company? 'Ark at that, honey, an' he used to 'old me 'an like yer boy's 'oldin' yours. That'll do Ebenezer, I wasn't talkin' to you, you look out at window. Used to call me his own damsel, an' I found it was 'im that was the damnsell. An' he used to kiss me in the tunnel like yer young man kissed you in the last one.

"'Twas Peter 'Enery sucking sweets? No, Honey, they ain't got no sweets. An' now look what 'olding 'ands and kissing's done, honey. Ten on 'em and a blotting pad for a husband. Yer young man said he'd be good to yer? Ah, that's what the spider said to the fly, honey, but then the fly got in the web.

"'Ere we are. Don't forget what I've said, honey. 'Elp the kids out, John, we're at Weymouth."

Mrs Crabthorn on the War-Path: Another Echo of the Swindon Trip Story
By George E Hobbs
(First published: July 16, 1920)

I have found it a fearful thing to rush into print: also that notoriety of the certain order is apt to prove very embarrassing. I write this with memories surging around me like gnats in a summer sky – and these are the circumstances thereof.

When I realised to what extent I had hurt the feelings of Mrs Crabthorn, I felt the only course open to me was to apologise. And I called at the house for that purpose.

Mrs Crabthorn answered the door in person, and when I revealed my identity – well, I can understand her husband's preference for the genial atmosphere of the "Blue Nose." "Come in," she vociferated, while a steely glare came into her eyes. I followed her in with feelings similar to what a profiteer will have, when, at the crack of doom, the gentleman with the trident and toil invites him into his well-heated den.

As soon as we got into the kitchen, Mrs Crabthorn grasped the neck of a quart bottle, and in that quaint vocabulary of which she is an adept said: "I'm going to biff you one on the napper, sonny!"

"One moment before you carry out your benevolent intention," I answered as amiable as I could; though my knees were behaving like a three-decker blancmange in a gale. "I have come round to apologise."

"Awhata?" she queried, mystified.

"Apologise, Mrs Crabthorn," I said. "I'm truly sorry if I have hurt your feelings."

For a moment it seemed that Mrs Crabthorn failed to understand my magnanimity. Then, realising my gracious capitulation, she fell forward on my neck to kiss me.

I trust the good lady will not be offended at my candour, but viewing the situation dispassionately, had I known of her intention I would rather have had the bottle shivered into a thousand fragments upon my head.

Mrs Crabthorn is an elf-like creature of sixteen stone burden, a head taller than myself, and built upon the lines of a thirty-six gallon cask. Whether she is patriotic upon principle or compulsion I cannot say: but certainly there is no "waste" about her. Not only so (forgive me, dear Mrs Crabthorn) but I feel certain that John – that is her husband, of whom more anon – must have courted her in the dark; never taking the precaution of providing himself with a lantern.

Of course, I quite realise there is no blame attached to Mrs Crabthorn in regard to her generous outlines – or her face. I believe in giving censure where censure is due. Dame Nature was the culprit, and she must have been either cross-eyed or had a momentary lapse when she gave Mrs Crabthorn her figurehead.

But to return to my narrative: I was quite unprepared to such an onslaught. To call it the "Charge of the Light Brigade" would be a misnomer. The metaphor nearer the truth would be "The scramble of the Heavy Brigade" or "the falling of an avalanche," or, "the inexorable crush of a Super Dreadnought". Fighting manfully, I retreated in good order until I came to a sudden and violent stop. I could retreat no farther, for the back of my head was in painful contact with the wall. Neither could I advance as her massive chin was pressed heavily upon my nasal organ.

It was far from a dignified position, and, just at the psychological moment, who should've come in but one of the Crabthorn tribe by the name of Ebenezer. Mistaking the circumstances, he yelled: "Father! Here's a strange man a-trying to murder mother!"

I was rather muddled and nearly senseless, but I am almost certain I heard John reply: "At last – Come away Eby and let the gentleman finish the job!"

Mrs Crabthorn must have heard it too; for, putting her engines in full speed astern and her helm hard-a-port, she waddled over to the window and looked out.

"John," she cried in a voice that boded no good for that worthy. "Come here!"

"Coming dear," said John and in another moment Mr Crabthorn appeared upon the scene.

"What was that you said?" asked Mrs Crabthorn, trying to ledge her hands on what should be her hips. "I understood Ebenezer to say you had a visitor," replied John innocently, "and I told him not to be rude and come away."

"I thought it sounded like something else," said Mrs Crabthorn, eyeing John as though she would read his soul, "and I'm so relieved to know it was not what I thought that you may come and kiss me."

"I'd sooner have a pint, missus," replied John, backing away from his beautiful wife. (How's that Mrs Crabthorn?)

"You'd what?" she screamed – and then another catastrophe occurred.

Ebenezer, naturally, had followed his father in from the garden, and had stood an interested spectator to the whole proceedings. His position was between his father and myself; and, as Mrs Crabthorn barged into her husband, Ebenezer, who evidently had witnessed such scenes before, turned to dodge between my legs. Before he could do so, however, his father cannoned into me, and down I went, all of a sprawl, on the top of the poor little chap. No sooner was I down than John fell on the top of me, and the avalanche, not being fitted with a back-pedaling brake, fell on the top of John.

All seemed over, and I resigned myself for the worst. I just managed to gasp out who was to have my German keyless watch when the thought came how unheroic the end was. The bitterness of the situation gave me new strength, and with a super-human heave I rolled John and the dread-nought under the table.

I gave first aid to poor little Eby, and after rolling and bumping him back into shape, he revived sufficiently to go into the garden and pull a few peas for himself, as his father was otherwise engaged. Poor John, too, looked pretty sick, but as soon as he had scrambled to his feet he went off to get a reviver at the "Blue Nose".

Now came the worst part. How was I, unaided, to get Mrs Crabthorn from under the table. Dear woman, she helped all she could, but, unfortunately, she tried to crawl through the legs of the table narrow ways.

If it had not been for the extreme pathos of her plight, I'm afraid I should have smiled. The table legs gripped her across the middle, and the table unresistingly followed. In my excitement I cried, "Gee back. Back pedal! Back water!" – then, recollecting myself, I lifted the end of the table, and Mrs Crabthorn stood upon her feet – or, at least, that which corresponds to feet in ordinary people.

"Sonny," said Mrs Crabthorn, shaking me until my teeth rattled, "I'm going to have my revenge. And this is my revenge. You've got to come round here and write a few of my experiences for the Advertiser."

"But Mrs Crabthorn, I can't write," I said, as soon as I could recover my breath. "I know you can't," she replied tartly, "but you've got to try."

"But" – I tried again – "I am sure the Editor would not publish anything you have to say."

"Wouldn't he?" she replied significantly, "then I'll just walk up and serve him like I've served you."

So there it is: And to save the Editor from a violent end, and myself from the ague, I suppose I shall have to do it.

Mrs Crabthorn and Her Neighbours: The Episode of the Needle and Sundry Explosions
By George E Hobbs
(First published: July 30, 1920)

Before writing of my second interview with Mrs Crabthorn I want that good lady to understand I shall not visit her house again unless I am supplied either with a pneumatic suit, or a substantial guarantee against personal violence.

For years I have suffered from a slight nervous disorder, and the experiences incidental to my second visit – to use a modern phrase – completely put the tin hat on it. It was one succession of fireworks and volcanic shocks; sharp, brilliant, nerve wracking. It is true I am now able to sit up and receive a few friends, but I trust I shall be exonerated from the charge of cowardice if I refuse to go again. Incidentally, I became initiated into the mysteries of classical feminine phraseology. I have heard men in a slanging match, but it was quite a tame affair compared to this display of sparkling rhetoric. It was deep, sincere, arid – but let me record the interview in a proper sequence; trusting that its nightmare effects will not be too much for me.

Arriving at Mrs Crabthorn's House I did as she requested me: knocked and walked straight in. Mrs Crabthorn informed me she was patching a pair of Peter Henry's trousers – he having fallen through the seat. "Sit you down," said she, "I shall be ready in a moment."

Before I could do as requested, there came a yell that almost split my eardrums. Looking over the table I saw Peter Henry stretched face downwards across his mother's knees, while the patch was being sewn on in position. "Oh! oh!" screamed Pete. "You've been and stuck the needle in my – "

"You shut up," said his mother hastily, giving him a resounding slap on the patch. "Bide quiet or I shall stick it in again. And don't forget we've company present."

As though in answer to that agonised cry, there came a voice from the garden: "Drot Mrs Crabthorn and them kids of hers! How can a body rest with murder going on under yer nose?"

The effect of this upon Mrs Crabthorn was nothing less than electrical. "That's that Johnson woman," said she. "Now we'll have the final reck'ning." And if the look upon her face had been intended for me I should have had urgent business elsewhere – and gone quickly too. So great was her anger that she failed to notice Ebenezer having a nap upon the sofa, and down she flopped Pete on the top of him.

I believe it is the custom of ladies when disturbed in their sewing to lay down their work and attach the needle thereto. This is done so that upon the resumption of work and no difficulty is experienced in finding the needle. Mrs Crabthorn followed the usual custom – but unfortunately it was Pete that found the needle! No sooner had he discovered it than he conveyed the knowledge to the sleeping Eby by kicking him vigorously upon the shins and yelling in his ear with the resonant blast of a foghorn.

It was enough to startle an unimaginative person; but Eby is a great reader of Indian stories. At this very moment he was dreaming that a Sioux war party, under their chief "Red Cloud", were attacking the stockade of the palefaces. White and drawn, Eby was defending the settler's daughter, when Pete's bloodcurdling yell penetrated to his sub-conscious mind. They had broken through! They were surrounding him! Bravely he struck out – and Pete had it right on the top of his chubby little nose.

What with Eby defending the white settler's daughter, Pete retiring before the rear attack of the needle, and Mrs Crabthorn attacking both hostile camps at once, pandemonium reigned. Presently there came a lull in the combat, when again that persistent voice was heard: "I'll have the perlice here I will!"

That was enough. Leaving the Indian raid and the needle to settle their several differences, Mrs Crabthorn sailed out determined "to have the final reck'ning". Naturally I went with her to see there was no overcrowding.

"What you doing with them kids of yours, rednob?" was the polite greeting Mrs Crabthorn received as she emerged into the garden.

"Red nob?" screamed Mrs Crabthorn. "I'll have you know it's auburn tresses I have, you fabricated old she-wolf! And it's real – that's more than can be said of your tangled old furze bush. I've seen better hair on a superanimated door-mat than what you got on that thing you calls a head."

"Yah!" sneered Mrs Johnson, "what did that writer chap call you in the Adver? 'Shaped like a thirty-six gallon tub.' He made a mistake. He meant a fifty-six. (Oh, dear, now I'm for it.) Old Giles the farmer only told me yesterday you'd be worth ten bob a day to him on his wheat patch. No self-respecting rook would come within fields of a dial like yourn. But I told him he'd lose more than he'd gain, for even the wheat would be afraid to come up while you was anywhere about."

In my anxiety to see and hear everything in connection with this interesting debate I approached rather close to Mrs Crabthorn. Luckily, I kept my wits about me or then and there I should have been counted out. The effect of Mrs Johnson's conciliatory remarks caused Mrs Crabthorn to become a cross between an irresponsible jazzer and a dancing dervish. I side-stepped just in time to avoid one of her propellers descending upon my devoted head. Her wrath was terrible to witness. "I'll get at you, you scum," she cried to Mrs Johnson, and suiting action to words she tried to scramble through a gap in the dividing fence.

Halfway through she unfortunately got wedged. It was a trying situation; but believing Mrs Crabthorn had right upon her side, I immediately commenced to devise some means to assist her.

As I pondered the problem I saw it was of little use to attempt to push her through. I had not the physical strength. Then, remembering a little engineering knowledge, I took hold of a clothes prop for a lever, formed a fulcrum with a piece of wood and, with a "heave altogether boys", I shot her right onto the Johnsons' onion bed. And I followed to see fair play.

Let me draw a veil over the scene that ensued. It is too delicate to me to dilate extensively upon. Sufficient for me to state Mrs Crabthorn somehow obtained the assistance of the frying pan. It was her intention to put Mrs Johnson's head through it.

Her first aim was a miss. Her second was a hit. But it wasn't Mrs Johnson's head that went through, it was mine! As I was losing consciousness I thought it must be the heavens that had fallen; for I remember counting all the planets, fourteen distinct stars, the Sun and moon.

As I say, I am now able to sit up and receive a few friends; but one resolution I have made and intend to keep. The next time I act as a war correspondent I intend to follow the lines of a modern general. I shall stand upon some adjacent promontory and view hostilities through a pair of binoculars.

Mrs Crabthorn on a Bike and Off: Here Endeth the First Lesson, and the Lady Executioner: George E Hobbs

(First published: August 13, 1920)

I have concluded my visits to Mrs Crabthorn and I am free to confess that happiness is once more mine. No inducement short of the amount Germany owes the allies will take me there again. She may send (if she recovers) wheelbarrow, donkey cart, brougham or Rolls-Royce; I shall stand upon my door step, wave away the proprietors of all means of locomotion and say in the picturesque phraseology of a continental student: "I go to her house not no more! Nevare!"

There are two reasons for this inflexible decision of mine: One is I have no desire to go; and I count it as foolishness to go where one's heart is not. The other, the more significant of the two, is that I am afraid to go.

I know it sounds paltry to acknowledge fear of one who is of the so-called weaker sex, but you do not know Mrs Crabthorn. There is little of the weaker sex about her. And after all Adam was afraid of Eve after she boxed his ears for staying out late one night. Of course none of the modern excuses had been invented then – "pressure of business at the office", "breakdown on the line, my dear", "train was booked but did not run", etc., etc. And so Eve gave him two – one for staying out later, and one because he was unable to formulate a reasonable excuse. My only regret is she didn't hit him more effectively before he foolishly invented work. Yes, I am afraid to go – and I will tell why.

John's punishment for the "milking" incident was the purchase of a bicycle for his dear wife. My punishment for believing him was to teach the said dear wife to ride the said bike.

Unfortunately I was too late with my advice as to the purchase of the right kind of bicycle. My advice was that one should be bought upon the lines of a steamroller; so that strength would be combined with self-propulsion and constancy to the perpendicular. In other words it should be non-collapsible and non-capsizable.

When I saw the bicycle John bought I wondered for the moment whether he had been smitten with cerebral depression or cerebral exultation. He had purchased with an utter disregard for requirements, and I was reluctantly compelled to think John anticipated an early return to single blessedness – with ten encumbrances.

I said as much to John when I met him, but he only smiled darkly and said; "I have completed my sentences; now you have to complete yours."

There was nothing else for it: so with very great reluctance I arranged an evening for teaching Mrs Crabthorn the art of bicycle riding.

The fateful evening came. When I saw her I fancied either she was mad or I was dreaming. It appears she once had a mistress whom she loved; and from whom, upon the mistress's decease, she received certain relics to keep her memory green. It certainly turned me green when I beheld her, for she was arrayed in a riding habit, while upon her left boot was a spur.

"Excuse me, Mrs Crabthorn," I said as politely as I could, "are you going steeplechasing, or to a fancy dress ball, or merely to have your photo taken?"

"Don't be daft," she replied inelegantly, "I am a-going riding."

"Ah, yes," I responded as inoffensively as possible for I did not want to arouse her anger. I understand you are going to attempt such an undertaking; but why the habit and spur? It is a bicycle not a horse – "

"Oh stow your jaw!" she admonished rudely. "I'm going as I am; 'fully accoutred', as they say."

I have learned wisdom in dealing with Mrs Crabthorn. I did not argue, but prepared myself for the job in hand.

The first difficulty that faced me was how to get her into the saddle. It was physically impossible for me to lift her, so I directed Pete and Eby each to bring a chair.

When these were brought I persuaded Mrs Crabthorn to stand with one foot on each so that I could back the bicycle into the required position. I fully anticipated that when this was done my lady friend could then descend gracefully into the saddle and we should be ready for the first trial.

Unfortunately it did not pan out as I intended. She mounted the chairs all right, and I got the bike into what I considered the right position. But I forgot that in her attempt to sit on the saddle she would have to perform a kind of semi-circular movement – and I had not allowed for this. The result was she came down flop on the rear mudguard which shot the bicycle out of my hand and with a terrible velocity along the road. Both the chairs capsized at the same time. One went on the top of Pete, the other on the top of Eby, and Mrs Crabthorn fell between.

I must confess I lost my head completely. In my anxiety to assist Mrs

Crabthorn I got entangled in the overturned chairs, and without going into details this made matters worse.

As my lady friend tried to attain a more dignified attitude, I heard a fearful rent. Her solitary spur had caught in her riding habit and converted it into what I should imagine would be the envy of a female "bronco buster".

To my great delight Mrs Crabthorn was not seriously hurt. And though she can deal in "language" she is far form being a pessimist. Very forcibly she commanded me to fetch her bike as she intended having another try.

This time the mounting part was successfully accomplished. Eby and Pete removed the chairs and there we stood, Mrs Crabthorn and I, in the middle of the road, a picturesque group. She like Ajax defying the lightning; I like a flying buttress preventing some venerable pile from toppling over.

With the assistance of Pete and Eby we managed to get a start. I did fairly well as long as she inclined towards me. I could then stumble along – flying buttress fashion – and keep her somewhere near the perpendicular. Once or twice I was too vehement in my support and nearly capsized her on the port bow.

Then came disaster. So bust was I keeping her in position that I failed to notice we were upon the brow of a fairly steep decline. The increased momentum of the bicycle and its passenger first revealed the danger to me, but what could I do?

I have been taught always to be cheerful when danger threatens, particularly when in the presence of others who may be inclined to give way to panic. I remembered this teaching now and called out: "It's all right, Mrs Crabthorn. You'll learn better going down hill than up" – and I gave her a good hearty push to help on her glorious joy ride.

Down she sailed like greased lightning, and undoubtedly by this time she would have made an excellent cyclist, but unfortunately she attempted too much.

Mrs Crabthorn must have thought that bicycles were made for cross country journeys and also to climb trees. Half way down the hill she swerved to the left in a wary attempt to run up a fair sized oak tree. The oak tree resented such an intrusion and shot her back into the road again. Evidently the road has no such scruples for it let her remain there.

No more need be said except that the road-men are busy repairing the road, the doctors are busy repairing Mrs Crabthorn. The bike is beyond repair – but I am free.

Mrs Crabthorn and Her 'Censhus': Popular Lady Brought Back
By George E Hobbs
(First published: June 17, 1921)

Last Wednesday evening, feeling somewhat jaded, I sat down intending to have a quiet and enjoyable evening with Jack London's "White Fang".

Jack London – my deepest respects to his memory – is an ideal tonic for jaded nerves. He grips the moment one begins to read him.

Settling myself comfortably I began to read: – "It is not the way of the Wild to like movement; and the Wild always aims to destroy movement. It freezes the water to prevent it running to the sea. It drives the sap out of the trees 'till they are froze to their mighty hearts, and most ferociously and terribly of all does the Wild harry and crush into submission MAN – '"

Rat-a-tat! went the front door knocker, and mechanically I went to the door, muttering to myself: "And most ferociously and terribly of all does the Wild harry and crush into submission MAN." Little did I think that in a few moments this very phrase would be verified in my own experience.

I opened the door – "So you've condescended to open the door at last 'ave you, young feller me lad," said a terribly well-remembered voice. "Open it wider, I'm comin' in!" And suiting action to word, bang went the door against my head and in waddled my old friend, Mrs Crabthorn.

"You can't come in here, Mrs Crabthorn," I protested wildly, filled with agony at the prospect of a spoilt evening. "Besides, I'm not at home to visitors tonight."

"Look you 'ere, Mr. Ananias," said Mrs Crabthorn, getting as much of herself as she could into my arm chair. "I don't want any more of yer gamoosh. Tellin' me yer ain't at 'ome, when I can see yer ugly dial straight afore me eyes. Sit you still! Put away that trashy nonsense yer readin', an' attend to me. I want yer to fill up me censhus paper!"

Head of the House

"But good heavens!" I ejaculated, "your husband, as the head of your household, is the one to do that: Please go, there's a good woman. Let me help you out of the chair, and – "

"Nuf said, sonny," replied Mrs Crabthorn. "Me and John 'ave decided long ago who was the 'ead of our 'ouse. An' I can tell yer it ain't John. 'Ere's the paper. Now get a move on!"

"Me 'usband's name's plain John – John Crabthorn an' 'e was fifty last tater plantin'. What's that? Is 'e a male? Course 'e is – married? Ain't I 'is wife you silly gawkin? No, 'e ain't in hemployment, 'e's on the Labour, drat 'im!"

"Me own name's 'Ria, Ma-ria in full. An' me age was thirty-two last fair 'iring. That was me age thirty years agone? What you mean? Where's me birth certificate? You'll want a death certificate if you try to be funny, young'un. Don't be stoopid. Course I'm a female.

"Ham I a British subject? What's yer joggrefy say? Ain't 'Vizes in Wiltshire? An' ain't Wiltshire in England? – fat head!

"Ham I in hemployment? What yer think with twelve nippers an' a 'usband what suffer wi' palpitations when work's talked about? No, I ain't in hemployment! Hi'm one of the idle rich. A non-prodoocer. Not 'alf!"

"An' then there's the nippers, bless 'em – an' drat 'em. I've forgot 'ow many there is. Any'ow 'ere goes.

"John Willie – no, 'tain't Will-yam – 'tis Willie, John after me 'usband, an' Willie after me sister's step-nephy. Peter 'Enry – no, 'Enery, Florrie Janet – no, 'tain't six, Mr Knowall, it's three up to now. Half my children 'as 'yphenated names. Then there's 'Kia Roger – 'Erzikia in full, with the haccent on the 'Erzi. What's that – 'ow many more? Git on with yer writin'. Gertrude Daphne – no I didn't call you a gurt rude dafty, though I shouldn't quarrel with anyone who did. It's me daughter's name is Gertrude Daphne. Me 'usband's sister's niece – a stuck-up wench she is – reads Charles Garvice to me, an' I took the name from one of 'is stories. What's that, was half my children chris'ened with these names? Course they was. I believes in chris'ning. Doctors knows better'n us. Half my children was chris'ened on their left arms – an' doctors do say they should be done ev'ry seven years. What you laffing at, you long-eared moke? Yes you was laffing! Hignorance that's what it is, hignorance!"

History in Names

"Now then, where 'ave we got to? Oh, I knows! The next is 'Oratio Francis. No, I don't know nothing about Mr. Bottomley. We called 'im 'Oratio because me grandfather knew a man who had fought under Hadmiral Nelson at Waterloo. 'E was a brave man was Hadmiral Nelson – an' 'e was not afraid to tell quizzy people off. Another Hadmiral named Nosey Parker told 'im to stop fightin' somewheres in Hegypt, an' little Nelson – 'Oratio that is – looked at 'im with 'is blind eye and told 'im to 'op it quick. An' we called him Francis after a man who walloped a Spanyard on Plymouth 'oe. They got a light-ouse there now, just where 'e walloped 'im. I loves to 'ear about brave men in 'istory.

"Then there's Grace Darlin' – yes, we named 'er after a girl what was plucky. She tackled nine men who was on the rocks. Hi've tackled John when 'e's bin on the rocks, an' tackled 'im easy, but to tackle nine on 'em was very brave.

"Then there's Samuel Fred'rick, Sally Liza and 'Erbert Hedward.

"Then there's the twins born'd durin' the war – yes, me 'usband served six months – no, jackanapes, not in jail – in the army. 'E would 'ave served longer only armistice came, an' 'e got demoralised. Oh the twin's names? One we called Arras Dixmude, an' tother, 'Ill sixty. Arras Dixmude is a girl an' 'Ill sixty is a boy. No, 'tain't funny names as I knows of. Other people gives names like it to their nippers. 'Ow about durin' the Bower war? I knows a chap name Spion Kop, an' a 'oman name Preetoria.

"As I was sayin', I named the twins like that so as to remind meself of the six months John did in the army. An' I can tell yer this, Nosey Parker, me 'usband was a C.R. for fower months out of the six, an' me nephy, who is a scholard, told me they gives them letters for special service.

"You silly ass! I always thought yer was a solemn bloke, but yer bin grinnin' all the time like a silly wench.

"Yes, that's all the nippers, an' anuff ain't it? Don't be imperdent! No, there won't be any more bornd before Satday. Bound to ask me, was yer? Well, don't ask any more daft questions. 'Ere, give us a 'and to git out of this chair, I'm fair wedged. Good day! Hi'll see you again some day."

Mrs Crabthorne's Grievance: Tale of a "Busted" Main
By George E Hobbs
(First published: August 12, 1921)

Few will dispute that Sunday should be a day of rest: But I fear that to a large number of folk, last Sunday was a day of unrest.

There are certain acts which are perfectly in order if performed between Monday and Saturday, but if performed on the Sunday the performer is said, by fastidious folk, to have broken the Sabbath. Those of us who may feel the Sabbath was broken last Sunday may find comfort in the fact that for necessity each day has an equal significance. Or, as my friend Mrs Crabthorne pithily put it: "A busted water main don't know Satdy from Sundy" – and thereby hangs a tale.

Last Sunday the district in which my villa is situated found itself without that precious commodity – water. It was a serious situation, for:

"From early morn 'till dewy eve,
No Adam's ale did we receive."

Now this in itself was sufficiently disturbing without the situation being aggravated by a person who ought to have known better.

When difficulties arise I always try to treat them philosophically. And last Sunday I was just recovering my mental equilibrium, after treating the matter of the water lock-out dispassionately, when it seemed to me that an unaware merchant had deposited his entire stock of unaware bang in front of my street door. Before I could ejaculate "Dear, dear!" or other equally violent expressions, in walked that annoying person Mrs Crabthorne.

"Water main's busted at Hogbourne, or Wraughton, or somewhere, an' can't get no water," said she without preamble.

"Well, I can't help it," I said, turning my back upon her "we're all in the same unfortunate position, and we must wait patiently until the water flows again."

"Can't wait!" she replied, "kids wants a drink, John wants a shave, an' I wants – "

"Yes," I broke in savagely, "I know what you want and want it badly. You want a wash. Go to the fire station and get one of the firemen to play the hose upon you. Do anything as long as you clear out. I'm busy."

"Now don't be cheeky young fella me-lad," said my lady friend in tones I dreaded to hear. "You've got to do as I tell yer or there'll be trouble. First, you've got to write to them chaps what looks after the Town, an' then you've got to 'elp me find some water."

"But what on earth has the Town Councillors to do with this question?" I asked, helplessly. "You'll make me the laughing stock of Swindon."

"No more than you are at present, so don't yer worry yerself," was her polite reminder. And then she blazed out, "Wot 'ave them chaps to do with it? Why, all in the world! Don't yer tell me as they didn't know their rickety old main wasn't goin to bust. Course they did, an' they ought to 'ave sent the crier round Satdy to let the people know. 'e could 'ave rung a bell an' yelled, "Water main's goin' to bust termorrer, so get your innards well saterated!"

"Why man alive, the rates is up 'igh enough to 'ave 'ad a new slap up main that wouldn't bust even if old Nick 'isself was pushing the water through. I 'eard John say only the other day as it wanted a bigger trunk main from Hogbourne an' Wraughton, an' a most up-to-date main service in the town. 'e was fuddled at the time I knows, still 'e says 'e knows a lot about pipes – an' 'e ought to seein' 'e's always a-sucking at one.

"Wot 'ave they chaps got to do with it?" she reiterated. "Ony two Sundays ago I took the nippers to the Town Gardens an' all of us wanted a cup o' tea. But no, them chaps said we shouldn't 'ave any tea in the Gardens on Sunday, an' so we 'as to go without. If I'd 'ad some of 'em there then I'd 'ave busted them.

"An' look wot a contropersy they 'ave caused over them dead cats an' things at the Savernake street dustbin! Sum it up, son! Sum it up! First they won't tell us when their old main's goin' to bust. Then they won't let us 'ave tea on Sundays in the Gardins. An' then they tries to poisin us. Wait – "

"Look here, Mrs Crabthorne," I interposed, wearily. "I have no wish to hurt your feelings, but I must tell you you are talking a good deal of nonsense. No one can tell when an underground service main is likely to collapse. And certainly, if such could be foreseen those in authority would give the community due warning. Whether there is logic in your statement that a larger trunk main is needed I cannot pronounce upon. I know very little of these things and therefore cannot give an opinion.

"As to the rates, I know they are terribly high. But you must remember that post-war conditions must always be very different to pre-war conditions. This is one of the inevitable effects of that glorious game – war.

"But what connection 'tea in the Town Gardins' and the 'Savernake Street tip' has with the present difficulty in the water supply, I really fail to see – "

"That's because yer be [one of] them chaps. Yer 'eads too thick," she broke in rudely. "Wait to the November 'lections, I'll wallop John to a pulp if 'e votes for any on 'em agen."

"That's nonsense," I replied. "And now clear out Mrs Crabthorne for goodness sake, I'm really busy."

"Not before you've 'elped me get some water, sonny," said she moving towards the door. "Come along, I've got a couple o' buckets, a bath and water can outside."

At that moment I heard the welcome air escape from the water tap and knew that they water would soon flow.

"Hurry up," I said to my lady friend, "the water is just come on again." And I pushed her towards the front door as vigorously as I could.

I am truly sorry for what happened and I can vouch I had no malicious intentions aforethought. Mrs Crabthorne had placed her buckets, etc. just in front of the doorstep. I must have closed the door upon her too abruptly for as I closed the door I heard a terrible commotion just outside.

I did not care to open the door to see what had happened, but glanced through the window. The sight I saw made me go to the door to remonstrate with Mrs Crabthorne.

"My dear Mrs Crabthorne," I said as gently as I could, "you must not have your bath in the street. You will – "

"It was your silly fault," she replied heatedly. "You banged the door aginst me an' I stepped in the bucket an' fell in the bath. But you wait sonny. You wait!"

So I suppose I am in the cart again.

Rodbourne:
A Topical Article by Mr George E Hobbs
(First published: May 4, 1923)

Sir – It is in sorrow more than anger I pen this letter to you as it deals with the "Rodbourne" controversy. I did not intend to take part in this regrettable debate, knowing there were many who would take up the cudgels in defence of dear old Even Swindon.

Even now I should not have written but for the fact that the controversy brought to me a most unwelcome visitor – Mrs Crabthorne.

It appears that her husband, John, has had what she inelegantly termed a "riz" and, as "Rodbern wernt class anuff, they 'ad moved to ware the helite lived – South Swindon."

Hoping to shut up her cackle (sorry sir, 'excessive verbosity' I should have written) and wishing to impress upon her the importance of my time, I told her I was exceedingly busy upon a scientific treatise.

Naturally, being a woman, she requested to know what it was. And I replied that the treatise upon which I was engaged was the relationship between face fungus and the divine art of osculation [kissing].

I was rather surprised at her swift comprehension. A changed expression journeyed over her vast expanse she calls a face and said, "Well, if you want my 'pinion, I'd sooner be kissed..."

"I don't want your opinion," I answered testily, "I want you to get out – at once!"

"Look you 'ere, sonny me lad," said the dear soul, grimly. "Ever since you writ them articles about me I've bin waitin' to get me own back, an' now I've got me chance. Wot do you think of Rodbern now?"

"Mrs Crabthorne," I replied as courageously as my temper would allow, "I had no wish to take part in this unfortunate controversy publicly, but as you have asked my opinion privately I will tell you.

" The district which is no longer graced with your charming presence – that is – residentially," and here I bowed to her, "unquestionably ranks as high in personal virtues as any other district in Swindon.

"And, except in very few instances, the houses compare favourably with any other district. There are no 'mean streets', no 'gin palaces', no 'slums'. I think that is about all. Good evening!"

Mrs Crabthorne unfortunately has a hide about as thin as a rhinoceros and she took as much notice of my dismissal of her as though I had not spoken.

"Half a mo', sonny me lad," said she, "not quite so fast. Then you say the Adver man was wrong?"

"He was not wrong by intent," I answered her wearily, "seeing he described what he thought to be true. But he was wrong in adding sarcasm in his reply after the mistake had been pointed out to him."

"Well, I agrees with 'un," said Mrs Crabthorne decisively. "If it wernt true, why didn't some o' them fellers wot got in with yer votes last 'lection protest against the description of the place they represent on the Town Council? Rodbern ain't no paradise, wot with the ash 'eap – an' t'other place."

"Mrs Crabthorne," I said patiently, "let me answer you and then please go. Perhaps the Town Councillors who represent Even Swindon thought the controversy too trivial? Perhaps they did not think of it at all, except votes at election time? I can't say, of course. I agree in so far as the ash-heap etc is concerned, that there are times when we are privileged to inhale a perfume somewhat inferior to attar of roses. But I can assure you that Rodbourne is a paradise, and..."

"Paradise?" queried Mrs Crabthorne. "Since when?"

I placed the table between the dear little darling and myself, and replied:

"Since you left the district!"

The crescent in which I live was quite shocked to see Mrs Crabthorne and myself roll out through the front door in quite an unconventional attitude.

As soon as I could disengage myself, I hurried indoors and shut the door. I trust I shall see the dear old lady no more.

Yours in sorrow,
George E Hobbs

Mrs Crabthorne in a New Role
By George E Hobbs
(First published: May 18, 1923)

I have performed many strange duties during my stay upon this interesting planet, but none more strange than the one of which I now write.

My old friend, Mrs Crabthorne, is responsible for this unique episode.

The other evening she sent me a bulky package, and with it a note. The note was peremptory in its demand; literally commanding me to criticise – favourably – some verses she had prepared for the press. The note ran thus: (I reproduce it as written.)

> Mister Obbs, – I ave writ some verses fer to be printed in the Advertiser if the stops commers an things aint rite then put em rite an wile youm at it fix up the spellin as well. mind you tell the editor tis the best youve ever red or it'll be the worst fer you. – S. Crabthorne.

When I opened the bulky package and saw its contents, so irrational became my actions that brandy had to be administered at once. My first task upon coming round was to try and decipher the meaning of its contents. For a time I could not decide whether it was a paper puzzle, in which sundry irregular portions duly fitted together would make a symmetrical figure, or whether it was the product of a cubist's nightmare.

There were dozens of pieces of paper, of every conceivable shape and size. And the quality of the paper was no less dissimilar than the shape and size. Grease proof paper, wallpaper – both new and old – brown packing paper, blotting paper; even a disreputable piece of emery paper was included amongst that brave array of manuscript oddities. And upon each and all were hieroglyphics such as would have made the ancient Egyptians envious. Mrs Crabthorne called the hieroglyphics "riteing" and the "riteing" she called pourtry".

Out of the chaos of paper I rescued one fragment on which was scrawled "Remernisences", which I here quote as near as possible to Mrs Crabthorne's diction:

> John courted I, I courted 'e.
> We courted one another:
> 'E kissed I on me ruby lips,
> An' said, 'Now Sal, you're mine fer kips.'
> 'Fer kips an' kips,' ses I to 'e,
> 'Now come an' tell me mother.'

I had just reached that far when, to my intense disgust, in walked Mrs Crabthorne. I suppose it was excitement, due to her anticipated literary success, which caused the good lady neither to knock at the door nor to ask permission to enter. She just barged in with as much grace as a hippopotamus attempting the swallow dive.

"So you 'ave started, sonny me lad!" chirped the old dame, exhaling breath like the exhaust of a superannuated engine.

"I have," I answered, and then added significantly, "But it is not usual for authors to assist in the criticism of their own compositions."

"Ain't it though," said Mrs Crabthorne. "Then you read the Sorrers of Satan. In that book Marie Corelli ses eny author can get writ up so as the mob'll take notice if 'e's rich enough to pay fer 't."

"Well, we will let that go," I answered, somewhat lamely, at the same time wishing an explosion would occur and blow her to – to – to the middle of the Sahara desert. Then an idea came to me, and smiling to myself, I said:

"This exquisite poem of yours Mrs Crabthorne, entitled 'Reminiscences'. It is excellent! Wonderful! But you know that a poet or poetess must not only obey the laws which govern metrical composition, but must also obey the laws of truth!"

"Wot you mean?" she demanded wrathfully. "Ain't I rit the truth?"

"Try and be calm my dear lady," said I gently. "I have no doubt you courted John – as your poem so entrancingly mentions. But it is certainly inconsistent with reason to think that John courted you. I – "

"Then 'ow could we be wed, you ass, if John didn't do 'is wack of the courtin?"

"That's easily explained," I replied, preparing for a deadly siege. "I have been told that when a tigress has sprung upon her victim she has no need to hold it. The victim is held by a baleful hypnotism, and – "

Oh, it was a merry dance! Round and round the table we went; in fact, she would have caught me, only I suddenly remembered the passage which leads from the front door to the kitchen. Mrs Crabthorne can only negotiate the passage sideways. Into the passage I ran, and the good lady, forgetting her limitations, got stuck.

Out of the front door I went, taking the precaution of leaving it open to its widest capacity. It was the work of a moment to go round the house and enter by the back door. There was the dear soul facing the street door and still tightly wedged like a cork in a bottle.

Perhaps I was a trifle too vigorous in my efforts to help her. I only think that by the velocity with which she shot along the passage out in to the street. You see she is so palatial in her physique – and I only charged her in the back.

And the worst of it is I am afraid I have not seen the last of her. I still have her wretched manuscript.

Mrs Crabthorne's "Robot":
How She Has Solved the Servant Problem
By George E Hobbs

(First published: May 25, 1923)

Mrs Crabthorne is nothing if not up to date. The other evening she came to my place, burst in upon me in the true unceremonious, Crabthornean way, and, without pausing to apologise or for breath, bellowed:

"'Fore you do eny more at my pourtry I want you to come to my 'ouse, I've got a Robot to show you. Come on, sonny, me lad, come on – "

And so she could have continued all the evening, so inexhaustible is she in the bellows department: only, as politely as one possibly could be with a lady, I requested her either to put a sock in it, change the record, or get out as quickly as she had got in.

My sturdy courage in addressing her thus must have convinced her I should stand no nonsense. She looked at me helplessly for a moment and then said: "But I've got a Robot to show you!"

"My dear woman," I expostulated, "I've very little interest in, and less knowledge of, botany, horticulture or agriculture. If you want expert opinion upon this rare plant you must – "

"'Taint nothin' of that, you silly ape!" responded Mrs Crabthorne politely. "It's a machine man – a hautomatic servant. When we shifted from Rodbern we decided to keep servants. But I 'ad to sack me maid cos I found John a kissin' of 'er, an' the nippers drove their nus to the loonatic assalum, an' John kicked the butler out fer pinchin' the wine. So I ups an' buys a Robot. An' this Robot butles for us, valets John, lady-maids me, an' looks after the nippers, as well as odd jobs about the gardin."

This, I need scarcely say, was most wonderful news to me, and I decided to go with Mrs Crabthorne to see it.

When I got to her palatial villa, she requested me to "get along in fust". I did as she wished and received quite a shock. A well-dressed and respectable young man was leaning against the wall in an attitude of anguished collapse.

"Quick! Mrs Crabthorne!" I shouted in my excitement. "Get medical aid at once! The poor young fellow has fainted or shot himself" – and dashing for a bottle upon the table, I was about to give the sufferer a drink when the fairy-like form of Mrs Crabthorne interposed between myself and that poor anguished fellow. The interposition must have been one of rather ponderous influence, for I found myself shot unceremoniously right under the dining room table. When I emerged from under the table, and scrambled, dazed and disheveled, to my feet, I could scarcely believe my eyes. It was not a faint the young fellow was passing through but a fit of the most violent type. The throes of madness were upon him, and Mrs Crabthorne was striving to keep him. Valiantly I dashed to the rescue, calling upon her to keep cool, and I would beat off his mad attack. He was head and shoulders taller than I. But the lust of battle was now in my veins. I closed with my big antagonist with the intention of releasing his terrible grip from my lady friend.

At that moment, Mrs Crabthorne, with a herculean effort, seemed to extricate herself from his embrace. Unfortunately, the extreme violence of the disengagement had disastrous results for me. Down on the floor I went again with the demented young fellow all a-sprawl on the top of me. A cold shudder passed through my being as his head came into contact with mine. His head not only rattled like a drum, but was of adamantine hardness. The whole solar system danced before my eyes, and in the midst of my bewilderment I heard the voice of Mrs Crabthorne raised in wrathful accents.

" x x x x x," represents her opening statement. I dare not write the actual words. My pen might stand it, but the class of type used at the Advertiser Offices would melt under its intense heat.

After consigning me to a place where no respectable people would think of going, she continued: "That aint a poor fellow, an' 'e aint fainted, an' 'e aint shot 'isself! That's my Robot – my hautomatic servant. An' the plaguey thing run down wile I come fer you. I was windin' 'im hup agen wen you shouted fer me to keep cool. Now pick 'im up agen an' let me finish a-windin' 'im hup."

I was still somewhat dazed and distressed, but Mrs Crabthorne has a way with her which soon restores confidence in oneself. Before I could obey her behest she "yanked" me to my feet and then picked up her "Robot".

"You won't see what 'e can do to-night," she said, "for you've wasted too much time over yer daft actions. But come up to-morrow night an' I'll show yer."

I went. Yes, I did. But that's another story.

Mrs Crabthorne's "Robot": First Demonstration a Disaster
By George E Hobbs
(First published: June 1, 1923)

I wrote last week that my second visit to Mrs Crabthorne's house in order to witness the capabilities of her "hautomatic" servant was another story. And it is another story with a giant capital "S". It is nothing but a chapter of unfortunate occurrences from commencement to finish.

There is no doubt that Mrs Crabthorne has implicit faith in her "Robot". And really, I know her faith. The unfortunate fiasco I attribute solely to the fact that my lady friend was over-anxious. It is so lamentably true that when one has a prized possession to show one's friends, something or other of a provoking nature will occur seemingly out of pure "cussedness". And so it was with Mrs Crabthorne and her "Robot".

When I arrived I found the exhibition of the Robot's capabilities were to be witnessed by the whole tribe of aborigines – sorry, I meant the whole of the Crabthorne family. Mrs Crabthorne was stage-manager and chief engineer. John, her husband, was a perfectly willing, though rather awkward assistant – called "Ass" for short by his loving spouse. Fred'rick James, John William, Ebenezer, Florrie Janet and I were presumed to be the audience.

Mrs Crabthorne explained that the Robot was full up "in 'is innards of deliket machinery". First the Robot was wound up with a key, similar to the operation applied to a gramophone. Then, according to the service demanded, switches were employed – of which I found there were several. One in particular took my fancy, upon which I read: "Four repeats".

In answer to my interrogation, Mrs Crabthorne explained that this particular switch was for bathing the children, when the Robot repeated its cycle of operations four times. And then, somewhat inconsequentially, added, "I told that fool of a shopman I wanted a five repeat un, an' 'e ups an' sends this un."

Naturally, and quite innocently I asked the dear woman why she had ordered a "five repeat", seeing there were only four young Crabthorne's in the hive.

"Mind yer own bisness, Nosey Parker!" was her characteristic, and disconcerting, reply.

"Now, Sal," mildly remonstrated John. "There ain't no 'arm in tellin' Mister 'Obbs the 'appy noos. W'em..."

"You shut yer rattle," broke in John's amiable partner. "An' don't think yer body everyself just because it 'appens to be true."

Not wishing to witness a family jar, I hastily assured Mrs Crabthorne of my sincere regret for asking such an irrelevant question. To which she replied, "Surely." And so came peace for a time.

The first demonstration of the Robot's activity was to valet John. He was to stand ready for his coat and vest to be removed, John stipulating that darling Sal should throw the switch out of contact when the second article of clothing was removed.

As the Robot was still somewhat of a novelty to the Crabthorne menage, it was perhaps pardonable though very unfortunate, that John should have exhibited such excited eagerness. Instead of remaining where his dear wife had placed him, he advanced to meet the Robot. The result was that both met in mid-field so to speak, with disastrous consequences. The equatorial region of John's anatomy arrested the Robot's advance with such a shock, that being unstable, it collapsed to the ground.

This in itself would not have mattered: only in the Robot's readjustment of posture from the upright to the prone, he gathered up poor little Ebenezer in his progress – and to my sorrow Eby was underneath.

"O-o-o! Muver!" shouted the distressed little Crabthorne. "'E felled on me stumick! I can't breave! O-o-o!"

In cases of emergency I always strive to keep my head. In this case I nearly lost it. Not by lack of nerve, but by violent impact.

Mrs Crabthorne and I, plus John simultaneously rushed to the rescue. Like three old friends, we met over the fallen bodies of Robot and Eby. As the trunk of each was at right angles to the legs, it was our heads that met – and the meeting produced a sound like unto the crack of doom.

"Goodbye, Sal!" I heard the despairing voice of John cry as he went down athwart the Robot. I went down next, and though my head was whirling like a buzz-saw, I believe I should have been quite comfortable with John as a pillow, only... whack came the elephantine mass of Crabthorne femininity upon the top of me. At the base of this human and mechanical heap there came a sound like the expiring shriek of a punctured bagpipe.

"Ah!" grunted Mrs Crabthorne, letting herself down gradually from the summit of the mix-up. "That's the Robot gone bust! Wait till I get John on 'is pins. I'll out 'im fer six!"

But it wasn't the Robot that had "gone bust". It was poor little Eby gasping the gasp of the lost.

I thought (naturally) that Mrs Crabthorne would reconsider her amiable intention of "outing" John, seeing that the poor fellow had not yet returned from his journey into space. So, as soon as I had recovered my dignity, I busied myself with the rescue of Eby. I found he was dented in one or two places, but twopence transferred from my pocket to his soon filled-up dents, and he was happy again.

But poor old John had to go through the "outing" business. When Mrs Crabthorne shook John's false teeth I left the house to show my disapproval, and I am not all certain I shall go there again.

Mrs Crabthorne's "Trip"
By George E Hobbs
(First published: July 5, 1923)

When Mrs Crabthorne informed me that she and her family would not be journeying by the G.W.R. "Trip" trains this year, but would be taking a week's tour by motor car, I certainly did not know what was involved. Had I known I should have "gone on the club" to have saved personal expense – and trouble.

Two fundamental reasons decided the tour by car. My lady friend "wouldn't 'ave to bath the kids overnight", and she "wouldn't 'ave to get up so hearly in the mornin'."

I must confess inability to see logic in her first reason even if there was a certain amount of that commodity wrapped up in the second. But there is one thing I have long since ceased to do. I never argue with Mrs Crabthorne. For one thing, it involves too much mental fag, and another thing; I always obtain the worst end of the argument. I just expanded my face into the broadest grin I could command, and trusted that she and her full equipment would have a jolly old time.

And then came the bombshell! Down upon the table she threw ten £20 notes, "Take that, sonny-me-lad," said she, "an' go an' buy me a mote-car to seat seven. See that you get a good un, an' then drive un up to our place!"

Knowing Mrs Crabthrone as I do I saw myself fairly in the cart. She would insist upon my following her behest: and yet I knew as much about a motor car as a motor car knew about me. Carburettors, radiators, friction-clutches, sparking-plugs, and all the other technical terms of the motoring fraternity was to me a foreign language.

But before Mrs Crabthorne, above all, I dare not reveal my ignorance.

At that moment I showed my aptness to copy from my friends. I saw it would be much more dignified to assume knowledge than to admit ignorance. The only unfortunate part about knowledge that is assumed is that it so often leads to a dickens of a mix-up. Still, I would chance that possibility happening, and so:

"All right, Mrs Crabthorne," I answered carelessly, "I will do as you wish, and bring the car up to your house."

The following evening I went to purchase the car, with my plan of procedure in an advanced state of maturity. After the purchase was completed I intended to obtain the assistance of a qualified man, who would drive the car up to Mrs

Crabthorne's residence. Then, changing seats, I would get him to knock at the door while I sat sedately at the wheel.

But my plan was negatived, and my heart sank to zero, when, upon reaching the showroom, who should I see but the bulky form of my lady friend. "I thought I'd come an' 'elp you choose," said she sweetly, in answer to my look of interrogation – and I wished her in – Halifax. I quilted my annoyance, however, as best I could and together we proceeded into the showroom.

I informed the young man who advanced I wished to purchase a motor car to seat seven. And, to make things clear, I further informed him the purchase was not for myself but for the lady who accompanied me.

My further information evidently caused his bumps of intelligence to expand to its fullest capacity. "Yes, sir," he said politely. "I see, please step this way."

Crabthorne and self stepped that way. I really could not blame the young man for his mistake but when I saw what he was about to show us I trembled for his safety.

"This will about suit the lady I think sir," he began pleasantly. "It's a steam-driven thing, and will easily carry forty tons. The price is – " Before I could intervene, Mrs Crabthorne got well away. "You fool! You ninny! You nincompoop!!!" she began in graceful language. "It's a touring car we want, not a steam-driven lorry! Wot you mean by such a hinsult? For two shakes of a lam's tale I'd serve you like Lady Astor did Mister Banbury – you – you snipe!"

Ample apology upon the part of the young man, and my own persuasive powers at last pacified the good lady, and we were able to conclude the purchase. But my trouble now was how to get the car home without revealing my ignorance.

Almost with tears in my eyes I besought the young man to put everything in running order and get the car out of the showroom into the street. When this was done – and I watched everything he did with feverish anxiety – I took my place at the wheel with Mrs Crabthorne sitting beside me. All around me were handles, switches, indicators and pedals of one sort or another.

The young man had informed me the car had a self-starting appliance, but where it was I had no idea. Pretending to see that all was in order I touched one thing after another hoping to find that miserable self-starter. I found it before I knew it, and a yell from the young man revealed we were going backwards instead of forward.

In a moment or two we stopped. We stopped, not because I had adjusted any portion of the mechanical appliance, but because a stone wall refused to get out of the way of the car. Unfortunately, the young man was between the wall and the car, wedged quite securely with his arms working like a monkey up a stick. How I wished Mrs Crabthorne had been there instead of that young man. She would have made a much better collision mat than he apparently was.

Mrs Crabthorne was just getting out of the car to go to the young fellow's assistance, when, quite by chance, I threw the lever into forward gear. The sudden jerk forward was too much for my lady friend, and without even saying "goodbye" she collapsed into the road. A rapid glance over my shoulder revealed to me the young man was down and out. But I could not stop. I had to reverse again to avoid the opposite wall.

Half way across the road I found the back of the car mount some obstacle and then stop. I got down hastily to investigate – and there was my poor lady friend lying comfortably in the road, with one of the back wheels resting upon her waist-band. It was the first time I had ever known Mrs Crabthorne unable to give free expressions to her feelings. She looked like a person with a heavy weight upon her mind, and it was probably this reason that kept her from speech.

But she found her speech afterwards. A band of wiling sympathisers assisted to take the car back again into the showroom. The young man was re-rolled into his pre-collision shape, and Mrs Crabthrone conveyed tenderly home. It was John who told me of his wife's recovery of speech. He said he had had twenty years' experience of his lady-love's tongue, but the incident of the car unloaded a vocabulary as sultry as the lava from Etna.

"Mrs Crabthorne will go away by the G.W.R. Trip trains" is the latest report from headquarters.

Mrs Crabthorne at the Seaside
By George E Hobbs
Told By Herself

(First published: July 20, 1923)

We went to "Trip" on Frid'y,
Down to the gay seaside:
We travelled fast,
And then at last -

"Year's Waymuff!" Eby cried.
I said, "Shut Up, you ninny!
Don't show yer ig-o-rance!"
An' on 'is 'ead,
Me temper shed,
Which made 'im squirm 'an dance.

A young man in the 'partment,
(Wiv 'im 'is lady-love)
Then called me names,
An' up I flames,
An' bashed 'im wiv me glove:
Me puttie was inside it
(O' course I mean me 'and),
I flopped 'im one,
An' wen I done,
'E could not sit or stand.

Down to the sands we wandered
'Twas 'ot – as 'ot as – well,
I went to sleep,
Told John to keep
'Is eye on Liz an' Nell:
I waked up in a 'urry,
'An found meself alone,
The kids 'ad gone.
'An so 'ad John
(I guessed ware 'e 'ad flown).

I found 'im in a boozer,
I found 'im – yes, I did:
I yanked 'im out,
Gave 'im a clout,
Right on 'is blinkin' lid –
I biffed 'im in the ear-'ole,
And grabbed 'im by 'is 'air:
Then lovin'ly,
Back by the sea,
I takes 'an planks 'im there.

I ast a bearded boatman
To take us for a trip –
'E scratched 'is 'ead,
'An then 'e said:
"My boat – it ain't a ship,
You'd need a gurt big wopper,
A warship or a barge"
I give a nick
An' biffed 'im quick
'E's sleeping now is Jarge.

I went to do some swimmin'
So donned a bathin' dress:
The costume bust,
The hind-part fust,
An' left me in distress.
The S.O.S. was signal'd,
The rescue party came:
They lugged me out
Wiv cheer and shout -
Me cheeks burnt red wiv shame.

I 'ad anuff of Waymuff,
Wot wiv the kids, an' John -
The next time we
Goes to the sea
We'll go to gay Pur-ton:
We'll start down in the mornin'
(For 'tis a long, long way),
We'll fish for crabs,
Or whales an' dabs,
We'll then be all OK.

Chapter 13

Selected Short Stories

Having been fascinated by Bible stories throughout his childhood, it probably seemed quite natural to George that he would become an author and storyteller himself, in later life.

In this chapter, the aim is to give a flavour of George's collection of short stories, some of which are single, standalone pieces, while two are formed in several parts.

As with many of his stories, they contain a twist at the end – whether it be making the case for moral rectitude in the form of an affirmation of broadly Gospel teachings, or an overt appeal for a community cause.

The first, *Judge Not!*, is about never making assumptions and thereby rushing to judgement, and ironic when one considers that George and his wife, Agnes, were not married when their daughter was conceived; *Outwitting Mr Sykes* tells the story of how a female victim of a burglary prevails over her tormentor; *A Little Story for Hospital Week* tugs at the heart-strings and is to be seen as a proxy fundraiser for the Victoria Hospital in Swindon; *Soul Mates* is a ripping yarn in five parts about love at first sight; and finally, *The Fear of Ridicule* is a mini murder-mystery.

Judge Not!
By George E Hobbs
(First published: February 24, 1922)

They were sitting in the back pew of the small, country chapel when the young minister saw them. That they were strangers and somewhat out of their true environment was obvious to his quick perception: and for some inscrutable reason his great heart yearned towards them. Frequently during the service he found his gaze wandering in their direction. Not in the way of facing each section of his congregation, as was his habit; but wonderingly, interrogatively, sympathetically.

From his position upon the raised platform he saw something that held his attention – they were holding hands.

Full of sympathy as he was towards the love of man and maid, in no circumstances would he tolerate love-making during Divine service. Yet the sight of those clasped hands, instead of filling him with disgust, caused him momentarily to falter in his discourse. He had grasped the psychological factor, and he knew that they clasped hands for strength, for mutual solace, and comfort. In that back pew by the door, tragedy sat unmasked.

He had been speaking of the restfulness of the sanctuary; encouraging his hearers in their attendance at the House of God. He did not intend to go beyond that one point; but those clasped hands could not be ignored. His diagnosis may be wrong, yet an inward impulse compelled him to pursue a further point.

In tones beautifully modulated he spoke of the restfulness that attended complete confidence and faith in God.

"The world," said he, "is often harsh and unjust in its judgements; but the Master revealed God to us as our Father. One who is infinite in knowledge and mercy. He sees us as we traverse the valley of affliction, and, bitter as the experience may be, He is waiting to help us if we but have confidence in Him.

"Some of us have wandered from Him. Yet so great is His love that He is ever waiting to give to us the kiss of forgiveness and reconciliation."

Tears were near his eyes as he concluded his discourse, and, dispensing with the last hymn, he bowed his head in prayer. Without appearing to be conscious of it he had seen the hands clasp tighter – and he knew that they suffered.

When he looked up after pronouncing the benediction they were gone.

The Steward

"I be main glad you spoke as you did to-night, sir," volunteered the steward in the vestry. "I do 'ope as the sinners present 'll profit an' mend their ways. 'Ow they can come to the 'ouse of the Lord – an' they livin' in open sin – beats me 'ollow. Why weem told as they baint married."

"I do not wish to know to whom you refer," said the young minister quietly. "And, Steward, remember this: The Pharisees had as much need of forgiveness as did those who betrayed and rejected the Master. I will wish you goodnight! Mr. Johnson."

"Won't 'e come an' have a bite o' supper?" asked the Steward on whom the reproof had been wasted.

"Not to-night, thank you, Mr. Johnson. I must be getting – "

"Just a moment, sir," said a quiet voice behind them – and there by the door stood the young fellow who had so strangely attracted the minister. "I should like to have a word with you. No, you need not go!" – seeing the Steward with a snort of dissent make for the door.

"What I have to say you may as well hear. We shall be quits, I think, when I tell you I overheard your remarks just now, and I knew you were thinking of me.

"It is true, as you inferred, we are living together. It is equally true that we are not married. But whether we are living in open sin is a matter not for you but for my conscience to decide."

"But there be a child a-coming," said the old man, shaking an accusing finger. "An' if that baint agin the Lord's 'Oly Gospel, then I don't know what is."

"That, too, unfortunately, is true," replied the young fellow patiently. "But, unfortunate though it may be, is there any sin in that?"

Such a question was too much for the Steward. He looked to the young minister for inspiration, but none came. He sat with bowed head, instinctively realising that the conversation had better continue without his aid. "Sin!" at last spluttered the steward, "Sin will be punished, so the good old Book says. And unless ye repent the Word declares ye shall perish!"

"Listen, you canting hypocrite!" said the young fellow with suppressed passion. "Listen and hear my story!

"When I was eighteen years of age, I unfortunately fell in with a fast set. Drink and gambling I tasted to the dregs, but thank God I have never harmed a woman yet.

"In that set was a man who professed a great affection for me. He was a devil incarnate – but I did not know it then.

"He fell in love with the dear girl who is living with me, but she refused him emphatically and finally. I was glad she refused him, for I loved her more than anything on earth, and I did not want to see her ruined.

"One night I was taken home in a taxi, oblivious of everything. When I came to in the morning I had no recollection of what had passed the previous evening. This friend of mine came to see me and told me I had killed a man whom I had detected cheating at cards. His regard for me was such that he gave me £200 to fly the country while he put the police upon a false scent. My nerve was broken by excess, and I took passage on a general cargo boat for South America.

The Sequel

"Two years I lived there in seclusion and in terror of detection. And then, out there, I met another of my former boon companions. He told me a story that made me experience hell! I had been a fool to fly. It was a concocted story – about my killing a man – for a purpose. As soon as I was out of the way, this friend of mine went to Alice – that is the girl I am living with, Mr. Pharisee – and told her the same story he had told me. If she would marry him at once he would keep my secret. If not, he would put the police upon my track. And the poor girl bowed to what she believed the inevitable and married him – to save me.

"As I say, he was a devil incarnate. Her soul was pure, and her nature sensitive in the extreme. Knowing this, he took a fiendish delight in torturing her day and night with his infidelities, his cruelties, and his animal propensities until she prayed to die.

"That was the story, and when I came home and saw her I could have killed him freely, and felt virtuous in the act. The world would be cleaner without such vermin. There was only one thing I could do short of killing him, and that I have done. I have taken her from him, and, Mr. Johnson, we are living in your sanctimonious village. She is all I have in the world," he concluded falteringly. "And I love her dearly."

"But you are livin' in open sin," said the steward doggedly. "An' you can't expect the blessin' o' the Lord to rest upon the child that be a-coming."

"The child is her husband's," replied the young fellow quietly. "And knowing who its father is I pray it may die."

"Mr. Johnson," said the young minister in deep emotion. "We both owe to this noble lad our sincere apologies. My brother" – holding out his hand to the young fellow – "I know now that this dear girl is – "

"My twin sister," replied the young fellow simply.

Outwitting Mr W Sykes
By George E Hobbs
(First published: April 1, 1921)

It was the hour of midnight. The time when deep sleep falls upon men – and women.

In a semi-detached villa, situated just off the main thoroughfare of Wicktown, there were two people upon whom the mantle of sleep had not fallen. Or, to be more correct, old Somnus had claimed one for a time, but something had happened which, suddenly, had rendered his claim null and void.

She – for the roused one was a lady – was now sitting up in bed, tense and drawn; listening, with fast beating heart, and breath which came and went in gasps.

What was it that had disturbed her? She was not usually so easily alarmed. But this was the first time since her marriage – now a year old – that she had been left alone. Her husband had been called away on urgent business; and though he knew her to be strong mentally and physically, he did not like the idea of her being in the house alone.

"Don't worry, dear," she said in reply to his worried countenance. "It's only for one night. You will be home again in the morning," – and he had gone.

After locking up for the night she had retired to rest and, being healthy in mind, had promptly fell asleep.

But she had dreamed an unpleasant dream. Jack, her husband, was in an aeroplane which had become groggy. He was falling and she was powerless to help. Down came the great winged plane, and – crash!

It was some moments before she realised that the sight just witnessed was but a dream. But with this realisation there came also the consciousness that the crash was real. Presently she became calmer, and slipping from bed she donned a becoming dressing gown and stood by the bedroom door listening.

Meanwhile, the cause of her momentary terror was standing in the drawing-room beneath, cursing below his breath with a volubility and expressiveness that was surprising in these days of more cultured phraseology. It proved him – this one was a gentleman – to be one of the old school. One to whom "top hole" – expressing delight and "bally" – expressing disgust, was a foreign and incomprehensible vocabulary.

I said the one in the drawing-room was a gentleman. But that is rather an ambiguous term. To particularise he was a gentleman only in the sense of sex differentiation. He was by no means a "gentle" man to judge by his facial expression, which was revealed by the aid of a bull's-eye lantern. In plain words he was a burglar. He was ferocious of aspect, burly and powerful, with a jemmy in his pocket and felt slippers upon his feet.

It was this latter fact which had caused him to forget his environment and indulge in one of his weaknesses – that of bad language. An unobtrusive pin-tack had penetrated into his foot just as he was quietly closing the door.

A vicious twinge of pain, a sudden backward kick – and the crash of the door and the crash of the lady's dream were coincident.

The language of Mr. Sykes suddenly eased. It had been to him like a safety valve. But while it had relieved concentrated pressure, it had also complicated his position.

"Good job there's no feller in the 'ouse," he muttered, "on'y a slip of a wench who'll be too sceered to blow the gaff" – which soliloquy revealed on the one hand cunning forethought, on the other hand – as the sequel will show – that Sykes had not calculated the unknown quantity.

At that moment Sykes received a shock. The drawing-room door opened and revealed to his gaze the "slip of a wench," clad in her dressing gown and holding an electric torch in her hand. It was a sight to move the heart of any man; for she was beautiful in the extreme. Around her shoulders her dark tresses had fallen in wild abandon, and these seemed to accentuate the sweetness of her face. But Bill was insensible to feminine beauty. The only beauty he appreciated was the commercial beauty of his swag.

"Now no nonsense!" said Bill, gruffly, holding the jemmy in a threatening attitude.

"No, no!" she replied tremulously. "Take what you want but don't hurt me," and overcome by the horror of the situation she sat down by what looked like an ordinary side table, encircled her dark head in her arms and sobbed.

Evidently she knocked something over in her anguish, but, William with a sardonic smile upon his face, went on with the collecting. Once she roused, lifted her head, then let it sink again upon her arms, with a muffled cry of: "Oh if the police were only here." There was a strong emphasis upon "police" – and then she sobbed again.

In the Central Police Station of Wicktown a telephone bell rang. The inspector in charge took the receiver and listened. "Hello!" he said, "what the dev – Here, Stanard" – this to a young constable standing near – "Here's a woman crying in a funny fashion, and I can't get her to speak a word. See if you can make anything of it."

Stanard took the receiver from his superior and he, too, listened.

"Why," he said, as he placed his hand over the transmitter, "she's sobbing like a poem, and," as a sudden light of comprehension lit up his face, "she's sobbing with a purpose. Army training's solved it, sir, for she's sobbing 'Oh's!' in Morse code. Take this down, sir. 'Burglar at number two Wessex road. Girl only in the house. Come at once.'"

Removing his hand from the transmitter, Stanard called: "All right, Missie, I've got your message. We'll be there in a few moments."

"However did you manage it sweetheart?" asked the bewildered Jack, the next morning, as he took his wife in his arms and kissed her.

"I did very little," she replied with a wan smile. "I simply knocked over the transmitter, placed the receiver between my arm and ear, and switched off the bell in what the burglar thought was my agitated fright. Luckily the girl at the exchange understood my muffled appeal and put me through to the police station.

"As you know I was on telegraphy during the war, and my only worry was whether anyone at the station would understand it as well. Someone did, dear – and that is all there is to tell."

"God bless him, whoever it was," said Jack fervently. "Never again will I leave you. And yet," he added, looking at her with pride, "If I had not, I should not have known what a brave little wife I had."

And being that she loved him, his praise was very sweet to her.

A Little Story for Hospital Week
By George E Hobbs
(First published: June 8, 1923)

Although it was summer time and wanted yet an hour before darkness enveloped the land, she went up to her bedroom precisely at 8 p.m. She went because mother said it was best that little folk should be early to bed. And mother should know what was best, for she herself had once been a little girl. Her prayers, beautifully sweet upon childish lips, had been said, and mother had given her the fond, good-night kiss, and had left her to sleep.

But strange to say, she could not sleep. She would like to have slept. She knew her usual sleep to be healthy and dreamless. It brought forgetfulness – and, at the moment, it was just what she wanted. Dear little soul! She was face to face with a supreme problem, and like so many older folk she put from her a definite solution until the morrow.

And then she did decide! Decided without equivocation. She turned back the coverlet a little way and looked into the cracked, cross-eyed face of her dolly. Fiercely she kissed the cracked face and hugged to her breast a form which was somewhat denuded of certain specific limbs.

"I nearly 'sented to give 'ou up!" she said tremulously. "But I ust tant! No, I tant!"

Having so decided and thinking the difficulty was now solved, she settled herself to sleep. But she found sleep to be as elusive as ever. From side to side she tossed, while all the time she clung tenaciously to her darling. Then came to her a vague glimmer of the reason she could not sleep. Her decision had been a selfish one!

And then she did a brave thing for one so young. Hungeringly she took her dolly, kissed again its cracked face, and then buried her beneath the clothes.

"I love ou' bestest – 'cept mummy an' daddy," said she with a pathetic droop of the lips. "But I tant fink properly wiv 'ou in my arms. Let me 'sider a minute."

Darkness had settled now. Mother had peeped in, and, thinking her little one asleep, had gone quietly to her room. Now was her time to have a real big think – and she would think of an incident that perhaps would help her.

She thought back to the time when her little body was wracked in pain. Mother and father, with all their great wealth of love, could not ease that infinite torture which throbbed through her being.

And then she remembered the young doctor, with his cheery manner and kindly smiles. Mother and father, for some reason or another, had turned to the window, and the young doctor had stooped to her so kindly and said:

"Little woman, we can't make you better here. But I know a place, with dear little snow-white beds, with beautiful flowers upon the tables, and big sisters who will love you. We could make you better there. And I shall be there with you. Will you come?"

Yes, she was sorry to be away from mother and daddy. She remembered how they had tried to speak to her, but their voices seemed muffled and broken. Perhaps they had had colds – she was not quite sure even now. But she had gone to the place where the young doctor said he could make her better.

She thought of the sweet-faced big sister who had put her so gently to bed. Though the pain had been intense she saw the flowers – just as her doctor man had described. The little cot, too, was snow-white and even rested her tortured body.

And then she remembered the day when nurse placed around her the little pink robe, and conveyed her, without even one tiny jolt, from her bed to another room. There was her doctor-man with that kind smile upon his face, and he had said, "Now, little woman, we are going to make you better!"

It was a strange experience! Even now she could not explain its details. All that she remembered was that a bewildering perfume came to her nostrils. No, it did not frighten her because nurse stood by her – and nurse – was smiling – at her. She remembered it just like that. Consciousness dimmed and then revived and dimmed again.

And then she remembered it was not nurse who smiled at her but an angel, with long, white, tapering wings, and her face was the most beautiful she had ever seen. The angel had gathered her to her soft breast – and her pain and anguish had vanished!

"Little sister!" the angel had said, "presently you will awake once more in your own bed. You will get quite well again, and when you are back with mummy and daddy, remember all the love and skill and patience that has been given you here. You were able to come here and get better because kind people gave their pennies to build this nice house. Remember, little sister, for the sake of other little children and grown up folk too, give the best you – "

Before the angel had completed what she wished to tell her, she remembered she awoke to find herself in her own little hospital cot. Yes, and from that day she gradually got better until at last she was back again with mummy and daddy.

Yes, she remembered – and remembering all, she decided anew. But if one could have touched the pillow beneath her sweet little face, one may have judged the value of her decision, for the pillow was moist with tears that could not be repressed.

She was early astir the following morning, and creeping from bed, proceeded to mother's room. Mother was naturally concerned at so early a visit, but before one question could be put the little quivering voice said:

"Mummy, I 'eard Mister Richardson tell daddy the 'toria 'ospital wanted lots and lots of pennies, 'cause they wanted to help lots more childrens and big people to get well. Here's Daisy, mummy. I loves her bestest 'cept ou an' daddy. Sell Daisy, mummy, then p'raps – "

With that wonderful intuition mothers have, mother saw at once what her little one had passed through. Before her darling could complete her broken sentences she gathered her tenderly to her breast.

"My dearest!" she said softly, "you are a noble little girlie. What you would do is this – you would give up that which you love best to help others. You will not quite understand me dear, but daddy and I will take your offer in spirit – and you shall keep Daisy. Daddy and I will see that you shall give something to the Victoria Hospital!"

She may not have understood all. But two little feet pattered along the landing, and mother heard her say: "Come on, Daisy! We'll say prayers agether 'smorning!"

* * *

Readers of the Advertiser, I have tried to tell you a story for a specific purpose. Will you at least try and remember the spirit of the story during the carnival week, and with your usual generosity give "lots and lots of pennies"!

Soul Mates (1)
By George E Hobbs
(First published: May 19, 1922)

Chapter 1 – The Man

"So you want a holiday, Seymour, eh? Yes, I think you deserve one. You have been of the greatest service to me. And now we are working upon a more solid basis, I think I can spare you – for a time. How long do you wish to be away?"

These words were spoken by a grey-haired man to a young, brown-haired giant in the manager's room of a remote Griqualand West diamond mine.

Four years previous, a prospector had found some very valuable specimens a few miles from where the great Kimberley diamond mines are now situated.

Many of the experts had believed the "find" to be merely isolated and superficial, and that the undersoil would not be commercially workable. But the prospector had been a lifelong friend of Sir Hedley Grey's, and had given him information which he had withheld from others.

Sir Hedley had believed it to be a valuable venture, and had promptly purchased several acres of the surrounding land, installed an up-to-date plant and commenced the work.

For a time the mine proved unproductive, but Sir Hedley, acting upon the advice given by his friend, plodded on and eventually a rich lode was discovered. The mine had now been working successfully for two years, and the real success of the venture was directly attributable to John Seymour – the young giant who now faced his employer in the manager's office.

John Seymour had passed out head of his year at the college set apart for the technicalities of mining engineering. Having nothing definitely fixed in his mind, he decided to take a trip to South Africa, nominally to spy out the land.

Sir Hedley Grey chanced to be travelling to Africa by the same boat. Just after passing the equator, one of the young stokers became temporarily deranged by the intense heat and would probably have killed Sir Hedley but for the timely intervention of John Seymour.

Very warmly Sir Hedley thanked him for the skilful and courageous manner with which he overcame his assailant, and learning of his credentials, had taken him into his confidence and offered him the post of manager to his new venture.

It was Seymour who had selected the requisite machinery. And who by patient zeal had worked the mine up to the present successful position. Everything was now working in first class order and Seymour, knowing he had an assistant upon whom he could depend, asked permission of Sir Hedley to take a holiday.

"How long do you wish to be away?" again asked Sir Hedley as Seymour hesitated.

"Six months, Sir Hedley if you do not mind," answered Seymour slowly.

"Ah!" – with a smile. "You are going home then. Are you thinking of bringing a wife back with you? I am rather hoping you are, then I shall be having you settled here."

"No, no, Sir Hedley! I do not even possess a sweetheart. I am only twenty-five. There is plenty of time yet for me to seek the doubtful joys of matrimony."

"Don't be cynical, lad," remonstrated Sir Hedley softly, while his eyes seemed to take a far away look. "A good wife is one of God's richest treasures." And to John Seymour's dismay, he saw the strong eyes of his employer suffused with tears.

"Forgive my weakness, Seymour. My wife was one of the best. Ten years of exquisite joy we had together, and then – I lost her. No, I have no children. I am practically alone in the world. No, I shall never marry again – her memory is too sweet that I could replace her. But your holiday!" he continued, tearing himself with an effort from the past.

"You shall have the six months you asked for. But you will come back again?" looking wistfully at his young manager. "You will come back again?"

"Yes, Sir Hedley, it will not be my fault if I do not return. Your kindness to me has been..."

"Never mind that, lad," interrupted Sir Hedley, hastily. "It is I who am indebted to you. By the way, how are you off for money? You will need a few extra pounds if you are going home. Let me be your banker, lad. I... I'd like you to have a good time – and then come back again!"

John Seymour saw that a refusal upon his part would have pained Sir Hedley.

Often had he noticed a sad expression upon the patient face of his employer, and during its cause had never ventured by look or gesture to break upon his reserve.

Seymour was a man of strict honour. He knew that the natives and the casual foreigner who came to the mine for employment would judge English ethics by the standard he set and lived. He represented English morals, and he saw to it that no stain came upon his country by any act of his.

The same moral sense that had pervaded his dealings with the employees and his employer at the mine was evidenced in his courteous acceptance of Sir Hedley's generosity. Had his employer been situated as other men, he would not have accepted. But understanding the circumstances, he knew that his acceptance would give to his employer a sense of satisfaction and even joy.

"Thank you, Sir Hedley," replied John simply. "I am obliged to you for your kindly generosity, and I accept in the spirit it is offered."

"Then that is settled, lad," said Sir Hedley, relieved by Seymour's simple acceptance. "You will want to start in a day or so, and as you will have several things to see to, you had better commence your holiday as from tomorrow." So saying, he drew out his chequebook and handed to his young manager a cheque for five hundred pounds.

"Cash that at Cape Town, Seymour – and God bless you, lad!" And with a hearty clasp of the hand, he was gone.

Seymour was not emotional by nature. He hated the weakness of tears. But as he turned to close the office for the night, there was strangely like a mist about his eyes.

"Poor old man," he soliloquised feelingly. "What a comfort a son would have been to him – or a daughter. How she could have cheered him. And strangely enough, this unsophisticated young giant found his pulse to quicken as, for the first time, he thought of a woman's embrace.

Upon reaching Kimberley, he found by the shipping news that the "Renfrue", a fine P&O boat, was sailing for home from Cape Town in seven days' time.

So, telegraphing for a first class berth, he made his way down to the port of embarkation.

(To be continued)

Soul Mates (2)
By George E Hobbs
(First published: May 26, 1922)

Chapter 2 – The Man

On the steps of an unpretentious farm house, a few miles south of Fraserberg, a girl sat in a pensive mood with a pen letter in her hand. Before her lay the wide, sunlit veldt, gradually ascending until the rugged peaks of the Nieuw Mountains seemed to kiss the heavens. The scene was beautiful in the extreme; with inspiration enough to infuse warm blooded life into a Pygmalion statue. But the girl, usually so sympathetic towards the divinity in nature, was at this moment unconscious of its call.

The letter absorbed her whole being.

Presently she came back to earth. Quietly folding the letter she replaced it in the envelope and conveyed it to where she had taken it from – within the lacy folds of her blouse. The face which had been so set in its pensiveness relaxed to normality, and when she stood up her queenly grace would be acknowledged even by the proverbial woman hater – if one should really exist.

Her beauty was not such as would startle by its boldness. Rather was it of that type which may be compared to the pure symmetrical beauty of the daisy – the sweetest, the most inspiring of English flowers of the field.

And now she was all animation. Going to her room she changed into her riding clothes, and was passing out to the stables, when she heard her mother calling to her.

"It's much too hot to go out riding dear, isn't it?" mildly remonstrated her mother, seeing her attire.

"Oh, no, mother mine!" answered she gaily. "I'm going for a canter on 'Prince'" – and then more soberly: "I've had a letter from Jim, mother, and I'm going over to 'Shadynook' to read it over again, and have a good big think all on my lonesome."

"And what is the great problem, Nesta dear?" asked her mother, smilingly, yet with anxiety revealed in her tone. "Jim will surely not ask you to go over to England to marry him. No, no, dear, if that is the problem you must not think of it. Jim must come here to Africa."

"Now mother, not a word. Here's Daddie coming. Let me have my big think first; and then I will tell you the contents of my letter afterwards. Just let me have an hour to myself mother dear," – and vaulting lightly into the saddle, away she flew to the place she often rested when faced with some perplexing problem. And evidently this one would need some very big thinking indeed.

There was no need to tether her horse. "Prince" knew the habits of his young mistress. As soon as he saw the direction they travelled, he knew under the restful shade of the trees bridle and saddle would be thrown off, and he could wander free within its shady limits. Not one step outside that belt of trees would he go until he heard that beloved voice say: "Come, Prince!" – and he was ready.

As soon as "Prince" was free of saddle and bridle, Nesta threw herself upon the ground, and taking out the letter that had so disturbed her, read through its contents again. And this is what she read:-

Dearest Nesta,
I am sorry I cannot come out to Africa as promised. I have a big contract which will keep me in England for another twelve months. If it is your wish to be married at the time we agreed, then you must come to England. I will send your fare, and we can be married as soon as you land. At the conclusion of my contract we will return to Africa. Love to you, Father and Mother.
Yours with love, Jim.

"No," she mused, "there's nothing wrong with the letter – and yet – there is. Jim, dear, I gave you my whole heart. Surely you have not tired of me. That cannot be – " and then realising that such doubts savoured of disloyalty, she turned from the letter to thoughts of the happy past.

No man had touched her heart until that fateful day when Jim Weston was carried into her father's house – his horse having thrown him through stepping into a rabbit burrow. Nesta nursed him with all the sweetness of her nature, and Jim, versed in the world's love, watched to his entire satisfaction, the gradual response to his wooing.

Nesta remembered as she lay upon the green sward that never-to-be-forgotten evening when Jim, impetuous and strong, declared his love for her. It was in this very spot – rendered sacred by that scene – with the golden orbs of the Southern Cross casting its gentle rays upon them, that this plighted their troth.

Yes, Jim was true to her. Yet as she glanced at the letter again, there seemed some vague apprehension of change. True, once or twice during the two months Jim spent with them after their engagement was announced, he revealed momentary traces of extreme selfishness. Rage gleamed, and as quickly faded if his will was thwarted. But, of course, that was due to his accident.

And so if Jim could not come to her, she was in honour bound to go to him. He needed her – and she would go.

"Mother, dear," said Nesta as soon as she arrived home. "You must be a wizard, for you divined the contents of my letter. Jim had written to say he cannot come out to Africa. He wishes me to go over to England and be married as soon as I land and he will bring me back in twelves months' time. I – "

"My darling, you cannot do such a thing!" gasped her mother. "You have never been farther than Cape Town by yourself, and how can you possibly think of going to England. Beside, it is selfish of Jim to ask of you such a thing. Remember, dear, we only saw him for three months. We know, after all, very little about him. And it would be strange people you would go amongst. If things are not what we believe them to be, what would be your position, a stranger in a strange land. Listen to me, Nesta dear, and if Jim cannot come out for twelve months, then wait that time."

Good, sound advice, and buttressed by a mother's love and yearning. It was met, not with defiance – for that would be contrary to Nesta's sweet nature – but with logic based upon age-old love and a keen sense of loyalty to him who had won her heart. Yes, Nesta knew her mother loved her. But Jim needed her. Needed her to inspire and cheer him in his great commercial undertaking. And the time would so pass. One twelve month and she and Jim, happy and radiant in their wedded bliss would be back upon the dear old farm again.

With a heavy heart her mother gave a reluctant consent, and Nesta, accompanied by her father and mother, went down to Cape Town.

And on the good ship "Renfrue" – the ship on which John Seymour travelled – her passage was booked.

(To be continued)

Soul Mates (3)
By George E Hobbs
(First published: June 2, 1922)

Chapter 3 – The Meeting

John Seymour was free to observe everything that went on around him. He had no one at the dockside to see him off or to bid him "God speed." His personal effects first engaged his attention, and after seeing these safely deposited in his cabin he returned to the deck.

The Renfrue was a splendidly equipped ship, and Seymour, being a good sailor, looked forward with a good deal of pleasure to the voyage home.

Having nothing particular to do, he stood some little distance from the gangway, watching the passengers come aboard.

Presently, with no curiosity in his glance, he saw a little group of three hesitating at the foot of the gangway. Mentally he fixed them as father, mother and daughter, but whether one or all were to be fellow voyagers he could not determine.

And then he saw that their indecision had vanished, for all three proceeded up the gangway to come aboard.

"Yes, Nesta, dear," he heard the elder woman say. "There is another hour yet to sailing time, so father and I will just see your cabin and then we'll go ashore again. But dear, even now I wish you would change your mind and not go."

To which the man made haste to answer: "Let her alone, Di. She will be all right. If things do not turn out well, Nesta can return to us at once. I have instructed Jenkins, my old lawyer, to meet her and watch her interests. And if..." But they had passed by, and John, not wishing to be guilty of eavesdropping, dismissed the incident from his mind.

In a quarter of an hour, however, he saw the mother and father proceeding down the gangway, so he concluded it was the daughter only who would be travelling.

Exactly to the minute of departure the four fussy little tugs at the Renfrue's bows began to strain at the hawsers, and the ship, amid profuse "Good-byes" and waving of handkerchiefs, slowly warped out into midstream. As the boat gathered weigh, John, leaning upon the taffrail, became absorbed in watching the gradually receding shore.

So absorbed was he that he did not notice a neatly clad figure standing by his side. Then, upon his sub-conscious mind, he seemed to hear "England! – Happiness!"

"Ah!" he exclaimed, unconsciously speaking aloud. "England! – Happiness!" Then, as it were, overhearing his own voice, and realising that someone else must have first spoken, he turned with a start to see a young girl standing by his side. It was the young girl whom he had seen at the foot of the gangway, and whose mother had addressed as Nesta.

"I beg your pardon," he said, raising his hat, and turning to move away. "I did not know you were there. I trust you will forgive my seeming rudeness. I assure you it was quite unintentional."

"It is quite all right," replied she with a smile. "I must have spoken my thoughts aloud. You quite startled me when you repeated the very words I used." And with a slight bow she turned and left him.

Astronomers may interpret the mysterious ring of Saturn, and geologists may interpret the age in which a fossilised Saurian flourished; but no living philosopher can interpret the subtle workings of the human heart. The one is interpreted by immutable law; the other is a law unto itself.

It must have been because Seymour's life was so full of study that no inclination for female companionship had crossed his mind. But now as he watched that graceful, receding figure, certain thoughts were taking shape in his mind. As yet they were fragmentary, and in no sense coherent or followed in consecutive order. There was something about that fleeting glance which those grey eyes had given him; and something about the presence of that willowy figure, which somehow had caused the sun to shine with a richer glow, for the very air to be fragrant with an indefinable joy of exquisite sweetness. Something, but he knew not what. He did not know it was the call of the ages: the call which had vibrated through the race since the first man, incomplete and dejected, found his completeness and joy in the first woman.

To Seymour's secret satisfaction he discovered they were to be next each other at meals; and as life aboard ship seeks to destroy formality and stiffness, it was not long before they gravitated towards real good friendship.

It was on the evening of the sixth day out that the inevitable crisis came to John Seymour. Nesta had gone to dress in preparation for a dance in the first class saloon, and Seymour was walking reflectively along the wide avenue of the promenade deck. The words of his old chief came back to him with startling vividness: "Are you thinking of bringing back a wife with you?" he had asked. And then to his unthinking satire he had again replied: "Don't be cynical lad, a good wife is one of God's greatest blessings."

He stopped short in his tracks. Revelation had come like a flash of light. He knew at that moment Nesta was to him more than fame or riches, even more than life itself. How glad he was now that no regrets had place in his thoughts. No episodes of which he would be ashamed. He could offer to Nesta a love pure and unsullied; a love in which knowledge and innocence were co-ordinate qualities.

As he mused, he remembered how restless Nesta had been all that day. There had been moments when she seemed far from her own bright self; even petulant at times. And John thought perhaps she grieved for the father and mother she had left at Cape Town, and blunderingly tried to cheer and comfort her.

He did not know that a greater crisis was pending in her life. The battle ground was her heart, and the contestants were love and duty, fidelity and dishonour.

When he met Nesta outside of her cabin to take her to the saloon she said hurriedly: "I am sorry if I disappoint you, Mr. Seymour, but I shall only stay for the first three dances. My head is aching rather badly, so I am sure you will excuse me."

"Only three!" exclaimed John, in dismay, the bottom knocked out of his world in a moment. "Oh, but you must stay for longer than that. I am sorry your head is so bad. But never mind, instead of dancing we can sit and watch the rest, and then perhaps the ache will go. Only do stay the evening."

"No, no!" replied Nesta firmly. "I will just stay the first three, after that I must really go, or I shall have to stay in my cabin all day to-morrow. In fact I think I ought not to attend at all."

"Oh, do come!" said John, alternating between hope and fear. "Just for three and then you may return to your cabin."

At the conclusion of the second dance Nesta said she must retire to her cabin. "No, Mr. Seymour," as he turned to accompany her. "I can find my way, thank you. You stay and enjoy the evening."

"I shall see you to your cabin," said John quietly. And Nesta felt sick at heart when she heard his tone.

At the door of her cabin she turned and held out her hand – "Good-night, Mr. Seymour, and thank you."

John took her hand within his grasp. And then, before Nesta knew, she was in his arms. "Nesta, darling!" he cried passionately. "I love you. I have wanted so much to tell you. You are all the world to me. Will you be my wife?"

For a moment she lay passive in his arms. Then a vision of Jim Weston came, waiting for her in England.

"No, no," she cried piteously, freeing herself from his embrace. "I am sorry, but it is impossible. No! Do not hold me again. Take this note and read it in your cabin – and if you love me as you say you do – forgive me!"

She was gone. And John was left staring stupidly at a letter which the moonbeams revealed in his hand.

(To be continued)

Soul Mates (4)
By George E Hobbs
(First published: June 9, 1922)

Chapter 4 – The Parting

John Seymour staggered rather than walked back to his cabin. Under no circumstances could he return to the saloon. Dancing was altogether out of the question. The brief moment in which Nesta had rested in his arms revealed to him how exceedingly precious she was to him, and how necessary she was to his happiness. Why had she been so emphatic in refusing him? But had she been emphatic? Certainly he had taken her at a disadvantage. Yet, for the moment, she had been passive in his arms. Had she already a lover? Was she married? No, no, such thoughts were treason. Fool that he was!

Why should he debate such questions when her letter lay in his hand? He would open it and read its contents. Perhaps after all she was only trying to discourage him until she had communicated with her parents. Of course that was it. She was alone – and certainly he ought not to have spoken; he should have waited with such a tremendous proposition until she was properly chaperoned. He might be an adventurer to her, and she must be protected until a responsible person examined his credentials. That was it. But he would read her letter first. Explanations would undoubtedly be there. He turned into his cabin and locked the door.

On account of the dance John knew that the electric lights would be left on until 11:30pm, so that he would have plenty of time in which to read her letter.

Switching on the light he sat on the edge of his bunk and broke the seal of Nesta's letter. And this is what he read:

"Dear Mr. Seymour, – I am afraid this letter will pain you. But please believe it was not my wish to do so – and forgive me.

"From the commencement of the voyage we seemed to have chummed together. I have indeed been grateful for your companionship, for I was lonely. It was not until to-day, however, I realised how foolish I had been in being in your company so much. And to-day you must have noticed a change in my manner towards you.

"I am afraid you have entertained thoughts in your mind which I dare not encourage. I value your friendship, dear friend, but it can be no more than that. I should have told you perhaps before, but I did not realise until to-day to where we were drifting.

"I am going to England to be married.

"Forgive me, dear friend, if I pain you. And God grant some dear girl will make you happy. It will be best for the rest of the voyage if we meet only in the presence of others. – Yours, etc., Nesta Lindon."

The electric light had ceased its illuminating rays two hours before Seymour realised its absence. Two or three times had he mechanically glanced down to where the letter was, as though to refresh his memory of its contents. The darkness enveloped him, though he knew it not. He thought he re-read some of its outstanding features, only because the words had seared into his throbbing brain.

"I am going to England to be married!" iterated and re-iterated like the metallic clang of a funeral bell.

No, he would not blame her, he loved her too well to have harsh thoughts of her.

And then through his dazed mind another sentence of the letter rang clear: "I did not realise to where 'we' were drifting." "We?" he queried wonderingly – "We? What made Nesta use the plural? She has not said 'you' but 'we'. Have I touched her heart? Has she commenced to love me? If so – No!" he concluded fiercely, and in that moment Seymour became again the man of honour. "No! she shall keep her tryst though it break my heart. God bless you Nesta darling, and give you happiness and joy."

Down upon his bunk he cast himself, but he neither undressed or slept, and the morning found him heavy-eyed and weary. Still he would try and meet Nesta as though nothing had happened. He would not embarrass her. He only wished for her happiness.

To his great surprise John found upon emerging from his cabin that the ship was proceeding at half speed, while all around lay a thick impenetrable mist. Incessantly sounded the siren so that other vessels in the vicinity should be apprised of the Renfrue's presence. There was no real danger, the first officer told John the mist would clear in about half an hour. It was rarely met with here, but when it did occur it was of short duration.

Scarcely had this information been given to Seymour when a violent shock threw him prostrate upon the deck.

"Good God! We've been run into!" cried the first officer, making a dash towards the bridge. "Call the Captain, one of you! Be sharp!"

But the Captain was there. Clear and sharp came his commands: "Crews to stations! Stand by! Locate the damage quickly, Mr. Menlin."

The sudden list of the huge vessel, however, told the extent of the damage much quicker than the First Officer could report. The Renfrue was sinking with a starboard list by the bows.

"Women and children first! Men stand clear of the boats. Shoot any man who attempts to rush!" – but there was no need of threats. The old law of the sea would be obeyed. The old tradition of chivalry would be upheld – and the men stood back as the women and children were hurried into the boats. There were a few women who disobeyed. They refused, by a right that none could deny, to be separated from those without whom life would be meaningless.

Wives who loved their husbands even unto death. Seymour stood back with the rest of the men praying that his Nesta may be saved. There was no harm now in thinking of her as his. Yes, she was – .

At that moment John was conscious of a hand laying softly upon his arm, and to his agonised alarm Nesta was standing by his side.

"Good heavens, Nesta, darling, you must not stay here. I thought you were in the boats. Run, sweetheart! For the love of God run and take your place or you may be too late!"

"Jack!" said Nesta quietly but firmly, using the more intimate form of his name, "death faces us both, there in the boats and here on the Renfrue. Yes, yes, dear, I am going because I know it will be more torture to you if I remain than if I go. Before I go I want to tell you that I love you with my whole heart and soul. I should not have told you had things been otherwise, because I am in honour bound to Jim. But here in the face of death I tell you. One kiss, Jack, dear, and I will go."

Even before Nesta had concluded what she was determined to say, Seymour had circled his hungry arms around her.

"You love me, Nesta!" he cried exultingly. "Then I am content. Let death come to me – I am happy!"

One passionate embrace and she was gone.

There was a moment's pause – "Now the men!" came the sharp command. "Quickly – God! Every man for himself! She's going under!"

Even as the cry came the Renfrue took a long shuddering dive. On the side of the ship opposite to the list John rushed and with an herculean effort sprang into the sea.

(To be continued)

Soul Mates (5)
By George E Hobbs
(First published: June 16, 1922)

Chapter 5 – "Amor Vincit Omnia"

When Seymour sprang from the fast sinking Renfrue, and plunged into the sea he made up his mind his last hour had come. Yet, terrible as the experience was, a strange exultation possessed his soul. Nesta loved him! That great, wonderful fact outweighed the fear of death and the agony of dying.

He knew what would happen to him. The mad vortex created by the disappearing ship would suck him down into the dark depths of the sea. He would be thrown hither and thither in the swirling race until the struggle of instinctive self-preservation would be calmed by the exquisite sweets of growing insensibility. Earth and sea, mist and darkness, would fade from his view, and then he would find himself in the limitless grandeur of the Paradise of God. There, stripped of gross elements and gross thoughts, he would wait for Nesta.

No, there was no dishonour in such thoughts. Nesta had given her promise to Jim Weston because she thought she loved him. But the shadow had to give place to the substance, at least in so far as knowledge went, and Seymour knew that love such as theirs could not be terminated by the mere intervention of death. They were twin souls; soul mates, and though one may survive the other for a few fleeting years upon the earth, release would come, and they would forever be together.

Yes it was all happening just as he thought it would. Scarcely had he reached the water and struck out as he thought away from the maddening race, when he felt himself sucked remorselessly into the vortex of the plunging vessel. Down he sank with sickening velocity, and then, beneath him, some powerful force seemed to arrest his descent. For a brief second he was held there, and then he found himself rushing madly to the surface.

He was fast losing consciousness. The force that had propelled him to the surface seemed to gather fresh impetus as it reached the higher waters, and, exploding at the surface, shot Seymour high into the air.

As he descended again to the sea, it seemed to his semi-conscious mind that two arms opened to receive him. They must have been malignant arms for a terrible crash came upon his head – and he knew no more.

∗ ∗ ∗

"Concussion, poor fellow," said the surgeon of H.M.S Plympton to the skipper in answer to the latter's enquiry as to "how the young un was doing?"

The morning before the "Plympton" had picked up the despairing S.O.S. call from the sinking Renfrue. Luckily she was homeward bound, going out of commission at Plymouth. Crowding on all steam she raced to the scene of the disaster. But all that met her skipper's view was a mass of floating wreckage. One piece proved to be a deck seat. It was awash, and within its spacious arms the huddled figure of John Seymour was found.

Since Seymour had been picked up the "Plympton" had received a further wireless message stating that another vessel had rescued sixty-nine of the Renfrue's passengers and crew, and was proceeding with all speed to London.

"Yes," said the surgeon again, "he's got it bad, poor fellow. I'm afraid even if he pulls through he won't know much of the world's happenings. I shall not be sorry to see him upon land."

And so it proved. Gradually Seymour recovered his physical strength, but his once robust mind was now almost a blank. To every enquiry he gave the same answer; "Nesta, Nesta, Nesta!" His whole vocabulary consisted of that beloved name.

One day, about six weeks after being landed at Plymouth, a sweet-faced girl rang the bell of the hospital in which Seymour was rapidly regaining his strength. Breathlessly she told her story to the doctor and asked if she might see the sufferer.

"I am glad you have called," said the doctor in reply. "For I confess this case has puzzled me. No, my child, I would rather you did not see him. In fact to be quite candid with you it will do no good. It is a strange case, I have studied it closely, and my considered judgement is that he will recover his memory, only if he passes through a similar scene to that which caused his loss of memory."

"Then I must return to Africa without seeing him," said Nesta – for it was none other – piteously. "The man to whom I was engaged has failed me. I did not love him as I thought, so I am not hurt. But Mr. Seymour and I were great friends coming over, and I thought… I thought I…"

"Do you love him?" asked the doctor abruptly.

"Better than life, doctor," said Nesta brokenly. "If only I could go to him. I…"

"The very thing!" exclaimed the doctor in great excitement. "Listen, Miss Nesta! A friend of mine is the Captain of the "Lanark", a sister-ship to the unfortunate Renfrue. She sails to-morrow from this port to Cape Town. I will book two passages for you and this young man. – Oh, yes, you can pay me, but never mind that now. And when I tell the skipper your story I think he will be pleased to arrange the little drama for me. No, no, dear child, I want no thanks. It will be thanks enough if Seymour recovers. Go and get a night's rest and see me here in the morning."

And so it was arranged. On the following day Nesta could scarcely repress her tears as she saw the Captain go forward and greet John.

"Come along, my friend," said the Captain. "I will arrange your comfort." To which Seymour merely smiled vacantly and said "Nesta! Nesta!" – and Nesta thought, as she remained hidden, her very heart would break.

Captain Johnson saw that every comfort was showered upon the sick man until after they had passed clear of the Bay of Biscay.

"Now, Miss Nesta," said the Captain on the following evening. "I think we can arrange our little experiment, and may God help us in the effort. I have arranged for every detail as you have told me – except the mist," he added smilingly, to help her. "Are you equal to your part?"

"Yes, Captain," she answered bravely. "I am ready."

"All right! I will see that all the passengers are at dinner first. I only want my first officer and two of the crew present – and may God bless you!"

At that moment Nesta caught sight of John aimlessly walking the deck and by his side was the first officer. With fast beating heart and tear-filled eyes she hid herself. And then something fell upon the deck.

"Good God," exclaimed the first officer as though in real fear. "We've been run into! Call the captain, one of you! Quickly!"

At that moment the Captain appeared.

"Men to stations," came the clear, sharp order. "Men stand clear! Women and children first! Shoot, if the men disobey!" – and one of the crew gently pushed Seymour back.

It was Nesta's turn now, and with face white with emotion and a prayer upon her lips, she went quickly to John's side.

"Jack!" she said brokenly. "I did not mean that last night. Here in the face of death I tell you of my love. I do love you, Jack – Jack! – I love – !"

Oh, it was good to be alive! Captain Johnson, nor any of the participants in that drama ever forgot the scene which followed. Hardened men of the sea as they were, each had to turn and walk away with tear-dimmed eyes.

With a terrible cry, John caught Nesta to him. "Girlie, mine. What has happened? Oh, save yourself, dear heart! God! Take her one of you and make her go into the boat. Nesta loves me! I do not fear death!"

And then with soothing words she quietened him and told him all.

Yes. "Amor vincit omnia." "Love conquers all things." And Nesta and John found it so.

(The end)

The Fear of Ridicule
A "Human Document" (Part 1)
By George E Hobbs
(First published: September 23, 1921)

It is ten o'clock on a Tuesday in September, in the year of Grace, 19– , and I sit alone with my thoughts. What memories surge through my throbbing brain, as, now and again, I try to realise lucidly my position. Here am I scarcely thirty years of age and ruined; an outcast and condemned to die.

Let me set in order the record of my life. It is no easy task, but as I realise it will soon be over, my one last wish is that someone by a perusal of these notes may be saved my fate. That some tired mariner upon the sea of life, seeing the rocks ahead, may be able to steer his barque into the fairway once more.

I shall, perforce, write under an assumed name; for, though I have forfeited their love, I still have a reverent affection for my parents. I am determined, therefore, that no word of mine shall suggest their identity. This is the truth of God – I love them still!

My name, then, is Ralph Glenson, and I am the younger son of wealthy parents. As I have already intimated, this is not my real name, but it will serve the purpose of this record.

Though the powers of heredity are prodigious, its malignant form, so far as I am capable of judging, has not been responsible for my shipwreck. I have no wish to excuse myself, but sometimes I wonder if I am a reproduction, not of an immediate but of a remote ancestor. Has the law of Atavism worked its fell purpose in my life? I cannot say. But I can speak with certainty of my parents.

My father was honourable to a fault; taking his part in the guiding policies of his country with a clear aim as to its advantages along legitimate and clearly defined moral lines. Subterfuge and prevarication he abhorred; nor would he allow himself to be cajoled or forced from the policy he believed to be right.

Though I have fallen I can still pay tribute to purity and sweetness. If God will hear a prodigal's prayer, I say: "God bless my Mother!" She was the sweetest woman that one could call Mother. Even as I write, hardened though I may be, the tears flow unchecked as I think of her.

In my boyhood's troubles, troubles that were so real to me then, my father would speak sternly to me of duty and discipline. But my mother would throw her soft arms around my neck and with winsome tenderness win my confidence. There in the inspiration of her loving embrace I poured out my troubles, and mother would point out with emphasis that went to my heart the misery attending wrong doing, and the joys of right living. God! If I had only remembered her loving counsel.

My weakness was the fear of ridicule. To be laughed at, to be made fun of would cause untold agony. Often in those far-off days I would absent myself from the company of my little friends, playing with myself rather than face the possibility of performing some act which would set free their ridiculing propensities. Even in those days my little friends, with that wonderful intuition that is native to childhood, discovered why I held aloof from them. Then they would seek me out, and goaded by their taunts, I compelled myself to do the most adventurous things – things that quickly brought me into conflict with my parents – out of sheer braggadocio.

And so time went on. Often I tried to grapple with and slay my foe, but it seemed that circumstances were ever such as to leave me crestfallen and beaten.

Then came the time when I was to go up to Oxford. I was then about eighteen years of age, and seeing that I should be with men whom I had not previously known, I determined to make one supreme effort to be master of my weakness.

There was one fellow in particular with whom I felt I could chum, and much to my secret delight I found it an easy task in persuading him to share rooms with me. With Jack Neremer beside me I felt there would be no occasion in which my weakness would be called into question – and for a time I felt happy.

Then, alas! There came disillusionment. Once or twice he was very late in returning, and knowing there would be trouble with the Prefects if he was detected, I waited anxiously for his return. Soon I heard stealthy footsteps along the corridor, and going hastily to the door I saw Jack with two companions creeping quietly towards our room.

Bidding his companions goodnight, he turned in with me, saying quite jocularly: "It's all right old boy, I dodged them all right, but it was a close shave!"

"I am glad you got in safely," I replied. "And now we will turn into bed." And apparently the incident was closed.

On the Wednesday of the following week, Jack suddenly exclaimed: "I say Ralph! What do you say to an evening's fun? I have friends living here in Oxford which will serve as an excuse. We can go ostensibly to visit them, catch the 6.15 and be in Town by 7.10. We can have our evening's fun, catch the 11 o'clock out of Paddington and be back at midnight. What do you say old chap?"

It was with a sinking feeling at my heart that I listened to Jack's proposal. To doubt the validity of his friends never entered my head. But now a thought came whether these friends were not after all mythical friends.

And, too, I saw that the struggle with my weakness was about to be opened again. What Jack proposed I knew to be wrong, but dare I tell him? Physically I was Jack's superior. In fact I had lately won the light heavyweight championship at the inter-college sports. But where moral stamina was concerned I was at fault. I feared Jack's ridicule more than I feared anything. So for the moment I was tortured between my hopes and fears.

(To be continued)

The Fear of Ridicule
A "Human Document" (Part 2)
By George E Hobbs
(First published: September 30, 1921)

My cogitation consequent upon the question Jack put to me – virtually, that we should break bounds – was painful in the extreme. Yet, I felt I would make one bid for the mastery of my weakness. Jack would surely understand because he was my friend; a friend in whom I had the utmost confidence. And so – "No!" I replied, quietly but with conviction. "I think neither of us will do that. The exams will be due in another month, after which we'll be able to have all the fun we need."

"Don't be a silly ass!" exclaimed Jack, nettled by the tone of rebuke I unconsciously adopted. "I thought I had chummed with a man, but it seems to me I have chummed with a squeamish girl."

Before I could reply, our room door opened and in walked the two whom I had seen with Jack on the night of his last escapade.

"It's all right, Neremer!" said the taller of the two, addressing Jack with a wink. "Mervel and I have each arranged for a telegram to be sent to us. He is to see a brother who has suddenly been called abroad; I to see a sick relative. So," he concluded with a chuckle, "we shall be quite a merry – ahem! – quartette."

"Ah, but we sha'nt," exclaimed Jack petulantly. "My young Apollo of a chum has contracted heart trouble, and will not allow himself to be mixed up with such wicked people as you and I and Streamer. On the night we have arranged our outing he will be conducting his little girl's class at the mission..."

But why should I continue? The upshot was that not having moral stamina sufficient to combat their bantering ridicule, I consented to join them in their adventure.

And was it any wonder that I fell? I had reached the age when I felt the thrill of primitive instincts surging through my blood. I tasted the wine – and I tasted more. Amid the soft dreamy music in the semi-darkened room I inhaled the intoxicating perfume of her who sat beside me. I was young, inexperienced, and plastic. To my already excited imagination she too was young – and beautiful. Moreover, she was experienced and she had little difficulty in moulding the yielding material to her desire.

With death but a few paces from my cell door, I swear by all I hold sacred it was never my desire to live a dissolute life. It was not that forbidden things had an appetising flavour for me that I did them. I adventured because I feared ridicule consequent upon my refusal. Oh how foolish it seems for me now – here with death awaiting me! I do not fear death! Not even in the violent form that awaits me. Yet I feared ridicule; and the balance of three pairs of mocking eyes weighed down my better judgement and the wine, calling up all the primitive passions within me, caused me to see alluring beauty in a sin-sodden she-devil.

Needless to say this was not the only escapade in which I figured during my stay at Oxford. But as my time grows short I will not weary the reader of these notes by repetition. God! If I'd only been a man.

Let me come quickly to the hideous thing for which I am now awaiting death. No, No! I cannot believe even now that I did it! The agony, the shame, is upon me as I write! But let me proceed as coherently as circumstances will permit.

During my scholastic career I had discovered an abnormal quality within me. I discovered a liking which grew into a passion for the hieroglyphic writing of the people who lived in the dawn of written communication. Tablets from the ancient library of Ashurbanipal at Nineveh, or yellow, partially faded papyrus from the tombs of Egypt, would create within me unbounded joy, as I mastered, deciphered and translated the almost unintelligible characters contained thereon.

Taking a six months' holiday in Africa, upon the completion of my studies at Oxford, I had the inestimable good fortune to discover a tablet upon which was impressed hieroglyphic characters that were unknown to any student of this branch of research. My thoughts immediately went to my old French Professor, who had three absorbing passions. One was an inordinate love of country, the second was a super-inordinate love for ancient hieroglyphics, and the third, an absorbing passion for his only child – a daughter.

In matters pertaining to hieroglyphics he was recognised as the world's leading authority. I knew he would be frantic with envy but did he but know of my discovery. But I made up my mind that none should know until I had mastered and deciphered its contents.

I will not weary the reader by detailing the work of the subsequent months. Months of hope and despair, and again of hope until at last, verging upon a mental collapse, I discovered the key to the whole of the written structure.

My delight was unbounded, for no writing upon this plan was known to any other person upon the globe. Writing out my key plan I knew without a vestige of doubt that any subsequent discovery could easily be translated therefrom.

I had left Oxford with my fear of ridicule still unmastered. Right to the end of my collegiate days that ever portent fear had made me perform many questionable actions. So much so that my sense of moral perception was dull in the extreme. But during my sojourn in Africa and the months I spent in elucidating the hieroglyphics mystery, there had been no occasion in which my weakness had been called into question. I little thought that my old college chum, Jack Neremer, would be the one to revive the struggle, or that my life, choked out upon the end of a rope, was to expiate the taking of his life.

Yet I was found dazed and incoherent in his chambers with a revolver clenched firmly in my hand and Jack lying dead before me. They said I babbled of love and honour and possibly I did – for I saw red when I found how devilishly I had been betrayed and trapped.

I can remember but little of what followed for a drug had speedily rendered thought imperfect. Yet, as coherently as I can, I will tell the reader of these notes the steps that led up to this supreme tragedy.

(To be continued)

The Fear of Ridicule
A "Human Document" (Finis)
By George E Hobbs
(First published: October 14, 1921)

I come now to the final episode in the tragic story of my life.

I thought the secret of my hieroglyphic discovery was well kept, but subsequent events proved that during the time I was laboriously deciphering their mystic symbols, information leaked out.

Having completed the translation I sought a publisher who would undertake the publication of my discovery. Journeying to Town for that purpose I chanced to meet Lord – , a friend of my father's, and one who stood high in the Diplomatic Service. (If by chance Lord – should read these notes, I pray for his silence.)

Believing he could help me in the choice of a publisher, I told him exactly why I had come to Town. For a moment he stood in deep thought, and then asked me if I had any objection to his looking over my MSS. "For," said he, "something of great importance has just occurred to me."

I went with him to his club, and in the privacy of his room I laid before him the sketch of the original symbols, my translation and the key plan.

For a quarter of an hour he closely examined my manuscript and then, obviously labouring under great stress of feeling exclaimed: "The very thing! Ralph, you have solved a greater problem than you imagine. If you are prepared to do your country a service, listen to me! I cannot go into details but it is very imperative that a certain document should be in the hands of our Representative in Berlin before a week tonight. French secret service men are already on the watch to prevent its passage or, at least, to know its contents. We do not know of a code safe enough from them. This is the very thing.

"Make out a copy of the document in these symbols. We will send a misleading document in code with one of our men, and will see that this is captured. Immediately following we will send the one you make out. This also must go with one of our men as the Office would not allow me to use a stranger. But we can get over this difficulty, for on Thursday you could slip over to Berlin with the key plan."

I did as Lord – requested. The document in code was captured, as was intended. The second document, made with hieroglyphic symbols, got safely through. And I went to Berlin and gave to our Representative the key plan. I then returned to town.

And then I met again Roselle, my old French Professor's daughter.

As I took her little hand within the clasp of my own, the feeling I had for Roselle, and which I had striven to repress, reasserted itself with an increased vigour. I had loved her in my Oxford days; from the moment I had seen her when first introduced to her father's house. Yet even as the truth flooded through my soul there rose up before me the barrier of my follies. She was sweet and good and pure. And my foolish weakness had made of me a creature of loathsomeness. If my fear of ridicule had made me a moral coward, at least I was master of my will in this direction. And I determined to crush for ever my love for her.

There were times when I caught a shy, elusive glance from her eyes. A glance in which wonder, interrogation and sadness found expression. It caused me to wonder whether she had seen the love light in my eyes, and loving me in return, wondered at my silence. It was hard to resist her at such times, but knowing I could not offer her an unsullied past, I kept silent.

And this night I met her again. Tho' suddenness of meeting threw me off my guard. As I retained her little hand in mine, the touch of her fingers broke down the flood gates of my determination, and I told her of my love.

I did not realise my offence until she said: "Yes, Ralph, and I am not ashamed to tell you I have always loved you. But dear, why have you kept silent so long?"

It was then I realised what I had done.

"My dear one," I said brokenly, "I did not intend to reveal my love for you. God knows I love you dearly, but you must put me out of your life. My past..."

"Never mind your past, Ralph," said Roselle quietly. "Some of it I know. The rest I do not wish to know. I am satisfied to know that you love me and that I love you. Let the dead past bury its dead. Ralph, I am paying an important call, but come and see us in the morning and tell Papa our news. Tonight he is dining with Mr. Neremer, your old chum. They will both be pleased to see you for they are anxious to know about your new discovery."

"Neremer? Your father? Discovery?" I exclaimed, while a thousand doubts and fears rushed through my mind. "What do you mean, Roselle?" But she only waved her hand. "See you in the morning, Ralph." And she was gone.

What happened at Neremer's rooms I have only a hazy recollection. The atmosphere was suffused with pleadings, recriminations and threats. But I dared not give my secret away now.

At last Roselle's father said: "Well never mind, Glenson. I have other news to tell you. Roselle knew of your movement and she got you here by a fluke. She and Jack here are engaged to be married, so you need not trouble yourself..."

It was then that I saw red. I cursed Roselle and Jack and her father. After that I know no more. The trial has taken place. I am condemned to die because I was found alone with Jack and he was dead. In one sense I am glad, for life without Roselle would be impossible for me. Let death come. I am ready.

Thank God I can write a postscript to my narrative.

I write these lines thankfully because I am free. Free of the awful stain of bloodshed. By some mysterious means, Roselle's father knew of my discovery and the use it was being put to. It turned out that he was one of the astutest of French secret service men. One to whom love of country was greater than filial affection. And Roselle had been his dupe.

Before my dread sentence was carried into effect, he met with an accident and lay dying. Before he passed into the inscrutable future he sent for Lord – and confessed that it was he who shot Jack Neremer – shot him in a fit of perverseness because Jack could not extract from me my secret. He confessed that but for his accident, he would have let me die.

Thank God Roselle was innocent of duping me. She does not even know now what her father charged her with before me. And she shall never know.

I love her. And soon, please God, she will be my wife. Then, I trust, the look of sorrow upon her dear face will vanish.

Ridicule will never hurt me more. I have learned my lesson. And Roselle is with me.

The End.

Appendix A:
The Known Works of George E Hobbs

Poems

The following were published in the *Swindon Advertiser/Evening Advertiser/Swindon Evening Advertiser* (unless otherwise stated); those marked with * also appeared in *The British Soldier and Other Poems*, a booklet containing 24 poems, published in 1915:

Britain's Response (October 28, 1914)
No Conscription (November 13, 1914)
The Subtle Request (November 24, 1914)
Don't Criticise! (December 5, 1914)
Commander Holbrook & the B11 (December 23, 1914)*
The Last Goodbye (December 28, 1914)*
The British Soldier (January 2, 1915)*
The Brave Northamptons (January 15, 1915)*
Heroes All (January 22, 1915)*
The Soldier's Letter (January 29, 1915)*
The Foolish King (February 12, 1915)
My Need (February 19, 1915)*
To The Despondent Ones – Part I The Question (February 26, 1915)*
To The Despondent Ones – Part II The Answer (March 5, 1915)*
To The Despondent Ones – Part III The Conclusion (March 12, 1915)*
Love Fills The Void (March 26, 1915)*
In Memory of the Scott Expedition (April 2, 1915)*
In Memory of 2nd Lt WGC Gladstone (April 23, 1915)
Where Dwelleth Peace? (April 30, 1915)*
Trust (May 2, 1915)*
Watchman, What of the Night? (May 7, 1915)*
I Will Repay (May 14, 1915)
The Wanderer's Vision (May 28, 1915)*
Ode To The Sun (June 4, 1915)*

The Central Sun (June 11, 1915)*
True Love: Life's Greatest Blessing (June 18, 1915)*
Britain's Need (June 25, 1915)
Lance-Corpl Gee (July 2, 1915)*
The Stream of Life (July 9, 1915)*
Meditation (July 23, 1915)*
The Desert Shall Rejoice and Blossom as the Rose (July 30, 1915)*
A Year of War (in booklet only)*
Triumph of Love (November 5, 1915)
Clemanthe & Ion (November 12, 1915)
Ode to the Moon (December 3, 1915)
The Air Raid of January 31st 1916 (March 31, 1916)
Faith (March 10, 1916)
Nurse Cavell (October 13, 1916)
My Sleeping Boy (October 20, 1916)
T'was Ever Thus (November 3, 1916)
A Column of Verse – David & Goliath/The French Soldier (May 4, 1922)
The Crucifixion (March 29, 1923)
Mrs Crabthorne at the Seaside [Crabthorn 12] – Told by Herself (July 20, 1923)
The Eventide (undated, not previously published)

Prayers

Published in the *Advertiser*:
Intercession (October 29, 1915)
O God Bless the Mourners (April 16, 1915)

Newspaper correspondence

The following letters to the editor were published in the *Advertiser*:
Poets & The War (April 16, 1915)
An Appeal (December 15, 1916)
The Story of the Creation (March 1, 1917)
The ASE and the Government – A Warning (February 1, 1918)
Communion With The Spirit World (June 19, 1918)
An Open Letter to Mr H Day Headmaster of the Even Swindon Mixed School (August 1, 1919)
An Answer, Please (October 14, 1921)
Christmas Carollers (December 8, 1922)
Why Planet Swerved (January 13, 1938)

Published in the *Derby Daily Telegraph*:
Toy Soldiers (September 17, 1936)

Newspaper articles in the style of a letter

Published in the *Advertiser*:
Kaiser Roused – Mr GE Hobbs Humorous at Wilhelm's Expense (December 22, 1922)

A Suggestion For Aiding the Hospital – What the Men In The GWR Works Could Do (February 2, 1923)
Prehistoric Life (April 27, 1923)
Rodbourne – A Topical Article [Crabthorne 7] (May 4, 1923)
Peace Disturbers – Discord at Services on Sundays (June 1, 1923) + *Mr Hobbs Taken to Task* (June 8, 1923)

Newspaper articles

Published in the *Advertiser*:

For Young People – Article No 1 (January 10, 1917)
For Young People – Article No 2 (January 19, 1917)
For Young People – Article No 3 (January 24, 1917)
To Young People – No 4 (February 2, 1917)
The Story of the Creation 1 – North American Indian and Grecian Narratives (February 6, 1917)
The Story of the Creation 2 – The Biblical Narrative (February 13, 1917)
The Story of the Creation 3 – The Biblical Narrative Continued (February 21, 1917)
The Story of the Creation 4 – The Creation Narratives Compared (February 27, 1917)
The Story of the Creation 5 – Comparison of Creation Narratives concluded (March 8, 1917)
The Story of the Creation 6 – The Interpretation of the Biblical Narrative (March 15, 1917)
The Story of the Creation 7 – The Interpretation of the Biblical Narrative continued (March 23, 1917)
The Story of the Creation 8 – Interpretation of the Biblical Narrative – concluded (March 27, 1917)
The Story of the Creation 9 – The Scientific Interpretation of Creation (April 6, 1917)
The Story of the Creation 10 – The Scientific Interpretation of Creation (Continued) (April 13, 1917)
The Story of the Creation 11 – Scientific Interpretation of Creation continued (April 27, 1917)
The Story of the Creation 12 – The Geological Periods, concluded and the Advent of Man (May 1, 1917)
The Story of the Creation 13 – The Origin and Development of Life (May 16, 1917)
The Story of the Creation 14 – Organic Evolution (May 23, 1917)
The Story of the Creation 15 – Organic Evolution continued (May 31, 1917)
The Story of the Creation 16 – Organic Evolution part III (June 5, 1917)
The Story of the Creation 17 – Organic Evolution – Man (June 15, 1917)
The Story of the Creation 18 – Concluding Remarks (June 19, 1917)
Usefulness – A Parable Part I (August 18, 1917)
Usefulness – Part II (August 28, 1917)
Conversations 1 – The Moon (September 5, 1917)
Conversations 2 – The Moon continued (September 12, 1917)
Conversations 3 – The Moon continued (September 18, 1917)
Conversations 4 – A Voice from the Past (September 25, 1917)
Conversations 5 – A Voice from the Past part II (October 2, 1917)
Conversations 6 – A Voice from the Past (October 9, 1917)
Conversations 7 – The Moon concluded (October 17, 1917)
Conversations 8 – Tiny and I (October 25, 1917)
Conversations 9 – Just a Common Stick of Pencil (October 30, 1917)

Conversations 10 – Truthfulness (November 14, 1917)
Conversations 11 – Tiny asks a Question (November 22, 1917)
Conversations 12 – I Try to Solve Tiny's Question (November 28, 1917)
Conversations 13 – I Continue My Explanation (December 6, 1917)
Conversations 14 – Higher Wages Not The Remedy but "Equality of Sacrifice" (December 12, 1917)
The Late Mr TR Bray – Memorial Tablet Unveiled In Swindon (February 1, 1918)
Conversations 15 – Deeds Not Words Prove The Worth Of A Man (March 29, 1918)
Conversations 16 – Tiny Asks The Meaning Of Pandora (April 5, 1918)
Conversations 17 – I Try To Interpret Pandora In A Practical Way (April 12, 1918)
Conversations 18 – Can Mortals Hold Communion With The Spirit World? – Yes! (April 19, 1918)
Conversations 19 – A Record Of My Second Visit To The Spirit World (April 26, 1918)
Conversations 20 – A Record Of My Third Visit To The Spirit World (May 3, 1918)
Conversations 21 – My Fourth Visit To The Spirit Land Leads Me To A Strange Experience. The Revelation of Love Part 1 (June 7, 1918)
Conversations 22 – The Revelation of Love Part 2 (continued) (June 14, 1918)
Conversations 23 – The Revelation of Love Part 3 (June 25, 1918)
Conversations 24 – The Revelation of Love Part 4 (August 30, 1918)
Conversations 25 – The Fox and the Cat (March 14, 1919)
Conversations 26 – Sirach – His Mission (Friday 21st March 21, 1919)
Conversations 27 – Sirach – His First Adventure (March 28, 1919)
Conversations 28 – Sirach – Areta fights for his Downfall (April 11, 1919)
Conversations 29 – Sirach – His Fall (April 18, 1919)
Conversations 30 – Sirach – He Seeks Peace in the Only Way (April 25, 1919)
Conversations 31 – Sirach – Awaiting Sentence (May 2, 1919)
Conversations 32 – Sirach – His Success (May 16, 1919)
Even Swindon Schools – Presentation to Mr Day (August 8, 1919)
Other Worlds Than Ours Part 1 (November 7, 1919) (General Intro)
Other Worlds Than Ours Part 2 (November 14, 1919) (The Solar System)
Other Worlds Than Ours Part 3 (November 21, 1919) (The Solar System)
Other Worlds Than Ours Part 4 (November 28, 1919) (Mercury)
Other Worlds Than Ours Part 5 (December 5, 1919) (Venus)
Other Worlds Than Ours Part 6 (December 12, 1919) (Mars)
The End Of The World (December 19, 1919)
Other Worlds Than Ours Part 6a (The Asteroids) (January 9, 1920)
Other Worlds Than Ours Part 7 (January 16, 1920) (Jupiter)
Other Worlds Than Ours Part 8 (January 23, 1920) (Saturn)
Other Worlds Than Ours Part 9 – The Mysterious Satellites of Uranus (January 30, 1920)
The Marconi Sensation – Signals From Whence? (February 7, 1920)
Other Worlds Than Ours Part 9a – Neptune (February 27, 1920)
Other Worlds Than Ours Part 10 – Some Personal Views Upon The Plurality Of Worlds (April 9, 1920) (Final Part)
Trip Eve & Trip Day – A Comedy of the Train and of the Washtub [Crabthorn 1] (July 1, 1920)
Mrs Crabthorn On The Warpath – Another Echo of the Swindon Trip Story [Crabthorn 2] (July 16, 1920)
Mrs Crabthorn And Her Neighbours – The Episode of the Needle and Sundry Explosions [Crabthorn 3] (July 30, 1920)
Mrs Crabthorn On A Bike And Off [Crabthorn 4] – (August 13, 1920)

Pen Pictures Of The Pulpit 1 – Universal Unrest, Solution and Consolation (September 3, 1920)
Pen Pictures Of The Pulpit 2 – A Discourse on Knowledge v Love Dissected (September 10, 1920)
Pen Pictures Of The Pulpit 3 – Eating the Bread and Drinking the Wine (September 17, 1920)
Pen Pictures Of The Pulpit 4 – The World and Its Need of the Visionaries (September 24, 1920)
Pen Pictures Of The Pulpit 5 – Where Broadmindedness is a Vice (October 8, 1920)
Pen Pictures Of The Pulpit 6 – A Discourse on Habits, Good and Bad (October 19, 1920)
Pen Pictures Of A Heavy Cast – A Notable Event at the GWR Works, Swindon (October 22, 1920)
A Day's Effort & its Results 1 – Amusing Article (February 4, 1921)
Swindon GWR Shopmen at Dinner (January 28, 1921)
A Day's Effort & its Results 2 – The Second Chapter (February 11, 1921)
A Day's Effort & its Results 3 – The Third Chapter (February 18, 1921)
A Day's Effort & its Results 4 – The Fourth Chapter (March 4, 1921)
Pen Pictures of the Pulpit 7 – A Forceful Preacher (March 1921)
Outwitting Mr W Sikes – A Short Story (April 1921)
Nemesis, or Truth Will Out – A Short Story (April 22, 1921)
To Seekers After Trouble 1 – Instructions (April 29, 1921)
To Seekers After Trouble 2 – Further Instructions (May 6, 1921)
To Seekers After Trouble 3 – Further Instructions (May 13, 1921)
To Seekers After Trouble 4 – The Final Instructions (May 20, 1921)
Algy's Riding Lessons – The First Attempt (June 3, 1921)
Algy's Riding Lessons – The Final Attempt (June 10, 1921)
Mrs Crabthorn and her Censhus – Popular Lady Brought Back [Crabthorn 5] (June 17, 1921)
Pen Pictures of the Pulpit 8 – The Problem of Suffering (June 24, 1921)
Pen Pictures of the Pulpit 9 – Steps Leading Upwards (July 7, 1921)
A Cricket Match Record – Tale of Two G Shop Teams (July 15, 1921)
Eaves Dropping & A Lesson – George E Hobbs and the Kiddies (July 29, 1921)
Mrs Crabthorne's Grievance – Tale of a Busted Main [Crabthorn 6] (August 12, 1921)
The Landing of J Caesar – History as Wrote (August 26, 1921)
A Vision – Heirs to a Wondrous Inheritance (September 2, 1921)
The Fear of Ridicule 1 – A Human Document (September 23, 1921)
The Fear of Ridicule 2 – A Human Document (Part 2) (September 30, 1921)
The Fear of Ridicule 3 – A Human Document (Finis) (October 14, 1921)
Reminiscences – George E Hobbs strikes a Poignant Note (November 4, 1921)
The Genius of Algy – George E Hobbs In Lighter Vein (November 11, 1921)
Can You Help? – Moving Pen Picture (November 25, 1921)
The Copper Parade – It's Educational Value (December 23, 1921)
A Good Riddance – The Message of 1921 (January 6, 1922)
Interviewing a Stranger – George E Hobbs as a Journalist (February 3, 1922)
Judge Not! (February 24, 1922)
The Mysterious Message – Chapter 1 (March 24, 1922)
The Mysterious Message – Chapter II (March 31, 1922)
The Mysterious Message – Chapter III (April 13, 1922)
The Mysterious Message – Chapter IV (April 21, 1922)
Soul Mates – Chapter I The Man (May 19, 1922)
Soul Mates – Chapter II The Man (May 26, 1922)
Soul Mates – Chapter III The Meeting (June 2, 1922)
Soul Mates – Chapter IV The Parting (June 9, 1922)
Soul Mates – Chapter V Amor Vincit Omnia (June 16, 1922)

Battle of Giants – A Picture of "G" Shop at Cricket (July 14, 1922)
Story of Sunday Sport – How Johnny Bilson's Future was Spoilt (July 21, 1922)
Pen Picture of a Mission Service (October 27, 1922)
Remembrance Day in the GWR Works (November 17, 1922)
Making a Success of Life – Mr GE Hobbs' Letters to a Young Lad (November 24, 1922)
Spirit to Achieve (December 15, 1922)
Abolish Death Penalty – Convincing Arguments by George E Hobbs (January 12, 1923)
A Nature Note 1 (May 4, 1923)
A Nature Note 2 (May 18, 1923)
Mrs Crabthorne In a New Rôle [Crabthorn 8] (May 18, 1923)
Mrs Crabthorne's Robot – How She Has Solved the Servant Problem [Crabthorn 9] (May 25, 1923)
Mrs Crabthorne's Robot – First Demonstration a Disaster [Crabthorn 10] (June 1, 1923)
A Little Story for Hospital Week (June 8, 1923)
Beauties of the Isle of Wight – Swindon Party's Happy Outing (June 15, 1923)
Carnival Night (June 15, 1923)
Truth Unadorned – Mr George E Hobbs and Adult School Movement (June 29, 1923)
Mrs Crabthorne's Trip [Crabthorn 11] (July 5, 1923)
Cricket Through Expert Eyes (July 13, 1923)
William Shanks' Wooing – A Sad Story (July 27, 1923)
Educative Factor of Games (August 3, 1923)
Record of a Visit to the Moon [Intro] (August 10, 1923)
A Visit to the Moon – Part 1 of Journal (August 17, 1923)
A Visit to the Moon – Part 2 of Journal (August 24, 1923)
A Visit to the Moon – Part 3 of Journal (August 31, 1923)
A Visit to the Moon – Part 4 of Journal (September 7, 1923)
Men of G Shop Honour Their Dead – War Memorial Unveiling in the GWR Works (September 7, 1923)
A Visit to the Moon – Part 5 of Journal (September 14, 1923)
A Visit to the Moon – Part 6 of Journal (September 21, 1923)
A Visit to the Moon – Part 7 of Journal (September 28, 1923)
A Swindon Product – Mr Percy Lewis of "Laughter (Un) Limited" Musical Director (September 28, 1923)
A Visit to the Moon – Part 8 of Journal (October 5, 1923)
A Visit to the Moon – Part 9 of Journal (October 12, 1923)
Does Boxing Brutalise? (October 19, 1923)
A Visit to the Moon – Part 10 of Journal (October 26, 1923)
A Visit to the Moon – Part 11 of Journal (November 2, 1923)
Doctor Nickols 1 – A Tale of Weird Happenings (November 16, 1923)
Doctor Nickols 2 – A Tale of Weird Happenings Chapter II (November 23, 1923)
Doctor Nickols 3 - A Tale of Weird Happenings Chapter III (November 30, 1923)
Doctor Nickols 4 – A Tale of Weird Happenings Chapter IV (December 7, 1923)
Answers to Correspondents (1) (April 17, 1924)
Answers to Correspondents (2) (April 25, 1924)
Answers to Correspondents (3) (May 23, 1924)
The Conversion of Z – A Little Story for Hospital Week (June 13, 1924)
Trip (July 3, 1924)
Beauties of Wye Valley – A GWR Shop Outing (September 5, 1924)
A Pen Picture of the Pulpit 10 – Rev W Clifford (January 14, 1927)

Victoria Hospital – Impressions of a Visit (April 1, 1927)
Pen Picture of the Solar Eclipse (June 30, 1927)
The Solar Eclipse – Impressions of a Swindon Lecture (November 2, 1927)
The Significance of 11 November (November 9, 1927)
(Subsequent articles are the subject of ongoing research)

Other articles

Published in *Great Western Railway Magazine*:

The Heaviest Casting Ever Made at Swindon Works (1921)
The Erection of a Stirling Water Tube Boiler at Swindon Works (1922)
Heating Installation at "A" Shop, Swindon Works (1923)
A Pen Picture of the Royal Visit to Swindon (June 1924)
A Relaying Gang at Work (December 1928)

Published by GWR Mechanics' Institute/Swindon Engineering Society:

Transactions 1928-1929 Pamphlet 169: Permanent Way Fittings and their Manufacture (February 5, 1929)

The Virtue of Gratitude (not previously published or publication date unknown)
The Life of Charles Bradlaugh (not previously published or publication date unknown)

Appendix B:

Glossary

Archaic words and phrases used by George E Hobbs

Acme: the point at which something is at its very best
Adam's ale: water
ASE: The Amalgamated Society of Engineers
Atavism: reversion to an earlier type; throwback
Bairnsfather: Bruce Bairnsfather was a prominent cartoonist of the era
Benedict: a newly married man
Bole: tree trunk
Braggadocio: boastful or arrogant behaviour
Connubial: relating to marriage
Crowding: To spread a large amount of sail to increase speed
Dilutees: Unskilled workers performing a task previously performed by indentured tradesmen
Essayed: attempted
Expiate: make amends for
Fain: gladly

Frank Moran: early 20th century American heavyweight boxer
Griqualand West: an area of central South Africa
Groggy: unsteady
Lodgement: a place where a thing is located
Masterman: a master craftsman
Osculation: the act of kissing
Paravane: a streamlined, submersible, mine-sweeping device towed by a ship
Peg: a measure of spirits
Pinnace: a small boat used as a tender
Press his/her suit: seek out a romantic partner
Pygmalion: a king of Cyprus
Quietus: death
Quilted: covered, ie concealed
Rake: A man habituated to immoral conduct
Refulgent: shining very brightly
Rift within the lute: an apparently minor piece of damage, likely to have fatal consequences
Saurian: an ancient type of lizard
Screed: a long piece of writing
Somnus: the Roman god of sleep
Sub rosa: In confidence or 'just between us'
Taffrail: a rail and ornamentation round a ship's stern
Terpsichorean: relating to dancing
Toluol: aka Toluene, used in the production of explosives
Vicissitudes: unwelcome changes of fortune
Visage: appearance as it relates to hair – in this particular context
Voluptuary: a person devoted to luxury and sensual pleasure
Warped: move or be moved along by hauling on a rope
Weal: a sound, healthy or prosperous state
Whilom: erstwhile

Appendix C:

Bibliography

Bridgeman, Brian & Squires, Teresa, *The Old Lady on the Hill* (Bradford on Avon: ELSP, 2001)
Child, Mark, *The Swindon Book* (Warminster: Hobnob Press, 2013)
Great Western Railway, *Swindon Works and its place in Great Western History* (London: 1935)
Great Western Railway Magazine (Swindon: Great Western Railway
Pringle, Mike, Swindon – *Remembering 1914-18* (Stroud: The History Press, 2014)
Swindon Advertiser/Swindon Evening Advertiser/Evening Advertiser (Swindon: multiple issues 1914-1927)

Swindon Engineering Society minute books
Swindon Heritage (Graham Carter, Frances Bevan, Andy Binks, Noel Beauchamp, Noel Ponting et al, various issues 2012-17)
www.brin.ac.uk
www.www.britannica.com
www.british-history.ac.uk
www.britishnewspaperarchive.co.uk
www.dailymail.com
www.encyclopedia.1914-1918-online.net
www.en.wikipedia.org
www.www.gcsehistory.org.uk
www.greatwestern.org.uk
www.gutenberg.org
www.humanities.uwe.ac.uk
www.iwm.org.uk
www.myprimitivemethodists.org.uk
www.mywesleyanmethodists.org.uk
www.rail.co.uk
www.rodbournehistory.org
www.staugustines-swindon.co.uk
www.swindonadvertiser.co.uk
www.swindonweb.com
www.totalswindon.com
www.unionhistory.info

About the Authors

Noel Ponting

Noel started writing for *Swindon Heritage* in 2014 and became a regular contributor to the magazine, all the way through to its final edition in December 2017. A dedicated fan of brilliant local band XTC, he is an authority on their history, and saw them perform live on eight occasions, including in their early days. Noel is a longstanding season ticket-holder at Swindon Town FC.

Graham Carter

A co-founder and vice-chair of the Alfred Williams Heritage Society, in 2014 Graham co-wrote (with Caroline Ockwell) *The Shadow of the Workhouse*, about the history of the institution at Stratton, near Swindon, based on Williams's observations made there on a visit, c1912. He was a co-founder and the editor of *Swindon Heritage*, and wrote, designed and edited *A Swindon Time Capsule*, which won the Chartered Institute of Library and Information Professionals' Alan Ball Award in 2018 for Outstanding Local History Publication. Like George Hobbs, Graham is a former journalist, and continues to write a weekly column for the *Swindon Advertiser*.

www.ingramcontent.com/pod-product-compliance
Lightning Source LLC
Chambersburg PA
CBHW070957160426
43193CB00012B/1818